18-95

KARMA CHAKME'S
MOUNTAIN DHARMA

KARMA CHAKME'S MOUNTAIN DHARMA

VOLUME ONE

Entering Dharma's Gate (the four ordinary foundations) *
Renunciation * Various Greater and Lesser Vehicles * How to Keep
the Three Vows * Taking Refuge * The Generation of Bodhichitta *
Protection of the Three Jewels Through Meditation * Dispelling All
Obstacles * Purification of Karma, Vajrasattva Practice * Offering
the Mandala * Guru Yoga

VOLUME TWO

How to Recognize the Arising of Experience and Realization * Love
and Compassion * A Brief Explanation of Geomancy * Instructions
on Retreat * Chö Practice * White Tara and Tseringma * Kriya and
Charya Tantra * Yoga Tantra for Those Skilled in Ritual and Mudras
* How to Purify the Obscurations of the Dead

VOLUME THREE

A Concise *Liberation Through Hearing*: Introduction to the Bardo *
Signs Arising Through Practice * Avoiding Deviations * Dispelling
Obstacles and Removing Impediments * Instructions on
Improvement to Increase Experience and Realization * Five
Poisonous Kleshas

VOLUME FOUR

Instructions on Conduct in Order to Behave in Accord with the
Victors' Dictates * Instructions on Benefiting Beings * How the Best,
the Intermediate and the Least Practitioners Die * Choosing a Pure
Realm * How to Reach a Pure Realm

VOLUME FIVE

Ri Chö, original text in Tibetan

For the complete list of contents of *Ri Chö*, see "Precious Garland:
A List of Contents to Prevent Disorder," page 27

KARMA CHAKME'S
MOUNTAIN DHARMA

VOLUME ONE

AS TAUGHT BY
KHENPO KARTHAR RINPOCHE

TRANSLATORS:
LAMA YESHE GYAMTSO
CHOJOR RADHA
NAMGYAL KHORKO

KTD PUBLICATIONS
WOODSTOCK, NEW YORK USA

This book is dedicated to
His Holiness the Seventeenth Karmapa,
Ogyen Trinley Dorje

༄༅། །ཨོཾ་སྭ་སྟི་ཀརྨ་ཀ་བི་ཛྫ་ཡ། །མི་འགྱུར་རྟག་པ་རང་
བྱུང་ཆོས་ཀྱི་སྐུ། །སྐྱུ་འཕྲུལ་གཟུགས་ཀྱི་སྐུར་བཞིངས་
གཙོ་བོ་འདི། །གསང་གསུམ་རྡོ་རྗེའི་ཁམས་སུ་རབ་བརྟན་
ཅིང་། །མཐའ་ཡས་ཕྲིན་ལས་ཕུན་སྒྲུབ་དཔལ་འབར་ཤོག །
རྒྱལ་ཚབ་སྐུ་ཕྲེང་བཅུ་གཉིས་པ་གྲགས་པ་མི་འགྱུར་གོ་ཆ་སྨོན་འདི། །མངྒ་ལཾ།། །།

OM SWA STI KARMA KA BI DZA YA

From the unchanging, permanent Dharmakaya
appears the magical body of Karmapa.

May your three secrets of body, speech, and mind
firmly remain in the vajra realm.

May your boundless activities be blazingly
glorious and spontaneously accomplished.

Aspiration by the Twelfth Gyaltshap Mingyur Gocha.
Mangalam

Published by:
KTD Publications
335 Meads Mountain Road
Woodstock, NY 12498 USA
www.KTDPublications.org

Distributed by:
Namse Bangdzo Bookstore
335 Meads Mountain Road
Woodstock, NY 12498 USA
www.NamseBangdzo.com

ISBN 0-974-10920-7

This book is printed on acid free paper.

Contents

Preface

The students of Khenpo Karthar Rinpoche wish to express their gratitude to Rinpoche for bringing *Karma Chakme's Mountain Dharma* to us. As always, Rinpoche presents his teaching with infinite generosity, wisdom, and compassion, and we appreciate his confidence in us to receive this teaching.

His Holiness the Sixteenth Karmapa (Rangjung Rikpe Dorje, 1923–1981) indicated that it was his wish that Khenpo Karthar Rinpoche present *Karma Chakme's Mountain Dharma* to Western students. In accordance with this wish, Khenpo Rinpoche began teaching this text in the Year of the Earth Rabbit, February 1999, at Karma Triyana Dharmachakra, the North American seat of His Holiness, located in Woodstock, New York. The teachings took place on weekends over the subsequent four years, concluding in the Year of the Water Sheep, April 2003.

The original text by Karma Chakme Rinpoche was written in 1659. The text that Khenpo Karthar Rinpoche taught from was printed and published at Tashi Jong, Himachal Pradesh, India, and consists of 595 pages in fifty-four chapters. Karma Chakme requested that the text always be copied and presented in its completeness, thus ensuring that nothing be lost. Because *Karma Chakme's Mountain Dharma* is a complete work of the complete path, Khenpo Karthar Rinpoche follows Chakme Rinpoche's instructions in maintaining the integrity of the original text. We also respectfully follow their wishes and instructions; however, due to the length of the text and commentary, we will publish Khenpo Rinpoche's commentary in four volumes, with a separate volume for the Tibetan text.

Rinpoche followed the same order as the original Tibetan text with two exceptions. He began with the namthar (spiritual biography) of Karma Chakme, which in the Tibetan original is placed at the end of the text. Rinpoche also omitted the restricted chapters, which, at some point, will be published separately for use by qualified students. The result of these efforts is that the entire contents of *Karma Chakme's Mountain Dharma* will be available in English for the first time.

We would like to express our appreciation and gratitude to our translators, Lama Yeshe Gyamtso, Chojor Radha, and Namgyal Khorko, to Jeanette DeFries for transcribing the oral teachings as well as for her invaluable support and guidance, to Louise Light and Sandy Hu for their generosity in helping us get started, to Naomi Schmidt for her technical assistance, to Wendy Harding for the line drawing of Karma Chakme Rinpoche, to Chojor Radha for his calligraphy, and to Tenzin Chonyi for his kindness and encouragement.

The editorial and production staff—Maureen McNicholas, Peter van Deurzen, Daia Gerson, Barbara Majewska, and Mary Young—also wish to thank all the many others who helped in so many ways to bring to fruition the wishes of His Holiness the Sixteenth Karmapa and the wishes of Khenpo Karthar Rinpoche. This would not have been possible without the extraordinary talents and efforts of all. Our most special thank you is for Khenpo Karthar Rinpoche for his blessings and guidance.

Together we have made our best effort to present Rinpoche's teachings as accurately as possible. However, if any parts are incorrect or unclear, we take full responsibility. We hope that, despite our shortcomings, all beings may benefit from these teachings.

Maureen McNicholas and Peter van Deurzen

Advice from Khenpo Rinpoche

The following paragraphs are taken from the Question and Answer sessions that were a part of Khenpo Karthar Rinpoche's teaching on Karma Chakme's Mountain Dharma. *During these sessions, Rinpoche personally engaged with his students, answering their questions and offering his advice. Here Rinpoche comments on how the teachings were given to Tsondru Gyamtso, the uniqueness and value of this text, and how to use the information and practices contained in the book to instruct and support their practice.*

Karma Chakme Rinpoche was in lifelong retreat when Tsondru Gyamtso requested teachings on mountain Dharma. Traditionally, when someone was doing a lifelong retreat, provisions were made for limited communication with the outside. When a practitioner had completed all of the graduated practices of the various yidams and had achieved signs of realization, it was appropriate for them to teach even though they were remaining in retreat. They would speak through a small aperture in the wall, and as in the case of Karma Chakme Rinpoche and Lama Tsondru Gyamtso, the teachings would be received and written down by a student sitting outside, often in the cold. In some cases a blessing would be given, with the retreatant actually sticking his hand out and blessing the person. The reason it was appropriate for Karma Chakme Rinpoche to teach while he was still in retreat is that he was in lifelong retreat and he had completed all of the necessary practices.

❖   ❖   ❖

This book is almost unique in its clarity of presentation. The various topics that are dealt with are also to be found in other texts; however, most of these are so long and detailed that it is possible to get lost and not come to any real understanding of the subject. The presentation here is concise and very clear. As Karma Chakme Rinpoche wrote in his introduction, "If you place this volume on your pillow, then you have gotten hold of the one teacher who will never get mad at you." If people have this text available, then they will truly have an understanding of how to practice and how to approach the many different practices we do. They do not need to use the whole book. They can select the parts that correspond to their particular practice and get a much better idea of the purpose of it.

◆　◆　◆

This text is designed as a means of general guidance. It presents the whole path common to any system of practice in which you might be engaged. For example, when the text explains the preliminary practices, they are presented in their usual sequence. When it reaches the yidam practices, they are presented in a general way that can be applied to any major yidam practice, although you would need the empowerment for that particular yidam.

◆　◆　◆

When you make tea, you have to know what you are doing. You have to know how to use the stove. If you do not know what you are doing, you are going to burn your house down. When it comes to practicing Dharma, you think that you do not need to know what you are doing. You do not need to know anything. You do not need to study. This is incorrect. You may wonder why I am teaching all of this. Surely, the contents of any one of these chapters would be enough. It is not enough. Everything presented in this text is necessary and is here for a reason. You need to know these things in order to do your practice and to be able to deal with the problems that arise. Therefore these practices and these chapters are not redundant. They are not irrelevant. They are not outmoded. They are here for a reason.

◆　◆　◆

It is best if these practices are done by someone who has finished ngondro because the function of ngondro, as its name indicates, is to prepare you for other practices. However, there is no rule that says you cannot perform these visualizations until you have completed ngondro. In the case of the practices to benefit others, it is best if you have the seed of empowerment and the required mantra recitations, but it is most important that you have compassion.

◆   ◆   ◆

The practices that have been described in this text are a specific type of visualization practice called an application. To do an application connected with the practice of a specific deity, you should have received the empowerment of that deity. Strictly speaking, in order to perform an application practice, you must not only have received the empowerment, you must have performed a specific number of recitations of the deity's mantra. This is called being "fit for activity." The usual requirement is 100,000 multiplied by the number of syllables in the mantra. Thus if it is a ten-syllable mantra, it would be 1,000,000, and so on. That is considered the minimum requirement to be "fit for activity." The reason for this is that your faculties have to be empowered and familiarized with the visualization to the point where the application of that visualization and the benefit of others will actually be affected.

◆   ◆   ◆

I would like to say something about this whole question of signs or indications in practice. Sometimes it happens that practitioners will experience some positive signs in their practice, some indication that the practice is taking effect. They assume that that means they are done, that they have attained the result, and they therefore stop practicing. This is incorrect. Signs in practice do not indicate that you have reached your destination. They indicate that you are heading in the right direction and that therefore you should continue to practice as you have been. It is as if you were driving for the first time to New York City, and you were not really sure if you were taking the right highway or not. All of a sudden you come across a sign that says,

"New York City this way, so-and-so many miles to go." You would not stop at that point but would just realize, "Well, at least I am on the right road and if I continue, I will eventually get there."

Introduction

Mountain Dharma, Oral Instructions for Mountain Retreat, by Karma
Chakme Rinpoche is, on an outer level, a comprehensive manual for
all aspects of practice by the great mahasiddha Karma Chakme
Rinpoche. In essence it is a text on how to reveal our own buddha
nature. Buddha nature is who we truly are. It is our own genuine
nature, and it is absolutely essential that we understand this as the
basis of motivation to practice.

Simply knowing that we possess buddha nature, however, is not
sufficient to bring about awakening. If we know this but do not practice, it will not change anything. After all, this has always been our
nature. We have always possessed buddha nature, or sugathagarba,
but we have not yet attained buddhahood. Just its being there is not
enough. This is like the way it is with water in Tibet. It is now evident
that there is a lot of water underground in Tibet. We once thought
there was a problem getting water, but now we know that if we dig
in the ground, we could readily gain access to it. Nevertheless the
water just being there does not do us any good unless we actually
drill the wells. In the same way, the only point of studying buddha
nature is to be inspired to practice Dharma, because it is the practice — not the knowledge — that reveals our buddha nature and
enables us to attain buddhahood.

What we call buddhahood is nothing more or less than the full
revelation of our own innate qualities that have always been present.
"Buddha" is not something external to us. As long as we have not
discovered our own buddha nature, we can only regard "Buddha" as
external because we have no experience of "Buddha" as something

within ourselves. This text, *Mountain Dharma, Oral Instructions for Mountain Retreat* by Chakme Rinpoche, is concerned with every stage and every detail of the process of discovering our own buddha nature. It describes how to remove every type of adventitious obscuration and other impediments that in any way conceal or prevent the recognition of it.

Nevertheless it is possible to misunderstand the point of this text. Because the text is called *Mountain Dharma, Oral Instructions for Mountain Retreat*, some people may think that it is only useful for those who are in strict, isolated retreat, but that is not what this title refers to at all. *Mountain Dharma* refers to the fact that this is an all-sufficient, single text of instruction. Once you have received the necessary transmissions and initiations from a qualified teacher, if you were then to take this text into isolated retreat and had no other resources—no other literature and no living instructor—you would still have access to all of the guidance and all of the instruction you would need. The reason why this is called *Mountain Dharma* is that it is a text that will give you whatever instruction you need whenever you need it. It contains within it all the tools you will need at different stages of your practice in order to realize your own buddha nature. Therefore this title does not mean that this text is only for those in retreat; rather, it means that it is sufficient for those in retreat.

Furthermore the text is not designed for advanced practitioners only. It begins with the most fundamental aspects of Buddha-dharma—the vow of refuge and so forth—and continues all the way through the path, explaining everything you need to know and everything you need to practice in order to attain buddhahood. It contains all of the teachings of both sutras and tantras, an explanation of all of the stages of discipline and practice corresponding to individual liberation (Hinayana), the bodhisattva vow (Mahayana), and secret mantra (Vajrayana). Because of its completeness, this text is therefore regarded as superior to almost all other texts of this type.

The historical period in which this text was written was a remarkable and difficult one for our lineage. It was the time of the Tenth Karmapa, Choying Dorje, who because of political circumstances was unable to directly benefit beings in any significant way.

He said that Karma Chakme Rinpoche was the emanation of his activity in upholding the teachings of our lineage and spreading them widely. In addition, based upon the vision of the Fifth Dalai Lama, Karma Chakme Rinpoche is considered to be an emanation of the mind of Amitabha. During this era, the time of the Tenth Gyalwa Karmapa and the Fifth Dalai Lama, the writings of Karma Chakme Rinpoche spread like wildfire throughout Tibet, especially in Kham, forever changing the character of our practice.

From Rinpoche's teaching in which he introduced some background to the text.

Short Biography of
Karma Chakme Rinpoche

Karma Chakme was born, in accordance with the prophecies of Guru Rinpoche, in the Do-Kham area of Tibet in the year 1613. His father was the mahasiddha Pema Wangdrak and his mother, Che Kyong Kye, was a wisdom dakini. At the moment he was born, his father gave him the name Wangdrak Sung and bestowed upon him his first empowerment. As a child he was very accomplished in all aspects of study and Dharma practice, and by the time he was nine years old, he had received many empowerments and had become well known for his supreme intelligence and knowledge.

When he was eleven, Wangdrak Sung met Prawashara, from whom he received many empowerments, transmissions, and pointing-out instructions. When he was thirteen, he began a solitary Chenrezik retreat. After completing this retreat, he began to bestow empowerments and give reading transmissions and instructions to everyone who requested him to do so. At the age of twenty he received full ordination vows from the Tenth Karmapa, Choying Dorje, at Tsurphu Monastery, and received the name Karma Chakme. From that time, he diligently served the sangha at Thupten Nyinling, a monastery of the Surmang tradition.

For the next few years Karma Chakme studied with and received many empowerments, transmissions, and pointing-out instructions from His Holiness Karmapa, including Mahamudra, Chakrasamvara, Medicine Buddha, and Dorje Phakmo. He became quite well known and his fame greatly increased with his public examination at the Karma Kagyu Monlam in 1635. Between the ages of eleven and thirty-seven, Karma Chakme entered into solitary retreat for at least a few months every year in order to accumulate root and accomplishment mantras. There was not a single mantra he had not accomplished. During this time, he also received many auspicious visions, dreams, and signs of accomplishment of various deities.

At some point Karma Chakme returned to his native region and built a retreat house at Palri. He resolved to accomplish Gyalwa Gyamtso, and received the four empowerments in a dream from the Tenth Karmapa, Choying Dorje. Soon after this, in 1650, at the age of thirty-seven, he began a strict thirteen-year retreat, persevering in the practices of Gyalwa Gyamtso and Mahamudra. During this period, he wrote many texts and commentaries including *Ri Chö, Instructions for Mountain Retreat* written in 1659. In the same year Karma Chakme recognized and enthroned the great terton Mingyur Dorje, who gave oral transmission lineage teachings for which Karma Chakme was the scribe.

In 1663, at the age of fifty, Karma Chakme ended his thirteen-year retreat. He continued to greatly benefit beings, performing ceremonies and giving empowerments often attended by over four thousand students. Karma Chakme perfected all possible stages of practice and every miraculous deed for the sake of benefiting others.

In 1678, the Year of the Earth Horse, at age sixty-six, Mahasiddha Karma Chakme Rinpoche announced to thousands that the time had come for him to change realms, and he passed away. Many signs occurred at the time of his death, including rainbows, clouds in the shapes of the eight auspicious symbols, and countless images of Gyalwa Gyamtso and Dorje Phakmo embossed on his bones.

Adapted from the "Biography of Karma Chakme" by Jampal Gyepai Loden, Garland of Immortal Wish-fulfilling Trees, *Snow Lion Publications, 1988.*

Biography of
Khenpo Karthar Rinpoche

Khenpo Karthar Rinpoche was born in Rapshu in the province of Kham in eastern Tibet. He was born at sunrise on Mahakala Day, the twenty-ninth day of the second month in the Year of the Wood Mouse, 1924. On this day, very early in the morning, immediately after Rinpoche's mother went to fetch water from the stream and carried the full vessel of water back by herself, Rinpoche was born without giving any pain to his mother. According to Tibetan tradition, all of these special circumstances indicate a very auspicious birth.

Rinpoche's father was a devoted Manjushri practitioner who constantly recited the Manjushri sutra. He would go to sleep reciting the sutra and when he'd wake up he would simply continue with his recitation. His practice was so strong that he was known to benefit even animals when they died. When Rinpoche was quite young, his father taught him to read and write and to study and memorize Dharma texts.

Rinpoche decided at a young age to follow the path of his older brothers, who were both monks. At the age of twelve he entered Thrangu Monastery in Tso-Ngen, eastern Tibet. For the next six years Rinpoche studied and practiced at this monastery.

When he was eighteen years old, he went to Tsurphu Monastery to visit the seat of His Holiness, the Sixteenth Karmapa. His Holiness, who was also eighteen, was not yet old enough to give full ordination vows, so the following year Rinpoche received his Gelong vows from the Eleventh Tai Situ Rinpoche at Palpung Monastery.

After the Gelong ordination, Rinpoche returned to Thrangu Monastery and participated in the annual Yarnay (three-month summer retreat). Soon after this, he joined the year-long Vairochana group retreat, which was special to Thrangu Monastery. By the end of that retreat, Rinpoche was very enthusiastic to participate in the traditional three-year retreat, which he began shortly thereafter.

After completing the three-year retreat, Rinpoche expressed the heartfelt wish to stay in retreat for the rest of his life. He went to his uncle's cabin to begin his lifelong retreat, but after one year the Eighth Traleg Rinpoche strongly advised him to come out in order to receive transmissions from Kongtrul Rinpoche and to join Thrangu Rinpoche and other lamas in the newly formed shedra (monastic college) at Thrangu Monastery, which was under the directorship of Khenpo Lodro Rapsel. Traleg Rinpoche felt that Khenpo Rinpoche had attained insight and realization in his years of retreat and that this further education would be of great benefit to many students in the future.

The Second Jamgon Kongtrul Rinpoche, the Eighth Traleg Rinpoche, and His Holiness the Sixteenth Karmapa are Khenpo Rinpoche's main teachers.

In 1954, when Rinpoche was thirty years old and had completed his advanced training, he received the title of Khenpo. For the next four years he was an attendant and tutor to Thrangu Rinpoche. They traveled together teaching, studying, and benefiting others.

By the late 1950s the threat of the Communist Chinese was creating an increasingly dangerous situation for the Tibetan people. In 1958 Rinpoche left Thrangu Monastery along with Thrangu Rinpoche, Zuru Tulku Rinpoche, and the three-year-old Ninth Traleg Rinpoche.

With a few horses and some provisions, the party began their long trek. After two weeks they realized they were surrounded by Communist soldiers. They managed to escape, but for seven days they had to survive without food. During this time the elderly Zuru Tulku Rinpoche fell from his horse, so Lama Sonam (Khenpo Karthar Rinpoche's younger brother) carried him the rest of the way. Eventually they met a group of nomads who gave them some provisions.

After two and a half months, they arrived at Tsurphu Monastery. His Holiness the Sixteenth Gyalwa Karmapa, with his profound vision, was aware of the dangers and told them they must leave immediately for Sikkim. He provided them with the necessary provisions, and in March 1959 the lamas left Tsurphu.

Thrangu Rinpoche, Traleg Rinpoche, and Khenpo Karthar Rinpoche,
Karma Triyana Dharmachakra, New York, 2002.

The group quickly reached the border between Tibet and Bhutan. At this time the Bhutanese were unwilling to grant passage, and as a result, the party spent one month at the blockaded border until His Holiness the Dalai Lama could secure permission for the refugees to enter India. The rinpoches then traveled to Buxador, located at the border of India and Bhutan, where a refugee camp was set up by the Indian government.

More than fifteen hundred monks were gathered at Buxador. Their vision was to maintain and preserve the Dharma. During this time, due to the heat and unhygienic conditions, disease spread rapidly through the camp, and by the eighth year of residing there, Rinpoche was terribly sick. In 1967 Rinpoche went to Rumtek Monastery in Sikkim, the seat of His Holiness the Karmapa in India, where he taught the monks and performed various rites for the local Buddhist communities. As the state of his health worsened, Rinpoche was sent by His Holiness to teach at Tilokpur, a nunnery in Himachal Pradesh founded by His Holiness and Sister Palmo. After this, Rinpoche traveled to Tashi Jong Monastery, also located in Himachal Pradesh, where he received the Dam Ngak Dzo empowerment, transmission, and teachings from Dilgo Khyentse Rinpoche.

Rinpoche's health improved while he was there, but once he returned to Rumtek, his condition worsened once again. His Holiness then sent Rinpoche to Tashi Choling Monastery in Bhutan. Unfortunately, his health again grew worse, leading to a long and serious hospital stay.

Upon His Holiness's return from the United States in 1975, Rinpoche returned to Rumtek. In this same year Khenpo Rinpoche received the title of Choje-Lama, "Superior Dharma Master," from His Holiness the Sixteenth Gyalwa Karmapa.

For so many years Rinpoche had been ill with tuberculosis and now he was close to dying. He asked His Holiness the Sixteenth Karmapa if he could go back into retreat for the rest of his life. Instead His Holiness requested that Rinpoche go to the United States as his representative to establish Karma Triyana Dharmachakra, His Holiness's seat in North America.

Initially unable to obtain a visa due to his illness, Rinpoche soon acquired a special type of visa enabling him to enter the United States specifically for the purpose of receiving medical treatment. Nonetheless, sick as he was, Rinpoche boarded an airplane in February 1976 to begin a different life as teacher of the Dharma in a culture and environment far removed from his home in eastern Tibet.

When Rinpoche arrived in New York City, he was greeted by Tenzin Chonyi and Lama Yeshe Losal, who had been sent ahead by His Holiness while Rinpoche awaited approval of his visa. Immediately upon his arrival, Khenpo Karthar Rinpoche was taken to a hospital in New York where he spent one month receiving treatment. It would take another year for him to regain his weight and become strong and healthy again. Years later when His Holiness the Sixteenth Karmapa visited the United States, Rinpoche thanked him for saving his life. His Holiness responded by telling Rinpoche that if he had stayed in India he would surely have died. After his initial recovery, Rinpoche, along with Tenzin Chonyi, Lama Losal, Lama Ganga, and Yeshe Namdak, moved into a house in Putnam County that had been offered by Dr. Shen, a devoted student of His Holiness. From there Rinpoche traveled to New York City every week to offer teachings at what was to become one of the first KTC (Karma Thegsum Choling) centers in the United States.

Soon more centers were established and when His Holiness visited in 1977, the search began for a permanent site for His Holiness's seat in America. His Holiness had told Khenpo Rinpoche that he should open the new center on the auspicious day of Saga Dawa in 1978. Early in this year they located a good property and purchased the Mead House located on a mountaintop in Woodstock, New York. The day Karma Triyana Dharmachakra opened was the very day (the fifteenth day of the fifth Tibetan month in 1978, May 25, 1978) that His Holiness the Sixteenth Karmapa had commanded Rinpoche to do so. Ever since this time Khenpo Karthar Rinpoche has been teaching extensively with a warmth and directness that communicates the compassionate wisdom of the Kagyu lineage.

The Venerable Khenpo Karthar Rinpoche is the Abbot of Karma Triyana Dharmachakra in Woodstock, New York, the North American seat of His Holiness the Gyalwa Karmapa, head of the Kagyu lineage of Tibetan Buddhism. Rinpoche is also the retreat master at Karme Ling in upstate New York where he is now leading his fourth traditional three-year retreat.

རི་ཆོས

KARMA CHAKME'S
MOUNTAIN DHARMA

NAMO GURU DEVA DAKINI SARVA SIDDHI HUNG

Karma Chakme Rinpoche begins with homage and supplication to all dakinis, asking them to bestow siddhi and spiritual attainment, and pays homage to his own kind guru, Chokyi Wangchuk, "the one who is the knower of everything, who is the master of the mandala, who is always gazing upon every sentient being with tremendous compassion."

Karma Chakme Rinpoche

Namthar: The Spiritual Biography of Karma Chakme Rinpoche

The mahasiddha Karma Chakme Rinpoche, who lived at the time of the Tenth Karmapa, was one of the most highly realized and accomplished individuals in scholarship and meditation of the time. In order to benefit all practitioners pursuing the path of the Dharma, he composed over one hundred volumes of teachings, of which this text, *Mountain Dharma*, represents the essence.

During his lifetime Karma Chakme obtained teachings from over fifty great masters, including the Tenth Karmapa, His Holiness Choying Dorje, as well as the Tenth Karmapa's root guru, Chokyi Wangchuk. The text begins with the traditional Sanskrit invocation NAMO GURU DHARMESHVARA, "Homage to the guru." After Karma Chakme pays his respect and offers devotion to the guru, he supplicates all of the lamas and the yidams, whom he visualizes above him in the open sky, inseparable in mind from the guru.

Before beginning the actual instruction, Karma Chakme describes his own life, presented in the tradition of a spiritual biography, which is called a namthar in Tibetan. A namthar is actually much more than a mere biography. It is an explanation of the complete path to liberation and is presented at the beginning of a teaching in order to build confidence on the part of the students.

Traditionally, great realized beings humble themselves before presenting a definitive teaching in order to make it clear that they do not approach the task with any sort of ego or pride. Thus Karma Chakme begins by stating that he himself, born into a very poor, destitute family, has no realization whatsoever in either worldly or spiritual matters. Although people have given him the title of lama, he says that he is simply an ordinary person with no qualities at all. "My qualities and realizations are so rare that if you say that I have any of these right now, you might as well say that a rabbit has antlers."

"Despite my background and my lack of any qualities in meditation and realization, a person who has complete trust and confidence in me has requested me to teach and to write. Not only has this one individual requested this teaching and biography, but many great, reincarnated lamas, many great diplomats, and many great geshes have also made the same request. So, even though there is a crowd of students gathered to hear me teach, I take no pride in that fact. I am simply teaching with the hope that what I say will be of some benefit and that it will be of some use to students, like chewing on a radish." There is a saying in Tibet that even if you are totally destitute, at least you can chew on a dry radish, which in Tibet is considered among the worst of foods. In other words, at least you can survive. Karma Chakme is saying that by depending upon his teachings, even if worse comes to worst; you will at least have the minimum you need.

Responding to these requests to teach, and wanting to benefit all beings, Karma Chakme says he has the responsibility to present these teachings because he has obtained all the transmissions for them from many incarnated lamas and teachers. Therefore it is his responsibility to continue to bring forward the oral tradition, word by word, without allowing the stream of transmission to break. Furthermore he claims that he himself is not really the one giving the transmission. "I offer this transmission to all the people attending this teaching in the same way that you offer mandalas to the deities. I myself have no special quality empowering me to give this transmission; nevertheless, because I have received it from others who do have such qualities, I offer this continuous lineage of the stream of the teachings to all of you with my full, complete respect."

Next Karma Chakme describes some of the prophecies about his own present and past incarnations. He writes, "There is a great Tibetan teacher and terton named Mingyur Dorje, who discovered many termas, including the Buddha Amitabha sadhana. Mingyur Dorje and I have had a very close relationship as teacher and student over hundreds of past rebirths. Even when we both reincarnated in lower realms, we still had relationships as friends." According to Mingyur Dorje, the reason Karma Chakme was known for his displays of compassionate energy is that he is an emanation of Chenrezik. This also explains why people sometimes say that Karma Chakme is an emanation of the Karmapa, since the Karmapa is also an emanation of Chenrezik.

Another great master in Tibet, named Dudul Dorje, has said that along with Vairochana, Karma Chakme was one of the lotsawas (translators) during the period of Guru Padmasambhava. His name during that lifetime was Sena Lek, and he was also a very famous terton at that time. In addition, Karma Chakme was also said to be connected to the lineage of King Songtsen Gampo of Tibet. Karma Chakme says that although he may be called "an emanation of this and an emanation of that," he himself interprets the situation differently. In the six realms of samsara, the six buddhas are present, signifying that all beings have buddha essence. "Therefore I must have buddha essence too. The past masters must be referring to the buddha essence in me, not the realization aspect of my practice. In the sutra teachings we talk about tathagatagarbha, the buddha essence, which we all possess. In this way, even though the great masters have said that I am an emanation of some great terton, I do not present the teaching with any arrogance."

"If you really want to know who I am and what I am, I can say that I am a person from the ignorant caste." At the time of this writing, the caste system was very strong and the lowest caste was known as "the ignorant caste," so here he is putting himself in the lowest social sphere. "Nonetheless there was a practitioner yogi named Pema Wangdrak, who claimed that I was his son, a yogi. There were four other well-recognized realized beings with supernatural power who also said that I belong to the yogic lineage. Even if it is as the great masters say, that I belong to the line of a great yogi, what does that make me? It makes me nothing. It is as if I am a great ruler and have no subjects. What is the benefit?" In this way Karma Chakme asserts again that he has no feelings of arrogance or pride in giving these teachings."

"My only quality is that from childhood I took the full ordination of a bhikshu monk. In the full monastic ordination there are 253 precepts, and I am happy to be able to say that I have kept the four root precepts and have held them more precious than my own life. I have not even come close to breaking them. The rest of the branch precepts are very difficult to keep. There is a Tibetan expression that says that the causes for breaking the branch precepts are like raindrops, falling from everywhere. I have perhaps come close to breaking the branch precepts, but I have kept the root precepts very pure and unbroken."

Karma Chakme Rinpoche was a very popular teacher, and in reflection of that he says, "Wherever I go and wherever I sit to expound teachings, I am showered with offerings and gifts. I do not know whether such offerings are a hindrance or a benefit to me, whether such gifts are demonic or divine." Whatever they may be, he says that he has never broken the samaya of bodhichitta. With the Three Jewels as his witness, he declares that he has never misused or wasted any offerings. "I used these material and financial gifts to build great statues of the Buddha and to make offerings to my teachers and gurus. When making such offerings or building such statues, I have always remained humble. I have no arrogance or pride in thinking that I am doing a great thing. In any case, any ability I have to make such offerings is really a blessing of the guru and yidam."

Providing details about his own practices, he continues, "I have practiced one hundred deities, and in every one of these practices, I have gained some sign of experience or realization in dreams and other nonordinary signs. However, even with all of these signs, I have felt no arrogance and have lived a simple, humble life. I have not bragged about my qualities or experiences to others.

"In undertaking these practices, I have accomplished the recitation of the mantras of many deities, and because of this I have experienced many powers. Such powers may be misused by ordinary individuals to subdue their enemies. I could easily have done this because there are many people who have annoyed me and who could have caused anger or hatred to arise in me, but I have never used the power and strength of mantra in this way. Believing in the protection of the Dharma whenever hindrances or negative influences arose, I did not regard these as the enemy. When you do not regard them as the enemy, the negative feelings of animosity are instantly burned away like the wings of a moth burned by fire.

"I have studied many other practices. There is nothing that I have not turned over to study, in all cases relying upon fifty very extraordinary teachers. I feel that I am very rich because of these studies, transmissions of the yidam practices, and accomplishments of the mantra practices. I have made the utmost effort to complete every subject I have undertaken. Having studied, learned, and also accomplished all these subjects from many teachers in my young age, now I can be of benefit because students have so many different needs. In this way, I am like a merchant with many goods—whatever the student wants, I can provide, thanks to my great teachers in the past."

Speaking directly of his own meditative experience, Karma Chakme says, "When I myself obtained the teaching introducing the nature of the mind from my teachers, I was by then so well prepared to receive these teachings that I was completely free from any distractions. In fact I had no awareness of the state of distraction or nondistraction. Being in a state beyond 'is' or 'is not,' I was able to rest in the state of the dharmakaya inseparable from myself. Being inseparable from the dharmakaya, free from distracting mind, I was able to receive from my teacher the introduction to the nature of the mind. Resting fully in the goodness of that state, I was free from all arrogance and pride. As I was receiving the instruction on the introduction to the nature of the mind, I felt the inseparability of the minds of all the buddhas and myself. Not only did I feel the inseparability of the buddhas' minds and my own mind but I also felt the inseparability of the minds of all the beings of the six realms and my own mind. Not only that, I actually felt inseparable from, or beyond, all time and space—past, present, and future. Everything, my mind and the minds of enlightened and sentient beings became inseparable like mixing water with water."

This is Karma Chakme speaking about his own experience. He warns that sometimes when beginning practitioners reflect on the inseparability of their minds and the minds of enlightened and sentient beings, they may think, "Well, then everything becomes one,

one whole cosmic mind." Karma Chakme says that this is not so. "Although I felt or experienced this inseparability, I could at the same time clearly experience the innate energy and essence of all beings separately and individually, just like a clear, precise reflection of something in a mirror. The reflection of something in a mirror has no substance. Similarly, although each thing is so precise and so distinctive, it is also empty of existence." Karma Chakme states that since he has experienced all this, it may be quite all right to call himself a meditator. He is not really saying that he is a great meditator, but he does say, "It may be acceptable to say I am a meditator."

Karma Chakme says that having practiced the sadhanas of the great yogis of both India and Tibet, he has never experienced the direct or physical manifestation of these realized beings when he was practicing. "But I have experienced many realizations and manifestations of these realized beings in dream states or in other magical or miraculous ways. I cannot say for sure whether these are manifestations of demons or whether they are really the yogis themselves, but whenever I experience such manifestations, I also experience calmness of mind. It heightens my spiritual realization, so this is definitely a sign that it is not a manifestation of a demon but rather a definite realization of and blessing of past realized beings or yogis.

"Although I am not qualified to give teaching to others on any worldly or Dharma matters, because I have maintained a very strong bond with the great master Mingyur Dorje, because I have attended to many teachers, and because of my past prayers and aspirations, it seems that I have the ability to benefit beings right now through giving teachings. Whenever I give an empowerment, lung, or instruction that I have received from my teachers, the student always receives benefit.

"Further evidence that these transmissions are unbroken is that my students benefited, and many have already attained higher realization. The sole reason the students are able to experience quick realization is the result of my very strong, pure samaya with all my teachers. Feeling the immaculate purity of my samaya with my teachers, the students gain a sense of confidence and trust in the teachings. Based on this, many are led to higher realization. There are students who have not yet developed calmness or stillness of mind but are constantly distracted and unable to remember their past lives. Even all of these people, having received and applied the practices of this unbroken transmission, are gradually led to experience their previous births in the form of dreams and other miraculous or magical illusions.

"My guru, Chokyi Wangchuk, taught me to abstain from criticizing people, whether they are good or bad, whether they are friend or enemy. By abstaining from criticizing people, it is possible that you may be accumulating positive karma, but even if you are not accumulating anything positive, it is definite that you are not accumulating negative karma. As instructed by my guru, whenever I speak to anyone, whether they are close to me or not, I try to explain everything in a manner that is humble, straightforward, as truthful as possible, and free of any criticism."

Earlier in the text Karma Chakme stated that by practicing correctly, one will not only experience realization in the present but will also remember the experiences of past lives. Now he relates some of his own past-life memories, which he remembers very vividly.

"I have seen Buddha Shakyamuni at Bodhgaya. I have seen Ananda as well. I have seen Lord Nagarjuna. I have seen Pandita and the dakinis." When Lord Nagarjuna passed away, Pandita, his principal disciple, was very depressed and he sat down and wept. At that moment many dakinis appeared and explained to Pandita that it was not necessary for him to weep or to feel sorrow because in the future there would be great teachers who would appear and who would be of equal benefit to beings. Karma Chakme is acknowledging that he was a monk at the time of Buddha Shakyamuni and of Nagarjuna. These are not merely visions; they are actual memories.

Karma Chakme also remembers that he was at the cave of Milarepa, called Yolmo Khangri. This sacred cave is located between Tibet and Nepal, and today many students of Khenpo Tsultrim Gyamtso practice there. When Milarepa was meditating at Yolmo Khangri, Karma Chakme was present as an emanation of Zhing Kyong, one of the five female Dharma protectors. He remembers being in this form, which is like a mountain goddess, and along with the other four female protectors, participating in a ganachakra offering to Milarepa.

"I remember that I was the youngest of the three sons of the king of Tibet known as Trisong Deutsen. My name was Jing Yon Sena Lek. I remember being a personal attendant to the First Karmapa, Dusum Khyenpa. I remember being the emperor of China and being a student of Karmapa Rangjung Dorje. I invited him to China. I was a yogi in the Tibetan province of Kongpo, where I discovered one of the great holy termas of the Dzokchen teachings. As a yogi I had many sons, and I offered one of them to Karmapa, hoping that the child would learn the teachings and realize the body, speech, and mind of Karmapa, and that he would accomplish the realization of the three kayas, the dharmakaya, sambhogakaya, and nirmanakaya. I remember being a businessman in the streets of Lhasa, the capital of Tibet. During that period I remember sponsoring people to do one billion recitations of OM MANI PEME HUNG. I remember many things like this, scattered all over here and there, not only one rebirth but many; not only a few experiences but many. Nevertheless I have neither fear, hope, pride, nor arrogance in any of these memories."

Having told us about some of his past lives, Karma Chakme now turns to his current life. When he was young, he was very dedicated to Dharma practice, alternating between doing retreat and participating in pujas. When he was thirteen, he began a solitary Chenrezik retreat. After completing this retreat, he began to bestow empowerments and give reading transmissions and instructions to everyone who requested him to do so. "The people seemed to enjoy hearing both the teachings and what I had experienced in retreat, and many students made material and financial offerings to me.

"Even though I was now accumulating many students and they were making many offerings, I still maintained the lifestyle of a fully ordained monk living very simply and in perfect accordance with the Buddhadharma. People often developed a tremendous trust and confidence in me because my lifestyle was so consistent with the discipline of the Dharma. Because of this trust and confidence I gathered more and more students and also more and more offerings. I gave all of these offerings back to monasteries and to the high lamas, by making personal offerings to them and by building statues and so forth. I have never kept a single offering for myself."

Karma Chakme Rinpoche continues, "It is wonderful if I am able to dedicate my life to the practice of Dharma and able to go into retreat. If I am unable to dedicate my life to the practice of Dharma, however, if I am unable to go into retreat, and if my mind just wanders around in complete distraction, then I might as well be dead. I have come to the point where I really have no concern whether I live for a long time or a short time. The prophecies record that because of my dedication to practice, the moment that I die I will immediately be reborn on a lotus in Dewachen, the pure land of Amitabha, and having been born there I will obtain direct teachings from Amitabha. Because of my complete confidence that this will happen as predicted, I neither care nor wish to live for either a long time or a short time.

"Since some students may not be familiar with these predictions from Amitabha that are found in the sutras, in the teachings of the great master Mingyur Dorje, and the ancient terma teachings, I would like to give a short account here in order to enhance your understanding and to eliminate any doubts in your minds.

"The predictions state that at the moment I die, I will experience the rebirth of my consciousness appearing on a lotus in front of Amitabha in Dewachen. My form will be one of a bhikshu, a fully ordained monk, and from that form five emanations will radiate out in five directions. The first emanation is blue in color and radiates in the eastern direction penetrating to the Medicine Buddha realms and conducting the activities of Medicine Buddha to benefit others. The second emanation goes to the northwest, in the direction of Uddiyana, Guru Padmasambhava's birthplace. Green and wrathful in appearance, this Buddha activity is to protect all beings who practice the teachings of Mingyur Dorje and my other teachers, as well as all Dharma practitioners. The third emanation is born into the family line of the great terton Mingyur Dorje and his activity is to develop the tantric teachings during the time of degeneration. The fourth, from Dewachen, emanates as the nephew of my guru (Chokyi Wangchuk), and works to fulfill my guru's activity, especially preserving the Karma Kamtsang tradition of the Buddhist teachings. It is said that this nephew, because of past prayer and aspiration, is able to bring peace to Tibet. The fifth emanation will be born in Bodhgaya in India during the time called the Good Kalpa, when the people are experiencing life spans of six hundred years. My activities during this Good Kalpa will fulfill the sixteen arhats' activities.

"When the activities of the fifth emanation, the one born in Bodhgaya in the form of a fully ordained bhikshu, are complete, and when I have passed into parinirvana, all five emanations will unite back into the main source, the one who appears as a fully ordained monk on the lotus in the front of Amitabha in Dewachen. At this time I will cease to take rebirth anywhere in the world. I will have become fully enlightened, a buddha who will have the name Immaculate Pemo Chukye. Although I will be in the Amitabha realm, my complexion will be white in the nirmanakaya form. At the moment I attain full enlightenment, all those who have built a connection with me through my teachings, or through any of my emanations or activities, will, at that very moment, immediately experience rebirth in my buddha field.

"In recounting all these prophecies about myself, it may seem as though I am bragging, but any qualities that I may have developed are also found within all beings. To fabricate a story simply for personal gain and fame would be hypocritical and totally contradictory to Dharma practice. Especially in this case if I, as your teacher, were to lie to you, my students, the negative karma would be so immense that not only I but also anyone who believed and acted on such falsehoods would fall to the lower realms. Because of fear of causing such negative karma, I assure you that I am not exaggerating or lying about any of this. Rather, at the request of my vajra friends, I have simply explained my true life story.

"Because these predictions are true, I feel comfortable in presenting them to you. What I have presented here is very short and I am telling it to you as I remember it, so it is not in a very orderly form. Those who are interested in a more orderly, precise text should read the biography I have written at the request of my teacher, Lord Mingyur Dorje. Because these subjects are so precise, there is a chance that readers might develop wrong views that will cause them harm. For this reason I request that my biography be read only by those who have the empowerment and the lung."

Questions and Answers

STUDENT: Karma Chakme seems to be putting himself forward as the type of person who has no learning and behaves poorly in retreat. Is that just a formality, or is there a deeper meaning to that presentation?

RINPOCHE: Self-denigration in this way is characteristic of the speech and behavior of all great individuals. Somehow they always say those things about themselves. They will never praise themselves. This goes against how we normally are in the world. Individuals like Karma Chakme Rinpoche actually hate any kind of position. They dislike receiving the respect, adulation, and praise of others. Nevertheless, while they may claim to be degenerate, when they teach, their quality is evident in their teaching, even though they will make all attempts to deny and conceal it in every way. This is simply how they all are. In fact this is almost the only way we can determine when someone is such a great individual. Whereas an ordinary person, a mundane person, will always seek to emphasize, promote, and show their best qualities, and hide their defects, these great teachers will always denigrate themselves and will always avoid any kind of situation of grandeur or position.

STUDENT: The writer of the text begins by telling us that he has no realization whatsoever, and then he goes on say that when he received pointing-out instructions, he was able to remain undistracted in the dharmakaya. How is this possible?

RINPOCHE: When a teacher gives the instructions on the introduction to the nature of mind, they will include teachings on how to sit and meditate, how to rest in the state of no concept, and so on. When ordinary students like us receive these instructions, we go back home, practice the instructions repeatedly, and do many practices for purification and the accumulation of merit, such as ngondro practice. Eventually we get a glimpse of the nature of our own buddha mind and at that very moment we experience a special wisdom that we have never experienced before. That wisdom is actually the first stage, the first bhumi of enlightened wisdom. Did we acquire that wisdom from someone else? No, it came from ourselves. Was this wisdom that we acquired absent before? No, it was always there. Our consistent practice led us to see our own wisdom and our own buddha nature that was always there. Therefore we got to the first bhumi, the first stage of enlightenment. That is how an ordinary practitioner evolves to enlightenment. In the case of Karma Chakme, because of the degree of purification and accumulation of merit he had achieved in his previous lives, the moment the teacher talked about what to do, the moment the teacher gave the instruction, Karma Chakme was able to accomplish it. The ability to experience that wisdom at that very instant was the outcome of his previous accumulation of merit, and it was also a sign that previously he had purified all obscurations. Such instructions are really like a precious jewel that has been placed in our hands. We know that there is something in our hands, but we have no idea what it is. In the case of Karma Chakme, however, he realized its preciousness. It is nothing external, nothing new, it is something that was always there but now it is recognized. Thus because of past-life accumulation of merit and purification, Karma Chakme was able to have this experience instantly.

STUDENT: Isn't it unusual to start a teaching by telling the story of your previous incarnations? Why is it done here and why don't other teachers do this?

RINPOCHE: There are several reasons why teachers might not speak of their past lives. Often when you talk about your own life, you may indulge yourself by dwelling on what you see as your positive qualities, your accomplishments, your perfections. When you do this, unless you are really a very highly developed individual, it can lead you to develop personal arrogance. Furthermore, by exaggerating your own qualities over and over again, you come to believe what you are saying, and then you tend to exaggerate even more. In addition, even if what you are saying is not exaggerated at all, if you speak the truth of what you have accomplished in your Dharma practice, then there are many beings who will be jealous. Again, unless you are very accomplished, when you end up talking about your biography, there will be a hundred people who will hate you because of your accomplishments, and not only will they be jealous but they will also try to attack you, to bring you down, because of that jealousy. In the case of Karma Chakme, even when there were evil beings who would try to bring him down out of anger and jealousy, because he himself was highly skilled, the evil beings and all their negative emotions were rendered harmless. Karma Chakme was also able to plant a seed of virtue in them. To receive such a seed of virtue, the person must have some connection, good or bad, with the teacher. Maybe they hate him or are jealous of him, but because he does not respond in kind, he is able to plant a seed of virtue in them to establish a connection. That is the method of highly realized beings. When teachers talk about the details of their lives and accomplishments, it may look to ordinary people that they are doing this simply to accumulate students, offerings, and other types of personal gain. This causes doubt in ordinary people. So again, for this reason, many lamas do not talk about their biographies. We are beginning to study a new and very important text by Karma Chakme, who is unknown to many students. When a teacher is being introduced, it is beneficial to know who he is, what emanation he is, and so forth. Therefore to give you some sense of enjoyment and confidence in this text, I have shared this spiritual biography of Karma Chakme with you.

STUDENT: Could you say more about the long list of connections that Karma Chakme had with the Karmapa?

RINPOCHE: Karma Chakme says that he always had some sort of connection with his teachers throughout his many lives. Sometimes the teacher was just a friend, and sometimes there was a teacher-student relationship. Whatever kind of relationship it was, he was always able to maintain a very pure samaya. That ability to maintain such a pure samaya for life after life not only helped him but it also helped his students and future students like ourselves, who follow his teachings so that we will also become free from any hindrance or obstacle on the path to enlightenment. This is due to the force of the purity of his samaya, life after life. Another connection between Karma Chakme and his teachers is illustrated by the fact that he is known as an emanation of Chenrezik. His Holiness Karmapa also spoke of Karma Chakme as an emanation of Karmapa himself. In reality what this refers to is that they are both the emanation of Chenrezik, so one is not really different from the other. In essence there is no difference between them. We separate them, but for them there is no dualistic view. Therefore with all these connections as well as with the compassionate energy of Chenrezik, the activities of Karma Chakme and Karmapa have become very vast and continue into the present.

STUDENT: When Karma Chakme appeared in the form of the Zhing Kyong during the time of Milarepa, was he actually reborn in that form, or was he an emanation?

RINPOCHE: He was actually reborn in that form as one of the five female protectors. He was not an emanation. Often great realized beings make the prayer "May I be able to benefit every sentient being in accordance with every one of their needs." In order to fulfill every need of sentient beings, you have to experience many different births, many aspects of form and birth. In that lifetime Karma Chakme, as a result of his prayer, was benefiting beings as a female Dharma protector. Such protectors, with their outer fearsome appearances, are able to protect the Dharma and Dharma practitioners from evil beings. The protectors also bestow siddhi upon serious practitioners, and help to maintain the continuity of the transmission of all the teachings by destroying or subduing whatever adverse conditions arise.

STUDENT: Your explanation of how Karma Chakme realized that his mind was the same as the minds of all the beings in the six realms was very powerful. I know that we should be remembering beings in the six realms and praying for them, but I find myself forgetting that and praying mostly for beings in the human and animal realms. Could you give us suggestions for remembering beings in the other realms?

RINPOCHE: In our case as beginning practitioners, all we can really do is pray for the welfare and happiness of all sentient beings, that they may be liberated from any negative karma that they have created and that they may come to the realization or experience of enlightenment. Our prayer is the best thing we can do as beginning practitioners. Once we are able to remove our own mental obscurations, then of course we can do more. Great mahasiddhas like Karma Chakme demonstrate for us that enlightenment is not like passing into an unconscious state. Enlightenment is becoming aware and clear about everything, developing the wisdom state of our mind. That is the way we can be of great benefit to beings. This is possible for all of us, but in order to get to that point, we have to really overcome all obscurations. Until then it is best to always pray for the happiness and enlightenment of all beings.

STUDENT: The text mentioned at one point that there are six realms in samsara and six buddhas in the six realms. What is meant by that?

RINPOCHE: In Buddhism we talk about the six realms, or sometimes it is translated as the six existences. These are the human realm, the animal realm, and so on. Within each of these six realms, there are six types of beings, each having different aspects of suffering and experiences, and each having its own type of outer appearance. When we consider the different physical appearances of the beings of the six realms, we come to the point of asking, "Who gives us the physical appearance we are born with? Are we shaped by some external being to look the way we do?" In Buddhism we say that no one shapes us except our own afflictive emotions—our attachment, anger, ignorance, pride, jealousy, and greed. Whichever is strongest in us, and whichever we participate in more, creates the karma that will determine within which realm our subsequent rebirth will occur. With regard to the six buddhas, the six tathagatas within the six realms, there is an outer meaning and an inner meaning. The outer mountain Dharma meaning is simply that within each of the six realms there is a buddha who benefits the beings of that realm. The inner meaning of these six buddhas is the six wisdoms, which are nothing more than recognizing the absence of each of the afflictive emotions that we just described — anger, attachment, and so on. Thus when we are overcome by an afflictive emotion, the inner meaning, or the innate nature of that afflictive emotion, is wisdom. When we have not recognized this wisdom, then it becomes an afflictive emotion — anger, jealousy, and so forth. When we recognize it directly, that is wisdom. Whether in the lower realms or in the higher realms, all beings have this buddha essence, and this is what Karma Chakme describes.

STUDENT: From the perspective of one who has realization, could you give us some sort of insight as to what it is like to look at beings without criticism or judgment?

RINPOCHE: Every religion is worthy of respect; however, I am not qualified to comment on other religions. It is not that I do not respect them, but I have no knowledge of them, and I do not want to talk about something I do not know. However, I am very comfortable in Buddhism because I was brought up from childhood in this religion. Have I accomplished anything in this practice? No, nothing whatsoever. But I have developed a tremendous trust in Buddhadharma, as well as in the laws of karma. Through this trust I have realized that if I keep up with the Buddha's teachings or try to follow in the Buddha's footsteps, then it will be very beneficial for me in this lifetime and future lifetimes and also that I could be of benefit to other beings. Without any doubt, I have a very strong, complete trust in that. At the same time, being a Buddhist has also caused me to realize the preciousness of this human birth. When we have a human life, we have a choice to direct our life to virtuous or to nonvirtuous actions. Therefore it is very shameful for me to think of wasting my life by not doing something virtuous. This is also because, as much as we respect this precious human life, we also know that it is impermanent. It is subject to loss, to death, at any time, any moment. Therefore if we do not do something with this life to establish virtue while all the opportunities are there, it may be that when death strikes, we will not have another such opportunity to do good or virtuous actions. Sometimes when we think about studying the Dharma and doing our practices, we think, "Why do we have to struggle through so many hardships? Can't we just enjoy our life?" Consider the following analogy: If you have a child and you don't send them to school but instead let them watch television all day long, the child would enjoy it very much. He or she would love you. At that moment it seems that the child who is enjoying television, not going to school, is really having a great time. However, if this were to go on year after year, and you did not make them go to school, your child would have no education. Did that time of enjoyment really help them or did it harm them? Definitely it will have caused that person tremendous harm. Therefore understanding the meaning of precious human life and also of impermanence is important. Furthermore we are not talking just about this life. We are talking about life after life. With that sort of understanding it becomes extremely important to engage in the virtuous action of practice, not wasting this precious life, and understanding or remembering the impermanence of it. Because of my upbringing, I have definitely developed that sort of devotion to Buddhadharma.

STUDENT: Can a teacher of lesser realization bring a student to full awakening?

RINPOCHE: Yes. This is possible because if someone sees their teacher as the embodiment of all buddhas, and has one-pointed faith in the teacher as Vajradhara, then that individual will receive the blessing of Vajradhara, even though their teacher has not attained the state of Vajradhara. This is why we visualize our root guru as the dharmakaya Vajradhara and not in the flesh-and-blood form in which we normally perceive them. Some teachers actually are fully awakened beings, whereas some are ordinary beings, but in either case if you see the teacher as an utterly ordinary person, you will not receive any blessing from the relationship. If you see them as Vajradhara, you will receive Vajradhara's blessing. There is a story that illustrates the truth of this. There was once a woman who had tremendous faith in Buddhist teachings but who had a merchant son who did not have much interest in the Buddhadharma. Every year as part of his business the son would go on a long journey to a trading location that was also known to have a lot of relics of the Buddha. And every year his mother would say to him, "Well, you know you're pretty wealthy. As long as you are there, you could find a relic of the Buddha and bring it back for me. I do not think that is too much to ask." Every year he promised to do so and every year he would forget and return without the relic. Finally one year she said, "Well, this is it. If you don't bring a relic for me this year, I will kill myself." So again he made the promise, and again he went on his journey, conducted his trading, and then came right back, having again forgotten his mother's request. When he was almost home, he suddenly remembered her words and he got very scared, thinking, "Now my mother is really going to kill herself." At that moment he happened to see the skull of a dog lying by the side of the road. Thinking that he had to try to fool his mother, he took a tooth out of this dog's skull, wrapped it up in silk brocade, and brought it to his mother, saying, "Look, Mother, I have brought you a relic of the Buddha. In fact I got one of the Buddha's teeth." She believed him completely, and she prayed to the tooth one-pointedly. Over time, the relic started to produce miracles, including sacred relics called sharira, or rinsel. In addition, the mother herself reached a high level of attainment. There is a Tibetan saying that if you have enough faith, even the tooth of a dog can bring blessing. The tooth of this dog obviously carried no blessing of itself. The blessing was in her attitude.

STUDENT: So even if there is no skill in the teacher, it is the blessing of the buddhas that can bring the student to awakening.

RINPOCHE: Although it is not necessarily entirely due to the skill of the teacher, the teacher is nevertheless a necessary condition for that development to occur. It depends a great deal on the perception of the individual. For example, there is no one with a greater blessing than the samyaksambuddha, the "perfect buddha," yet his own half brother, Devadatta, perceived him as negative. The Buddha's qualities only inspired jealousy and competitiveness to the point where Devadatta attempted to kill the Buddha and ended up driving himself into the lower realms. Thus even though the teacher may be perfect, the student's devotion must be there. Teacher and student must both be there. For example, Tilopa's training of Naropa would, by most standards, seem somewhat odd, as would Marpa's training of Milarepa. But through the unflagging devotion of Naropa and Milarepa and the unlimited compassion of Tilopa and Marpa, things worked out very well, to say the least.

STUDENT: Could you explain why the texts sometimes refer to the three kayas and sometimes to the four kayas?

RINPOCHE: The bodies of Buddha can be divided into two, three, or four. The rupakaya, the form body, is part of the twofold division, not the fourfold division. I will review the four and then explain the others. The buddha who appeared in this world of Jambudvipa as a human being, demonstrating the twelve deeds and manifesting unexcelled qualities, is a nirmanakaya, or an emanation body. As an emanation body, he appeared to take birth, to attain awakening, to teach, and to pass into parinirvana. However, this nirmanakaya—this appearance of the Buddha among us—was just a display of the qualities of the Buddha in a way that we as sentient beings could experience. Ordinary beings experience the Buddha as the nirmanakaya, but bodhisattvas, that is to say those who have attained spiritual levels or bhumis, perceive the Buddha somewhat differently. Bodhisattvas are beyond the world, they are supramundane, but they have not yet attained buddhahood themselves. Bodhisattvas do not perceive the Buddha as being born, attaining awakening, and passing away. They perceive the form or body of the Buddha as something that is constant and everlasting, beginningless and endless, and that is called the sambhogakaya, or body of complete enjoyment. However, this, too, is merely an image that is displayed for the benefit of beings, in this case beings who are bodhisattvas, who are very close to awakening. Ultimately the Buddha is really what we call dharmakaya, or the body of Dharma. And dharmakaya is the quality or the nature of all things. You can also think of it as the nature of the Buddha's mind or the mind of the Buddha. We call the dharmakaya a "kaya" or a body, but this is metaphorical. It does not have form; therefore it has no color, faces, hands, scepters, costume, and so on. Nevertheless it is the qualities of the dharmakaya that manifest in the experience of those of purified karma as the sambhogakaya, and in the experience of relatively impure karma as the nirmanakaya. Since displays of the qualities of the dharmakaya— which is anything we call buddha—is a display of the same qualities, it is called the fourth kaya, the svabhavikakaya, which means "the body of the essential nature." It is not a separate thing. It is merely a way of pointing out that the other three are not separate things either. *Rupakaya* is a general term that includes both the sambhogakaya and the nirmanakaya, because they are both form.

STUDENT: What is your own karmic relationship with Karma Chakme?

RINPOCHE: Well, that is a very interesting question because I cannot say that I do not have any connection at all with Karma Chakme. I have the transmission of these teachings that I am giving to you, and when you have received such a transmission several times, you have already built a connection. However, if you are talking about my mental connection with Karma Chakme, he is a fully realized being and I am a completely ignorant, ordinary individual. There is no relationship whatsoever. Nevertheless because I have received this transmission and am teaching this text, I can say that I do have a connection with Karma Chakme from the transmission or lineage point of view.

STUDENT: First I want to thank you for your great sacrifice in coming to America and making the teaching available to us. Would you tell us, after so many lives and studying and staying on the path, how would any human being know within themselves when they have taken that first step, that first step toward becoming a realized being?

RINPOCHE: In response to your first comment, I came out of Tibet to India not because I wanted to teach, but because I was afraid of the Communists. I had to escape from my country; it was not a choice. In addition, my coming here from India was the command of my guru, His Holiness Karmapa. If such teaching is of any benefit, you must thank His Holiness, not me. In answer to your question, the step-by-step explanation of the path to enlightenment often makes it sound as if enlightenment is very difficult. Even one step toward enlightenment sounds very difficult. But in reality enlightenment is not as difficult as it sounds. It all depends upon an individual's exertion and diligence in the practice. There are several positive circumstances in our favor. First of all, as we explained, there are beings in all six realms. As beings in the human realm, we are the most fortunate because we can receive the teachings of enlightenment. We are all human beings and therefore we are able to study and practice. Second, even if one is a human being, having the wish or thought to participate in Buddhadharma is very rare. The mind that is drawn to Buddhadharma has a tremendous accumulation of merit developed in previous lifetimes. We ourselves are participating now in Buddhadharma, so it is obvious that those of us who are participating now and who have participated in the past have accumulated such merit. Third, it is said that you have to have a tremendous accumulation of merit not only to participate in Dharma but especially to participate and to engage yourself in the practice of Tantrayana. All of you are practicing Tantrayana teachings, showing both ability and a willingness of mind or an interest in Tantrayana practice. This definitely shows that you have participated in the accumulation of tremendous merit in the past. Enlightenment is not really that far away. It is said that if you are using the Sutrayana tradition of sincerely practicing pure loving-kindness and compassion toward all sentient beings, in one second that practice can burn away the accumulation of the negative karma of many lifetimes. That is the power and strength of such pure love and compassion. If you sincerely participate in deity practice, you can burn the accumulation of negative karma for hundreds of kalpas in a single instant. In my own understanding, we are not walking step-by-step to enlightenment. In some sense, I feel, we are jumping to enlightenment. However, as you jump, whether you remain where you land or jump again higher and farther depends upon you as an individual. Will you be diligent in your practice? That is the question that you have to ask yourself. You must not think of enlightenment as merely a slow step-by-step process but understand it as being totally possible in one instant if your mind is put into the practice. So you see, enlightenment is not really that far away.

Precious Garland: A List of Contents to Prevent Disorder

NAMO GURU DEVA DAKINI SARVA SIDDHI HUNG. Karma Chakme Rinpoche begins with homage and supplication to all dakinis, asking them to bestow siddhi and spiritual attainment, and pays homage to his own kind guru, Chokyi Wangchuk, "the one who is the knower of everything, who is the master of the mandala, who is always gazing upon every sentient being with tremendous compassion."

Karma Chakme begins by describing the place and circumstances under which he did retreat. In the eastern part of Kham, where he was born, in the direction of the Yangtse River, there is a very special mountain named Phal Ri, or "Glorious Mountain." Everyone who gazes at this mountain experiences a feeling of happiness and amazement, so the mountain itself is often referred to as being like an entertainer for people. Karma Chakme undertook his mountain retreat in Phal Ri, in a place that is shaped like a triangle — that is, not only did the land come together in the shape of a triangle but the mountains framed the sky in the same shape. Karma Chakme says that it was like doing retreat within the mandala of Vajrayogini. He started teaching from his retreat in 1659. Tsondru Gyamtso, a monk whose name means "Oceans of Tremendous Diligence," began to write down Karma Chakme's teachings.

He begins with the profound expression "E MA HO! I, the monk called Bhikshu Karma Chakme, born during the time of a dark kalpa, am not an expert in the studies of the science of philosophy. I am not an expert at all in the science of poetry or art. I have not composed this teaching based on research from great scholars, nor research from books. I have not composed this teaching to please the scholars or learned ones. I am not a master of the winds, nadis, and channels. I have not composed the teachings in order to gather students or to attract beings."

As always, Karma Chakme writes in the tradition of a great teacher, that is, one who always humbles himself. There is a famous story about him in this regard. During the time of the Fifth Dalai Lama, Karma Chakme visited Lhasa, the capital of Tibet. By then he had already become very popular and had written and delivered many teachings. The Dalai Lama sent a monk to see who this individual was who had written so many explanations of the Dharma. Consequently Karma Chakme went to visit him. After they paid each other respect by offering scarves, His Holiness the Dalai Lama said to Karma Chakme that in order to have the right to compose commentaries or explanations on the Lord Buddha's teachings, an individual must have three qualities. First, the person should be very learned in all the fields of philosophy and science in Buddhism. Second, he or she should have achieved a direct vision of the deity. Third, this individual should have achieved a high realization in meditation. The Dalai Lama asked, "Which do you have?" Karma Chakme answered, "None. I have none of these qualities."

The Dalai Lama was taken aback by this answer and thought that it would not be appropriate for such a person to write commentaries on the teachings. After all, did Karma Chakme himself not say that he lacked the necessary qualities? If one person did this, then another one would, and soon Tibet would be filled with teachers who were not really realized at all. Because Karma Chakme seemed to be a very nice, humble monk, the Dalai Lama said, "Come back tomorrow and we will discuss this."

The Dalai Lama contemplated what to do. He knew that it would not be appropriate to let the teachings of an unqualified teacher spread around Tibet. There must be some punishment that would also instill fear in other people who lack the necessary qualities and thus deter them from writing commentaries. The problem was what punishment to give. The Dalai Lama came to the conclusion that perhaps cutting or breaking Karma Chakme's thumbs and index fingers would be effective because then the monk could not write anymore, and the punishment would be severe enough to be a deterrent to others. This was what the Fifth Dalai Lama was thinking as he went to sleep.

That night the Dalai Lama dreamed of Amitabha. In the dream he saw himself carrying a knife and trying to cut the thumbs and index fingers off of Amitabha's hands. He awoke immediately, with the certainty that the monk he had interviewed that day was an emanation of Amitabha. The next day when Karma Chakme came before him, His Holiness paid respect and homage to him as an emanation of Amitabha. The Dalai Lama then told Karma Chakme there would be no restrictions on his writings and teachings. Therefore when Karma Chakme begins this chapter by saying, "I am not a master of the winds, nadis, and channels" and so on, we need to remember that this is the manner in which this teacher always presents himself, and that what he really is, is an emanation of Amitabha himself.

Returning to the text, Karma Chakme answers the question of what it was that convinced him to actually undertake these teachings on doing retreat. He says that because of his daily guru and yidam practices, and by the blessings of his guru and yidam, all of the teachings of the Sutrayana and Tantrayana became very familiar to his mind. He also became very aware of all the experiences based on applying those teachings. In fact the main points of every teaching of the Sutrayana and Tantrayana had become so clear in his mind that they became like the reflection of something in a mirror. "Now that I have become so old, I do not remember all these teachings precisely. Nevertheless by the blessings of the lama and yidam, the main points that are necessary for practicing and for achieving enlightenment are very clear in my mind. Therefore I have not composed these teachings through revising existing books, nor have I given them based on memorizing the texts so that the next day I would be able to recite them back to you. It is just flowing out of me based on what I have experienced through my own practices. If I let it flow, it flows ceaselessly like a river. Sometimes I have no idea myself where this endless river of thought comes from. Some scholars may not like these teachings, but I have presented them in the hope that other ignorant individuals like myself will benefit."

It is said, and it is very true, that if you become familiar with all fifty-four chapters of *Ri Chö,* you will have everything you need concerning how to conduct a proper solitary retreat. Karma Chakme himself notes that there are so many topics and so many texts available to the interested student, that it would be very difficult to obtain them all. Even if you could obtain all of them, you would not have enough time to really read and study them.

Think about all that is necessary to practice Dharma properly, particularly all that is necessary in order to conduct oneself in a retreat. Consider that you cannot possibly be with your guru for your entire lifetime. You will be away from your teacher sometimes doing retreat or practicing alone. What will you do if you always have to rely upon the physical presence of your guru? Karma Chakme Rinpoche answers that if you become familiar with all fifty-four chapters of these oral instructions for mountain retreat, it is like having a guru right there with you. "Just carry this textbook," he says. "The moment you are not clear, read that chapter. It is like having a guru there ready to explain everything. You do not have to obtain fifty or sixty different volumes of textbooks. If you become well acquainted with this text, you have everything necessary to achieve enlightenment. You have all you need to successfully undertake any practice, from the most basic to the complete Tantrayana."

Karma Chakme Rinpoche now provides a table of contents for each of the fifty-four chapters in the retreat manual.

Chapter 1. The Precious Garland: A List of Contents to Prevent Disorder

Chapter 2. To See It Is to Smile: An Introduction to *Mountain Dharma* Serving to Guide Ordinary People into Dharma's Gate

Chapter 3. Putting Away the Dice: How to Abandon the Paths of Samsara and Generate Stable Renunciation

Chapter 4. Gandi of the Nobles: A Clarification of the Practices of Individuals Immersed in the Various Greater and Lesser Vehicles

Chapter 5. Disk of the Sun: How to Keep the Three Vows Easily, Having Received Them in Sequence

Chapter 6. Protection from All Danger: Instructions on Taking Refuge in Order to Be Protected from All the Dangers of Samsara

Chapter 7. The Main Path to Awakening: Instructions on the Generation of Bodhichitta in Order That All One Does Be Brought to the Path of Awakening

Chapter 8. The Cooling Shade of Compassion: Placing Oneself and Others under the Protection of the Three Jewels Through Meditation

Chapter 9. Dispelling All Obstacles: Visualizations for Practice Sessions Used to Help the Weak, the Sick, and So On

Chapter 10. A River of Amrita: Instructions on the Purification of the Karma, Wrongdoing, and Obscurations Accumulated Throughout All One's Lives

Chapter 11. A Mountain of Merit: Instructions on How to Easily Complete the Accumulation of Merit by Offering the Mandala

Chapter 12. A River of Blessings: Guru Yoga, Practiced in Order to Receive Blessings and Increase Experiences and Realization

Chapter 13. The Traveler's Song: The Result of Long Experience, Recounted So That Beginners Can Recognize the Arising of Experience and Realization

Chapter 14. The Armor of Love and the Breastplate of Compassion: How to Protect from Obstacles Using the Buddhas' Truth

Chapter 15. All Jewels Included: A Brief Explanation of Geomancy, Since One Must Know What Places Are Good for Retreat

Chapter 16. The Good Path to Freedom: Instructions on Retreat, Easily Practiced by the Unintelligent

Chapter 17. The Axe That Cuts Through Self-fixation: Giving Away One's Body in Order to Gather the Accumulations and Bring Sickness and Spirits to the Path

Chapter 18. The Conjunction of Life and Fortune: The Generation of Life and Prosperity in Order to Prolong the Lives of Gurus, Friends, and Patrons

Chapter 33. Gold from Jambu River: The Root Words on the Physical Exercises for Establishing Interdependence in the Body

Chapter 34. The Magic Mirror: An Essay on Indications Enabling One to Determine Whether or Not One Has Accomplished the Three Roots

Chapter 35. Showing the Unmistaken Path: Avoiding Deviations, So That One Remains on the Flawless Path to Awakening

Chapter 36. A Rain of Amrita: Instructions on Removing Outer, Inner, and Secret Impediments

Chapter 37. The Wish-Fulfilling Jewel: Instructions on Improvement, So That Experience and Realization Increase Like the Waxing Moon

Chapter 38. The Great Peacock That Conquers Poison: Supporting Instructions on Abandoning the Obscuration by the Five Poisonous Kleshas

Chapter 39. The Practices of the Victors' Children: Instructions on Conduct, So That One Behaves in Accord with the Victors' Dictates

Chapter 40. Ocean of Activity: Instructions on Benefiting Beings, So That One Accomplishes Great Benefit for the Teachings and for Beings

Chapter 41. The Fruit of the Wish-Fulfilling Tree: How the Best, the Intermediate, and the Least Practitioners Die

Chapter 42. The Guide on the Quest for Jewels: Choosing a Pure Realm, So That One Knows Where One Is Going

Chapter 43. The Steed Balaha: How to Reach a Pure Realm If One Dies Without Leisure for Meditation

Chapter 44. Letter of Royal Command: Reminding Someone of Their Meditation So They Recognize the Ground Clear Light at Death

Chapter 45. Great Waves of Activity: the Practice of Protectors in General, So That the Buddhas' Teachings Flourish

Seeing It Makes You Smile: Ordinary Beings Entering the Gate of Dharma

The next chapter serves as an introduction to *Karma Chakme's Mountain Dharma*, which is intended to guide ordinary beings entering the gate of Dharma. The function of this introduction is to explain why and how this text came to be written.

Karma Chakme Rinpoche begins, "I will set forth here, briefly and in verse, the causes and conditions for the composition of these instructions for retreat, or mountain Dharma. I am someone who composes things because I wish to be renowned as a scholar. I am a hypocrite who wishes to be seen as a good person. I am someone who builds things out of the belief in permanence. I am someone who assembles a retinue out of nepotism. I am someone who pretends to benefit beings out of the wish to become wealthy. I am someone who remains in retreat out of the fear of death." He then says that all of these things refer to himself, Raga Asya, which is Sanskrit for the Tibetan word *chakme*, which means "nonattachment."

"In the presence of four wise and accomplished gurus, I offered the promise to practice one-pointedly, and to many prominent individuals and patrons I promised to remain in retreat my whole life. I left what domestic animals I had on the mountain and went to live in a hut built in an isolated place. There I remained in great concern that I might become ill or that I might die. I pretended to be in retreat but secretly slept the time away."

"While I was doing this, toward the end of one year, Lama Tsondru Gyamtso, of excellent family, good intelligence, great faith, respect, and diligence, came to the door of my retreat cabin and said the following: 'This year I almost died and I was tormented by the agony of apparently mortal illness. I discovered that I could not over-power this suffering with the realization I may have from practice. If the suffering of sickness is like that, then when the suffering of death arises, when Yama, the Lord of Death, approaches, I am very afraid that whatever experience and realization I possess will be insuffi-cient.

'By the compassion of the Three Jewels, I did not die this year. But, given the nature of this illusory body, I know that there is no way of avoiding death forever. I wonder if I have done enough retreat and practice so that I will have no regret at death. I have a place to practice, but because I do not know how to analyze the qual-ities of that place, I do not know if it is really appropriate or not. I have received many empowerments, transmissions, and instructions, and I know a great deal about the generation and completion stages, but I have not really accomplished them. I have no real experience. I have always thought that I would want to live only in retreat, but I have never received the practical instructions of mountain Dharma, of how to be in solitary retreat. I have texts of mountain Dharmas composed by the Kagyu predecessors, but I have not even received the reading transmissions, let alone experiential instruction. Furthermore the methods described in these texts are very difficult to put into practice.'

"Tsondru Gyamtso addressed me in this way and then made this request: 'You have compiled a great deal of instructions for use in retreat, but up to this point you have not composed a written text about retreat, or mountain Dharma. Please compose such mountain Dharma now. It is said that you have harmed your hands by writing so much. Therefore, since physically writing this yourself would be tiresome for you, I will write it down if you will dictate it to me.'"

Chakme Rinpoche continues, "Having said that, Lama Gyamtso requested the composition of this text, making a mandala offering of a thangka painted with gold paint bearing great blessing as the result of being consecrated with the footprints of Kagyu masters. Lama Gyamtso also offered a volume of his own compositions. He then performed many prostrations and offered one hundred actual man-dala offerings.

"At that time I, Raga Asya, laughed and then responded as follows: 'Heh, heh, Tsondru Gyamtso, the essential point of the mountain Dharma as composed by our Kagyu predecessors is to abandon all concern with this life and, having done so, to abandon your birthplace and go into solitude; to be terrified by impermanence and the thought of death; to relinquish all concern for food, clothing, and conversation such that you drink water, gnaw on stones, and wear the clothing of corpses.'" This last point need not be taken absolutely literally. It simply means that you are satisfied with whatever you acquire in the way of food and drink and that you are content with even the worst of clothing. "Having done that and sustaining the experience of the nature of your own mind, there is nothing else for you to do in retreat.

"As far as recitations are concerned, a few words or a few stanzas of supplication to your guru are sufficient. Aside from waiting for the coming of death, there is nothing else to think about in retreat. If those with faith in you should come to see you, then you should just flee like a wounded deer or antelope and go somewhere else where they cannot find you. We see this in the examples of great masters such as Jetsun Milarepa. When he was in retreat and pursued by patrons and students, he would make sure he was somewhere else by the time they found out where he was. That is the mountain Dharma of our Kagyu predecessors. That is being a Dharma practitioner who is, without destination, carried by the wind." By this he means that you have abandoned all concern with where you live and therefore you have no agenda of establishing anything or maintaining anything.

Chakme Rinpoche continues, "Unfortunately I myself have been unable to do this. I have remained for a long time here in my birthplace, so that even the name of the place has attached itself to me." During his lifetime Chakme Rinpoche was commonly referred to as the Yogi of Bari, which was the name of the place where he lived. He uses this as proof that he had not moved around very much. "I have been surrounded by my relatives and monks, so I have never lived alone for a single day. From the age of eight onward I have consumed the food of the sangha." Here he is intending to disparage himself, but in fact the statement means that he was ordained at the age of eight.

"'Death has never touched me in the heart. I have even accumu-lated some horses and cattle. My remaining in retreat has merely been the building of a residence. Therefore how could I possibly com-pose mountain Dharma? I could, I suppose, compose it in imitation of the writings of our Kagyu predecessors, but if I did so, everyone would recognize this and it would only be extremely embarrassing. It would be like 'your nose being embarrassed by what came out of your mouth.'" This is a Tibetan expression that refers to the fact that when someone says something inappropriate, those around them will be embarrassed. What he means is that if he were to teach the Dharma that he has not practiced himself, no one would have any confidence in that. Thus he concludes, "Therefore there is no way I can compose the mountain Dharma."

Tsondru Gyamtso thought about this for a day and then he came back and said the following: "Lama Raga Asya, you were ordained at an early age, and you have possessed flawless morality your whole life. You have relied upon many gurus, both renowned and unknown. You are rich with the empowerments, transmissions, and instructions of the new and ancient traditions. In your early years, even when you were busy performing rituals in villages, you completed innumerable yidam practices in retreat. After that you remained in retreat for thirteen years. Innumerable earth termas and sky Dharmas prophesied that you would appear. In many of these termas, which were hidden in the ground, and also in the Sky Dharma of Namchö Mingyur Dorje, Karma Chakme was predicted by Guru Rinpoche himself to be the holder of these teachings. Thus in innumerable terma teachings you were prophesied as the holder of the teachings and a fortunate vessel. For seven years now you have performed incredible benefit for countless people in many places. You are respected and depended upon by many, many people, and even now you have renewed your commitment to remain in retreat for the rest of your life. Therefore please compose a mountain Dharma in accordance with your own personal experiences of retreat practice. Even if there were a teaching that exceeds your own experi-ence, how could we put it into practice? We are incapable of even emulating your example. Dharma texts that are not used in practice are merely a heavy weight in the bookcase. Therefore please bestow instructions that we can actually use." Thus Tsondru Gyamtso made this request, and in response Chakme Rinpoche composed this text.

By the time Karma Chakme agreed to this, it was the middle of winter, with few daylight hours. He continues, "The days were short and I had many different daily practices to perform, as well as many practices and rituals to perform for the benefit, health, and protection of others. I did not have time to look at any source text, such as earlier compositions of mountain Dharmas, and had not ever really studied them. I did not have time, given my own retreat schedule, to think very much about what I was writing or dictating. Nevertheless each day at the end of the afternoon session, just before sunset, whatever I said, which was whatever I thought of at the time, was written down by Lama Tsondru Gyamtso, who did this in the attitude of faith that it was profound Dharma. This involved great austerity and patience on his part, since he was wearing very light clothing while sitting outside my retreat hut taking dictation in the middle of winter. His fingers rode the horse of the wind, writing down exactly what I said as I was saying it."

Chakme Rinpoche continues, "This text will not contain any quotations from the sutras and tantras, therefore there is no danger that it will be studied or read by the learned. I think it is not in contradiction with authentic sutras, tantras, and shastras. Nor will it contain any high-blown talk of emptiness, so there is no danger that it will be read by those with high realization. I think it is free from falling into deviation or error about the view. It will not contain any elegant composition or poetry, and therefore does not possess all the fit characteristics of composition. I think, however, that it will be beneficial to the mind. If someone properly practices what I have taught here, then even if they do not come to be renowned as a siddha, I am confident they will travel on the path to awakening. In other words, these instructions contain everything you need to know in order to attain awakening. Therefore we did not spare ink, paper, or quills in writing it down."

This concludes the introductory section of *Karma Chakme's Mountain Dharma*.

THE SONG OF PRECIOUS HUMAN BIRTH

The section begins with the invocation NAMO GURU, "Homage to the Guru." In response to the request of his disciple, Chakme Rinpoche begins, "Lama Tsondru Gyamtso, if you really want to wander in isolation, if you really want to remain in retreat, if you really want to make meaningful use of your body and your human birth, if you really want to have no regret at the time of your death, if you really want to have the assurance that you will be reborn in the pure realms, if you at least want to be certain that you will not be reborn in the lower realms, if you really want to eliminate the bardo, if you really want to accomplish the happiness of future lifetimes, if you really want to pass from happiness to greater happiness each lifetime, if you really want to accomplish your own ultimate good, if you really want to finally attain buddhahood — if you really want all of this, then place the following words of advice from my heart in your mind.

"Like a crop that ripens once every million years, we have been born human beings this once after innumerable births. We must make this rare human birth and this human body meaningful. Not only is a human birth itself rare, but for thousands of aeons there is no sound of the Buddhadharma, not even its name. Throughout most of time, buddhas do not appear, there is obviously no teaching of Dharma, and thus no opportunity to practice.

"We have been born in a fortunate aeon, however. Even though one thousand buddhas will appear in this aeon, in between their appearance there will be long periods in which the doctrine of the previous buddha will have disappeared and that of the subsequent buddha will not yet have appeared. We have been born during the time of the doctrine of Buddha Shakyamuni and therefore we have encountered his teachings.

"Although there are many countries within Jambudvipa (this world), the Dharma is not found in most of them. In some, it never appeared, and in others it has disappeared. Now, however, we have the opportunity to encounter the Dharma. Nevertheless, if our faculties are unclear, if our minds are so obscured that we cannot understand the teachings, then even though we have contact with them, we will technically have a human birth but it will be of no use. This is not the case for us, as we are fortunate enough to be born with the necessary intelligence to understand the teachings.

"With all of these favorable conditions, if we do not practice Dharma now, we will definitely never get such an opportunity again. Since the acquisition of this precious human existence is based upon the accumulation of its causes, if we do not accumulate the causes of a future precious human rebirth, we will definitely not get one again. Therefore make your present human life meaningful.

"You may ask, 'What makes a human life meaningful?' It is protecting the roots of your three vows. The three vows are the pratimoksha vow (individual liberation), the bodhisattva vow (bodhichitta), and the Vajrayana vow (samaya). You should protect the root commitments of these vows as attentively as you would protect your own life. Although you maintain the root vows, if minor branches of the vows become violated, you must immediately confess this and restore the purity of the original vows.

"Thinking of your body as an employee, you should not allow it to be idle even for a moment. When you are employed by someone, during the hours when you are working, he will not just let you sit idle. He will make sure that you are working very hard for him when you are supposed to be doing so. Think of your body as the employee of your mind and do not let it goof off. Make use of your body by performing prostrations and circumambulations, by training the winds, and by training in the yogic exercises. Make use of your speech by reciting mantras in formal practice or by reciting supplications and various liturgical practices. Make use of your mind by meditating upon the generation and completion stages, and especially by performing the practice of tonglen, through which compassion is cultivated. Just as you must pay a salary to an employee, the salary you pay your body for its service in your practice of Dharma is whatever food and clothing are necessary to survive physically. The payment need not be excessive. Simply give your body enough food and clothing so that it does not die."

Chakme Rinpoche goes on to say that when you cannot get adequate food and clothing, you should cultivate the yogic practice of austerity. This refers to using the nutritive substances found in minerals and elements for survival without consumption of conventional food. Even when you have good food, such as meat, yoghurt, and tea, after one day they become excrement. Reflect on how meaningless such food is and that it is without any substantial essence. Before you eat certain foods, they look really, really good to you. They look good, they smell good, and you think of them as good. Nevertheless, once you have eaten them, they do not look good, they do not smell good, and you do not think of them as good anymore. "Cast aside the depression that comes from hunger and thirst," says Karma Chakme Rinpoche. In other words, do not worry and become depressed about how much you have to eat and drink. You can generate physical vitality by visualizing the essences of the winds, learning to absorb the essences, the nutritive or vital essences, of the four elements through breathing them in.

On the other hand, he tells us, when you do get what you need to survive, such as adequate food and clothing, you do not need to throw these things away, because they can become a means for your gathering the accumulation of merit. Offer them to the yidams, the deities who abide within your body, and dedicate this to the accumulation of merit of yourself and others.

Karma Chakme concludes this section, "In short if you do all of this until you die, your human life will have been meaningful and you will have no regret at the time of your death." This concludes "The Song of Precious Human Birth."

THE SONG OF DEATH AND IMPERMANENCE

Karma Chakme Rinpoche begins this song with NAMO GURU, "Homage to the Guru," and continues, addressing Karma Tsondru Gyamtso, the person who requested the composition of the text, "Listen, Karma Tsondru, if you are really going to remain in retreat, then it is important and necessary for you to recollect impermanence and death, which, although it is described as a preliminary, is important to do all of the time." The recollection of impermanence and the imminence of death are introduced at the beginning of any course of instruction, and therefore are considered a preliminary, but this is simply because of the sequence of instruction. Chakme Rinpoche reminds us that it is necessary to constantly maintain this recollection. "If you do not remember death in the depths of your heart, your having entered the gate of Dharma will be meaningless."

Karma Chakme says that there are people who undertake the novitiate ordination for the sake of food. There are also people who undertake final ordination for the sake of social position, so that they do not have to sit at the end of the row with the other novices. Such people are merely the reflections, or empty images, of the ordained, because they are without Dharma. Even if you learned all the artistic and scientific knowledge that exists, you could be doing this simply to become wealthy and famous. Even if you remained in retreat your whole life, practicing intensively, you could simply be doing this to accomplish the power of mantra to pacify sickness and demons. In other words, you could practice with the motivation of achieving some benefit in this life, which would not be a cause of awakening or benefit in future lives. Furthermore, "You could even keep your vows and your samaya merely through the desire not to be embarrassed in the presence of others. If whatever you do is done only for your own benefit or for some purpose of this life, you have failed to recollect impermanence."

All composite things are, in their most essential characteristic, impermanent. Even that which we regard as the toughest and most stable, for example, these billion worlds, will eventually be destroyed by fire, water, or wind. If even the vajra body of the samyaksambuddha must display the manner of passing away, then what need is there to affirm that our pathetic little human bodies, the result of such little merit, will die? In other words, if even the Buddha himself must display the manner of passing away, then obviously ordinary individuals like ourselves are definitely going to die. If even such powerful individuals as Brahma, Indra, and chakravartins must die, then what need is there to say that all other beings must die? In comparison with such powerful beings, we are really like insects; our lives are that weak.

Not only is it definite that we are going to die, but human life is of uncertain duration. Especially now, in this age of degeneration, Chakme Rinpoche says, "There are many who do not even reach the age of forty. Everyone, from the most learned, the most moral, the most benevolent, and the most powerful, such as kings and queens, down to the least powerful, such as beggars and so on, will die. No one has the ability to remain."

Using the Tibetan word *kye ma*, which means "oh" and is an expression of great sadness, Chakme Rinpoche continues, "Oh, Tsondru Gyamtso, everyone knows about death, of course, but it is the thought that we do not need to worry about it that deceives us. This deceives everyone. It seems that I myself am deceived by this. You must be careful not to be deceived by thinking that you do not need to remember death."

There are several methods we can use to remind us that we are not exempt from death. Whenever you hear that someone has died, think of it as a sign of your own future death. Whenever you hear that someone young has died, recollect that there is no certainty to the duration of human life. Whenever you see a corpse or bones, whether it be that of a human or an animal, recollect that that is the nature of your own body. Whenever you hear that someone died in spite of all efforts at medical treatment, recollect that medicine cannot avert death forever. Whenever you hear that someone died in spite of all the rituals that were done for their benefit, recollect that nothing can avert death forever. Really, we are like travelers who will stay in a hotel one night only. Recollect that we are going to pass from this life as quickly as that. Remember that death is certain.

Consider, furthermore, that even if you accumulate an ocean of wealth, do you have the power to take any of it with you as provisions after death? Even if you have hundreds or thousands of employees surrounding you, do you have the power to enlist the aid of any one of them after death? Even if you amass a private or state army consisting of millions of people, can you use it to stop yourself from dying? Even if you could fill the whole world with food and wealth and own all of it, could you take even the slightest crumb with you after death?

We never know when we will die. It is always a surprise, like a stroke of lightning shooting down at us from the sky. Karma Chakme says, "When it happens, *atsamay*! Ow!" Consider the agony of death. Even if you are surrounded by all of your friends and all of your family, you cannot parcel this experience out to them. Even if the people who are surrounding you when you are dying would like to relieve you of your suffering, they do not have the ability to do that and you do not have the ability to give it to them. Remember that at the time of death nothing you have created in this life can help you, not your possessions, not your friends, and not your family.

Furthermore, when the elements dissolve one into another as you die, none of the bewildering and terrifying experiences that you undergo will be alleviated by your intelligence or your clarity of mind. The various appearances of the bardo are like the experience of a criminal who has been captured and thrown into jail. It is terrifying. He says, "It is horrendous and it is horrible. Ow!" You are thrust into an environment that is completely unfamiliar to you and you are utterly alone. In such a situation, what will you do? Will you have any sense of destination? Although you may have developed the intention during your lifetime to be reborn in a certain realm, there is no guarantee that you can do that. Once you are in the bardo, you react with fear, you panic. You have no idea where you are or where to go.

Karma Chakme warns, "When you are in the courtroom of Yama, lies are of no use." In other words, when you are in the bardo, you experience yourself as being judged for what you have done in your lifetime by Yama, the Lord of Death. It is said that Yama is omniscient. You cannot lie to him. You cannot claim to have done what you did not do nor claim not to have done what you did do. "Yama sees everything on the small print of his mirror. Tsondru Gyamtso, from now on act and live in such a way that you will have no fear and no shame on that day."

This concludes "The Song of Death and Impermanence," which is a necessary provision for remaining in retreat.

THE SONG OF KARMA

Most of the Buddha's teachings of the four noble truths are actually an explanation of karma—cause and result. This is the primary message of the first part of the Buddha's teaching. Chakme Rinpoche begins this song with the invocation NAMO GURU, "Homage to the Guru."

Karma Chakme warns us that this is a vast subject. A complete, precise understanding of the subtle workings of karma is unique to the samyaksambuddha, the "perfect buddha." Even arhats do not really understand all the workings of karma, so how could we? The point in the path where one develops a direct knowledge of the workings of karma is the level referred to as the realization in one taste. At this level, one achieves a definitive realization of the single nature of all phenomena beyond good and bad. At the same time, as a result of that realization, there is also a direct perception of the working of karma, which is called "the manifestation of interdependence."

Chakme Rinpoche says that although such direct realization of karma is not within his experience, through the kindness of his gurus he will explain karma here, taking the Buddha's teachings, the words of Buddha Shakyamuni, as a source. He begins by describing the three types of karma: common, individual, and immovable.

Everything in the external environment, including the entire world and universe is the result of karma. The external environment does not come about for any other reason than what is called *the karma common to the sentient beings that will experience that environment or that world*. This is the first type of karma.

Second, the experiences of individual sentient beings, the various joys and sufferings that we each undergo, are the result of the particular actions of each of us as individual beings in the past. Virtuous actions lead to rebirth in the three higher realms, which are the human realm, the asura realm, and the realm of the gods. Unvirtuous actions lead to rebirth in the three lower realms, which are the hell realm, the preta realm, and the animal realm. Thus *individual karma* is the second type of karma.

The third type of karma is called *immovable karma*. This refers to the karma of abiding one-pointedly in meditation with an attachment to the experience or to the taste of meditation. This causes immediate rebirth as a god of either the form or the formless realm, depending upon the exact meditative state in which the person was immersed.

After introducing the three types of karma, Chakme Rinpoche describes the various methods of determining how specific actions lead to certain specific types of rebirth. The first explanation considers the motivation for an action. In general, unvirtuous actions lead to rebirth in the three lower realms, while virtuous actions lead to rebirth in the three higher realms. Any unvirtuous action motivated primarily by anger or aversion will lead to rebirth in hell. Just as anger is the worst of the afflictions, the hell realm is the worst of the six realms. In the same way, an unvirtuous action of body or speech motivated by greed will lead to rebirth as a preta and the experience of extreme hunger and thirst. An unvirtuous action motivated by apathy or bewilderment will lead to rebirth as an animal, the particular type of animal depending upon the particular action.

Virtuous actions that are somewhat corrupted by or mixed with desire will lead to rebirth as a human being, in the human realm, which although relatively pleasant within the general samsaric context, is marked by unceasing endeavor and struggle. In the human realm we are extremely busy from the moment we are born until the moment we die, always trying to achieve or accomplish something. When we do actually accomplish anything, we are so addicted to the struggle that we then compulsively go on to try to accomplish something else, moving constantly from one thing to another. This is one of the fundamental characteristics, or marks, of the human realm.

A virtuous action that is corrupted by jealousy will lead to rebirth as an asura. Asuras, although they are powerful and wealthy, and theoretically could experience some degree of pleasure in their realm, are tormented by constant warfare. Consumed by the need to go to war against the more powerful gods, they suffer greatly from the inevitable failure.

Virtuous actions that are corrupted by pride or arrogance will lead to rebirth as a god. The sufferings of the god realm are basically the sufferings of loss and downfall. A very long time before the gods die, they become aware of their oncoming death and can see when and where their life as a god will end. They also become aware of where they are going to be reborn in their next life and of all the sufferings they will experience there. They are tormented for the rest of their life as gods by knowing what is going to happen. They are utterly unable to prevent it and they know that they are going to lose the pleasure of being a god and will experience a lot of suffering. This concludes the explanation of how actions based on specific motivations such as anger, greed, desire, jealously, and pride lead to specific types of rebirths.

Another way of correlating unvirtuous actions with rebirth in the lower realms is based on the intensity of the action. Just as unvirtuous actions motivated by aggression in general lead to rebirth in hell, so also very strong or extensive acts of wrongdoing will lead to rebirth in hell. Intermediate wrongdoing, which is pretty intense and extensive but not too bad, will lead to rebirth as a preta. Minor wrongdoing will lead to rebirth as an animal. This is because the hell realm is the worst, the preta realm is horrible but somewhat better, and the animal realm is somewhat better than that. In the same way, great virtue will cause rebirth as a god, intermediate virtue as a human being, and minor virtue as an asura.

A third way of understanding karma is to correlate the ten different unvirtuous actions with their specific results. Every action brings three different types of result, so each of the unvirtuous actions committed by the body leads to three different unpleasant outcomes.

The first unvirtuous action is to intentionally kill. This means to do something with your body, your speech, or your mind that intentionally and successfully kills another being, which is typically some kind of aggression. The primary result of killing, which is called *ripening, or maturation, of the deed*, is to be reborn in hell. The secondary result of an action is called *the result of the power of the action*, a literal translation that does not really communicate the meaning. The secondary result of killing is that in the future, if you become a human being again, you will have a shortened life span. This is possible because you might have done some other virtuous things, so after you have been reborn in hell as a result of killing and that karma is completed, then you are reborn as a human being. The tertiary karmic result is called *the similar result*. This refers to a result that is similar to the action itself. Thus in the case of having killed, the tertiary result is that thenceforth you will delight in killing. You will have the habit of wanting and liking to kill.

In the same way, each of the other nonvirtuous actions has three results. The maturation of stealing, of taking what is not freely given, is to be reborn as a preta in the realm of the pretas. The secondary result is that even though you might eventually be born as a human being because of some other virtuous action, you will be impoverished and you will live in a type of human environment where the necessities of life are very scarce. The similar result is that you will like to steal.

The ripening or maturation of sexual misconduct or adultery is to be reborn as a preta. The secondary result is when you are born as a human being again, you are reborn in a harsh, desertlike environment, where it is extremely hot and dry, water is scarce, and it is dusty and unpleasant in every way. Born in such an environment, you are likely not even to have what normal human beings have to shield themselves from the harshness of the environment, such as hair. The similar result is that you delight in adultery. These are the results of the three unvirtuous actions related to the body: killing, stealing, and sexual misconduct.

The four negative actions involving speech are lying, slander, verbal abuse, and mindless talk. The karmic maturation of lying is to be reborn as an animal. The secondary result is that once you are again born as a human being, you have terrible bad breath. The similar result is that you like to lie.

The maturation of slander is to be reborn as an asura. The secondary result is that once you are reborn as a human being, you cannot get along with anyone; for no apparent reason your friends and family are always in conflict with you. We can see such a situation arising when things happen to us for no apparent reason, because then we blame the other people involved since we believe that we ourselves have not done anything wrong. However, the truth is that it is usually not so much the other person's initiative as it is the result of our own actions in previous lives. The similar result of slander is that we enjoy slandering others because we enjoy divisiveness.

The maturation of verbal abusiveness is to be reborn in hell. The secondary result is that even when you are born as a human being, you are constantly verbally abused by others for no apparent reason, without your having done anything to bring it on. The similar result is that you will just naturally find yourself being verbally abusive all the time. You will like it and it will be very natural to you.

The maturation of babbling, or mindless talk, is to be reborn as an animal. The secondary result is that once you are again born as a human being, even when you tell the truth, no one believes you. They think you are lying. The similar result is that your speech will be ignoble. Your words will be ineffective; you will never be able to speak with any kind of authority.

The three types of mental negative actions are covetousness, spite or maliciousness, and wrong view. There are two varieties of covetousness. The first is coveting one's own possessions, which is really a type of perverted self-esteem where we overvalue our possessions and situation, which results in our becoming obsessively attached to them. The other, more conventional variety of covetousness is to covet that which belongs to others. This is basically seeing the excellent or abundant possessions or situation of someone else and thinking, "Why couldn't that be mine? I wish that were mine and not theirs."

The maturation of covetousness is to be reborn in any one of the lower realms, depending upon the specifics of the situation. The secondary result is that even when you are born as a human being, your wishes are never accomplished. Everything you try to do becomes the opposite of what you intend. We often see this. There always seem to be people who, without any apparent effort, just accomplish whatever they set their minds to, and then there are other people who, no matter how hard they try and no matter how carefully they plan, never seem to be able to accomplish what they want. Usually we assume that there must be something extraordinary about the person who accomplishes everything so easily and something really wrong with the person who seems ineffective. However, it is not necessarily true that there is something wrong or right with either of them in this lifetime. Their situation is the result of their actions in previous lives. The similar result of coveting is that you will naturally covet. You will naturally want what belongs to others.

The second form of mental wrongdoing is spite. The maturation of spite is to be reborn in hell. The secondary result is that even when you are once again reborn as a human being, you are never without enemies. You are constantly in a state of fear and anxiety, sometimes even terror. You always feel that there is somebody out to get you, and in fact there usually is. The similar result is that you will be naturally spiteful in your future lives.

The third form of mental unvirtuous action is wrong view, which also has the connotation of antipathy or dislike for the truth. The maturation of wrong view is to be reborn as an animal. The secondary result is that even when you are reborn as a human being, you will be born into a society where you naturally develop a wrong view from the influence of others. The similar result is that, innately, you have a wrong view, or a tendency to go against the truth.

These are the karmic results of the ten unvirtuous actions: the three unvirtuous actions of body, the four unvirtuous actions of speech, and the three unvirtuous actions of mind. To abandon these unvirtuous actions and, by implication, engage in such actions as saving lives and being generous, which are the exact opposite, is to engage in the ten virtuous actions. Just as the ten unvirtuous actions lead to thirty unpleasant results, three for each action, so also the ten virtuous actions lead to thirty corresponding pleasant results. These are the exact opposites of the unpleasant results. For example, if killing leads to a short life, saving lives leads to a long life, and so on.

The text to this point has described how to understand karma based on the motivation of the action, on the intensity of the action, and in correlation to the ten unvirtuous and the ten virtuous actions. To further understand the way karma functions, Karma Chakme instructs us to consider the four ways in which actions can ripen. Here we are not looking at the four different types of results, as presented in the foregoing discussion. Rather we are talking about how long it takes for an action to ripen.

The first type of karmic ripening is called *evident and manifest karma*. This is when an action in one life manifests in the next life. For example, the experience of happiness and all sorts of good things in this life can be the result of virtue accumulated in the life immediately preceding this one. When a virtuous action is powerful enough that it will ripen in the subsequent lifetime, that ripening cannot be stopped by anyone else. Even the most evil mara who wishes to make you unhappy and obstruct you in every way can do nothing to prevent the ripening of that virtuous action.

Unfortunately, in the same way, wrongdoing that is of such intensity or strength that it will ripen in the subsequent lifetime also cannot be stopped for you by anyone else, even by the Buddha. This is a very important point. Buddha cannot remove your karma. Only you can remove your karma in reliance upon Buddha. If Buddha could remove your karma, he would have done so already. We would all have attained buddhahood by now because, of course, Buddha is perfectly benevolent. However, to purify karma, two things must come together. First, the Buddha's qualities and compassion make him a fit basis for your own faith and gathering of the accumulations. Then, based upon that, you exert the appropriate effort from your side, and in that way your karma can be purified. Buddha cannot just save you without your doing anything.

The process of purifying karma is a little bit like trying to grow a flower. When a seed is planted, it needs to be fostered with the right conditions: the proper soil, enough water, sunlight, air, and so on. These are like the various causes and conditions that must come together to purify an action. Just as the growth of a plant is dependent upon certain conditions, the eradication of negative karma is a function of many conditions. Primary among these are your own wish to purify the karma, your effort in doing so, and then the qualities of holy beings as bases for accumulation of merit.

The second type of karmic ripening is based on the actions, either virtuous or unvirtuous, that are less intense or less powerful than those that ripen in the subsequent lifetime. The results of these less intense actions will ripen in the lifetime after that and they are called *results experienced after one more birth.*

The third type of actions includes the very small or apparently insignificant actions, and again they can be either virtuous or unvirtuous. These are of uncertain ripening. *Uncertain* does not mean that whether or not they will ripen is uncertain, since one of the characteristics of karma is that it is certain. Rather, the name here means it is uncertain when they will ripen. It is uncertain how many lifetimes it will take before they ripen. So these are called *results that will be experienced at some other time.*

The fourth type of karmic ripening is called *straight-through,* and is divided into two parts: an *upward straight-through* and a *downward straight-through.* These types of actions are also called *actions of uninterrupted, or immediate, consequence.* The five negative actions of uninterrupted consequence are actions that are so negative, so egregious, that they cause a ripening right after you die. This is different from ripening effects that are experienced in the next lifetime. These results are "uninterrupted" in that the moment you die, you start to experience the result and assume immediate rebirth in the lowest of hells without passing through the bardo. The five negative *straight-through* actions are killing one's father, killing one's mother, killing an arhat, intentionally causing a buddha to bleed and doing so with the desire to harm, and causing a schism in the sangha. These actions are so powerfully negative that at the moment of your death, you enter the worst of the hell realms, which is called Avichi, which means "uninterrupted torture or torment." Therefore this is called *negative uninterrupted consequence,* meaning "downward right away, downward straightaway, or downward straight-through."

An example of this type of karmic consequence is found in the story of Buddha's half brother, Devadatta, who attempted three times to assassinate Buddha. The last time Devadatta made the attempt, the earth opened up under his feet and he fell to hell. You can think that his body was destroyed and he was immediately born in hell or you can think that his actual body fell to hell. It does not matter. The point is that without going to the bardo, Devadatta went straight to the worst possible hell realm. When the earth opened up under Devadatta's feet, there was hot magma that immediately began to burn him. As he was starting to fall and was burning, he looked at the Buddha, realizing that he was wrong—a little too late—and he screamed, "Gautama, I'm burning," and then he fell down to the hell realm. The result of that moment of regret, born of unimaginable agony and terror, was that at the end of this aeon or kalpa, after the doctrine of the last of the thousand buddhas has vanished, he will attain the state of pratyekabuddha, a solitary realized one. Until then he is in Avichi.

On the more cheerful side, there is also the upward straight-through immediate karmic consequence. This is of two types. In the first type, because of a person's realization, through their accumulation of virtue and the strength of their practice of Dharma, at the time of death they recognize the ground clear light. Recognizing this, they therefore remain in what we call thukdam, which in this context means "meditation." Thus when someone recognizes the ground clear light, they do not go through the bardo.

The second type of upward straight-through is when the transference of consciousness is effectively performed by or for someone so that their consciousness is shot out of their body like an arrow being shot out of a skylight straight to the pure realms. In that case the person also does not go to the bardo before being reborn. For example, if, at the moment of death, through the practice of phowa, you see Amitabha and are immediately reborn in Sukhavati, then that is an example of upward straight-through. You go immediately to a pure realm without experiencing the bardo.

Those are the four ways of examining karma based on the ways in which actions can ripen: in the subsequent lifetime (evident and manifest karma), in the lifetime after that (results experienced after one more birth), in some future lifetime (uncertain karma), and uninterrupted ripening (straight-through karma).

Another way of looking at karma is to consider the recipient of the action. The intensity of a karmic imprint depends to some extent upon to whom the action is directed, whom it affects. Actions, both virtuous and unvirtuous, directed at your parents, your vajra master, bodhisattvas on any of the ten bhumis, or buddhas are the most powerful. They are so powerful, in fact, that virtuous and nonvirtuous actions that are directed at those four types of people can even ripen in the same lifetime. For example, you can think of Devadatta's falling to hell as something that ripened in that very lifetime, since he had not died yet when he fell.

Another complication of the way karma works is that the basic trend of all of your actions—to the extent that your actions have a unified trend—can change at some point in your life. These events are called casting actions and completing actions. *Casting actions* are those that determine the fundamental question of where you will be, and *completing actions* determine the details within that.

For example, it is not uncommon that someone could devote their early life to extensive wrongdoing and then devote the latter part of their life to virtue. An example of this is Angulimala, who spent a certain part of his early life engaging in serial killing but still managed to attain arhatship at the end of his life. In that type of situation the virtue you accumulate toward the end of your life becomes of primary power; therefore that will ripen first, even though the negative actions were committed first. The term for this sequence of events is *negative casting and positive, or virtuous, completing actions.*

Unfortunately it is also possible that someone could devote their early life to virtue and then their later days to negativity. This happens, for example, when someone practices Dharma in their early life with some sincerity and intensity but at some point they regret having done so and they think, "Oh, because I spent my youth practicing Dharma, I am poor. I do not have a social position. I do not have a real job. I wish I had not wasted my time. I am going to do everything I can to make up for that." The attitude of turning against the virtue they performed in their youth becomes the predominant karmic tone for the rest of their life. This is called *virtuous casting and negative completing karma.*

There is another extremely important point to consider about actions and their results. Virtuous actions that are not dedicated to the awakening of all beings are very fragile and can be quickly exhausted. Virtuous actions get used up very easily by being experienced as a pleasant result, unless they are sealed by a dedication such as "through the power of this virtue may I attain buddhahood so that I can bring each being without exception to the same state."

Any positive result is not only used up quickly when you fail to dedicate it, but it can be used up even more quickly by your attitude. For example, if you become arrogant or vain about the virtue you have engaged in, that will exhaust it — and even more so if you regret it. Regretting a positive act will immediately use up all of that virtue, unless it was sealed with an impartial dedication. If it was sealed in that way, even your own negative attitude cannot really destroy or use up the virtue itself.

Correspondingly, negative actions can be used up or eliminated through admission or confession. *Confession* here refers to all of the four powers or processes that make a confession valid. These are the power of support (the object of refuge), the power of regret, the power of resolution or commitment, and the power of remedy. Among these, of foremost importance is commitment. What primarily destroys the imprint of the negative action is the sincere thought "I will never do that again." That is the primary force. Without that commitment, confession is ineffective.

Those are the ways that the imprint of a virtuous action can be used up or removed and the ways that the imprint of a negative action can be used up or removed. Aside from those situations, if the imprint remains, even though it may be dormant for a hundred or a thousand aeons, it is not gone. It will definitely ripen for that individual at some point in some future lifetime if it is not counteracted.

What you do ripens for you and not for anyone else. Likewise, you can never experience something that is a result of someone else's karma. You can never experience something that is not a result of your own karma. Everything you experience that is karmic is the result of your own actions, and everything you do, unless it is counteracted, leaves an imprint of one kind or the other. For virtuous actions not to lead to positive results and for unvirtuous actions not to lead to negative results is even more impossible than for the sun and the moon to fall to the ground, or for the wind to be captured in a lasso, or for fire to be cold. Even those things, Chakme Rinpoche says, are comparatively possible, but for a virtuous action to lead to suffering or an unvirtuous action to lead to happiness, these are absolutely impossible.

This is the fundamental teaching of all buddhas: the consistency of actions and their results. A person who denies cause and result will lose the faculty of communication. Denial of karma is the most fundamental and worst form of incorrect view. Such an incorrect view causes one to be born for innumerable lifetimes in a situation where they are incapable of understanding karma. That is the result of being exposed to this concept and refusing to accept it.

Chakme Rinpoche concludes this section saying, "Therefore if you want to remain in retreat, then think very carefully and precisely, again and again, about karma and put your knowledge into practice. Make appropriate choices of actions based upon your understanding of their results. This is the little song that gives the basic meaning of the results of actions."

THE SONG OF THE MEANINGLESS NATURE OF SAMSARA

At this point Karma Chakme has completed an explanation of three of the four ordinary preliminary practices as a basis for undertaking solitary retreat: precious human birth, impermanence and death, and cause and result. Now he discusses the fourth, which is the meaninglessness of samsara.

There is a very good reason to consider the meaninglessness of samsara. Everyone knows that if you want to shoot an arrow at a target, you need to see that target very clearly. If you do not know where the target is, it is very unlikely that you will hit it. However, if you can see the target and if you make the utmost effort, it is quite possible that you may hit the very center of the bull's-eye. In the same way, although we know that the idea of practicing Dharma is to overcome the cause of suffering, until we also know what it is that is actually causing our suffering, we will never be successful in our practice. We need to clearly see the target.

To put this another way, if you are suffering from an illness, you must first identify the symptoms and then you must find out from a skilled physician what exactly it is that is causing those symptoms.

Having identified the symptoms and the cause of your illness, you will then learn what actions you should avoid that may exacerbate the condition, such as eating certain foods or undertaking certain activities. Finally you will take medicine to heal, to overcome your illness completely. The primary reason why you take the medicine is to overcome the pain associated with the illness and to experience the resulting happiness that is free from that disease or that type of suffering. In the same way, when we practice Dharma to overcome suffering, we first have to understand the cause of our suffering, and to do that we have to understand the meaninglessness of samsara. Once we understand that the cause of our suffering is afflicting emotions and karma, we will be very motivated to apply the antidote, which is the Dharma.

Many students engage in Dharma practice for a long time, but they still experience no positive results. Often they get discouraged, thinking there is no benefit to their practice, and sometimes they give up altogether. When we ask these people about their practice, we find the problem is that they do not know the point of why they are doing the practice in the first place, nor do they even know the proper manner of doing the practice. If we do not know why or how to practice, we will never achieve an effective result, no matter how long we engage in the practice.

For all of these reasons Karma Chakme presents here the explanations on the meaninglessness of samsara. His purpose is to help us clearly understand why we have to practice without a distracted or confused mind. Karma Chakme begins by saying to his disciple, "Listen, Tsondru Gyamtso, think properly. If you really think properly about the sufferings of samsara, your mind will not be peaceful in the daytime and you will not sleep well at night. If you really think properly about the sufferings of samsara, you will see that samsara is like a limitless ocean. We, the beings of the six realms, have fallen into this endless ocean, and none of us can escape from its churning waves. Having fallen into this endless ocean, we all experience the suffering of birth, the suffering of old age, the suffering of sickness, and the suffering of death. These sufferings are like the waves of the ocean that hit us constantly and unavoidably."

Not only are we subject to the four types of suffering, we are constantly creating new causes for further suffering through our actions within the ocean of samsara. When we participate in nonvirtuous actions, we are creating the cause for rebirth in one of the lower realms: the hell realm, the hungry ghost realm, or the animal realm. The strength of our negative karma pulls us down, like an alligator pulling an animal down under the water. We try to escape, we try to pull ourselves out, but the strength of our karma is so powerful that we are pulled down into the very depth of suffering. This is the true nature of samsara.

How do we become liberated? How do we escape from this ocean of suffering? First we must be motivated to find someone to show us the method of escape and then we must take refuge. But this in itself is not sufficient. Motivation and finding an authentic teacher are the initial, primary steps, but in order to experience true liberation, we have to maintain with great clarity and precision whatever precepts or vows we have taken, such as refuge precepts, lay precepts, and bodhisattva precepts. These precepts become like our boat in the ocean of samsara. If you have a strong boat, then you have the possibility of experiencing liberation from the ocean of suffering. If your boat has lots of holes or cracks in it, you have no guarantee of reaching your destination safely. You have no guarantee that you will experience liberation. In this sense, the purity of your precepts becomes of utmost importance, equivalent to having a very strong and proper boat.

Even if you have a strong, flawless boat, if you do not have and use paddles, the boat will just go wherever the waves take it, floating without direction. You need the paddles, which in this analogy are equivalent to the lama's instructions. Furthermore even if you have paddles, you still have to work consistently and with much effort in order to guide the boat to your intended destination. The meditation practice instructions of an authentic teacher become like the paddles of the boat. It is you who must make a real and consistent effort to liberate yourself from the ocean of suffering. The diligence and effort is totally up to you.

We may ask, "What's the point of causing ourselves anxiety by thinking of the sufferings of samsara? What is the point of thinking so much about this so that we cannot sleep at night and we cannot have fun during the day? Why not just relax and enjoy life?" When people say this, it is because they do not really believe that there is experience beyond this present experience. They do not really understand the immense suffering of the lower realms.

As described earlier in the text, the lowest of the three lower realms are the hell realms. In the hot hell realm one physically experiences the feelings of being burned in boiling water and of melted lava being poured down one's throat. That experience goes on continuously, not just for a year or two but for thousands and thousands of years. As we sit here, enjoying life, if a small flicker of fire should fall on us, we would immediately rush to extinguish it because the pain of fire burning our skin would be so intense. Imagine the pain if your whole body were being burned. Imagine if your whole body were submerged in boiling water. Consider also the cold hell. In the wintertime we put on many layers of clothes to protect ourselves from the pain caused by the cold. In the cold hell you experience complete nakedness in a place that is so cold that your whole body cracks open. There is no one to rescue you. There is no help, and again you experience that painful suffering from the cold for thousands and thousands of years. Even if it does cause us to feel a little uncomfortable, we really should think about the actual experiences of being in the hells. If we do, we will want to do whatever we can to prevent falling into such places of intense suffering.

The next realm is the preta, or hungry ghost, realm. Imagine ourselves today when we come home and say, "I haven't eaten all day. I'm really hungry. I'm starving." If we do not eat much or drink much in one day, when we get home, we think that we must have everything in the refrigerator. Imagine if you are in a realm where for thousands and thousands of years you do not get anything to eat or anything to drink. The hunger and thirst are the same as we experience here, but the possibility of obtaining food and drink is completely different. Here you can obtain what you need, but think how you would feel after one day of not eating or drinking and then multiply that by thousands and thousands. The suffering is unimaginable.

Consider also the animal realm. All animals live in constant states of intense nervousness and fear. Every sound they hear, every action around them, is intensely perceived as potentially threatening. They never experience a state of true calmness or rest. They are constantly expecting attack from other animals, and usually for a very good reason. It would be a very painful experience if we had to live our lives in that way, in consistent, unrelenting fear and anxiety.

Beings in the demigod, or asura, realm experience thousands and thousands of years of constant quarreling and fighting. Whatever happiness they might enjoy from their possessions is totally negated by their pride and attachment and the resulting fighting with one another. There is not a single moment of peace in this realm.

Finally, consider the god realm, which is also a samsaric realm. One experiences rebirth in the god realm from having accumulated virtuous karma from positive actions, but these actions were undertaken with obscured motivation, that is, for personal benefit and without knowing the proper way of dedicating that virtue. Thus although there is happiness in the god realm, the karma causing that happiness will eventually run out, and the resulting suffering will be immense. For example, think about how it would be to be involved in a major legal battle. You put tremendous effort and resources into winning the case, but your opponent wins and you therefore become extremely angry and depressed over your loss. Now think about the gods at the end of their lives in the god realm. Everything they once had will now be completely lost. Not only that but because they are omnipotent, they begin to realize that they are not going to be gods anymore. They can clearly see the end of their lives in the god realm and also their rebirths in one of the lower realms. Seeing all that they will lose, their pain and suffering is therefore very intense.

From these descriptions, we see that the actual sufferings of beings in the hell realm, the hungry ghost realm, and the animal realm are greater than we can really comprehend. Beings in the human, demigod, and god realms may experience some happiness compared to the three lower realms, but that happiness becomes mixed with afflictive emotions, creating more unhappiness. This is like having very nutritious food that would otherwise be good for our health except that we add poison to it. The food is nutritious, but because of the poison we have added, the food is now very dangerous for us, potentially causing us much pain and trouble. The poison we add in the higher realms is our attachment. In the god, demigod, and human realms, we may experience joy and happiness, but we become attached to it, and from that attachment we develop other emotions such as anger, jealousy, and pride. In order to protect our happiness and to try to create more happiness, we now indulge in more and more afflictive emotions, which is like adding poison to what was once good. The karmic result is to have continual experience of the different levels of suffering in the six realms.

When we really look at the intense suffering of the realms, we may ask, "Who has created such a depth of suffering? Who is the creator of these realms?" The answer is we ourselves, or—to be more precise—our own afflictive emotions. For example, the karma that you have accumulated through intense hate or anger causes you to experience the suffering of the hell realm. This hate and anger comes from you, your own afflictive emotions, not from an external creator. If you have accumulated karma through tremendous greed or miserliness, you will experience the suffering of the hungry ghost realm. If you act in a way that you think is virtuous but actually is rather stupid, the strength and karma of that stupidity results in rebirth in the animal realm. Even if you are practicing Dharma, if you become jealous whenever other people seem to practice better or seem to have better results, you will accumulate the karma to experience the suffering of the demigod realm. Finally, even if you have practiced Dharma and also great virtue, if you have a feeling of pride and arrogance about it and if you are preoccupied by your own personal needs alone, you then accumulate the karma to experience the god realm.

In all of these cases, there is no external creator of your suffering. Rather, because you participate in certain actions, you will accumulate the results of those actions. It is infallible. It is definite. Once you understand this, you know that it is absolutely necessary to engage in Dharma free from any of these afflictive emotions. Sit down quietly and think honestly about your actions from the moment you can first remember until now. Consider how many positive actions and how many negative actions you have been involved in. It may be rather painful to remember all the negative ones, but you will clearly see that we are constantly participating in afflictive emotions and negative actions.

In addition to accumulating karma in this life, we have also given rise to afflictive emotions over uncountable previous lives, and thereby we have accumulated the resulting karma. Even if you think, "Well, I haven't done too badly in this life," you must realize that in past uncountable lifetimes we have all participated in many negative actions. Do not simply give up, thinking, "Oh, I have accumulated so much bad karma. There is no hope for me." The accumulation of negative karma has no advantage whatsoever except for one positive characteristic. If you recognize your negative actions and confess them sincerely, then the accumulation of the resulting karma can be completely uprooted and purified. This is the one positive attribute of negative karma: it can be purified and totally negated.

How does one purify negative karma? If you acknowledge and sincerely regret your actions and make the strong commitment not to repeat them in the future, purification is possible. Mere words are not enough; you must make a real effort. If you are very accustomed and attached to the negative actions, it may not be possible to give up everything all at once. However, if you make a conscious, continuous effort, then after some time, when you examine your actions, you will realize that you are making success in decreasing and eventually overcoming the afflictive emotions such as jealousy, greed, and anger. It is a good idea at the end of each day, before going to sleep, to examine your behavior for that day. When you recognize your negative actions, generate regret and resolve not to engage in those actions in the future. When you recognize the positive actions that you have undertaken that day, then rejoice and dedicate the virtue to the benefit and enlightenment of all sentient beings. When you do this, the virtue becomes indestructible because you have let it go and have dedicated it for the benefit of all sentient beings.

Please remember that when we talk about negative actions, we often think only of physical and verbal actions. However, negative actions also take place in the mind as negative thoughts. Thus when you review the events of your day, you may conclude, "Well, physically I did not engage in any negative or violent actions and verbally I did not really speak any harsh words." But your mind that day had many negative thoughts of attachment, anger, greed, and so on. These are also negative actions. The most important element in overcoming the afflictions that result in accumulation of negative karma is to be totally aware and mindful of your mental state.

The Buddha gave 84,000 collections of teachings, each of which is ultimately aimed at pacifying one's mind and overcoming the afflictive emotions. That is why it is said that the essence of the Buddha's teachings is "Commit not a single evil action. Practice virtue completely." When the Buddha says, "Commit not a single evil action," the meaning is very clear. He means to refrain from any action arising from the afflictive emotions. "Practice virtue completely" instructs us to practice loving-kindness and compassion very sincerely, with all our heart. He means that we should replace all negative actions with positive ones. The third line in this teaching by the Buddha is "Pacify your mind wholly." In other words, experience the pacification of your mind free from the afflictive emotions. The teaching ends by saying that if an individual is doing all of this, then he or she is a "true practitioner of Buddhism." These four lines are the essence of the Buddha's teaching. They clearly say who is to be considered a true practitioner of Buddhism. Whether one is a monastic (monk or nun) or a householder (layperson) makes no difference. What makes a difference is one's ability to "practice virtue completely" and to "pacify one's mind wholly." This is the person who is a true practitioner of Buddhism.

This concludes the section presented by the great master Karma Chakme, who was called Bhikshu Raga Asya, to his student, Tsondru Gyamtso, in the Year of the Horse. The teaching was written down by his disciple, Tsondru Gyamtso, who ends with his own dedication, "May these teachings be of benefit to many sentient beings."

Questions and Answers

STUDENT: The text refers to deities residing in the body and our making offerings to them. I understand there is reference here to advanced practices, but I would like to know what this really means and if it has any relevance to someone like me, who is not an advanced practitioner.

RINPOCHE: The basic meaning of this is that every sentient being possesses buddha nature, and it is for that reason that we all have the ability to attain the result of Dharma practice. The view that buddha nature is the essential nature of each and every being is common to the Mahayana of the sutras, or Paramitayana, and to the Vajrayana, or Tantrayana. The Vajrayana goes into detail about what this means. Vajrayana explains that buddha nature is the innate presence of the source of all of the realms and bodies of all buddhas and that these are innate within us. It talks about the presence of this as dakas and dakinis and so on. The Vajrayana explanation is essentially saying the same thing as the sutras. It is just saying it in a little bit more detail.

For example, if we say that buddha nature is like a seed and the attainment of buddhahood is like the flower that grows out of that seed, we must accept the fact that in some way the qualities particular to that flower are inherently present within the seed itself. The sutras present this same idea—that the qualities of the result (the flower) are present in the cause (the seed)—a little differently. Here it is said that there is this little dark seed and it is certainly not like the flower. It is very subtle. If you plant the seed in the ground and you water it in a certain way, then eventually you will get a flower. That is basically the way it is presented in the sutras.

The tantras go on to say that if you look at the flower, it has this kind of petal and this kind of stamen, it tends to be this color and to have this kind of stem. The tantric approach would be to explain that the reason why this kind of petal grows out of this kind of seed is that the seed has the qualities that have made the plant what it is. It is a matter of the qualities within the core seed. Therefore in the tantras, it is the equivalent of pointing out the potential already present in the seed for each quality evident in the flowers. Without going into more detail, basically the sutras and tantras are saying the same thing, which is that we all have buddha nature.

STUDENT: The text speaks about the preciousness of being born at a time when the Buddha's teachings are available. The Buddha himself predicted the end of his teaching in progressive stages. What stage are we in now?

RINPOCHE: It is very hard to say, because there are different systems, or ways of calculating the extent of the Buddha's teachings. Numerically, it is usually said to have been ten five-hundred-year periods, each cycle corresponding to the degree of presence and effectiveness of the teaching. At the same time, it is also said that these periods can be used up more quickly than that, even instantaneously. It is very difficult to correlate our present age with those predictions. However, based upon the state of things, I am guessing that the stage we are in now is probably one of the five-hundred-year periods enumerated by the Buddha, with merely the marks of the teachings, the merest signs of them, still being present in the world. Even so, what I have just said applies only to the general current state of the Buddha's teachings in this world today. For certain individuals this statement need not apply because there are still teachers available who carry the ultimate lineage of the Buddha's teachings. Those students who partake of that are acquiring more than merely just the external signs of the teaching. For example, although we could say that the Buddha's teachings are scarcely present in the world today, nevertheless we could not say that great teachers such as His Holiness the Dalai Lama, His Holiness the Gyalwa Karmapa, His Holiness Sakya Trizin, and so on are teachers who hold the merest sign of the Buddha's doctrine. Rather, they hold its full meaning and blessing.

STUDENT: We hear that overpopulation is a serious problem for our planet, but as Buddhists it seems that we should see increased human birth as a good thing, as rebirths from other realms into this precious human life where Dharma is available.

RINPOCHE: In general, of course, it is good when a being that has previously been in the lower realms is born human. Human birth is kind of middling within the scheme of samsara. It is not the most pleasant, yet it is far from being the most unpleasant. It is a fortunate birth by the standards of samsara. At the same time, not all human beings practice Dharma. In fact, not all human beings practice virtue, and the problem with a human birth is that it can be a positive support or it can be a resource of the accumulation of incredible amounts of negative karma very quickly. Human birth, if misused, is a very effective way to produce a great deal of wrongdoing. Consequently human birth is not always good if one accumulates a great deal of negativity while being human, ensuring an unpleasant birth thereafter. Furthermore the modern concern with overpopulation is based upon a scientific understanding of how many human beings this planet can reasonably hope to support and feed, which is based on an actual situation in the present and foreseeable future and is different from the question of the long-term karmic development of individual beings.

STUDENT: The text describes yogis such as Milarepa fleeing from their students. What was their motive, and do teachers today do this?

RINPOCHE: Before Jetsun Milarepa demonstrated the manner of attaining full awakening, he sought perfect isolation for the protection of his practice. Occasionally people would show up and he would try to avoid them. Once he had attained full awakening, naturally individuals flocked to him like swans to a lake, and at that point he was no longer so hard to catch; however, his desire for isolation is evident in his songs. For example, in the "Song of Aspiration" he says, "This beggar aspires to be utterly alone in caves and places where there are no people whatsoever."

STUDENT: There is a lot of encouragement/emphasis, in the Kagyu and Nyingma traditions, for practitioners to go into retreat. Is there any hope for those of us who are trying to practice in normal life, or is it essential that at some point we would have to go into isolation?

RINPOCHE: First of all, the whole reason why we usually do not have the opportunity to do retreat, to emulate the lifestyle of radical renunciation that is advocated in these lineages, is because our priority is this life. We prioritize success and pleasure based upon clinging to the permanence of this life, which is a mistake. It is bewilderment, and in the most extreme cases, we think that this life is all there is. Whatever we may believe, we tend to cling to it as the most important thing, since it is right in front of us. Therefore we prioritize success in this life, and as a result we do not have time to practice, whether in isolation or not.

Once you see that everything you cling to in this life and in this world is unreal, that it is impermanent, that it is insubstantial, and that your perception of these things as real and worthwhile is bewilderment, you will automatically find all kinds of time and all kinds of circumstances for practice. If we had not been born as human beings, that would not be the case. Or if we had been born as human beings but had no access to teachers and teachings, that would not be the case. But we have amassed all of these rare circumstances. We have been born human, we have access to teachers, and we have access to teachings. In spite of the fact that we do have the opportunity to pursue whatever amount of practice we are willing to do, the reason we do not do so is simply that we bind ourselves up with our own fixation on the permanence of this life and of our own misplaced priorities.

Practically speaking, this means that to adopt a lifestyle of renunciation, live in retreat, and practice intensively is of course best. But even if you cannot do that, you can still make time, provided you prioritize it. Even if it is a little bit of time in the early morning and late evening, there is always some time for practice. In addition, there are many practices that can be done under any circumstances, for example, the Chenrezik meditation practice, the recitation of mantras such as OM MANI PEME HUNG, Guru Rinpoche's mantra, Amitabha's mantra, and so on. For these to be effective, however, your motivation has to be that you are doing this practice, whatever it is, in order to bring all beings to a state of buddhahood. Through having that motivation and doing even a small amount of practice, there will be great benefit because you will definitely progress along the path to full awakening.

Nevertheless, while it is best to do retreat, there are two different outcomes to retreat, and the outcome depends basically upon your motivation for doing it. Someone might do a long retreat with the thought, "I must bring all beings to buddhahood. In order to do that, I have to attain it myself, and I am willing to do anything I have to do in order to attain that as quickly as possible." A person with that kind of motivation for doing retreat will get a lot out of it. On the other hand, you could go into retreat, especially in an organized situation where it is built into an institution, thinking, "I want to do retreat so that I can learn a little bit about Dharma, at least a few words and a few tricks, so that when I come out, I can be a lama and I can have a certain position, probably have free food, and impress people." If that is your attitude, then it is almost better not to do it because you will come out with a little bit of learning and a mountain of arrogance.

STUDENT: But motivation can be tricky. Sometimes it is mixed and seems to develop slowly. How does the initial motivation itself become purified?

RINPOCHE: The geshes of the Kadampa tradition certainly agreed with you. They made the gradual rectification of motivation one of the foundations of their practice. As you say, in the beginning, whoever you are, your motivation is mixed. There is a little bit of good motivation and usually a lot of impure motivation, so the Kadampas developed specific practices for the observation and rectification of motivation. One such practice was that they would sit with two piles of stones, a set of white stones and a set of black stones. Every time they had a thought that was a pure motivation, they would put out one of the white stones. Every time they had a thought that had an impure motivation, they would put out a black stone. What they found was that in the beginning of doing this practice, they would have a huge pile of the negative-motivation stones and maybe only one or two of the positive-motivation stones. However, if they kept on using this technique to observe their thoughts closely, then over time there would gradually be more and more of the positive ones and fewer and fewer of the negative ones, until finally they were even. Then if they kept on with it long enough, eventually they would get to the point where almost all their thoughts were positive and it would just be occasionally that they observed a thought of a selfish or negative motivation.

The point of this technique is that, as you say, motivation can be rectified – but it will not be rectified all by itself. You have to have the intention to rectify it. You have to recognize that your motivation is problematic and you have to be willing to change. You have to try. You have to put some effort into it. The problem with most of us is that we just kind of let our motivations be whatever they are. We accept them as they are and allow ourselves to abide in a state of the utmost negativity. Then, since we tend to associate with others who are in a similar state, we influence one another, and everybody just gets worse and worse as time goes by.

STUDENT: Is this text solely presenting guidelines for an actual retreat, or will it also begin to describe specific deity yoga practices?

RINPOCHE: It is really a combination of both. In the beginning Karma Chakme provides teachings on how to practice Buddhism in general – how to practice properly, effectively, and beneficially for all beings. Later the text will go deeper. It will explain how to prepare and undertake a proper solitary retreat. Therefore altogether the text provides instructions from the Shravakayana, Pratyekabuddhayana, Mahayana, and Vajrayana points of view.

STUDENT: Karma Chakme said that clarity of mind would not help alleviate the terror at the time of death. I was under the impression that that is not true.

RINPOCHE: That part of the text was referring to mundane intelligence and learning. The point was that no matter how intelligent you are, no matter how learned you are, it will all be irrelevant at the time of death. Your ability to traverse the bardo has no relationship whatsoever to your intelligence or education. What does affect your ability in the bardo is training in the Dharma, especially receiving the detailed instruction on how to work with death in the bardo, and then practicing this instruction to the point of confidence.

STUDENT: Is there a practice such as lucid dreaming that we can do when we sleep that will help us in the bardo?

RINPOCHE: It is true that lucid dreaming — knowing you are dreaming while you are dreaming — is cultivated as a preparation for the bardo. One of the best ways to cultivate lucid dreaming is to begin by seeing all appearances during the day as dreamlike or as illusory. That will help, but nevertheless the stable cultivation of lucid dreaming is a somewhat demanding, and therefore advanced, discipline or practice.

A more useful and in general a more effective way of approaching the preparation for the bardo is to dedicate the merit of whatever practice you do, and especially to pray for the compassion of the deities you practice, such as Chenrezik, for your successful traversal of the bardo and your rebirth in a pure realm. Supplicating Chenrezik to cause you to be reborn in a pure realm and dedicating your merit to that effect are very powerful practices. It will be much more powerful if the dedication and aspiration are made, not only for yourself but for all beings, recognizing that all beings die and go through the bardo. This makes it very effective. Therefore with the attitude that you are praying for all beings, you address your root guru or deity, and you think, "When the bewildering appearances of the bardo appear to me after my death, may you appear to lead me to a pure realm." If you make that prayer intensely and regularly, it will happen. It definitely can happen, especially if the supplication is directed to the Gyalwa Karmapa. He has proclaimed the assurance that when anyone supplicates him for liberation at the time of death, he will extend the hand of compassion and lead that being to the pure realm, to Dewachen.

This is something that anyone can actually accomplish through the force of aspiration, supplication, and dedication. By comparison, lucid dreaming as a preparation for the bardo is much harder to stabilize. It is much trickier, and therefore it is not particularly something you should rely upon. If you wish to pursue a practice in connection with the state of sleeping, the most effective and practical one is to go to sleep while very gently, quietly, maybe even mentally, saying a mantra, such as OM MANI PEME HUNG. By falling asleep with this mantra going through your mind, all of your sleep, whether dreaming or in a state of unconsciousness, will automatically become the cultivation of virtue. This is because that virtuous state of mind with which you entered sleep will be maintained until you wake up. This is the best single use of sleep for practice.

Another way to be benefited in the bardo is if a great lama or teacher performs the transference of consciousness, or phowa, for you. If your obscurations permit it and if you have a connection with that teacher, your consciousness can be transferred to a pure realm, or at least to a rebirth in one of the higher realms.

It is very good that you are thinking about this. It is always a good idea to keep in mind the thought that one day you are going to be in the bardo and that you have to prepare for it and to dedicate your virtue to that end.

STUDENT: Karma Chakme stated earlier in the text that he had fully abstained from any criticism or judgment. In our own daily lives, even if outwardly we do not say anything, mentally we are often criticizing. What are some daily exercises to really start cutting that habit down?

RINPOCHE: We must bear in mind that Karma Chakme was a fully realized individual who had come to a direct realization of dharmata. Therefore his state of mind or his mental abilities cannot really be compared with those of ordinary practitioners like ourselves. Because Karma Chakme has fully realized the state of dharmata, whatever he experiences, whatever he encounters, even those things that seem unfavorable to ordinary people like ourselves, cause him to have no reaction. He knows for a fact that those encounters are not real. There is no truth in them. They are like a dream, an illusion. Having come to realize the truth of nonreality, Karma Chakme is able to maintain a completely nonjudgmental state of mind. However, in answer to your question, for ordinary people like ourselves, there are some exercises, some practices that can be very helpful.

The first method is found in the Hinayana tradition. In this practice, whenever you encounter any negative circumstances such as ill will from individuals, becoming annoyed, and so on, you should think, "Because of my impure cultivation of karma in the past, as an outcome of that impurity I am encountering this negative circumstance." The negative circumstance could be an individual, a person, or just the circumstance itself. It doesn't matter. You simply know that whatever it is that has arisen, it is a result of your own negative karma. You do not blame the object. Why this helps is that when you think like this, you do not dwell upon the external cause, the object of the unfavorable conditions. At that very moment when you accept that it is your own negative karma, then you cease to dwell on the external negative circumstances.

In the Mahayana tradition, if someone is angry with you or criticizing you, then you try to recognize the negative emotion that in the circumstance is so powerful, whether it is anger, jealousy, or whatever. Then you recognize that because of this situation, the individual who is criticizing you is accumulating negative karma. Recognizing that, you see that really you yourself are the cause of this person accumulating this negative karma and that as a result this person may then be caused to take rebirth in a lower realm. Therefore, as a Mahayana practitioner, you develop some sense of compassion for the person who is criticizing you or is angry with you and then you dedicate your complete merit to him or her. By dedicating that merit, you may help stop them from accumulating further negative karma and therefore falling into the lower realms. You do this with a sense of love, compassion, and understanding. Remember that you must not think of the negative circumstance as being caused by the other person. Rather, you must think, "It is me, my existence, that is causing this person to criticize me, so I am to blame for the resulting negative karma." Now, you may not achieve success overnight. It is an exercise that you need to do over and over again whenever circumstances arise. However, definitely if you make an effort to do this, it will help you to pacify your own negative emotions, which will really be the outcome. You should do this gradually, over and over again, and eventually you will overcome your mind of judgment. One should try both methods, whether from the Hinayana or the Mahayana tradition, and alternate between whichever practice is more suitable. Either can be quite beneficial.

STUDENT: Based on what you just explained, if one accepts responsibility for one's own karma, then is this not saying that the person who is angry at us or criticizing us is not responsible for his or her own karma, but that somehow we are?

RINPOCHE: Yes, that is exactly the point. The individual responsibility here is that we make sure that we do not participate in the accumulation of negative karma on the part of the other person. That is our responsibility. Thus by thinking in that manner, when someone is criticizing you or is angry with you, if you do not participate with them in the angry exchange but rather understand the situation the way just explained, then you are free from accumulating negative karma yourself or from participating in the accumulation of negative karma by the other person. Not only do you not accumulate negative karma now, but your spiritual development is also enhanced through the sense of love and compassion that arises in you. So, yes, it is definitely your responsibility. If you say, "This is not my fault, it is the fault of the other," then you are now participating with that person in accumulating negative karma. You have *both* accumulated negative karma, so you have not fulfilled your own personal responsibility, which is not to participate in accumulating negative karma. That is really the key. What the other person does is another matter, but you have to be responsible from your side not to accumulate negative karma.

STUDENT: I think I understand your explanation that I am responsible for not furthering negative karma once a situation arises, but I still want to understand exactly how it is that I am responsible for the initial negative criticism, before the person even expressed it to me and the possibility for negative exchange arose.

RINPOCHE: Sometimes what is perceived as criticism comes from asking an honest question based on simply not knowing or on ignorance. Somehow that honest question is perceived as criticism and a negative circumstance arises. For example, I am walking down a street where nobody has seen a Tibetan monk before. An individual looks at me and sees a very funny-looking person, dressed oddly in a way they have never seen. That person comes close and asks, "What sort of dress is this? What country are you from?" In some sense this person is really asking an honest question of wanting to know, but the way it sounds is a little rude or negative in tone. This can create an atmosphere of anger. If you think about it, you yourself are to blame. If you were not wearing that unusual robe and walking down that street, he would not have developed that questioning thought at all. When you recognize this, you accept responsibility for the situation and do not engage in a negative interchange. That is how it is.

STUDENT: Sometimes terrible things happen to people who are good practitioners and good people. When this happens, they often ask, "What have I done wrong? Is this some kind of punishment?" How does one respond?

RINPOCHE: You must reach an understanding of the law of karma. First, you have to understand through inference that if you are enjoying a piece of fruit right now, it is because the seed of that fruit was cultivated in the past. If you are cultivating the seed now, you will not be able to enjoy the fruit right now. You have to wait for the future when the seed has grown and ripened. That is the basic nature of karma.

As you indicated in your question, it can be very disturbing to an ordinary individual's mind to notice that a person who seems so sincere and dedicated in the practice of virtue, who is a good student of the Dharma, who is living life so simply, and who is kind and helpful to others seems always to be experiencing negative karma. At the same time an individual who is engaged in negative and harmful actions seems to be enjoying good health and prosperity. This sometimes shakes one's faith in karma. What we fail to understand is that karma works in such a way that when you are creating positive karma, for example by practicing very diligently, you are burning away all sorts of negative defilements. Your past accumulation of karma, whether it is the previous lifetime or the lifetimes before that, has to ripen. When it does, you are completely exhausting that negative karma. Because you are practicing so hard, you are able to burn up or cause these karmas to ripen quickly, so that by the end you will have no negative karma whatsoever. All that will be left is complete purity. You are cleansing very quickly, therefore all this negative karma arises. The result is that it seems to the ordinary person's eye that this very diligent individual is going through more negative experiences than the person who is engaging in harmful activities.

Let me give you an illustration of what is happening here. A person in the United States suddenly decides to move to Tibet. This person has many debts to many people in this country. As he is about to move, all the creditors are calling him saying, "I need your debt paid before you move to Tibet because once you are there, it will not be possible to contact you." The analogy in this illustration is that you, as a sincere practitioner of the Dharma, are moving to a buddha field. In order to do so, you must be debt-free and you must be purified, immaculate. To reach that stage, all of your negative karma must be burned away, and that is what you are experiencing now. It is actually very good that you are reaping this negative karma.

The reverse of this is the individual who in this lifetime is indulging in negative actions of body, speech, and mind and who does not really practice. Such an individual is accumulating a lot of negative karma, piling it up on top of what he had accumulated in previous lifetimes. When this person dies, he will likely go to lower a realm. What we *see* is a person who is always engaging in negative actions but seems to be experiencing good health and to be free from bad karma. What is actually happening, however, is that the person's past accumulation of positive karma is burning up and all he is really left with at the end is negative karma. This can be very deceiving, but it is the truth about the law of karma.

STUDENT: We often hear in the teachings that even if a person has accumulated the karmic cause of being born in the lower realms, through the blessing of having met someone like His Holiness Karmapa, they would not be reborn in the lower realms. How does this take place? Does His Holiness actually remove the cause of the rebirth in the lower realms, or is it that through his compassion and power he is able to ameliorate the conditions through which the cause manifests?

RINPOCHE: You could say that it is both of those things that you mentioned, but it is something else as well. For an individual to have the opportunity to see His Holiness, or hear his speech, they must have accumulated vast amounts of merit in previous lifetimes. Their actually seeing or hearing His Holiness activates that merit. It is also because His Holiness manifests among us intentionally in order — purely and simply — to benefit beings. He has attained buddhahood innumerable aeons ago. Thus it is a combination of what is already present in the continuum of the person who sees or hears His Holiness and also His Holiness's own compassion.

STUDENT: Would you clarify why it is said that great virtue leads to rebirth in the god realm? I think of the god realm as being a place where one does not have the capability in that lifetime to achieve realization.

RINPOCHE: What you say is very true, but we need to look at the context. When it is stated that great virtue leads to rebirth as a god, intermediate virtue to rebirth as a human, and so on, the virtue being spoken of is ordinary mundane or defiled virtue. *Undefiled virtue* in this case means virtue motivated by the desire to attain awakening for the benefit of others. From a mundane point of view, the god realm is better because it is more pleasurable and more prosperous than the human realm; because of this it takes more mundane virtue to be reborn there. From a Dharmic point of view, the human realm is superior because it is a realm in which one may have the opportunity to practice Dharma. By no means, however, do all human beings have the opportunity to practice Dharma. Which is why we stipulate that the human birth we aim for is the "precious human birth," where one not only has a human birth but is born in a country where one has contact with Dharma and has the health and resources to access it.

STUDENT: The text says that ultimately we are the only ones who can purify our own karma. As you said, if the Buddha could do it for us, he would have done it already. On the other hand, we make the aspiration to liberate all beings in all realms. Can we, as future bodhisattvas, truly do that for a being in the hell or preta realm?

RINPOCHE: This depends on whether the particular being and the particular bodhisattva have formed a connection. If in cases where the being that is now in the hell realm has not formed any connection in previous lifetimes with a specific bodhisattva, then that bodhisattva cannot really do very much. In a case where the being has formed a connection, the bodhisattva can do quite a bit. Exactly how much they can do or how quickly they can do it depends on the type of connection.

There are essentially three types of connection that a being could form with a bodhisattva: a manifestly positive connection, a neutral connection, and an apparently negative connection. In the case of a positive connection, where the being already has faith in the bodhisattva, the bodhisattva may be able to lead that being right out of hell. In the case of a neutral connection, the bodhisattva will probably be able to shorten the being's sojourn in hell. If the being did something to harm the bodhisattva, thus forming a negative connection, which is the likely reason they are in the hell realm in the first place, it is doubtful that the bodhisattva will be able to help them out until the karma that got them in there is used up. It is a tremendous negative action to harm a bodhisattva, and the being that does so will be reborn in one of the hell realms. Bodhisattvas make powerful aspirations to benefit everyone with whom they have a connection, especially those people who harm them. Also, a bodhisattva's path is greatly enhanced by suffering harm from others because it is through this that the bodhisattva has developed increased patience and so on. Thus there is a connection between the two, so when the person eventually emerges from the lower realms, the bodhisattva, because of his aspiration, will be able gradually to lead the person up, eventually to the pure land and awakening.

STUDENT: What is the best thing that someone can do for a friend or relative who has recently committed suicide?

RINPOCHE: The best thing you can do is to pray for them. Since you are quite young, I want to say something to you about suicide. From one point of view, it is not hard to understand why people might take their own life, especially under certain circumstances. Nevertheless it is the worst mistake someone can make. From the point of view of how it affects them and from the point of view of how it affects others, it is an extremely serious mistake. The best thing you can do is to recite either the mantra of Chenrezik, OM MANI PEME HUNG, or the mantra of Amitabha, OM AMI DEWA HRIH. While reciting the mantra, focus on your friend and think that you are praying not only for him but by extension for all beings who have committed suicide and who are suffering in any way. Clearly bring your friend to mind based on your connection with him or her, and develop a sense of actually communicating with them, actually giving them something; the same way you would feel when feeding the birds. Then the mantra will help them. And your aspiration, because of your connection with them, will help them.

STUDENT: What is the point in visualizing the body or the face of a person who has died, since there is no longer any physical form to that person?

RINPOCHE: You should imagine him the way he was when you knew him. He does not have that physical body now, but he has a mental body that is a replica of it.

STUDENT: How do you avoid the immovable karma of being born in the form or formless realms?

RINPOCHE: Basically the deviation into rebirth in the form and formless realms is caused by fixation on our attachment to the peace or tranquillity that is the result of shamatha meditation. This occurs when someone practices shamatha so intensely that they generate a state of utter peace of mind, at least on the surface. The absence of the disturbance of thought generates a tremendous sense of well-being. This well-being is the primary object of attachment or fixation, and that is where the problem starts. Once the person has experienced that well-being, they start to become addicted to it. Being addicted to it, they suppress thoughts because they view them as threatening, as destructive to that tremendous sense of well-being. The suppression of thoughts is carried to the point where their mind is one-pointedly focused inward, without being distracted by thoughts that arise within the mind by anything external. That kind of deviation, if you are attached to it, can produce one of these kinds of rebirth.

The problem with being born in the form and formless realms is that once you are born there, since you do not do anything except remain in that continuous meditative state, you spend or use up all of your virtuous karma. When eventually you leave that realm, you are usually reborn in the lower realms because you have used up all of your virtuous karma and you still have all of your negative karma lying in wait for you. The way to avoid this is to cultivate a stable state in the practice of shamatha not as the final goal but as a means to an end. Do not fixate upon nor become attached to the well-being of tranquillity.

STUDENT: You said that the suppression of thoughts is the problem. How do you know when you are suppressing thoughts to this level?

RINPOCHE: The problem has two aspects: an aspect of aversion and an aspect of attachment. The aversion aspect is aversion to thoughts. The suppression of thoughts is occasioned by a feeling of rejection of thoughts. The attachment aspect is being attached to the well-being that is present in the absence of thought.

STUDENT: Can a person pray that any of the karmic consequences that they have accumulated happen as soon as possible?

RINPOCHE: Bodhisattvas constantly make the aspiration that all of the negative karma that they have accumulated throughout beginningless time ripen in this very lifetime. This is the beginning of their willingness to exchange themselves for others, for they extend their aspiration by saying, "And may all the negative karma accumulated by others only ripen for me, and may it do so in this lifetime." The result of making such an aspiration is that when their previous negativity does ripen sooner in this way, its result is much less than if it had ripened in its own, otherwise natural time.

There is a story about this. At one time a Sakya geshe was in retreat on the banks of the Zangpo River. Central to his practice was making the prayer "May all the suffering of others and may all my own previous negativity ripen for me right now." One evening this geshe became extraordinarily thirsty, much more so than he had ever been before. The strange and miserable thirst that he experienced that evening is said to be unlike human thirst at all. He knew he had a cup with water in it on his table, but when he reached over to take some water, the cup was empty. There was not a drop of water in it. He knew he had a container of drinking water in his retreat cabin, but when he went to get it, it too was completely empty. The geshe thought he had better fetch some water from the river and, desperately thirsty, he went outside. When he arrived at the river, it was completely dry. This river, called the Zangpo in Tibet, is the Brahamaputra River when it reaches India, and it is a very big river. Now it was completely dry. The geshe could see all the stones, pebbles, and sand on the bottom of the dry riverbed. When he saw this, he could not believe it. He thought something must be wrong. He tied one end of his monk's shawl to a tree and lowered himself into the riverbed. Sure enough, there was not a drop of water anywhere in sight. The tree itself was completely dry. Everything was dry.

By now he was almost dying of thirst, but there was absolutely no water to be found anywhere. He went back up into his retreat cabin and prayed, "May I take onto myself the karma of all the beings who experience this kind of thirst, especially pretas. May only I have to experience this." This prayer somewhat relieved his suffering of thirst, and finally he was able to go to sleep. When he awoke the next morning, he no longer felt thirsty. He looked at his cup and it was full of water. He looked at his water container and it was full. He went outside; the Zangpo was full to overflowing. In fact now he could not even get his shawl back, since it was still tied to the tree that was now submerged in the flowing river. The geshe went to his teacher and told him what had happened. The teacher explained that in a previous lifetime the geshe had accumulated the karma that would otherwise have definitely led to his rebirth as a hungry ghost and that because of the power of his aspiration, instead of having an entire lifetime of such suffering, he merely had to experience it for that one evening, because in doing so he had used up all of that karma.

STUDENT: If I understand the teachings correctly, any pleasure we experience in this lifetime is the result of virtue in the past that was not dedicated toward enlightenment. If this is so, can we rededicate it now?

RINPOCHE: Yes, you can dedicate or rededicate any merit or virtue that has accrued in the past. In fact we do this all the time. Whenever we dedicate any practice or any virtuous thing we do, we always have the idea "I dedicate the virtue from this specific action, and by extension, all the virtue I have ever accumulated in the past, and all that I will ever accumulate in the future." We say, "Just as such virtue has been dedicated to perfect awakening by bodhisattvas such as Samantabhadra, Manjushri, and Avalokiteshvara, in the same way I make this perfect dedication to awakening." If you are sincere and have no doubt, then through the reference to the perfect dedication of bodhisattvas, and through your willingness to embrace all of your previous defiled merit or virtue within the dedication, your dedication of past merit will be effective.

STUDENT: During the Buddha's lifetime, there was one particular student who, as a result of karma, was very stupid. The only task he was capable of was sweeping floors, and the Buddha used that method to help him purify his karma. What is the difference between ordinary beings changing conditions, as it were, and the process of purifying karma? On the surface the two look similar.

RINPOCHE: There is a difference. When you are changing conditions, you change the conditions themselves. When you change the karma of result, you are working with the cause in order to change the result. For example, in the analogy you gave, the student's intelligence increased by the purifying of his obscurations through doing the sweeping. This is different from attempting to change the intelligence itself, which you cannot do. That would be changing the condition. Since it was karmic, it had to be approached differently.

Obviously, we can do something about our karma, not so much by working on karmic circumstances directly but by working on the imprints of the causes themselves. We do this whenever we confess or admit wrongdoing. All of the methods of practice we do center to a great extent on the purification of our obscurations. To the degree that one purifies one's obscurations, one will have experience and realization. The difference is simply that you are not working with circumstances. You are working with the causes of circumstances.

STUDENT: The story of Angulimala, the serial killer who became an arhat, was presented relative to negative casting and positive completing karma. Could you explain this a little more?

RINPOCHE: In the example of Angulimala, the casting karma refers simply to the beginning of his life, and the completing karma refers to the end of his life, what he did in the beginning and what he did in the end. As you indicated in your question, he did purify all of the tremendous negative karma that he had accumulated. He did it in an extremely effective way because he was actually a direct disciple of the Buddha, consequently he was able to purify by confessing in the physical presence of the Buddha himself. What really changed the outcome of his life is that he became convinced, under the Buddha's influence, that what he had done was wrong, and he became so thoroughly convinced that all of the four powers were present.

STUDENT: Are actions separate discreet units that produce separate discrete results?

RINPOCHE: Each action has its own separate result. For example, in respect to being born as a human being, the predominant karmic circumstance is your having been born human, which is the result of one set of actions, but there are many other things that happen to you that are the results of your previous actions. Each one of those circumstances is a result of a particular action. For example, all the different circumstances of happiness and suffering that arise, to the degree that they are produced by karma and are not random conditions, are a result of those individual actions.

STUDENT: What is meant by *group karma*?

RINPOCHE: Group karma is the sum of the individual karmas of those beings that make up that particular group. An analogy for this is the sand in a desert. When you look at a desert from a distance, all the sand in it looks like one thing with a certain shape, but as you get closer, you see that each grain of sand is a separate thing. In the same way, the world that we live in and share is a function of our group karma, nevertheless our individual experience of this world is entirely individual to us. For example, if we all drink a cup of tea, we are having a similar experience. Tea will taste like tea to everyone, but each person's experience of that taste of tea is individual and unique to them.

STUDENT: The teachings mentioned the concept of environmental karma. When a natural disaster occurs, such as an earthquake, fire, or flood, are these things transitory conditions or are they an environmental karmic result?

RINPOCHE: It is hard to say whether everything that occurs in the environment is definitely a function of common karma or instead is definitely produced by temporary or transitory conditions. One thing that you need to remember is that the common karma that produces the environment, for example this world, is not a unitary thing. The karma that affects this world, that produced it in the beginning, that causes it to remain for its duration, and that causes it to be destroyed when it is, is not due to a single karmic cause. It is a function or sum of the many karmas of the many beings that are involved with this world and that experience it. Any given environment contains different beings over time, some dying, some being reborn, and some being born in that world that were not previously in that environment. As a result, what we call changing times occur in the environment, and these changes really come from the different beings having different karma being born in that realm. The environment responds accordingly.

STUDENT: What is the ground that karma ripens in? Does it ripen in the mind?

RINPOCHE: It really takes shape or grows within the mind stream. Our mind is a continuous stream, holding the karmic imprints of everything we have done in past lives. The mind continues to experience the results or ripening of karmas in this and future lives. Whatever we do, whether we cultivate virtue or nonvirtue, it is the mind that experiences the outcome in the next birth.

STUDENT: The most immediate form of karma that you mentioned in the teaching was the one that went "straight-through" after death. What about the kinds of results that one experiences right away in this present lifetime, sometimes quite soon after the behavior?

RINPOCHE: That is not really a "karmic ripening." It is the "immediate effect" of the action, but not the ripening result or the maturation of the action itself. That is still to come.

STUDENT: That is a little confusing for me. Can you elaborate further on the difference between karma ripening and the immediate effects of actions in the same lifetime?

RINPOCHE: The kind of thing I am referring to is classified as a condition, a transitory or temporary condition, rather than a karmic result. It is not a karmic result if it is not the ripening of the imprint of an action within your being, which is what a karmic ripening or true result of an action is. My point was simply that everything that happens to us is karmic. We have to make a distinction between conditions and results of actions, or karmas. It is very difficult to be absolutely precise about this and to actually point to events in one's life and say with certainty that this is karmic and this is not. Only a buddha can do that. We can, however, have a rough idea of it by basically understanding that anything we can change, anything we can do something about, is not fundamentally karmic for the most part. That which we can do nothing about, that is karmic. For example, you have many choices and small changes that you can make in your life; however, these are not changes in the problem but changes in your conditions. What you cannot change are the facts of birth, aging, sickness, death, and so on. You can do nothing about the inevitability of these, therefore that is the karmic situation. All the things that you can change through all the various things you do, by whatever means, those are probably conditions.

STUDENT: The text draws a really bleak picture of samsara. Do you have to have the fear of being reborn in the lower realms as a prerequisite for seriously engaging in practice?

RINPOCHE: The fear is absolutely necessary and it is also appropriate, because the sufferings of the lower realms are real. They are as real as anything and they last for a very long time. Under ordinary circumstances we regard it as appropriate to fear, and therefore avoid, something that is unpleasant, even though it might be short-lived. It is even more appropriate to fear, and therefore attempt to avoid, something as horrendous and long-lived as lower rebirth. At the same time the fear itself is not enough. The fear needs to inspire diligence within us. In other words, through fearing rebirth in the lower realms, we exert ourselves in doing that which will prevent it. Without that fear, there will not be any diligence.

STUDENT: Is it that, not remembering experiencing the lower realms, one has to kind of create them in one's mind?

RINPOCHE: As you say, we cannot remember our previous experiences of the lower realms. Not only can we not remember but we cannot even comprehend the sufferings of the lower realms or the pleasures of the higher realms. We are incapable of holding these things in our minds and incapable of seeing them, which is an example of our obscuration, of our ignorance. However, if someone has confidence and trust in the truth of the Buddha's teachings, they can still avoid rebirth in the lower realms. This is because the Buddha explained how to avoid it, through the observation of the causes and results of actions. If you trust the Buddha's teachings, even though you cannot see these sufferings, you can still avoid them, just as someone who is sightless can be led to a place they wish to go to by someone who can see; however, they have to trust that person who is leading them.

STUDENT: Is it common for practitioners to remember their past lives? If so, is it helpful?

RINPOCHE: When a person practices well, the layers of mental obscurations begin to peel away. As these obscurations become purified, one's past lives become clearer and clearer. Not only do you become clear about your own past lives but you also become clear about the past births of other sentient beings as well. How clearly you see the past lives of yourself and others depends on how mentally pure you are of obscurations.

Is there any benefit in remembering past lives? Definitely. Remembering past lives gives one a very strong, unshakable confidence in karma. For example, we say that if you do this good action, the karmic result in the next life will be this good result. If you do this negative action, the karmic result in your next life will be this negative result and so forth. Right now we hear these words, but nobody is really one hundred percent sure about it. Nonetheless when you see or remember a past life, you will not only know what that life was like but you will also know what led you to that birth, what caused you that sickness or that suffering, and what caused you that happiness. Seeing this so clearly with your own mind you become absolutely certain about cause and effect, the laws of karma. With this certainty, you will become even stronger in your practice and stronger in disciplining yourself to refrain from engaging in any negative actions. Now you know for sure that if you engage in a negative action, the result will be negative for you.

This is very similar to the difference between an adult and an infant. For example, let's say an adult eats something that is poisonous by mistake and it makes the person very ill. They go to the emergency room and the doctor helps them to recover. Now they know that this particular substance that they ate is poisonous and they will never touch it again. However, an infant having the same experience of eating the poison and going to the doctor and getting better will nevertheless eat the poison again and again if it is placed in front of them. The infant has no understanding, no discernment, in regard to the previous experience. At present we are like that infant. We are not remembering the lessons of the past. We participate in negative patterns over and over again, unable to discipline ourselves completely because we do not really have total trust in the laws of karma. Therefore knowing past and future lives does help a great deal, not only to discipline oneself but also to be able to understand the best way of helping others.

STUDENT: In the West we often hear stories about ghosts, who are usually described as being sad, confused, or attached to a particular house or place, but we never hear that they are particularly suffering from hunger. In what realm is such a ghost or spirit residing? Are they bardo beings?

RINPOCHE: Before we talk about ghosts, let me first address your question about bardo beings, which are entirely different. *Bardo* means "gap," or "in between." A bardo being refers to the spirit or consciousness that is in between the stage of death and the stage of rebirth. So these beings are not yet in one of the realms of samsara, such as the hungry ghost realm.

The actual word *ghost* is really a collective term as it is used in Buddhism, and there are many levels or classifications. As we have discussed, there are beings called hungry ghosts, but there are also demigod types of ghosts. These beings are very powerful, jealous, angry, and hateful individuals who try to use their power to cause harm to other beings. The "hungry ghost" type of ghost, on the other hand, is rather powerless and very timid in many ways. They are so timid that even if food is given to them, they cannot eat it unless it is offered in a certain way, at a certain time, or with certain special prayers. Some of these ghosts have no capacity to accept food at all even when it is dedicated; however they are able to experience some satisfaction through smell. That is why we undertake the practice of sur, in which we burn the food so that the smell provides relief to these beings. These are a few of the many classifications that are included in the general term *ghost* in Buddhism.

The specific rebirth that you described, in which a being is attached to a certain place, is usually the outcome of negative karma accumulated as a result of greed and stinginess, which are synonymous in the Tibetan language. Consider, for example, an individual who is very greedy and also very stingy. Such a person is unable to make appropriate offerings to the buddhas or to give generously to the poor, and may even be so stingy and so greedy that they cannot practice generosity with their own family. When such a person dies, through the force of the negative karma accumulated from such attachment, they experience a rebirth that sometimes may be in the form of a "ghost." We use the term *ghost*, but really there is no "ghostness" here. This is an actual being who, as a result of stinginess and greed, now has nothing, no food or clothes, and who experiences many more negative results of being unable to let go.

STUDENT: During the practice of chö we make offerings to beings that are only able to enjoy food through that specific practice. What category of beings are those?

RINPOCHE: They are another type of hungry ghost, as described in the previous question. This spirit is among the most timid of all the spirits, and suffers greatly. If you offer them the food first, they are unable to touch it because of their shyness and their feelings of inferiority. They do not feel that they deserve to eat food that is given before we eat, so only when we offer them the leftovers can they relax and enjoy it. Whenever you are performing any sort of practice, however, you must remember that compassion is essential. This is particularly true when you are doing this practice of giving the leftovers. You need extraordinary compassion.

STUDENT: I know that I have had pain and suffering in my life, and over the years I have experienced a lot of afflictive emotions, but I do not really remember these events clearly when I look back. The teachings say that we have all experienced all of the six realms. Why do we not remember the intensity of the pain and suffering? Why do we forget?

RINPOCHE: The major characteristic of the level of samsara in which we now exist is that we consider ourselves to be so real, so true, so concrete, and so permanent that we forget that we and everything in samsara are impermanent. We forget that all of samsara is subject to change. We are so preoccupied with thinking that everything right now is real and permanent that we forget what has happened in the past, and even ignore the changes that are taking place right in front of us. We are so fixated on the idea that nothing changes that we cannot acknowledge that everything in samsara is really eventually subject to deterioration. We believe that everything in samsara is true, real, and concrete. Therefore, based on that mental block, we are simply not open enough to remember things. This is why meditation on impermanence as described in the four ordinary foundations is so important. This helps remind us over and over again that everything is impermanent, that everything in samsara is subject to change. Such meditation ultimately awakens us from our deep sleep of confusion and forgetfulness.

STUDENT: What is the role of optimism in the context of samsara?

RINPOCHE: It is really a question of how you use optimism, not just the optimism itself. Suppose you are optimistic and you think, "I can practice. My practice will get better." Then you are using optimism properly. On the other hand, if you are optimistic about events or achievements in samsara, of course the optimism itself is good, but one day you will find that you have accumulated a lot of possessions and power and then you will die, and that is the end of that.

STUDENT: I have read that there are god realms where Dharma is practiced. If this is so, how is rebirth in such a realm less advantageous than a precious human birth?

RINPOCHE: Any god realm in which the Dharma is prevalent, such as Tushita, while it is still technically within the geography of the god realms, we would consider it to be a nirmanakaya realm, because it is the place where Dharma is available. Places where the Dharma is available, where there are perfect teachers, as there are in Tushita and as there are in this world, are considered nirmanakaya realms, not really pure realms but nirmanakaya realms. Being born in such places is as valuable as being born in a human realm in which you have the opportunity to practice Dharma.

STUDENT: You said that we create the six realms with our minds, as a result of our negative and positive actions. In that case, is the mind able at some point also to destroy these realms? Is this what we mean by enlightenment, liberation?

RINPOCHE: Yes, the mind is the essence of everything. The question of going up to an enlightened state is really one of mind. The question of falling down, experiencing birth in the lower realms, is also one of mind. Thus it is really a question of how you utilize this mind. If you make an effort to do good, to minimize and eventually totally cut off all the unvirtuous actions, that is mind. If you spend a lot of effort to engage in unwholesome actions continuously, that is also mind. Really it is the mind that goes through all of this. Remember that the mind makes choices; it makes the commitment as to which way to go. When we talk about walking up the mountain and walking down the mountain, the walking is the same, but the motivation, focus, and effort are different. You are using two feet that are taking steps one and after the other. One path takes you one way, one the other. It is similar with the mind. However the mind is concentrated or motivated, that is where it takes you.

STUDENT: Is it possible to help another person when their time comes to die?

RINPOCHE: Whether an individual is living or not living, we can only help them if we have the power to do so. Our good wishes are not enough, and that is why we have to practice Dharma. One can definitely obtain such strength and power by practicing Dharma. If you are a practitioner, then you should consider the person you wish to help with a true and sincere sense of compassion, and then with that true cultivation of compassion and love you should make a sincere prayer of dedication. The benefit will be much deeper if the individual has some connection with you, whether it is a physical connection, such as a relative, spouse, or friend, or a Dharmic connection, such as a sangha member. If you are doing a dedication prayer for someone that you have no connection with whatsoever, then the benefit will be rather minimal.

STUDENT: In *The Jewel Ornament*, or the *Dakpo Tarje*, Je Gampopa says in the first line, "Samsara is emptiness. It is shunyata. But its primary characteristic is ignorance." If we overcome this ignorance, do we overcome karma?

RINPOCHE: There is no contradiction in that statement. Samsara is emptiness. That is its ultimate nature. However, because of our attachment we are unable to experience the true nature of the emptiness of phenomena, or samsara. What prevents us from experiencing the true nature of the emptiness of all phenomena is partly attachment, but what causes that attachment is ignorance, ma rikpa. If you purify ignorance, then what you have left is wisdom mind, and wisdom mind is always free from any pollution, free from any karma.

Nevertheless, there is a risk in the statement "all phenomena is emptiness" (normally this quote is translated "all phenomena" rather than "all samsara"). Sometimes when we say that all phenomena is emptiness, people think that everything is void or hollow, that samsara disappears. That is not the emptiness we are talking about. *Emptiness* here refers to the truth that there are not any phenomena, which includes everything we perceive in samsara, that have any true concrete existence. Once you come to the complete realization of buddhahood, you can still perceive samsara. Samsara does not disappear, but you have gotten to a point where you have gone beyond attachment, anger, jealousy, and all the afflictive emotions. Samsara becomes free from all that. Samsara does not simply disappear to the mind of an enlightened individual.

STUDENT: As I understand it, samsara is a cycle of rebirths driven by our karma. How did samsara start? Did it always exist or did something happen to cause it to exist?

RINPOCHE: The question of when samsara began is very similar to asking when space began. Samsara is beginningless, and because it has no beginning, it also has no end. If there were a beginning, then we could also find an end.

Putting Away the Dice: Abandoning Samsara's Path

Karma Chakme Rinpoche now turns to an explanation of the path by which one learns how to abandon, or how to escape from, samsara. The main paths within Buddhism are the Hinayana, the Bodhisattvayana, and the Vajrayana. It is said that the ways to obtain liberation from samsara are as countless as the fine lines that are found on a mushroom.

The chapter begins by paying homage and respect to Shakyamuni Buddha, the one who has fully accomplished and fully perfected the paths. Addressing his disciple, Karma Chakme says, "Listen without distraction Tsondru Gyamtso. In order to successfully undertake solitary practice or retreat, you must first learn to cultivate the enlightened mind. In the absence of enlightened mind, you cannot successfully practice any tradition, much less the Vajrayana tradition. You must also understand the many classifications of the path. It is essential to follow the proper path and to know how to face in the right direction in order to be free from wrong direction and confusion."

In the first place we must understand the dangers of mistaken paths. The first mistaken path is called *the wrong path, the path of no virtue, or the path of negative actions*. The second mistaken path is called *the path of the circle*. This is when, not knowing the proper methods, you might believe you are on the right path but as you travel, you are actually just spinning around and coming back to the same point again, simply moving in circles and never making real progress. In addition to the path of no virtue and the path of the circle, there is also *the inferior path*. On the inferior path one engages in mistaken activities and, like the other two paths, does not arrive at the intended destination. If we recognize the dangers of these three mistaken paths, we can avoid them.

As mentioned earlier, it is only in the human realm, which in Tibetan cosmology is known as Jambudvipa, that the Dharma is available. The human realm itself is divided into twelve continents that consist of four major continents in the east, west, south, and north, and each of these has two subcontinents. Of these twelve divisions, the Dharma is available only in the southwest continent. During the period of Shakyamuni Buddha our own planet Earth was divided into ninety-nine great countries. Of these, the Dharma was only available in 24 nations, which were referred to metaphorically as middle, or center, nations. Around this center were 188 nations, but the Dharma was not available in any of them. In a circle, around the outer edges of the 188 nations, were another thousand worlds, and the Dharma was not available in any of them either. This is the very old traditional explanation.

During the time when the Buddha was in India, the Dharma did not reach Tibet; however, Chenrezik made the compassionate prayer that once the Buddhadharma was firmly established in India, it would become firmly established in the snowy country of Tibet. As a result of this prayer by Chenrezik, and due to the accumulation of merit by many individuals, the Buddhadharma flourished in Tibet. There were many great, perfected yogis and practitioners in Tibet. In this way, with the blessing of Chenrezik and all the bodhisattvas, we see that the activity of the Buddhadharma never ceases. Consequently we know that the great master, Buddha, existed and we are able to hear the teachings.

At the same time, because we understand that there is such a possibility as an enlightened being or buddha, there is also the possibility of a mara, an obstructer of enlightenment. Since a great teacher like the Buddha exists, we cannot deny that great evil also exists. Good and bad exist simultaneously, just like light and dark. Because of the possibility of the existence of many pure buddha fields, we can also infer that there are many impure realms as well. These possibilities lead us to infer that there are virtuous beings and there are unvirtuous beings. There is the possibility of afflictive emotions (kleshas), and the possibility of the absence of those afflictive emotions. There is the possibility of pure, authentic Dharma and the possibility of impure, fabricated Dharma. There is the possibility of pure view and impure view. There is the possibility of beings that maintain pure precepts and those who transgress or break their precepts.

All of these possibilities exist because everything is interdependent. *Interdependent* in this sense means that if we say that something is tall, we must also say that something else is short, because without short there is no tall. If there is something good, there must also be something that is bad. In the same way, if there is a quality that we call virtue, then there also exists nonvirtue. That is what we mean by interdependence. Even the great panditas, the great scholars of India in the past, began by studying this very basic logic.

The key here is to understand that there are both favorable and unfavorable paths. By recognizing and understanding this fundamental point, we can avoid following negative paths. For example, if you are walking on a very narrow path in the dark and if you know that the path is narrow and that on each side is a very long drop to the valley below, then you will be very cautious and mindful as you walk. If you are not warned that there is a dangerous narrow path, then you will just walk along freely and you will definitely fall. At that point it is really too late for understanding. To help individuals not fall into the wrong path, these explanations are given in the beginning.

In order to follow the correct path, it is important to understand the circumstances in which the teachings took place and how and why they were labeled in certain ways. One way to describe this is to consider that in India there were both Buddhist and non-Buddhist traditions, in China there was Mahayana Buddhism and Taoism, and in Tibet there was the Bon religion and Tibetan Buddhism. The text issues a warning here. In order to choose the right path, we need to understand that there are various paths, or religions. At the same time, we must be careful not to develop feelings of superiority or dislike toward other traditions. If as a Buddhist in the Mahayana tradition we develop aversion to practitioners of other traditions, then we are breaking the precepts of the Bodhisattvayana. According to the Bodhisattvayana, all beings are equal and one is required not to exclude any sentient being. In addition, such a view would also be breaking the samaya of the Tantrayana, because in the Tantrayana every sentient being has buddha nature. To develop aversion to buddha nature is the most profound breaking of the samaya of the Tantrayana. We must accept that there are many paths, each of which tries to direct the practitioner toward virtue. It is not appropriate to dislike or to denigrate other traditions.

The situation of Tibet at this time illustrates some of the pitfalls involved with the various paths. The text says that it is true that great masters like Padmasambhava, who compassionately commanded the twelve local gods of Tibet to protect the Buddhadharma that was being established there, have blessed the land of Tibet. As a result of such blessing, some people may believe that everyone in Tibet is practicing the virtues of Buddhism. Of course, this is not the case. There are people born in Tibet, where Buddhism is firmly established, who because of their accumulation of negative karma in previous lives, follow a nonvirtuous path. They do not turn themselves or their minds to the Dharma; therefore they definitely are not practicing the Buddhist path. There are others who because of past karma have strong negative habitual patterns and enjoy sacrificing animals to deities. Even in a rich Buddhist country such as Tibet there are some people who deviate from or do not follow the virtuous Buddhist path.

We have no knowledge of what will happen to us in this lifetime as a result of our past actions. Because we do not remember our past lives, we do not know whether we will experience a long and virtuous life or sudden, untimely death. Because of these uncertain conditions, we do not have any idea about our next birth. We cannot be certain that we will be reborn in a higher realm or not. Since we have no knowledge of the past or present conditions of our lives, what is really appropriate is to practice virtue and Dharma in order to prepare ourselves for our future lives. Nevertheless, instead of preparing ourselves by practicing Dharma, we are completely caught up with the worldly accumulations of wealth, position, power, and friends. Consequently we are constantly engaging in various types of unvirtuous activities and we have no time to practice the Buddhadharma.

The result is that we are no different from one born in a realm where Dharma is not available.

Black Bon practitioners, because of their past karmic habits, believe that by giving the flesh and blood of a particular animal to a certain deity the practitioner will experience long life, healing of their illness, and happiness. This is an example of wrong view or wrong path. Although one is born in a Buddhist country, if you participate in animal sacrifice, it is the same as if you were born in a country where Dharma is not available at all. There is no difference whatsoever.

Another example of non-Buddhist activity in Tibet concerns the way some people recite the six-syllable mantra, OM MANI PEME HUNG. Every individual in the country knows this mantra, even those participating in animal sacrifice and other nonvirtuous paths. They all know how to recite it, but they lack the empowerment, oral transmission, and instruction in the meditation of Chenrezik. They recite it often because they know that the six-syllable mantra is very powerful. Although they think they are reciting the entire mantra of Chenrezik, they recite the mantra inaccurately and they become like a satisfied horse lying on the ground in the sun chewing happily and mumbling "MANI, MANI, MANI, MANI." Of course, there is no benefit in that. People who practice in this category are not classified in the category of wrong view, but rather in the category of "not finding the path" or "no path." Here "no path" means that they are not really searching for any right or wrong path.

There are four basic categories of wrong view that can be expanded to three hundred sixty categories. The four basic categories are: (1) believing in eternalism; (2) believing in nihilism; (3) believing in both eternalism and nihilism; (4) believing in neither eternalism nor nihilism.

Believing in nihilism is the most serious. If one really has a strong nihilistic belief, there is no opportunity for enlightenment or rebirth in the higher realms of samsara—the human realm, the demigod realm, or the god realm. If you have a strong belief in eternalism, although you do not have the possibility to experience enlightenment, you do have the possibility to experience a higher rebirth within samsara.

It is important to be able to discern authenticity when you receive teachings because sometimes we are unable to recognize when someone is deceiving us. They are only interested in their own personal wishes and use the concepts of wrong view, nihilism, and eternalism simply to gain support and followers. There is one well-known story that warns of teachings that were fabricated for personal satisfaction.

Once there was a very intelligent and well educated individual in India. Because he was also very skilled in presenting his ideas, people always listened to him. One day he realized that he was very attracted to his own sister and he decided that he wanted to marry her, which was against the law and culture of the time. Knowing this, the man created a new theory. He began to teach that we have only one life to live, and this is it. He taught that there was no such thing as past or future and that when we die, it is the end of everything. There is no reincarnation or rebirth. He argued that we can clearly see that our body deteriorates when we die, that it just turns into dust. He said that our mind itself just becomes part of space. Therefore he concluded that there is no such thing as legal or illegal. There is no such thing as physical relation or no physical relation. There is no such thing as incest or not. With that theory he eventually convinced not only his sister but also many others, who all became his followers. His main motivation for developing this view, however, was that he wanted to marry his own sister. This is one example of how entire false paths can be formulated and how one must be extremely cautious and wary of false ideas and teachings.

In Tibet they often tell another story to illustrate the importance of discerning the authenticity of the words of a teacher. There was once a very smart man who lived in a small, prosperous village. This man decided that he would like to own all the land in the village, so he devised a scheme to encourage the other villagers to move to a different place. He began to tell his neighbors that he had come to truly believe that someday soon many wolves would come to the village and eat everyone. He suggested that people move immediately. Because the man was very smart, he was respected and the people listened, although they did not immediately pack up and leave.

Nevertheless they began to have concerns and spoke among themselves, saying that perhaps the words of this great teacher were true. Perhaps they really were in danger and should move. Other people had doubts, and this very smart man could see that he would have to make his story more believable. He went up to the mountains, killed a wolf, took its paws, and made footprints in the snow, encircling the village. The next day he said, "See, there are a few footprints. This is just the beginning. Soon there will be hundreds of wolves and they will eat all of us." In a couple of days the snow started falling, and again he made more footprints. People really started worrying, and some began to move away. Then one wise individual arose saying, "Well, we do see the footprints of wolves in the snow, but I would be very interested in the origin of these footprints. I would like to know where they are coming from and where they are ending. Let us check this out." Some of the villagers joined him and they followed the footprints to where they began, which were right at the doorstep of the very smart man who had made the prediction. In this way the villagers overcame the dogma presented by the teacher, whose real motivation was to drive the people out of the village. Please remember that we must not always trust what someone says; we must examine it thoroughly and ascertain if it is authentic.

We will now discuss the various philosophies and beliefs that were followed in the past. One philosophy believed only in the law of interdependence. Another belief stated that there is no enlightenment, no Buddha, no virtue and no nonvirtue, no cause and no result (karma). When one dies, that is the end. They believed that animal sacrifice to the appropriate deity is necessary to ameliorate and improve difficult circumstances in one's life. It is through pleasing the deity that one overcomes negative influences, afflictive emotions, and physical obstacles. Although this is not a Buddhist belief, it existed in both India and Tibet.

In another tradition, they do not believe in enlightenment, buddhas, or bodhisattvas. Not believing in buddhas and bodhisattvas, there is definitely no way of accepting the teachers of the Kagyu lineage. They do not take seriously the great stories of the enlightened beings of the past, in whom miraculous powers are so obvious. The reason these individuals are so resistant to accepting or believing in enlightenment is due to their past accumulation of negative karma. The result of this immense accumulation of negative karma is immense obscurations that prevent them from seeing the truth. Because of this deep confusion, they believe in a false reality. That is the answer to the question why some people cannot believe in enlightenment, buddhas, or bodhisattvas.

There is a non-Buddhist group that has a similar belief but that also believes in rebirth. This rebirth has nothing to do with the positive or negative accumulation of karma, but is based on the ability to please their gods. If you are able to do so, you take rebirth in the special god realm that exists in the sky like an upside-down umbrella. To please the deity, it is necessary to sacrifice the fresh blood of an animal or human heart. In some cases they would need to sacrifice five hundred to one thousand hearts in order to please the deity. At the time this was written, such practices existed in both India and Tibet.

Another belief says if you eat the food offered to you by another, or wear clothes given to you by another, you accumulate negative karma. To be free from such negative karma, you must not wear clothes. Being naked, you are then required by this system to apply ashes to your body. This particular belief did not exist in Tibet.

The belief of the Brahmins in India is closer to Buddhism. Although they do not take refuge in the Three Jewels—the Buddha, the Dharma, and the Sangha—we say that they are closer because they do abstain from the ten unwholesome actions and adopt the ten wholesome actions. They do this in order to please the god Brahma. To further please the god Brahma, they are very strict in maintaining the purity of the Brahmin caste. They believe that one must study the gods' language (Sanskrit) including sounds, etymology, and poems. By maintaining this purity, and through the proper aspiration prayers, one experiences rebirth in Brahma's pure realm. Through this aspiration prayer, it is possible that they can experience rebirth in a higher realm, but this realm is not the ultimate realm, because their enjoyment in such a realm will become exhausted and they will fall back to the lower realms of samsara.

There is a belief in Tibet that people completely trust. They do not take refuge in the Buddha, the Dharma, and the Sangha, but rather take refuge in the local deities they believe inhabit the mountains, water, and all of nature. They worship these local deities and do everything to please them, in the same way that the Brahmins try to please their gods. What we come to understand is that they are taking refuge in worldly gods, so they are all subject to falling back. They are subject to experiencing temporary benefits from the worldly gods, but receive no ultimate benefits.

In Tibet, the Bon religious beliefs are similar to the non-Buddhist beliefs, and like the Brahmins, they practice the ten virtuous actions. The Tibetan king, Trisong Deutsen, requested the great scholar Vairochana to bring Buddhism to Tibet. The king was very supportive of this authentic Buddhism; however, since the majority of the ministers were practitioners of Bon, it was clear to the king that if he proclaimed that Bon should not be practiced, his life would be in danger. King Trisong Deutsen used skillful means by maintaining the name Bon and changing the practice to the essence of Buddhist practice. The ministers were quite content that they still had their Bon religion.

During this period Guru Padmasambhava hid many teachings, which we call termas, and labeled them Bon, although they actually contained teachings for Tantrayana practice. Later the Bon practitioners discovered these termas labeled Bon and they followed the instructions that were actually for Tantrayana practice. Many attained enlightenment, and because of this they claimed that Bon practices lead to enlightenment, whereas in reality the practices were Tantrayana. Guru Rinpoche used skillful means in naming the terma Bon.

There is a belief in China known as Hashang. Although this path does not take you to enlightenment, it is not negative. The Hashang tradition uses something like shamatha meditation, but they do not have any emphasis whatsoever on vipashyana. If you believe in the higher realms, that is samsara; if you believe in the lower realms, that is samsara. They are both suffering. They give the analogy that it does not matter if you are bitten by a white dog or a black dog because both are equally painful. Therefore it is necessary to abandon both virtuous actions and nonvirtuous actions. They believe that shamatha is the ultimate meditation and that when you are able to sit still, free from all thoughts, it is the perfection of shamatha meditation. That is the belief of this particular tradition.

In Tibet there is a practice that uses shamatha meditation to block the feeling of the eight aspects of consciousness. When you are sitting so still and you block the aspects, if someone calls your name, you cannot hear because you are so deep into that meditation. That is their shamatha practice, which is very similar to the Hashang tradition practiced in China.

There are practitioners who claim to practice the ten wholesome actions, generosity, and Mahamudra. Nevertheless, no matter how extensive their virtue, merit, and practice, if they fail to take refuge in the Three Jewels, they will not experience enlightenment. Regardless of how many millions of times they practice virtue; it cannot help them to achieve complete liberation. Failing to take refuge in the Three Jewels, everything is for one's own personal benefit and is based on selfish notions that one can be completely free from sickness, misfortune, and obstacles. They have not taken refuge in the ultimate—the Three Jewels that are beyond samsara—but have taken refuge in worldly gods that are in samsara and subject to ups and downs. Their practice has virtue, but such virtue is limited and subsequently subject to deteriorate, so they are not able to experience enlightenment.

If you take refuge in the Three Jewels, then there is every possibility for enlightenment because you are taking refuge in beings who have actually experienced complete liberation from samsara. When you become Buddhist by taking refuge in the Buddha, the Dharma, and the Sangha, the outcome of the virtue and the merit leads you to enlightenment.

In Buddhism there are two main vehicles, the Hinayana and the Mahayana. In the Hinayana the emphasis is on individual liberation from samsara. The Mahayana path emphasizes an altruistic attitude, the wish to attain enlightenment for the benefit of all sentient beings and to establish all beings in enlightenment. Once you wholeheartedly take refuge in the Three Jewels and make a firm commitment, then you are on the bodhisattva path, the Mahayana path.

Karma Chakme concludes this chapter by telling his disciple, Tsondru Gyamtso, "You must properly cultivate the Mahayana tradition of taking refuge and precepts and trusting one-pointedly and whole-heartedly in the Three Jewels. I, Raga Asya, old and feeble, have given these very heartfelt teachings in the form of a Dharma song, to my disciple, Tsondru Gyamtso."

Questions and Answers

STUDENT: When you were explaining that Guru Rinpoche had hidden teachings for Bon, it sounded like he was doing a little trickery or deception. He was teaching Tantrayana and telling them it was Bon. I wanted to be clear about this and the use of deception for Dharma.

RINPOCHE: When you direct someone away from negative action toward positive action, that is not really a deception, but rather skillful means. If you confuse someone more, then of course that is deception. Padmasambhava knew that traditional Bon practice could lead these practitioners to accumulate negative karma and that they would therefore be unable to be liberated from the lower realms. Out of love and compassion, he provided the path to liberation in this terma, or hidden teaching. The Bons were practicing what they thought was Bon, but it was actually no different from Dzokchen practice or Maha Ati practice. It was the result of Guru Rinpoche's skillful means that many attained rainbow body and reached the highest level of realization. For example, a person is very sick and the doctor realizes that the cause of the sickness is addiction to milk. The person is unable to give up milk, but the doctor knows that milk is causing extreme harm to the person and the person may die. The doctor produces a white liquid just like milk and tells the person that it is milk and to drink it every day. The person, thinking it is milk, drinks it and is cured of the disease and gains perfect health. Here we have deception as skillfulness coming from an altruistic and benefiting mind, in contrast to wanting to hurt others and acquire gain for oneself.

STUDENT: This morning you said that negative and positive are interdependent. Is this a Buddhist belief?

RINPOCHE: We cannot call it a Buddhist view. All things are dependent upon each other. When there is short, there has to be tall. When there is high, there has to be low. When there is good, that means there must be bad. It is just a natural thing. It is not anybody's specific view. We cannot say it is a Buddhist view. The benefit of knowing that everything is interdependent is that we do not overreact to what we encounter—good, bad, positive, or negative. We know that "good" things happen and "bad" things happen. If you do not understand interdependence, when something negative happens, you become frightened or angry or depressed, thinking someone else is making you suffer. That is really a sign of weakness and not recognizing the interdependence of things.

STUDENT: Is there within the concept of interdependence of positive and negative actions the germ of an idea that will evolve into an understanding of the interdependence of the two truths?

RINPOCHE: You could say that, but the idea of relative truth and ultimate truth is interdependent because without "ultimate" there is no "relative." Interdependence is a natural thing as it is. The reason we are introducing this is that by knowing the interdependence of phenomena we do not suffer from changes when they occur. We do suffer from changes when we do not understand why the changes occur. For example, when there is day there has to be night. That is interdependent origination.

I have not really seen anybody falling on the ground saying, "Gosh, it's night. I hate this." They know it is night. Therefore if they still like to work late, they turn on the light and they do not complain that much. If they do not know that, then they think that somebody caused the darkness. They complain and they suffer. It is unnecessary pain and suffering. To overcome that, the knowledge of interdependence is very important.

STUDENT: I would like to ask something about the cultivation of bodhichitta. It seems like it is not too hard to cultivate bodhichitta during meditation. Sometimes during the day you are faced with hostilities and tension in the work environment. I am wondering if there is some kind of practice that we can do while working that reminds us to cultivate bodhichitta.

RINPOCHE: During practice it is not that difficult to cultivate bodhichitta. The advice is that after your practice, you make the commitment "I will maintain a strong mindfulness, and I will not react to any adverse situation that I might have to face." Because you have made the commitment to maintain mindfulness, you will decrease the anger and negative reactions you would ordinarily produce when you go to work. It is a repeated practice that you need to commit to. In the evening before going to sleep reexamine how you have reacted and how well you have kept your commitment. "Well, I was not able to keep all my commitments today, but tomorrow I will do much better." If you find you have participated in negative circumstances with anger, jealousy, or other neuroses, try to purify that by doing Vajrasattva practice or saying OM MANI PEME HUNG. Then make another confirmation of the commitment that tomorrow you will improve. It does require a lot of practice. If we can overcome hostility and harshness in the world, however, then enlightenment will not be that difficult. So it does take time, and we have to practice and commit over and over again.

STUDENT: You talked about how, with karma, you have the action, and then you have the result of that action. I want to know where this karma ripens. You have a seed planted in the ground and then the result of that seed is a plant that grows up.

RINPOCHE: When we commit a negative action, we plant the seed of negative karma. The ground is where we plant the physical seed, but we plant the seed of karma in our consciousness. For example, if you kill a human being and are not caught by worldly law, you are free. You are not free from the law of karma, however. The negative karma of killing a person is planted in your consciousness, and because of the weight of the negative karma you experience rebirth in the hell realm. The existence of the hell realm comes from your own karmic manifestation. It is not that somebody has created the hell realm.

STUDENT: Does karma always ripen?

RINPOCHE: Yes, definitely. Sometimes the more positive karma ripens, and sometimes the more negative karma ripens. Once you have created karma, it always has to ripen. The only time when you do not have to experience the ripening of karma at all is when you are enlightened.

STUDENT: I have been told that if you accumulate a lot of merit, you can cause karma to ripen prematurely. I believe that, but I don't have a logical understanding of it. How does merit cause karma to ripen prematurely?

RINPOCHE: Actually, the more merit you accumulate, the faster you purify the negative karma. If you are really very, very diligent in the practice of accumulating merit, then you are able to experience the result of your karma in one lifetime. When the result of action is very slow, one experiences rebirth after rebirth. If you read the life story of Milarepa, you will learn that early in his life he killed many human beings. Later on he felt regret for the negative actions he had performed and practiced extremely diligently and one-pointedly. Consequently he reached enlightenment in one lifetime. That is the symbol of the strength of merit that can purify the karma.

STUDENT: In Christianity there is a concept of grace, which is divine mercy reaching down and helping. With grace one is always going toward God. I know that it is different from Buddhism. I am wondering, with all the karma we accumulate and try very hard to purify, is there any concept of grace?

RINPOCHE: Yes, in Buddhism we have what is called "blessing." I cannot say if it is exactly the same as grace. In Buddhism there is enlightened blessing continuously penetrating every sentient being out of compassion from the enlightened beings. It is always there. Getting back to interdependence, in Buddhism blessings are only beneficial if the sentient beings are open to the blessing. What we mean is that blessings are always powerful, but if you are not open, it cannot help you. The sentient being's trust or confidence in the blessings of the enlightened beings is equally important, and when that and the blessing meet, then, yes, there is possibility. The analogy used to illustrate how those two things — openness of the sentient being and the blessing of the Buddha — are necessary to overcome negative karma is that the sun is always shining. When the sun shines, we can see the light of the sun, but those who are underground cannot see it. It is not that the sun is not shining. If they come up from underground, they receive the sun. The action of coming up from underground is the trust and confidence.

STUDENT:You have said that bodhisattvas are everywhere. Do bodhisattvas sometimes act through a regular person? Occasionally someone will say something to me and it will be a very profound and clear message. Then the person turns back into the regular person they were before. I was wondering if bodhisattvas work through regular people, or whatever you want to call that.

RINPOCHE: Yes and no. We have to keep in mind that bodhisattvas' activities are unimaginable; therefore, in that sense, yes. In saying yes, we must not expect that everyone who says something wise is a bodhisattva. In that sense, no. It is said in Tibet that bodhisattvas often predict things through a regular person — a non-practitioner — who gives a very precise prediction, and then becomes an ordinary person again. Since this has happened before, I do not want to say it is not possible.

STUDENT: Is there any way that we can be aware of buddhas and bodhisattvas everywhere?

RINPOCHE: It might be helpful to learn more about bodhisattva activity by reading the biographies of realized beings. In this way we come to realize that bodhisattvas don't only give messages to other individuals, they can manifest as anything, even sometimes a tree or a plant, if doing so will benefit others. Their activity is unimaginable, and the way that they benefit others is not necessarily through verbal communication. One really needs to get a strong understanding of bodhisattva activity through studying the lives of the bodhisattvas.

STUDENT: I am hoping you can help me understand about samaya relations in past lives, and when we take a vow in this life. I have to guess that in a past life I might have had some connection to you or to His Holiness Karmapa. Let us say in a past life I had taken the bodhisattva vow or the lay precepts or even the precepts of a monk or a nun. I took this as a Mahayanist, so I took them for all future lives. In this lifetime I have certainly broken the vows and precepts. Is this the purpose of the purification practices of Chenrezik or Vajrasattva, to purify our samayas and our vows that we have broken from beginningless time? I have had a hard time relating to what might have happened in a past lifetime.

RINPOCHE: I really do not know about the past; however, I am very certain of and completely trust the teachings of the Buddha. Based on that I am sure you have had a karmic connection with the Buddhadharma in a past lifetime, and as a result of that you are now also interested in this lifetime. Based on Buddhist teachings I am also sure that you have taken many precepts in past lives. We do not know specifically what precepts you have taken, but you have definitely taken vows and precepts in previous lives. Whenever we take precepts in the Mahayana tradition or the Bodhisattvayana tradition, we are taking them not only for that particular lifetime but also until we attain enlightenment.

The bodhisattva vow of the Mahayana has one root and many branches. As an ordinary unenlightened being we tend to break the branches. The root of the tree is still there even if you break a branch. You have not yet destroyed the root. The reason that we say you have never destroyed the root of the samaya from your past life is that you have taken a human birth. If you take precepts and vows and destroy the root, you will not have a human rebirth. If you maintain the root, you will have a human rebirth, and from there you can develop in Buddhism. In the Mahayana tradition, vows last until you reach enlightenment. As long as you do not give up wanting to help all sentient beings, then you do not destroy the root. If you become angry or jealous, you do not disconnect from the Buddhadharma at all. Those are just branches. The root is intact. In the Mahayana, bodhichitta is definitely the root. Giving up the Dharma, or giving up wanting to help and benefit all sentient beings breaks the root, breaks the samaya. Furthermore, if you do not have a proper establishment of bodhichitta, there is no way to practice Tantrayana at all.

STUDENT: Someone comes to you and says, "Forget about all the other sentient beings. Help me and make me happy." You answer, "I cannot abandon one single sentient being." How do you respond?

RINPOCHE: When we say "benefiting all sentient beings," we are not saying that we should be under the influence or control of someone else. When an individual comes and says, "Help me," and you have the power to do so, then you should help him. You do not have to agree not to help others, because you do not have to be under the control of this person. This person could be a mara—a demon—appearing in front of you saying, "Help me and do not help any other sentient being." Sometimes maras manifest in different disguises to prevent others from following the path of the bodhisattva.

STUDENT: I have been engaged in Dharma conversations on the internet, and many questions come up. One of these questions is, what specifically incarnates? Also, if upon extinguishing all cravings and desires and there is nothing left to incarnate, how does the bodhisattva fit in with that—because there is still desire to help all beings?

RINPOCHE: What reincarnates is the consciousness of the individual who experiences death and who experiences rebirth. The conditions of rebirth depend on karma. One's rebirth is based on one's karma and on one's consciousness. Our parents help us to experience that physically, but the mind or consciousness is very individual. It is the consciousness that continues to reincarnate or to experience rebirth.

Desire to help others is most often accompanied by personal interest. We have the tendency to help our friends and relatives. You say, "I really want to help my friends or my relatives." The problem with this approach is there is "my," and if another person or group tries to hurt your friend or relative, you develop anger toward that person or group. On the bodhisattva level, since the bodhisattvas are realized, there is no personal concern whatsoever. An example is the person who cut off his hand to give to another. That is impossible for us. We say, "Me first, then my friends." On the bodhisattva level there is no concern for me or my. On our ordinary level there is concern for me and my, consequently there are attachments and anger that go together like the two hitters of the damaru. Even if you want to help, if there is attachment and someone is harmful to your friend, you give rise to anger and depression. When you have developed compassion for all sentient beings, if you love and are concerned for all sentient beings, there is no space for anger. Since you are not concerned for your own personal welfare whatsoever, this does not fit into the category of desire. This unconditional, unlimited compassion for all sentient beings is completely without discrimination. If you discriminate between whom you love and whom you do not love, that is very limited.

STUDENT: What are demons? Are demons sentient beings?

RINPOCHE: Yes, they are definitely sentient beings, those that have accumulated an immense amount of merit in previous lives. You may ask how it is possible to accumulate merit and then become a demon or a mara. We must always be aware of our motivation, because motivation is most important in our practice. Even if you practice and accumulate a great deal of merit, if your motivation is negative, you may become a mara, or a demon with tremendous power. Unlike ordinary beings, a mara has the power to manifest in different forms.

There is an old Tibetan story that took place about ten generations ago in the village called Nyarong. There was once a boy who was very short and very ugly. Everyone in the village teased him from the time that he was a child until the time that he grew up. They never stopped teasing him. There was nothing he could do. He received many initiations, among which was a protector initiation. He also received the lung and instructions for this protector practice. He went to the mountains and did retreat for many, many years. Although the practice was genuinely authentic, his motivation was negative. He said, "By doing this practice may I be born in this village as a very powerful individual so that I can destroy everyone. When people hear my name, they will become frightened to death. Now because I am so ugly nobody takes me seriously." After many years in retreat he died. He soon took birth into a large aristocratic family in that village. From childhood he was very angry, hateful, and cruel. By the time he was an adult he was killing everyone, including his own parents. Toward the end of his life he was destroying and killing everybody. There was a Nyingmapa lama who approached him and explained that he was completely following the wrong path. By persevering in this way this highly realized Nyingmapa lama was able to convince this person that he had taken the wrong path. He repented before his death, and because of his repentance, although he had many subsequent births in the lower realms, he was finally reborn in the human realm and was able to pursue the Dharma. In Tibet when they tell children about the person from Nyarong, the children shake with fear.

This story illustrates the idea of a mara, and the importance of motivation in our practice. There are individuals in our own time, such as Mao Zedong, who have great power. Without such power they would not be able to control and destroy so many people. Whatever merit they have previously accumulated is destroyed by wrong motivation. Mao Zedong's motivation was to destroy religion—not just Buddhism, but all religions.

Gandi of the Nobles: The Three Vehicles

He begins with NAMO GURU ARYA MAITRE YE, by paying homage to Maitreya Buddha, the emanation known as the lord of unconquerable being, and by praising his root teacher, Dharmeshvara, paying homage to his very lotus feet. Having done so, he requests Tsondru Gyamtso to listen carefully.

THE SHRAVAKAYANA TRADITION

All the eighty-four thousand teachings of the Buddha are contained in the two vehicles known as the Hinayana and the Mahayana. The lesser vehicle, the Hinayana, is divided into two parts, the Shravakayana and the Pratyekabuddhayana. The Shravakayana tradition emphasizes the discipline of vows and precepts. Altogether there are seven vows, three for the male practitioner and four for the female practitioner. The upasaka and upasika are the vows of the layman and laywoman, who are accorded this status by going for refuge. The getsul, or shramanera, vows are those of the novice monk, and the getsulma, or shramaneri, are the vows of the novice nun. The vows of full ordination for a monk are gelong or bhikshu, and full ordination vows for nuns are gelongma or bhikshuni. Women have a fourth vow called gelopma, a training vow that is taken after the novice vow and before full ordination.

Recognizing that life is very short and that time is very limited, the Shravakayana practitioners do not indulge in superfluous activities and they limit their needs for food and clothing. They understand the suffering of the three lower realms and they understand the sufferings of birth, old age, sickness, and death. They are frightened by these sufferings and they have an immense desire to liberate themselves from samsara. With the desire to experience liberation from samsara, they emphasize the importance of not becoming attached to anything, particularly pleasure. They give the analogy that as you are walking to your death, the executioner offers you a delicious feast. How can you enjoy it? This is to remind you to cut off all attachment and give all your attention to achieve liberation from samsara and attain nirvana.

Shravakayana practitioners understand enlightenment and they also know that enlightenment is very far away. According to them, it takes three limitless kalpas to come to the realization of complete enlightenment. Consequently they are very strict and very disciplined, especially in regards to abandoning negative actions and strictly adhering to the precepts and vows they have taken. The strictness of the Shravakayana practitioner is similar to a very strict king who establishes laws and, if his subjects break these laws, they are executed. Based upon fear everyone follows that law. Similarly, because of the distance of enlightenment and fear of the lower realms, the shravakayana practitioner understands the need to be strongly disciplined in order not to accumulate any negative activities that hinder one's development toward freedom from samsara. That is why the practices, disciplines, and vows of the Shravakayana practitioner are very strict. There is no contradiction in the practice of the Shravakayana practitioner and the Mahayana practitioner except that the Shravakayana do not have a strong emphasis on wishing to lead others to enlightenment.

Understanding the negative aspects of attachment to sensuous pleasures and the great distance to enlightenment, the Shravakayana practitioner realizes there is no time to waste in pleasure and enjoyment. According to the Shravakayana it takes three kalpas to reach enlightenment. Accumulating negative karma by means of attachment will throw one to the lower realms, consequently they strictly maintain their discipline.

They also try to overcome and purify their very subtle faults and mistakes by applying the practice of sojong. *So* means "to restore" and *jong* means "to purify." You engage in virtue and purify all mistakes and wrongdoings, including the very subtle mistakes done without awareness. Sojong practice is for maintaining the purity of the disciplines and vows taken.

There are two classifications of sojong: *Full-Moon Sojong* or the *Sojong of Certain Time*, and the *Sojong of Uncertain Time*. The Full-Moon Sojong is practiced at a specific time, which is the fifteenth day of the lunar month according to the Tibetan calendar. Occasionally the fifteenth day is missing, in which case the Full-Moon Sojong practice is done on the fourteenth day of the lunar month. Sojong is purifying by confessing vows broken and by renewing vows. It is necessary to have four fully ordained monks present in order to perform sojong practice.

The second type of sojong is called the Sojong of Uncertain Time because you practice the sojong at the time when you realize you have broken a precept or vow. According to the Shravakayana tradition, when you have broken a precept or vow or have done something wrong, you practice the Sojong of Uncertain Time. The individual sits in meditation posture in one-pointed concentration recognizing that all conditioned existence is impermanent, and at the same time understanding the nature of suffering and that afflictive emotions cause our suffering. Recognizing this, one tries not to produce further attachment to anything. Having established that idea, one further recognizes that all phenomena are empty and that there is no self. At this point one rests the mind in the natural state; all phenomena are void of self.

What are the benefits of sojong? First you have to understand that every negative action performed strengthens and increases with time if it is not purified. It is just like a house. If you are able to repair things as they break, then you are able to maintain the house. If you let even minor repairs go, soon the house deteriorates, and if you go so far as to let the foundation deteriorate, then the next thing that will happen is that everything collapses. In the same way, the practitioner will be completely purified by applying the sojong practice for minor wrongdoings, errors, and transgressions of the precepts. Furthermore, by the power of sojong you have prevented your major transgressions from increasing, and by repeating sojong practice even major transgressions to the vows will decrease so that slowly one can be rid of them. That is the benefit of the sojong practice.

In the Shravakayana tradition the idea of strong discipline is to prevent attachment to and craving for worldly things. The Shravaka does not complain or make a fuss over worldly existence. For example, the method Shravakayana practitioners use to overcome the afflicting emotion of attachment is that whenever they have the temptation to be attached to their own physical body, or to someone else's body, they meditate on that very body. In contemplating one's own body, or that of someone else, one realizes that the body is nothing but a skeleton. One comes to the point of understanding that there is no point in becoming attached to a skeleton.

To take this contemplation further, of course the skeleton is covered with skin and underneath the skin there is meat and blood. It is said that there are 84,000 bacteria underneath the skin. If you think further, you see that there is pus and all impure things in your own body and in the bodies of others. Consequently there is no point clinging to or craving for something that is so impure and filled with filth. Our bodies are like rotten meat filled with uncountable maggots. How can one be attached? They conclude that it is completely a delusion to become attached to your own body or to that of somebody else. This is the meditation to overcome attachment.

In addition to seeing the impure nature of our body or object of our attachment, we must also understand that if we become attached to such an object, we will experience pain and suffering. For example, when our body experiences illness, swelling, or infection, the pain can be almost intolerable. Our body sometimes prevents us from dedicating ourselves one hundred percent to practice because we have to take care of it all the time, especially when we are sick. When we are cold we have to wear warm clothing, and when we are hungry, we have to eat. They are not saying that you have to completely abandon concern about your well-being. The point that they are trying to make is that you should not be overly attached to your body. You must maintain good health and well-being so that you are strong enough to concentrate and to practice Dharma. If you are overly attached to the well-being and beauty of your body, that time is taken away from practice time. In general, having food and wearing clothes is like applying medicine. We do these things so that we can have a good healthy body and are able to practice.

There is also a meditation practice that the Shravakayana practitioner performs as an antidote for hatred and anger. In Tibetan we use the term *she dang khong tro*, "anger and hatred." The Shravakayana practitioner is not saying that you must go to a place where there is no object for your anger. We cannot go anywhere where we cannot experience some frustration or anger. What is being explained here is how to understand the nature of hatred and anger. First, we need to understand that if we continue to engage with anger, it will deepen into hatred, and that the karma we accumulate from hatred will take us down to the lower realms. Understanding this consequence, we have some sense of compassion for ourselves, thinking, "I do not want to hurt myself, I do not want to make myself fall to the lower realms by engaging or participating in hatred or anger." With the knowledge of having compassion toward oneself and understanding the consequences, you know you must not participate in *the four points*.

The first point is that anger should not be met with anger. The second one is that harsh words should not be met with harsh words. If someone speaks harsh words, and if you reply with harsh words, then it builds up and deepens the anger. The third point is that you must not reveal the faults of others. If someone is pointing out all your faults and mistakes, do not participate in this degrading situation. The fourth point is that violence should not be met with violence, physical or otherwise. The reason why you should not participate in these four points, anger with anger, harsh word with harsh word, revealing the faults of others, and violence with violence, is you understand that by doing so the karma you accumulate makes you fall down to the lower realms. It is not that you have overcome the emotion of anger, but you do not want to participate because you do not want to go into deeper pain and suffering in the hell realm. Having some sense of compassion toward oneself and having the fear of falling into the lower realms, you abstain from participating in such activities.

Next is how to handle ignorance in the Shravakayana tradition. It is important to recognize that ignorance is the major problem for those practitioners who waste time and are thus prevented from practicing. One example of this would be wasting forty years of an eighty-year life span in sleeping, and thus not practicing. Recognizing this, one must make an effort to get up early in the morning and go to bed late at night. One must engage in whatever practices one has been given, such as chanting sadhanas, sitting meditation, and walking meditation.

For those individuals who have the problem of falling asleep while doing meditation practice, the following technique helps to overcome this. As you sit in full lotus meditation posture, have a vase full of water on your right shoulder, and meditate. If you fall asleep or make any movement, the vase falls and of course you feel the water pour onto you.

It is good to do practices such as circumambulating stupas, monasteries, and statues; reading the Buddhist teachings; and writing and copying Buddhist texts. It is also important to establish a strong respect for all practitioners.

One must recognize that the root of one's being in samsara is attachment or fixation to the self, the fixation to "I." Recognizing that, you examine your body to find the existence of this "I." You will find there is no really solid, concrete identity that you can find as this "I" that causes you to wander in samsara. Not finding this "I" within the physical body, then examine the mind to find this "I." Mind is empty. There is nothing there that is solid or concrete. You cannot find "I" or "self" in the mind. Not finding that solid "I" in the physical body or in the mind, you realize that the whole notion of your feeling this strong existence of "I" is simply from the result of your fixation on "I." Recognizing that, you must meditate without any distraction on the selfless nature. Here we are practicing the meditation of no personal self.

In the Shravakayana tradition, when a practitioner comes out of meditation, they recite a dedication prayer in order to realize arhatship. Because of their connection to the practice, and through the power and strength of their dedication prayer, they will experience human birth, and when Maitreya Buddha comes they will be present at his first teaching. At the very moment that they hear Maitreya's teaching, they will experience the realization of arhatship. Similarly, anyone who has made a connection with the Dharma through practice or circumambulating stupas and Buddhist statues will experience arhatship during the second appearance of Buddha. Even if they have not been diligent in practice, with the proper aspiration prayer, by the virtue of the accumulation of merit, and by having made a connection with the Dharma, they will experience realization.

It is of the utmost importance to maintain connection with the Three Jewels — the Buddha, the Dharma, and the Sangha — because by maintaining the connection with the Three Jewels you have the opportunity to experience liberation during the appearance of the next Buddha. How do you know such a connection will really help you to experience liberation? It is not Karma Chakme's fabrication, but rather it is a prediction from Maitreya. Karma Chakme goes on to say that it is predicted that the Red Hat Situ Rinpoche will appear as the fifth Buddha, and the sixth will be Karmapa himself. If you have made a Dharmic connection with His Holiness Karmapa or His Eminence Situ Rinpoche by receiving names, cutting of the hair, or receiving precepts such as the shramanera or bhikshu vows, you can experience liberation immediately at the moment when either the fifth Maitreya Buddha or the sixth Buddha appears.

If you make a Dharmic connection by receiving teachings in the Shravakayana tradition, you attain the realization of arhatship. If you make your connection through the Mahayana tradition you attain the bodhisattva level of realization. If you make your connection in the Tantrayana tradition you will attain complete realization. This concludes the Shravakayana section.

THE PRATYEKABUDDHA TRADITION

This next section begins with NAMO GURU SINGHA NADA YE, introducing the Pratyekabuddha tradition. Again, Karma Chakme pays homage to his teacher and requests his student, Tsondru Gyamtso, to listen carefully.

The Pratyekabuddha tradition is very similar to the Shravaka-yana tradition in that they are frightened of the suffering of samsara and strongly emphasize discipline and maintaining the purity of the vows and precepts. Because of their strong sense of discipline, they emphasize adopting the ten virtuous actions and avoiding the ten unvirtuous actions.

The difference between the Pratyekabuddha tradition and the Shravakayana tradition is that the Pratyekabuddhas use their intellect to understand the idea of our wandering in samsara. By using this wisdom they conclude that the root of samsara is ignorance, the first of the twelve links of interdependent origination. Because of ignorance one accumulates karma, which is the second link. Karma leads one to experience conditioned existence, and the means of experiencing conditioned existence is through consciousness, which is the third link. This conditioned "stream of consciousness" exists by the influence or power of our accumulation of karma. This leads to the fourth link, called "name and form." This refers to the five aggregates, of which form is the first, followed by feeling, cognition, mental events, and consciousness. These five aggregates are the basis for the fifth link, the five perceptual entrances or sense faculties—eye, ear, nose, tongue, touch, and mind. Through development of the senses, one experiences contact with the world. This is the sixth link, where there is contact between the sense organ and the sense object. The sense faculty and the mind faculty contact the object. All three come together. After that happens, one has feelings, which is the seventh link. Through experiencing this sensual contact you experience feeling, which can be pleasant, unpleasant, or neutral. These feelings lead to the eighth link, craving or grasping to that which is pleasant and rejecting or avoiding that which is unpleasant. Having developed this craving or rejecting through feeling leads to the ninth link, which is adoption or attachment. You make definite plans to acquire the desired object or to avoid the undesired object. Through clinging you come to the tenth link, of becoming. It is here that one performs an action that creates karmic consequences leading to the eleventh link, birth. Birth naturally leads to the twelfth link, old age and death. Once you are born, you cannot avoid old age and you cannot avoid death. This includes all the problems, sufferings, and difficulties of life. The twelve links are what is called the wheel of interdependence. *Khorwa* is Tibetan for "wheel," the endless circle of cyclic existence or samsara. *Tendrel* is Tibetan for "interdependence." All twelve links are interdependent and interconnected.

The Pratyekabuddha practitioner, recognizing that the cause of samsara is ignorance, comes to the point of questioning what ignorance is. If ignorance is the root of samsara, then you must look at the nature of the mind. We know that there is no true concrete identity of mind, but through ignorance, through not knowing, we believe that there is a mind that is truly concrete. It is ignorance that makes you strongly believe in the existence of the mind. By looking at the nature of mind you will see that there is no solid form of mind. Recognizing this and understanding that ignorance causes you to believe in the existence of the mind, whereas actually the mind has no concrete form or identity, results in you uprooting your fixation on the personal self. If you practice this frequently, through the wisdom that builds by such meditation, you are able to uproot your fixation on the phenomenal self as well. *Phenomenal self* is defined here as "the outer phenomena or being." Understanding those possibilities, the Pratyekabuddhayana practitioner develops a sense of pride that, "I will not experience rebirth in samsara again. Because of this method I will overcome my ignorance by uprooting my fixation on the personal self." They feel so confident and they feel strongly they can do it all alone. They do not feel they need assistance from teachers or lamas. That is why they are called Pratyekabuddha, "self-victorious Buddha," because they feel victorious over everything. The Pratyekabuddhayana practitioners dedicate the merit so that they will experience the highest goal, which is arhatship.

In the Pratyekabuddha tradition, they do not give teachings and they tend to prefer isolation. There are two categories in the Pratyekabuddha tradition. The one called "group oriented" is a very strict group of five hundred to one thousand Pratyekabuddha practitioners. The category called "individual oriented" do not mix or practice with others, even other Pratyekabuddha practitioners. These practitioners do not benefit others through teaching but go from house to house and to their sponsors begging for food. They will sometimes spontaneously perform miraculous activities, such as levitating or producing flames around the body. The sponsor is impressed and becomes quite devoted, "Oh, this is an individual who is very realized." Consequently they pay respect with folded hands, thinking, "May I be able to become a realized being like this individual." That sentiment alone can plant a seed that will help the sponsor and donor to accumulate merit. At the present time there are no practitioners of the Pratyekabuddha tradition in either category. It is said that when Shakyamuni Buddha's teaching era ends and before the next buddha, Maitreya Buddha, appears, eighty thousand Pratyekabuddhas will appear.

THE OUTSTANDING QUALITIES OF THE BODHISATTVAYANA

Karma Chakme begins by paying homage, NAMO GURU KARUNI KA LO, and explains the outstanding qualities of the Bodhisattvayana to Tsondru Gyamtso. "One has to understand why the Bodhisattvayana is called the greater vehicle, the Mahayana."

It is important to know the difference between the lesser and the greater vehicles. The Shravakayana and the Pratyekabuddhayana practitioners of the lesser vehicle do not have the altruistic motivation of wanting to liberate every sentient being from the suffering of samsara. In terms of prajna, their wisdom is such that they have come to the realization of the personal no self, but they have not come to the realization of the phenomenal no self. That is why the Shravakayana and Pratyekabuddhayana are called the lesser vehicle, or the Hinayana.

The greater vehicle is called the Mahayana. The Mahayana practitioner has a tremendous sense of courage, the courage to bear whatever suffering, physical or mental, that is necessary in order to liberate every sentient being from samsara. The Shravaka and the Pratyekabuddha practitioners do not have this courage to bear the suffering of our pervasive pain, the experience of ups and downs of the physical body, let alone the courage to bear the sufferings of all beings and to liberate all beings. Consequently the Shravakayana and the Pratyekabuddhayana practitioners do not want to live in samsara. Instead they aspire to go beyond samsara and aim to attain nirvana in order to go beyond suffering and reincarnation. They are frightened by the experience of suffering and aspire only to attain personal nirvana, called arhatship. Because Shravakayana and Pratyekabuddhayana practitioners have subdued the five afflicting emotions, they do not have to experience rebirth.

Having subdued the afflicting emotions and having accomplished profound meditation, they have given birth to the higher abilities of clairvoyance and performance of miracles. While in a deep meditative state they are able to see past and future lives; however, this ability is limited to when they are in a profound meditative state. By contrast the bodhisattvas are always omniscient; they see and understand all past and future kalpas.

In order to properly engage with the greater vehicle, the first thing one needs to do is to take the bodhisattva vow. There are three types of individuals, and each one pursues the bodhisattva path in a different manner. The highest type of bodhisattva practitioner has the intention and wish to liberate every sentient being so that they attain enlightenment before he or she does. The average type of intention is when the bodhisattva practitioner wishes that all attain enlightenment together. There is some emphasis on "me" here, whereas in the first one, you do not care if you attain enlightenment or not. That is why it is the highest category. The third one, the lesser type of intention, is when the practitioner attains enlightenment first and then leads all beings to enlightenment. In all three types, the highest, the average, and the lesser type, the practitioner always has the intention of liberating others, of benefiting all sentient beings. This is the Mahayana path, not to exclude any sentient being. If you do not include all sentient beings, complete enlightenment is not possible. By cultivating the mind of wishing to benefit all sentient beings, which includes yourself, you really work to benefit every sentient being, to establish every one in enlightenment. If you work sincerely for the benefit of every sentient being, the merit you accumulate is so powerful that you are naturally evolving toward realization. In the Mahayana tradition, if you establish the

mind that wishes to establish all beings in the state of enlightenment, it takes limitless kalpas to realize complete buddhahood. This
may sound like a very long time, but if you are not a Mahayana
practitioner, you wander in samsara for millions of limitless kalpas.
Compared to that, three limitless kalpas is nothing. It is like the difference between going to prison for three years or going to prison
for your entire life.

Even Shakyamuni Buddha, before he was fully enlightened,
practiced the bodhisattva path and was able to cultivate the altruistic
mind within any kind of birth. We must understand the advantages
we have in this human birth with all of its positive conditions and
endowments and we must endeavor to practice the Bodhisattvayana
of perfect buddhahood. We must develop the willpower and courage
to cultivate bodhichitta. Once you have taken the bodhisattva vow
from a qualified teacher, it is important to renew it as often as possible because you will probably make mistakes and do things that are
contradictory to the vow. The Shravakayana and Pratyekabuddhayana precepts are very much like a ceramic pot. If you break it, it is
broken. The bodhisattva vow is like a pot made out of pure gold: if
you drop the pot, the precious quality of the gold does not disappear.
Even if the pot is dented or misshapen, the gold never loses its quality. That is the outstanding quality of the Bodhisattvayana; if you
break your vow, you can renew it. The manner of renewing the
bodhisattva vow is to visualize yourself in a buddha field like
Dewachen and invoke all the hosts of enlightened beings right in
front of you, feeling their very presence. Then confess whatever
wrongdoing you have committed, applying the seven-branch prayer.

Having learned to purify any wrongdoings against the bodhisattva vow, next you learn how to continue to practice on the
Bodhisattva path. Although you have now engaged with the Bodhisattvayana, the afflicting emotions such as anger, hatred, attachment,
and passion are not immediately uprooted. An outstanding quality of
the Bodhisattvayana is learning to cope with the afflicting emotions.
If anger arises, you apply the remedy for anger, which is loving-kindness. Loving-kindness is not solid and concrete like a hammer you
can use to crush your anger. Anger is simply an idea of the mind.

Loving-kindness is simply an idea of the mind. What you are trying to do is to simply transform the idea of anger to the idea of loving-kindness. When a person causes you to be angry, it is important to remember that you have taken a vow to benefit all sentient beings and that this person is a sentient being. If you become angry, you are going against your vow. You understand that the person causing you to be angry may not be in the Dharma and is acting out of confusion. You need to realize that you are on a different level because you have taken the bodhisattva vow and you have knowledge of the Dharma. Thinking like this, you must not react with anger to whatever is causing you to be angry.

Suppose you have a very good mother that you dearly love. She contracts a mental disease and due to the nature of the mental disease becomes completely crazy and from then on continually irritates you and makes you angry. You realize that you love your mother very much and that you want to help her however you can. You know that it is not her but rather the mental illness that is making you angry. Understanding this, you will try to help her even more, rather than avoid her. In the same way, you understand that it is not the person but rather the confusion and lack of knowledge of the Dharma that is making you angry. Knowing this, you have understanding and compassion rather than frustration and anger.

The remedy for passion and attachment is quite similar to the remedy used by the Shravakayana and Pratyekabuddhayana. This view of the impurity of the body of self and others does not mean that you degrade yourself or others. If you look directly at your body, outer to inner, you will not find anything solid or concrete. When passion or attachment arises, use this technique of looking at your body, knowing that it is impermanent and has no reality or truth.

The next afflicting emotion is ignorance. We often use the word *ignorant* to describe someone who is uneducated; however, in Dharmic terms *ignorance* is used to describe not knowing the cause of why we are wandering in samsara. In the Pratyekabuddha tradition, they use the method of contemplation on a corpse. From this they develop an understanding of the twelve interdependent links. The bone reminds them of death. Death has to come from birth, and so on.

They work their way back through the twelve links to the first link of ignorance. If one link is undone or eliminated, the chain of birth and death is broken. For example if there is no ignorance, which creates karma, then there is no cultivation of karma. If you cease to engage in one, you are able to cease everything. This is very profound, and to understand this is supreme wisdom. These techniques and the example of the twelve deeds of Buddha Shakyamuni will help you to overcome the ignorance of not knowing why you are wandering in samsara. All twelve deeds of the Buddha explain that there is nothing that is permanent or solid. Traditionally in Tibet, people would recite the sadhana of *The Twelve Deeds of Buddha Shakyamuni* as a reminder of impermanence.

It is not sufficient to apply the remedies we have given for attachment, anger, and ignorance. You must also meditate. Meditation is divided into two categories, shamatha, or sitting meditation, and vipashyana, or insight meditation. We will first introduce shamatha, or sitting meditation. In shamatha you are developing concentration using the image of Buddha Shakyamuni as the object of your concentration. If you are doing shamatha meditation and you begin to feel dull or sleepy, concentrate on the forehead of the Buddha. If you look at the statue of Shakyamuni Buddha, you will see there is a white dot between the eyebrows. Think that there is a very brilliant, almost intolerably brilliant, light that radiates from this spot. Concentrate on that brilliance of the light and continue to maintain the concentration. On the other hand, if while doing shamatha meditation your mind becomes agitated and excited, concentrate on the crossed legs of the Buddha, at the point where they cross. Concentrate and maintain that concentration. If your mind is somewhat settled and you are not in either extreme of feeling dull and sleepy or excited and agitated, then simply concentrate on the heart of the Buddha, and continue to maintain the stillness of your mind. These are the techniques used to overcome the problems you may have while doing shamatha meditation. It is said that if you are able to maintain stillness of the mind, you are really achieving the results of shamatha. The teachings that explain these remedies are from the Buddha's sutra known as *Samadhi Raja*.

Shamatha is Sanskrit and *shinay* is Tibetan. *Shi* means "calm." *Nay* means "abiding." Therefore *shinay* means "calm abiding, free from any disturbances, simply abiding on whatever you have chosen to concentrate on." It is said that through development of calm abiding, one acquires some ordinary supernatural power, which is called common siddhi. Some practitioners are able to foresee the future or perform a quick miracle, and there are people who regard this as a very high accomplishment. These are actually ordinary and conditioned accomplishments, not regarded as the ultimate level. Nevertheless shamatha, or calm abiding, is used in Buddhism to develop to a higher level of meditation such as vipashyana, lhaktong or insight meditation.

With insight meditation the Shravakayana and Pratyekabuddhayana come to the point of realizing *no personal self.* "No personal self" means that there is no true concrete identity that you can pinpoint and say, "That is the self; that is the I." They come to this point through the use of their logical intellect. Taking one's body and looking at each part, from crown to toes, one tries to find what we call self. Although each part of our body has its own name, you cannot find the location of an "I." Consequently you come to the conclusion that everything is simply the accumulation of many particles that you have labeled as "I" and that, in reality, there is no true "I" or self. Recognizing this, you intellectually understand that there is no personal self, no personal identity of the self.

In the Mahayana tradition, in addition to recognizing that there is no personal self, they go deeper and recognize that there is no phenomenal self as well. For example, there is a pillar, which you can all see. It looks so concrete, so solid, and so real, but there is no such thing as "pillar." If you divide the pillar, it has a top, bottom, and an in-between. If you say "top-pillar," that is not the pillar. It is the top part of the pillar. If you say "bottom," is that the pillar? No, because it is the bottom part of the pillar. In between is also not the pillar. Then you think, "What is this very solid-looking pillar made of? Many, many material things." If you know how to break it down, there are names for all the materials, but there is no such thing as "pillar" that stands on its own terms. In short, one gets down to particles of atoms. Next you ask, "Who is aware of these atoms? Is it the mind or is it awareness? Has mind itself a solid, concrete identity?" No. You realize, therefore, the emptiness of the phenomenal self in addition to the realization of the emptiness of the personal self. If you are aware of *no phenomenal self* for one particular object, for example the pillar, then through logic you know that all phenomena have no true self. You do not have to examine every individual phenomenon. It is like cutting bamboo. If you cut one bamboo tree and see that the inside is hollow, then you know that all bamboo trees are hollow inside. The great panditas used this analytical meditation to come to the point of intellectually understanding no personal self and no phenomenal self. This idea of self is simply labeled and fixated in our mind as truth. Beyond that there is no true concreteness of the personal self or the phenomenal self.

The intellectual understanding of the empty nature of phenomena and the empty nature of self can be developed through analytical meditation, the logical means of meditation. The actual realization of the meditation develops in the following way. Using analytical meditation to come to an understanding of emptiness or shunyata brings you to the first bhumi and takes one kalpa. In the second kalpa you climb to the seventh bhumi. Then in the third kalpa you climb to what is known as the three pure bhumis—the eighth, ninth, and tenth.

There are the three obscurations: the obscuration of kleshas or afflicting emotions, the obscuration of wisdom, and the obscuration of habitual patterns. From the first to the seventh bhumi, you are overcoming the obscuration of the kleshas and the obscuration of wisdom, and by the time you actually reach the seventh bhumi, you have completely purified both the obscuration of kleshas and the obscuration of wisdom. From the seventh bhumi to the ninth bhumi, you are overcoming the obscuration of habitual patterns. By the tenth bhumi you are free from the obscuration of habitual patterns, and by the eleventh bhumi, the buddha bhumi, you have completely purified all three obscurations. In the eleventh bhumi you are developing enlightened qualities, such as the qualities to perform the twelve deeds of the Buddha.

His Holiness Karmapa is a fully realized being; the obscurations are completely removed and he is the embodiment of all enlightened beings. He is fully enlightened and manifests in many different forms to benefit sentient beings. Because we are not enlightened, it is very difficult for us to see and meet him at his level. For this reason he has come to us in nirmanakaya form in order to teach and benefit us. We must also keep in mind that His Holiness Karmapa not only manifests buddha activity as a human being but also manifests as an animal, bird, or insect in order to benefit those beings. Sometimes he manifests as a medicinal plant to cure disease. The manner and extent to which His Holiness manifests is unimaginable.

There is a difference between enlightenment and complete enlightenment. When you are enlightened, but not ultimately, your personal realization is complete. It is not called ultimate enlightenment because you still have to accomplish the qualities of the twelve deeds of a Buddha in order to benefit the limitless sentient beings. In the absence of afflicting emotions and obscurations, one's enlightened qualities, one's buddha qualities are fully developed. When you are completely and ultimately enlightened, you can turn the wheel of Dharma just like Buddha Shakyamuni and benefit all beings of all capacities.

Karma Chakme explains that all his teachings and all his commentaries regarding the Shravakayana tradition, the Pratyekabuddhayana tradition, the Bodhisattvayana tradition, as well as that of the personal no self and phenomenal no self were done without pride or the feeling that he had any ability to present such a teaching. Karma Chakme continues to explain that his teachings are based entirely on his guru the omniscient Dharmeshvara's teachings, and because of that he feels confident that what he presented has some meaning and will bear fruit.

These teachings were given by Karma Chakme, who describes himself as old and ignorant with a defective memory, to his student Tsondru Gyamtso, who with devotion and realizing the preciousness of the teachings, wrote them down.

Questions and Answers

STUDENT: I have seen the symbol of the eternal knot and I was wondering if you could explain why we visualize this in the heart of the Buddha.

RINPOCHE: If you look at the symbol for the knot of eternity, there is no beginning and no end. This symbolizes the truth that the Buddha's knowledge and wisdom has no beginning and no end; it is limitless. It also symbolizes your own state of equipoise, which is neither dull nor excited. Your mind is in an equal state, so you concentrate on the knot of eternity that has no beginning and no end.

STUDENT: My question is twofold. As you taught earlier, it is clear that if you orient yourself toward self, as the arhats do, you will eventually short-circuit your movement toward complete enlightenment. Is it also possible to do the reverse, to get so wrapped up in other people and doing things for others that you lose sight of your path and your own self? Even in Christian teaching it says that you shall love others as you love yourself, not less than but not more than either. To give a concrete example, in a work situation I tend to be a nice person. I try to be compassionate to someone and they repeatedly take advantage of me over and over again. How is it possible to gracefully deal with that situation in terms of compassion? Eventually you cannot let people take advantage of you either.

RINPOCHE: Yes, in some sense it is very true what you have quoted from Christianity. You should love others as much as yourself. This is not contradictory to the bodhisattva wish. We have said that there are three types of bodhisattva practitioners. Today we were explaining the highest type. The average type is exactly what you have said, love others or benefit others as much as you can benefit yourself. What we have to keep in mind is that there are two aspects to the bodhisattva path, commitment and practice. We are beginners on this path, and if you maintain your commitment, you will see what power and strength you have. Do your best and at the same time keep the wish that sooner or later you will be able to benefit every sentient being. By the time you attain full fruition of bodhisattvahood, at that moment you will have no resistance. Whatever people do to you, taking advantage of you or annoying you, nothing can shake your mind because you have achieved that level. Even if someone asks for his hand, flesh, or bone, the bodhisattva, without a moment of hesitation, when he knows that it is beneficial, will actually give his own flesh and bone to the person. We are not at that level, so we must not think that we have to act that way. We have to act according to our level, but mentally we have to maintain the commitment "I want to benefit every sentient being."

STUDENT: I am thinking of taking the bodhisattva vow and agree to refrain from absolute enlightenment until every sentient being in the universe has also attained enlightenment. Is there some contradiction there? If there are an infinite number of beings in all the universes, then how can you ever reach that point of absolute final enlightenment?

RINPOCHE: The interesting part is that the less you expect, the quicker the result. The more you expect something, the slower the fruition and result. The commitment not to attain full enlightenment until all sentient beings are established in buddhahood is true unconditional love and compassion to all beings and a true and sincere sign of selflessness. There is no mark of personal need. When we say that we want to reach enlightenment together with them or before them, there is some string, a little bit of a stain of selfish notion. To say "until I empty samsara and all sentient beings are enlightened" is a true sign of love and compassion toward all beings, and there is no selfish motive whatsoever. When there is no selfish motive, the merit that you accumulate by working free from expectation is unimaginable. You are, day by day and week by week, developing merit and you are climbing to the bhumis of enlightenment naturally. You are climbing up because of true selflessness. The more you think "I want," the more slowly you climb up. This is really the outcome of the selfless nature or selfless quality. This kind of bodhisattva actual-ly attains enlightenment faster.

STUDENT: It is said that the buddhas do not liberate anyone. We have to practice and that is why they teach. If we take the vow not to attain enlightenment until all beings have attained enlightenment, how can I do that unless I teach everyone how to be enlightened when I am not enlightened?

RINPOCHE: Traditionally the idea is that by taking the bodhisattva pre-cepts you promise that until all beings are enlightened you will not attain enlightenment. Now that you have the strong determination to really bring beings to enlightenment, you should be very willing to first dedicate your time to developing the qualities of learning. Through developing the qualities of learning Buddhism, whatever you have learned and understood well you can teach, from a philo-sophical point of view, to others. Having learned well and because of your determination to benefit all sentient beings and establish all beings in enlightenment, you are also willing to practice and do retreats. When you put what you have learned into your practice, you gain actual experience. Now you are no longer simply a scholar but a teacher. At the beginning you teach the literal meaning and later when you gain experience from practice you teach the experien-tial meaning. Taking the bodhisattva vow means that, if you are able, you should be willing to teach. If you are able to teach and you are not willing to do so, then you are not on the bodhisattva level.

STUDENT: Are there buddhas who did not teach?

RINPOCHE: No, there are not really any enlightened beings who have never taught. When enlightened beings spontaneously teach, each individual hears at their own particular level. When Buddha Shakya-muni taught, those who were not fully developed in the wisdom aspect of their mind heard only the Hinayana teaching. At the same time, the Mahayana-level student, who was more developed, heard both the Hinayana and the Mahayana levels of teaching. Those at the

Vajrayana level heard all three levels of teaching—the Hinayana, the Mahayana, and the Vajrayana—together at the same time. The Buddha spontaneously taught all three levels at exactly the same time.

STUDENT: You spoke today about how arhats have to practice for eighty thousand kalpas before they achieve enlightenment. Suppose I attain enlightenment in this lifetime and I do so for the sake of all sentient beings. Do I liberate those arhats even though they have not practiced for eighty thousand kalpas?

RINPOCHE: The bodhisattva prayer says, "May I be able to provide happiness to those with no happiness and liberation for those not yet liberated." If you were to attain liberation in this lifetime and you had the sincere aspiration to liberate all those not yet liberated, then yes, you could liberate them. Through prayer and the help of enlightened beings, the arhats do not always have to exhaust all those kalpas to be liberated. This is a general explanation.

STUDENT: I was not quite clear on something. It seems like you were indicating that if you are a bodhisattva, you are potentially engaged in a process that may never end. Once you take the bodhisattva vow and you have attained a certain state, you have got a job and that job is for eternity. Is that a possibility? Based on that, even Gautama Buddha may not have attained absolute enlightenment because he still may be out there working somewhere too. Is this a correct assessment?

RINPOCHE: The bodhisattva precept is a goal, and one tries to always keep this in mind. Leading the life of a bodhisattva, someone completely untouched by any stain of selfish motives, the accumulation of merit is unimaginable. Attaining enlightenment in this manner, by simply working for the benefit of others, is not against our commitment. It is merit that powers us to our goals, and based on that, it is similar to one individual trying to benefit and liberate all beings. In some sense your question is very true. If Shakyamuni Buddha has taken bodhisattva vows and has attained enlightenment, is this against the bodhisattva precepts? Not really. Having established the mental goal of wanting to liberate every sentient being and working with that mental goal, by the power of the merit and wisdom, having come to full realization of buddhahood, Shakyamuni's buddha activity is unimaginable, benefiting beings everywhere. This is the outcome of such motivation. It is said that Buddha Shakyamuni, having attained full enlightenment, can emanate a hundred billion emanations to benefit beings in the hundred billion different realms. This power and capacity is the outcome of the altruistic mind. Although bodhisattvas have power, it does not equal the power of the enlightened beings that emanate to a hundred billion realms. This is the result of the bodhisattva aspiration and commitment.

STUDENT: First, can a person be a real Buddhist if she does not believe in reincarnation, and second, would you please explain reincarnation to me?

RINPOCHE: An individual who does not believe in reincarnation or rebirth does not see the need of developing themselves for the next birth. Because of not being able to see the need for improving oneself for the next birth, one does not really feel the need to adopt virtuous actions and avoid nonvirtuous actions. One does not feel that it is necessary. In Buddhism we practice virtue and try not to intentionally engage in nonvirtuous action. Based on that, we cannot put down a really firm line and say that if you do not believe in reincarnation, you cannot become a Buddhist. It is difficult. In order to understand reincarnation, we need to understand that all beings are made up of body, speech, and mind. You could say that your parents gave you your body. Regarding the mind, there is no direct connection between the mind, or consciousness of the parents and the mind, or consciousness of the child. According to Tibetan Buddhism, the mind is the consciousness of the continuity of our previous lives. The consciousness of mind goes along with one's own habitual patterns that have developed by virtuous and nonvirtuous actions. As a result of the karma that you have cultivated, you experience pain and suffering or happiness in this lifetime.

The mind is independent and personal. It is similar to planting crops; when you cultivate a seed, it produces the same: rice becomes rice and corn becomes corn. Sometimes the condition of the soil or the weather affects the quality, but otherwise it does not change. Reincarnation of the consciousness is different. Since the karmic seeds planted and cultivated include the afflictive emotions, it is not certain we will be reborn in the human realm. The fruition of whatever we cultivate, including our afflictive emotions, is how we experience rebirth. Good or bad rebirth is based on how we have cultivated proper karma and improper karma. This is the idea behind reincarnation or rebirth. If you have not cultivated any karmic seeds, you will not have to experience rebirth. If you have cultivated good or bad karmic seeds, the results will show in your rebirth as success or failure, pain or happiness.

STUDENT: You said that the Pratyekabuddha often performs miracles for the patron in order to give inspiration. Why shouldn't a bodhisattva do that?

RINPOCHE: Bodhisattvas perform miracles when they see that it is necessary or beneficial. Bodhisattvas benefit beings by teaching and providing the method. When people are not ready to open themselves to the teaching, even a miracle would not help. It is very much like when we see our reflection in a mirror and we recognize ourselves. Some mental reaction is there. If you put a stone in front of the mirror, the stone has no reaction. Showing a miracle to an individual who is not at all ready is like putting a stone in front of a mirror. There is no reaction whatsoever.

Bodhisattvas perform miracles in many ways. Sometimes we are not pure enough to see the miracle in the sense that our mental obscurations are too strong. Before Buddha Shakyamuni passed away, he said that his teachings would continue without breaking the transmission and that great teachers such as Asanga and Nagarjuna would maintain the continuity.

There is a story about Asanga. He was given the practice of the bodhisattva Maitreya. Unless he was able to perfect the practice, he would not have the ability to strongly establish the Buddhadharma and continue the transmission. Having received this practice, Asanga went into retreat for one year. In order to perfect the practice of the bodhisattva Maitreya, Asanga was required to actually see Maitreya. Until then he had to practice. Asanga practiced intensely for one year, yet there were no signs of seeing the bodhisattva Maitreya at all. He became very discouraged and walked away, thinking that it was not really possible to really see the bodhisattva Maitreya. As he walked down into the valley, Asanga saw an old man rubbing a very fine cloth on a big piece of metal pipe. Out of curiosity, Asanga asked the old man what he was doing. The old man explained that he needed a needle to sew his clothing and that by rubbing the metal pipe with fine cloth, some day the metal would become so well worn that it would be as fine as a needle. Asanga was astonished at the patience the old man exhibited just for the sake of worldly activity. Thinking that he had left his retreat after only one year, he decided to return.

During the second year there was no direct sight of Maitreya, and again Asanga walked out of the retreat. This time he saw a man rubbing a wet feather and sand against a huge rock. Part of the rock was slightly worn out through the constant rubbing. When Asanga inquired of the man what he was doing, the man responded that his house was behind the rock and that the rock prevented the sun from shining into his house. The man explained that by rubbing the rock with the feather and sand, he hoped to one day be rid of the rock. Asanga was once again astonished at the lengths to which people go for worldly activity, while he was leaving retreat after only two years, so he went back into retreat.

During the third year nothing happened again. Asanga really got discouraged and again walked out of retreat. As he walked, he saw a wounded dog. Half of the dog's body was filled with wounds that were covered with pus and blood. The upper part of the body was all right, but the dog was barking with anger. When Asanga looked carefully at the wound, every part of the wound was filled with maggots. Asanga was amazed that while half of the dog's body was so wounded, the dog still showed a great deal of anger. Asanga felt so much compassion, more than he had ever felt before, and he really wanted to help clean the wound and remove the maggots, but using his hands would mean harming the maggots. He thought the best method would be to gently scoop out the maggots with his tongue. With his limitless compassion, he knelt down and tried to scoop up the maggots from the wounds. Because there were maggots, pus, and blood, Asanga closed his eyes and tried to reach down to remove the maggots. As he reached down, he fell to the ground. When he opened his eyes, before him stood Maitreya. Asanga said, "So many years of practice; why did you not come?" Maitreya said, "I was with you all the time. I was never separated from you, but because your obscurations were so thick, you were able to see me only as a human. The intense compassion you have developed burned away your obscurations. The very patient men that you encountered were actually me, but due to your obscurations at the time, you saw me as an ordinary human being. Now you see me as Maitreya." Bodhisattvas are always there and they are sometimes performing miracles, but we are not pure enough to see them.

STUDENT: Bodhisattvas are always performing miracles, but we are too dense to see them?

RINPOCHE: Obscuration is like darkness. It is not something solid or concrete. Let us say that the building is always there, even at night. The reason you cannot see the building so clearly at night is because of the darkness. The building does not disappear, but the darkness obscures our vision.

STUDENT: Do bodhisattvas think that it is harmful to levitate in front of other beings?

RINPOCHE: Sometimes they do not perform miracles because, although it is not particularly harmful, it is not beneficial. Sometimes they may be performing miracles such as flying, but people cannot see it. An example of one bodhisattva who could perform miracles is Milarepa. Milarepa could fly from one mountain peak to another. He did not have to walk, he just flew. Some people could see this, but few people developed a sense of devotion. Some people who disliked him, such as his uncle, told others that it was magic being exhibited and warned them not to go under the shadow of the flying Milarepa or they would be cursed. Consequently people tried to run away from the shadow of Milarepa. For those people the miracle was of no benefit whatever.

STUDENT: You said that when we break any of the bodhisattva vows, we should try to repair them as soon as possible, that we should visualize the buddha field and feel the presence of the buddhas and confess and use the seven-line prayer. Was Rinpoche referring to making prostrations and offerings and so on?

RINPOCHE: The seven-branch prayer is included in the Chenrezik practice. While you are reciting the prayer, you can repent any wrongdoings and renew your vow. That is the advantage of the Chenrezik practice. You are renewing everything because the seven-branch prayer is included. You do not need to do it separately if you are participating in the Chenrezik prayers every day. If you want to do it separately, that is fine.

STUDENT: If we recognize our wrongdoing and we do not have time to meditate, can we do it later on?

RINPOCHE: Later on is fine. As a beginner it is important that you practice Chenrezik or renew your precepts once a day.

STUDENT: Sometimes when I do something wrong, I realize it and I confess it and I really feel regret. I have a problem when I get to the part of promising not to do it again. In some events I feel very strongly that I do not want to do it again, but in some events I feel that I am not certain. I might do it again because there are certain things that are so difficult to change. I do not want to be lying to the buddhas or to my guru, so I want to find a way to confess. Sometimes I say that I will try my best or something like that, but I do not know if that is appropriate.

RINPOCHE: That is a very honest question and it is not only you. Everyone suffers from this since nobody can guarantee that they will never repeat the action. If somebody really can guarantee that he will never repeat a wrongdoing, then from that moment they are completely purified from wrongdoing and negative activity. In your case, the best thing is to promise to try your best not to repeat it. At the same time, commit yourself to confessing every day. For a beginning practitioner, confessing and purifying every day helps one not to accumulate negative karma. We are committing ourselves to purifying every day, as well as doing our best not to repeat our negative actions. That is the best way.

STUDENT: If there is no inherent existence in anything except mind, as you said this morning with the example of the pillar, then what is it that we are experiencing right now at this moment? Is it a projection of primordial mind?

RINPOCHE: The appearance is always there. Right now what you see happening is the appearance, a perception of the appearance. When we are experiencing the appearance, not only are we experiencing the appearance, we have some sense of fixation that the appearance is true and real, whereas in truth it does not exist. Even when you attain enlightenment, you can still experience the appearance of this, but you go beyond fixation and attachment. From the point of view of emptiness there is no concrete permanence, but there is always appearance, which is free from any fixation. When you come to the point of recognizing that there is no reality or truth to the appearance that you experience, then you are able to overcome the attachment and grasping to that appearance. For example, you suddenly hit your head against the pillar and say, "The pillar hurt my head." In reality there is no pillar. There is no solid concrete pillar. In some sense, when you use your intellect and logic, that which we call "pillar" is really a combination of many small particles such as atoms. If you think of the head itself, there is no one independent identity that we call "head." The head is an accumulation of many parts, such as "bone" or "skin," and is also a combination of atomic particles.

There is no hitter and no thing to be hit. Neither is real. The pillar is not real. The head that felt the pain is not real. In some sense the form of the appearance is similar to a rainbow that has no solid concrete appearance. Realizing this, you come to the point of knowing that both the pillar and the head have no solid concrete truth to their existence. Understanding that there is no truth to the existence of anything you now experience, you do not cling or grasp to whatever you see. Usually we react in one of two ways. If we like something, we grasp and become attached to it, and if we dislike something, we reject it. Understanding the truth of existence, you are able to go beyond attachment and aversion. Whenever you feel something is good and knowing it has no reality, you do not grasp it. In the same way if something is bad, knowing it has no reality, you do not reject it. This is the whole point of intellectually understanding emptiness.

It is important to keep in mind that intellectual understanding and actual realization are very different. Of course, one has to start with intellectual understanding. We have explained the logic and intellectual understanding of nonexistence. It is only logical that if you quickly walk into a pillar, you will probably hurt yourself. Even though we intellectually understand the emptiness of phenomena, we still grasp and cling to their reality. With complete realization people can walk through walls. There have been many great teachers who have been able to do so. Another example is that of His Holiness the Seventeenth Karmapa, whose handprints are found in stone. Knowing that stone has no relative truth, he can make handprints or footprints in stone. Those are manifestations of realization, and that is the difference between intellectual understanding and actual realization.

STUDENT: Just a further question on this. In *The Dhammapada* it says, "Be a lamp unto yourself" and "Only you can free yourself, no other." We can be in the condition of ignorance and transcend it. If we can put an end to it, would it not stand to reason that at some point in some primordial archaic past, kalpas ago, we started it in the first place ourselves?

RINPOCHE: I am not familiar with *The Dhammapada*. It seems it is from the Hinayana tradition. In some sense, yes, there is always truth to the fact that if we individually do not make an effort, we cannot experience liberation. Liberation is only possible through individual effort. Nobody can give us liberation without our personal work and effort. Secondly, on the bodhisattva level, we are really practicing hard making an extreme effort in order to liberate all sentient beings. The mental state is different. Yes, we have been retaking birth for infinite kalpas. Ignorance and delusion never age and they will never bring us to the point of needing liberation. Until we really come to the point of understanding how important it is to experience liberation, we do not make the effort to experience enlightenment. And until then we are always under the influence, the power, of this delusion and ignorance, which is ageless. Time does not matter to this afflictive emotion.

STUDENT: Is my interpretation correct, then, that there really was no beginning to this process? And that even though we can attain a very high degree of liberation and enlightenment, there really is not an ending to the process either? Maybe I am thinking in terms of beginnings and ends on a relative plane, rather than on an absolute plane, like the beginning of ignorance and the end of ignorance.

RINPOCHE: Yes, in the general sense; no, in the individual sense. Generally, in all beings there is no beginning or end to ignorance. Individually, like Buddha Shakyamuni, at the beginning there was ignorance. Then he was able to end it, so there was an end to that ignorance.

STUDENT: Could you repeat and clarify what the approach to the three precepts in the Kagyupa tradition is?

RINPOCHE: Today we went over a description of the slight differences among the different schools of Tibetan Buddhism. In the next section we will discuss each school in detail. Because you asked this question, we will go over the Kagyupa briefly now. Then next time we will know a little more and it will easily become clear. In the Kagyupa tradition, first one takes the self-liberating precepts, which are very similar to the vinaya discipline. The vinaya precepts include all of the following: the refuge vow, the upasaka vow, and the shramanera vow applied to both men and women. It also includes the vows of fully ordained monk and nun, or bhikshu and bhikshuni vows. All of these are included in the vinaya precepts. Once you have taken them, then you come to the bodhisattva precepts. In the Kagyupa tradition the vinaya is strict physical discipline and the bodhisattva precept is mental discipline. The vinaya precept has to do with being mindful and aware of one's physical conduct and discipline, and the bodhisattva precept has to do with being mindful and aware of one's mental state. We include both the mental and the physical disciplines together. You do not leave one having obtained the other. Both are now integrated. Finally you engage in Tantrayana, called secret Mantrayana. When you are in the secret Mantrayana tradition, you do not give up the precepts of the vinaya or the Bodhisattvayana, but rather include both, maintaining the strong outer discipline of the vinaya and maintaining the strong inner discipline of the mind of the Mahayana.

What is the practice of the secret Mantrayana? Among many others, there are the secret practices of the nadis, chakras, and bindu. Because they are secret practices, it is sometimes necessary to practice in solitude or in the traditional three-year, three-month retreat. The accomplishment of such practices really depends on the individual. You cannot always say that those who have been in a three-year retreat will have it all accomplished. It depends on how well and how properly they practice. It is not that the years will give them a high degree of accomplishment, but rather it is the quality of the practice that gives accomplishment. An individual having accomplished this is someone who upholds the three precepts of the vinaya, of the Bodhisattvayana, and of the Tantrayana. Because of such high tantric accomplishments they can perform miracles. They would never perform miracles for the sake of amusement, but if they see it is absolutely necessary for the benefit of sentient beings, they would. For example, when Tilopa accomplished these practices, he went to a particular village. He knew that if he performed a miracle, all the people in this village would benefit. He levitated to the height of seven palm trees. Accomplished individuals can do this; however, they would not perform a miracle if they see that some people will get confused or irritated by such magic. If they are not open, it could arouse anger or antipathy in the people. An accomplished being would never want to plant a seed of anger in anyone. Even though they are highly accomplished practitioners, they live very humbly. His Holiness the Dalai Lama and His Holiness Karmapa are very accomplished, but live as simple, ordinary monks.

STUDENT: You said karma is strongly related to interdependence. Is one's experience, then, completely a result of karma?

RINPOCHE: There was a seed cultivated in the past and you are able to experience the fruition of that seed now. By cultivating a seed now, you experience the fruition of the seed in the future. We are at present experiencing the fruition of the past seed that we have cultivated. *Seed* refers to the karma that we plant and cultivate, and it is the fruition of this seed, this karma, that we experience as happiness, sadness, success, and misfortune. The experience that has happened is because of karma. Our reaction to that experience can plant more karma, either positive or negative. What is happening is that we are again sowing the seeds of karma, depending on whether we respond with frustration and negativity or if we respond cheerfully and with some degree of positivity. It is individual. *Karma, cause and effect* and *interdependence* are almost synonymous.

STUDENT: Does anything happen to us that is not a result of karma?

RINPOCHE: First of all, your being a human being is your karma. In addition to being human, whatever ups and downs, good or bad fortune that you experience, that is also your karma. In the human realm, by using the proper methods and remedies, one can sometimes overcome the ripening of karma. Everything experienced is related to karma.

STUDENT: Can one say that things are empty because everything that we experience is a product of our karma, because the experience is a projection of our karma?

RINPOCHE: That is quite right, because you have to completely exhaust karma in order to come to the realization of emptiness or shunyata. What we sometimes fail to understand is that there is a difference between intellectual understanding and actual realization. It is easy to hear about emptiness, but to really come to the realization is very, very different. When you exhaust karma completely, then you come to the complete realization of emptiness.

STUDENT: Can you have glimpses of emptiness before you exhaust karma?

RINPOCHE: As one progresses toward realization, one's obscurations sort of thin and one begins to have very vague experiences of emptiness. I am using the word *vague* here to show that the levels are so different. You cannot even have a glimpse of complete emptiness until you reach the high bhumis. On our level it is really difficult to have a glimpse of emptiness; however, once you come to the realization of emptiness, then you never fall back. You never lose that experience. That is the advantage of the true realization of emptiness. If this were not so, we could think that enlightened beings who have come to the full realization of emptiness may sometimes lose it and fall back. They never fall back. That is the true realization of emptiness. Once you realize it, you never lose that experience whatsoever. I emphasize that the realization of emptiness is very different from the intellectual understanding of emptiness. Many people make the mistake of thinking that emptiness means everything disappears and there is nothing. Consequently they do not really make much effort to actually realize emptiness.

STUDENT: I have always thought that Buddhism is not really a religion or a faith so much as an empirical system, a system whereby you are given a method, something to try out. You try it out, it works, and you move on. This is in contrast to some of the other religions where they say you have to believe this because we say so. Is it correct to describe Buddhism not so much as faith but as a system of realization that is not really on the same level as the other religions? They say you have to believe because it is a revelation from God and that you cannot question it. For example, in other religions it is not something you can discover because it is something only God knows.

RINPOCHE: Sometimes you have to identify something. Therefore maybe people classify Buddhism as a religion, although it does not belong in that category. On the other hand, we cannot say it is not religion. When we have to classify something, we do so by using the outstanding quality and identifying characteristic of that object. Similarly, the term *Buddhism* is used by the whole world to identify the Buddha's teachings. In Tibetan we use the term *nangpa* to describe those who practice the Buddha's teachings. *Nang* means "inner," and *pa* means "practitioner." The reason why it is called "*inner* practitioner" is that our mind has both defect and quality. The "defect aspect of mind" is simply all the neurosis and afflictive emotions that cause us to wander aimlessly in samsara. We do not simply end there by saying that the mind is bad. The "quality aspect of mind" is that we can overcome afflictive emotions and reach enlightenment. Buddha realized the "quality aspect of mind" and taught the method of how to do so and become free of the "defect aspect of mind" by following the vinaya, the sutras, and the tantras. One tries to practice exactly as the Buddha explained in the tradition that one is following. With consistency and some faith and confidence in the teachings and the practice, one experiences the results.

STUDENT: Many of us have been raised in the West, and in the Christian faith you simply have to accept and believe without asking questions. Nor do you need to practice to demonstrate internally whether something is real and true, you just accept it on blind faith.

RINPOCHE: We may use the same terminology, but the meaning of the term may be different. Your idea of faith is from the Christian background, whereas in Buddhism we do not use the term *faith*. In Buddhism faith is a clear, complete, total understanding that is developed by studying and asking questions and then cutting through all the doubt. When you come to the point where it makes sense and is true, your own mind becomes free from doubt and this is what we call faith. It is absolutely not blind faith. Blind faith is, like you said, that you cannot ask questions and you just simply have to believe. In Buddhism there is no such idea. Secondly, you study about Buddha and learn how the achievement of buddha-hood is getting beyond all the afflictive emotions. However, when Buddha did this, it did not mean that he had become a person who had no feeling. Enlightenment does not mean that you have to go to a level where you have no feeling whatsoever. You have tremendous love and compassion that is unconditional. Furthermore you have gone beyond the discriminative mind to an equal state of mind. You have developed a complete sense of wisdom, knowing what is best for the beings you want to benefit as well as what is not beneficial.

How Buddha reached that level is found in the Dharma, the teachings of the Buddha, which are precisely the way he practiced. The good thing about Buddha's teaching is that before he became enlightened, he was an ordinary, confused being like us, a being under the power of ignorance and attachment. Using this method of Dharma practice, he overcame afflictive emotions. It is encouraging that we all have the opportunity to reach enlightenment. When we come to the point that the teachings make sense and we have also developed personal confidence that we can reach enlightenment just like the Buddha, who was at the beginning a very confused and deluded individual just like ourselves, that is called faith.

STUDENT: To get beyond all afflictive emotions, do we have to get beyond all good emotions as well? Do we have to transcend everything? Isn't even compassion based on emotion?

RINPOCHE: There is always a big difference between helpful and harmful situations. In the world there is medicine and there is poison.

If you say, "Do not touch any poison," does that mean that you should not take any medicine?

Disk of the Sun: The Way of Protecting the Three Vows

In this chapter we will hear about the three precepts, the commitments or samayas, and how an individual practitioner will keep these precepts. Having knowledge of the precepts is like removing the darkness from the room so that you can see things more clearly. Karma Chakme pays homage to Shakyamuni Buddha and requests his disciple, Tsondru Gyamtso, to listen carefully. This time, however, Karma Chakme addresses his disciple as "gelong," which is an ordained monk, and asks him to listen carefully to the explanation of the precepts, which are vast and profound.

There are self-liberating vows, inner vows, and secret vows. There are many countries that have teachings regarding how to keep the self-liberating vows and there are many that only have teachings on how to keep the Mahayana commitment. Tibet is unique in that it has teachings on keeping the self-liberating vows, the Mahayana vows, and the tantric vows. Those who practice with these three samayas are known as "gelong Dorje Dzinpa." *Gelong*, or *bhikshu*, refers to the ordinary samayas kept by those who are fully ordained, and *Dorje Dzinpa* refers to the tantric samayas or commitments that one must preserve. Clear examples of ordained monks who are Tantrayana practitioners and turn the wheel of the tantric teachings are His Holiness the Dalai Lama and His Holiness the Gyalwa Karmapa. Next there is a group of teachers known as "genyen Dorje Dzinpa." *Genyen* or *upasaka*, refers to the lay practitioner vows. Genyen Dorje Dzinpa includes highly respected lamas such as His Holiness Sakya Trizin of the Sakya tradition and His Holiness Dudjom Rinpoche of the Nyingma lineage. They are not monks. They are married and they are highly realized and accomplished teachers who turn the wheel of Buddhadharma.

The various traditions and vehicles differ in the ways they observe the precepts. Karma Chakme's explanation of the precepts is based on *The Hevajra Tantra*, which is accepted by all without any disagreement. When the Buddha gave the Hevajra teachings, he clearly specified that one must first receive the self-liberating vow and then receive the bodhisattva vow . Only then can one receive the tantra or vajra lineage vows. These are the three different vows to receive and to observe.

According to the Nyingma lineage, there are nine different vehicles, or yanas. When one receives the teachings of the nine yanas, one automatically receives the three types of vows. The Sakya lineage also has a unique view relating to the vows. In the Sakya lineage, one first takes the self-liberating vow. Once you have taken the self-liberating precepts, when you take the bodhisattva precepts, the self-liberating precepts become part of the bodhisattva system. After taking the bodhisattva precepts, when you take the Tantrayana samayas, then the bodhisattva precepts become part of the Tantrayana system. That is the Sakya tradition of transforming one into the other.

There are differences in terms of preserving the vows. In the Kagyu tradition one says, *"Tong ne tha de."* If there is degradation of the commitment of the self-liberating vow, you still have the bodhisattva vow and the tantric vow intact. If there is a defect in the bodhisattva vow, the tantric vow is still alive. They are not damaged or defective. The crucial point is that there must be no violation of the commitment to the tantric vows. Problems with the earlier vows bear lesser consequences, and the damage will not have serious implications to the tantric commitments. The Geluk tradition says that these three different vows are interdependent. If one is damaged, the other two are also violated. It is similar to a building with a foundation, pillars, and roof. If the foundation is damaged, then the pillars and roof will collapse. Similarly, if the self-liberating vow is violated, then the bodhisattva and tantric vows are both automatically damaged.

When Buddhism first came to Tibet, there were two ways the teachings were presented: the pure and the impure. The impure lineage started in Tibet at a time when there was a teacher, Gayadhara, who was visiting from India. On his first trip to Tibet he worked with a Tibetan translator, and together they did wonderful translations of many tantric teachings. He was a genuine Buddhist practitioner and gave very good teachings at that time. On his second visit to Tibet he used the name Red Sadhu. This time, as his main purpose was to obtain gold, he distorted the teachings on the three samayas. He thought that such distortion would make the teachings more attractive to people with the result that he would receive more gold from them. He distorted the teachings on the vows by teaching that first one receives ordination vows and then after a few months one abandons those vows. One then takes the bodhisattva vow, keeps it for a while, and then abandons it. Then one takes the tantric vow, reaching a very high level. He taught that one could discard the two previous vows and keep the tantric vow in whatever way one wished. For example, ordinary monks and nuns could engage in sexual misconduct and people could do anything they wanted including killing and stealing. Red Sadhu thought this would be very appealing to many ordinary Tibetans. His teachings became very prevalent throughout central Tibet, in such places as U, Tsang, and Nyari but did not spread to Kham in eastern Tibet. Many Tibetan scholars objected to his teachings since they were clearly distorted and all the schools of Tibetan Buddhism—Kagyu, Nyingma, Gelukpa, and Sakya—opposed these teachings. Because all worked together, they were able to bring back the purity of the practices. They put an end to his teachings in Tibet.

You may wonder why we present the impure practices since they were not accepted by all traditions of Tibetan Buddhism. The answer is that as a practitioner, you should know both the pure and the impure sides, so when you encounter something of the impure aspects, you understand what to do. Otherwise one always stays in the darkness, not being clear what is pure and what is impure. When Buddhism first came to Tibet, there were many who presented impure teachings. Red Sadhu, for example, came to Tibet to obtain gold as quickly as possible. He did not worry if the teachings were pure or impure. We are fortunate that the great panditas, siddhas, and practitioners of Tibet were able to bring back the purity of the teachings.

Although this happened in the past, we cannot say it will not happen now. There are people, who want to become rich and famous, who use different techniques to present wrong ideas. The advantage of knowing about the impure teachings is that, with your knowledge and wisdom, you can distinguish right from wrong and consequently will not participate in what is incorrect. It prevents you from falling into the wrong hands or the wrong ideas.

The Sakyapas emphasize that, while there is transformation and advancement to the three levels of commitments, thoroughly keeping them all is a necessity. Even when one has reached the highest result, one must still observe these three commitments in the proper way. An example of this is Guru Padmasambhava and his twenty-five different followers. When they teach the tantric teachings, they act like tantric masters, but in general life they remain ordained monks.

Gyalwa Tsongkapa, the founder of the Gelukpa lineage, who was believed to be the emanation of Manjushri, very clearly and strongly emphasized that regardless of the number of practices one has realized, one is still subject to observing the three commitments in a clear and proper way. He gave an example of a crystal bowl without a crack that can contain whatever you put inside it, such as water. He compares this crystal bowl of water to the self-liberating vow that can hold the bodhisattva vow. If you take the crystal bowl of water outside, you can see the reflection of the moon in the bowl of water. The moon in this analogy is regarded as the tantric commitment. If you have a bowl with no defect and put water into the bowl, you can get the reflection of the moon in the bowl. If there is a crack in the bowl, then the bowl can no longer hold the water, and consequently you will no longer see the reflection of the moon. Just as the bowl without defects that holds water has the ability to reflect the moon, the three vows must be preserved and kept clearly and properly. That is the emphasis that is usually given by Gelukpas.

In the Kagyupa tradition you do not take the three vows simultaneously. First you take the self-liberating vow, then you take the bodhisattva vow, and only then do you take tantric samayas. Since you must take them separately, when one is lost or damaged, the other two commitments are not necessarily damaged or violated. There are differences in terms of the potency and effectiveness of these three commitments. The bodhisattva vow is more important and more effective than the self-liberating vow; the tantric vow has more potency and potential then the other two. Together the three act like the sun, the moon, and the star. When there is sun, of course, everything is illuminated. If there is no sun, there will still not be complete darkness because of the light of the moon. If there are no sun and moon, the stars will still shine with light. There will never be absolute darkness.

The self-liberating vow is for oneself. The bodhisattva vow is for the benefit of others. Buddha said that you might sacrifice the self-liberating vow if necessary in order to accomplish the bodhisattva vow. For instance, Tilopa was a fisherman and Saraha was a hunter. At the self-liberating level, they were violating the self-liberating vows because they were killing fishes and animals; however, they were highly realized, enlightened beings and were able to liberate those fishes and animals. This is a case in which the self-liberating vow is sacrificed in order to accomplish the greater aspects of one's practice, the special and unique practices of the Kagyu lineage.

A practitioner who is subject to afflictive emotions and defilements must continue to keep the three vows intact. Think of a chicken that is newly hatched and can do nothing for itself. Its mother must feed it through her own mouth and the chick must be protected all the time. Until it can fly, the chick is subject to all kinds of problems and dangers and must be protected against rain, wind, and other animals. In a similar way, in the beginning the commitments must be protected with this special vigilance. It is especially difficult to keep the vows during these degenerate times; however, if one is violated, it is not hopeless because you still have the other commitments. The self-liberating vows contain vows prohibiting stealing, murdering, lying, and sexual misconduct, activities that must certainly be abandoned. If we can observe just one, there is benefit; however, if one commitment is violated, we should not be discouraged. If we are able to keep the other commitments, it is still a source of merit and benefit.

In Tibet there was a lama who was known as Jikten Sumgon, which means "the protector of the three realms of the world." He was a monk who held the three kinds of precepts. For some reason, he had to resign his monkhood, and on that day he got married and soon had many children who grew up and became butchers. This lama, regardless of whether he lost his vows, still dressed in monk's robes all the time. Some of his friends questioned why he wore the robes since he had given up his vows. He replied that he still had the imprint of thinking that he was a monk. He believed that having that imprint could lead him to the ultimate, highest form of life.

At this same time, there was a monk known as Iron-Footed Monk, who was able to see Chenrezik in person and to travel to his realm, the Potala, every day. One day on his way to the Potala, he met a monk who had violated his commitments. This monk carelessly hung his robes and begging bowl in a tree and was plowing a field. In the course of plowing the field he was killing many beings; insects that lived under the earth were turned up and exposed to death and insects that lived on top of the ground were buried. He was destroying many lives. The Iron-Footed Monk told him it was no use to have monk's robes and a begging bowl if he was going to do such terrible things and suggested that the robes and bowl be given to him instead. The Iron-Footed Monk took the robes and bowl to a clean area, buried them, and continued on his way to the Potala.

When he reached the Potala, there was nothing but a mountain. As he wanted to see Tara and Chenrezik, he did prostrations and prayed, however he did not see either of them. He climbed to the top of the mist-covered mountain and still did not see them. He spent a great deal of time crying and eventually Chenrezik came. The Iron-Footed Monk asked Chenrezik why it took so long to see him, when in previous times it had taken no time at all. Chenrezik replied that the Iron-Footed Monk had completely eradicated a small imprint from the monk in the field. Since this was a terrible thing to do, Chenrezik was reluctant to come see him. The monk who was plowing the field, although he did not have any ordination vow of commitment, still had the imprint of thinking that he wanted to be a monk. By taking the robes and begging bowl, the Iron-Footed Monk had destroyed the imprint of the monk in the field. The Iron-Footed Monk returned to that field, dug up the buried objects, and returned them to their proper owner with the request that they henceforth be kept respectfully. The detailed explanation of this incident is given in *The White Lotus Sutra*.

There are many possibilities in one's lifetime. You can become ordained as a monk or a nun or you can be a layperson. Because of these possibilities, you can experience many different kinds of good and bad circumstances, but no matter what, as Buddhist practitioners you will, during the time of Sangye Mö Pa, the last of the thousand buddhas, become a buddha or the disciple of a buddha. No matter how much one has violated the commitments and no matter how serious the consequences, because of the imprint that continues and because of the potency of Buddha's teachings, eventually everyone will become a buddha.

The Kagyu lineage holders clearly see whether one is able to keep the vows or not. They will give the vows, knowing that eventually they will plant a seed that will lead to the practitioner's liberation. If one has never received any vow, one will never really be able to escape cyclic existence. If one has received vows, even if there are violations of the vows, there is still an imprint or seed that will eventually blossom and will certainly help the individual to become liberated.

There is a long white flower, the tsampaka, found in India that retains its beauty even after it has dried. Buddha said that hundreds of the most beautiful flowers could not compare to an old dry tsampaka. Similarly, no matter how old, ugly, or bad a disciple may be, hundreds of ordinary beings still cannot compare. When the world comes to an end, even the old wretched pieces of cloth that used to be monastic robes will not remain on the earth. The gods and other beings will take these garments and place them as sacred objects in the god realms. This will happen when Buddha's teaching comes to an end. Buddha's advice is to develop a genuine respect and equanimity toward monks, nuns, and sangha, with no thought of judgment, thinking that one is good or one is bad. There must be equal respect and understanding for all.

In Tibet there was a great translator (lotsawa) known as Bari Lotsawa. He had such genuine respect toward all monks and nuns that whenever he traveled, if he found pieces of red or yellow cloth, he would pick it up and touch it respectfully to his head, proclaiming that once this particular cloth was used by a Buddhist practitioner. He respected all practitioners.

Karma Chakme Rinpoche was a highly realized person and a scholar who had a genuine, unbiased attitude and respect toward all Buddhist practitioners. If he entered a shrine room, he would pick up a small bit of dust because he viewed it as sacred blessed dust. He would make prostrations so that he would receive blessings from the cushions in the shrine room. This is unbiased, genuine respect.

As Buddhists we take refuge in the Buddha, Dharma, and Sangha. Sangha can be regarded as those who have taken the self-liberating vows. It is therefore very important to have unbiased, genuine respect for all those in the sangha, since they are part of the Three Jewels in which we take refuge. Maintaining such an attitude can bring two benefits. One is that it will inculcate perfect moral principles and conduct and the other is that it will help us to accumulate incredible merit. Our aim is to progress, from bliss to greater bliss to unsurpassable bliss. We are not to be content with just a little bit of happiness. Now we have this beautiful precious human life, and on the basis of this we must progress. Our aim should be to reach buddhahood. One cannot just feel happy because eventually there is a possibility of getting out of this cyclic existence. That is the wrong attitude to adopt. We must be able to observe these commitments as seriously as possible. By observing proper commitments and by trying not to violate them we can bring about a better positive result. The final buddha, who will be known as Sangye Mö Pa, will be here in the future, but the number of aeons it will be until that time are uncountable. In the same way if we do not become proper practitioners, there is no way of counting how many sufferings, tortures, and ordeals we will have to endure until the last buddha appears. If we are not careful and do not behave properly, we may be subjected to sufferings that may also be infinite.

You may have a perfect view of the Buddha's teachings and a perfect attitude relating to others, but you must also have the absolutely purest conduct and principles of morality. That is very important. Even though you have vast knowledge, you should not become inflated by the thought that you are a very high and knowledgeable person. Your conduct must be subject to moral observance regardless of how perfect a view you have with respect to all beings and nature.

There was once a monk who meditated in a cave. His toilet was outside the cave. Between the toilet and his cave there were bushes, some of which had bad thorns. Whenever he left the cave to travel to the toilet, his robes caught on the thorns. Once he thought that perhaps he should cut the bushes, but he did not, since he knew that the bushes are a part of nature and he respected that. One time when he passed the bushes, his robes became torn, so he got very upset and cut the bushes. Since Buddha said that we should not damage trees or living things, by cutting the bushes the monk violated two vows: he not only became angry and was unable to overcome that anger but he also doubted the Buddha's objection to cutting the plants, which is a violation of his view toward the Buddha.

Since the monk had been very strict in observing morality up until he became angry and cut the bush, when he died, he was reborn in the naga realm as king of the nagas. The consequence of his extreme anger in the cutting of the bushes and his wrong view toward Buddha was that he had one of these trees growing up out of his head. When winds blew back and forth in the realm of the nagas, he had tremendous pain because his whole brain was shaken. From this we can understand the kinds of problems and sufferings to which one can be subjected if one is born in such a lower realm. It will help us to understand the consequences of actions and to observe morality in a more rigorous way. If one is a respected lama or teacher, it is unthinkable to allow oneself the kind of moments of anger and doubt that the monk went through. There is nothing worse than that. If one happens to violate tantric teachings, the consequences would be even worse. Violations of tantric vows result in rebirth in the vajra hell, (Nyalwa Dorje Den) where the sufferings are limitless and unbearable.

The reasons leading to an individual's rebirth as a devil, demonic force, ghost, or in vajra hell are as follows. To accept a lama, whether he is good or bad, receive all of his teachings, and subsequently develop wrong view and violate all the teachings received can lead to the worst kind of rebirth. If one happens to engage in such a violation, then one must have sympathy for oneself, saying, "Kye ma kye hu," a sad and pitiful exclamation. This concludes the section on taking vows, the benefits one receives, and all the consequences that can result from our failure to behave properly.

Now we come to the items we must observe. First we must accept the self-liberating vow, which includes the following points: not to destroy lives, not to steal, not to engage in sexual misconduct, not to become intoxicated, and not to lie to your teachers or mislead others by saying that you are an enlightened being or a teacher. Observe these five points for the layperson (genyen).

In addition to these, there are male gelong and female gelong, bhikshus and bhikshunis, fully ordained monks and nuns, who have ten essential elements to observe. Altogether, male ordained have 253 points to observe, while female ordained have 364 points to observe. Those who are bodhisattva vow holders have four white dharmas to be respected and four black dharmas to be given up. There are eighteen points, or poisons, that completely obliterate the blessings or vows. According to the tantric commitments there are fourteen points, or fourteen root downfalls, that can completely wipe out the vows. There are eight branches, or secondary downfalls, that can also harm and destroy.

According to the Nyingma lineage, based on the lama's body, speech, and mind, there are twenty-five different commitments that you must observe. If you elaborate on these commitments, it becomes about thirty-seven million points to observe, and if you go into further detail, there are billions of points to observe. All the commitments can be summarized into two simple points, which are not to harm others and not to be the cause of harm to others, and to fulfill the commitment of the bodhisattva vow by benefiting others.

Having at this point given an extensive and detailed explanation of the three vows, the chapter concludes with a summary of them. If all of what has gone before is summarized into its essence, then it could be said that all of the pratimoksha, or individual liberation, vows are included in abandoning that which is harmful to others. This means abstaining from any action that is directly or indirectly harmful to others. In the same way, accomplishing that which is beneficial to others with body, speech and mind, together with the basis of such benefit, is the essence of the bodhisattva vow. Doing everything you can, directly and indirectly, and especially dedicating the merit of whatever virtuous actions you have performed includes all of the points of the bodhisattva vow. Finally, in the same way, to have one-pointed devotion for your guru is the essence of all the Vajrayana vows or samaya. These three points—abandoning that which is harmful to others, engaging in that which is beneficial to others, and having one-pointed devotion for your guru—are inclusive of all the points of the three vows.

"If you feel that the long explanation was too long and the short one was too brief, and you do not know what you actually need to do about this, then here is more." There are people who find that the detailed explanation is difficult to remember, let alone accomplish, but the reduction of the three vows to their essence is a little bit too concise. For such people, an intermediate explanation that is shorter than the first and longer than the second now follows.

First are the pratimoksha vows. The four root vows are the basic commitments of an upasaka, or lay disciple, a novice, or a monastic. It is taught that someone who protects the four root vows with as much care as he protects his own life and who abstains from intoxicants and meat that was killed for his specific consumption has what is considered nowadays pure vows. When the text says *nowadays*, what it is pointing out is that at the time of the Buddha it was appropriate to consider someone who meticulously kept every minor commitment free of infraction to have pure vows. Nowadays, given the way things are, anyone who can keep these five vows is doing very well.

The second category is the bodhisattva vow. It is first necessary to understand that with the bodhisattva vow and the Vajrayana samaya vows, some degree of pratimoksha, such as the four root commitments and the abstention from intoxicants, is absolutely necessary, as it is only based on this that the other two vows can be maintained. The way that the bodhisattva vow can be maintained is, first, by having bodhichitta that sincerely wishes to benefit all beings and that causes you to dedicate your virtue for the benefit of beings. The benefit of beings is not merely the temporary alleviation of specific sufferings such as illness or poverty. It is the sincere aspiration to bring all beings without exception to a state of full and complete awakening. The essence of the bodhisattva vow is to preserve that bodhichitta that wishes to bring about the liberation of all beings and to dedicate all of your virtue to that end rather than holding on to it yourself. The generation of bodhichitta at the beginning of a practice, the maintenance of nonconceptuality for the duration of a practice, and the dedication of the merit to the awakening of all beings at the culmination of a practice are the ways of keeping and including all of the trainings the bodhisattva vow.

This is important to understand because you might think that as a beginner you are responsible for emulating the great deeds of awakened bodhisattvas, who are capable of giving their bodies or lives for the benefit of others. Clearly, as beginners, we cannot do these things. What we can do, however, is preserve bodhichitta and dedicate our merit to the awakening of all beings.

"Buddha Shakyamuni taught this extensively to the king." Karma Chakme Rinpoche is telling us that this summary of the bodhisattva vow into the maintenance of bodhichitta and the dedication of merit is not something he is making up but was how the Buddha explained it. The king who is referred to here would be one of the kings who served as patron to the Buddha and who requested the sutras in which the Buddha expounded the bodhisattva vow.

The next category, samaya, is divided into several categories. The first is the *samaya of the guru's form or body*, which is maintained by thinking of your root guru as inseparable from the lord of your family, whom you visualize above your head in meditation. In short, to visualize your root guru above your head, viewing him as an awakened being, is how to keep the samaya of the guru's body. This has nothing to do with whether the guru is a sentient being or is actually the Buddha. In either case, provided the guru has bestowed upon you authentic empowerment, transmission, and instruction, their kindness is identical. It makes no difference whether they are an awakened being or a sentient being, just as it makes no difference whether the person who hands you a bar of gold is a prince or a commoner, learned or ignorant. Their kindness in handing you that bar of gold is the same. In the same way, the kindness of the guru in bestowing the means of liberation upon you is the same whether or not the guru himself is fully awakened. The samaya of the guru's form, which is how we can close the doors to rebirth in the lower realms and open the door to liberation, is to visualize the guru above your head inseparable from the buddha that adorns the head of your deity. For example, if you are doing Chenrezik meditation, you visualize Amitabha above your head. At that point you would think of the guru as inseparable from Amitabha.

The second samaya is the *samaya of the speech of the yidam*. This refers to the generation stage in the practice of yidam meditation in which you visualize yourself in the form of the yidam, whichever deity it is. While visualizing yourself as the deity, with your speech, you either recite that deity's mantra, do special breathing practices, or the combination of mantra repetition with breathing called vajra repetition. In any case, visualizing yourself as your meditation deity and reciting that deity's mantra is the way to keep the samaya of the yidam's speech.

The principal practice in our lineage, of course, is Mahamudra. Through the kindness of our lineage in general, and especially of His Holiness the Gyalwa Karmapa, and through the specific kindness of His Eminence Situ Rinpoche, many students here have had Mahamudra pointed out to them. The first point in keeping the samaya of mind, called the *samaya of the mind of the dakini*, is to look at your own mind in accordance with the instructions of Mahamudra. Depending upon your degree of training, this may be a coarse or a more refined practice. To look directly at your own mind is the first point of keeping the samaya of mind. The second point is to celebrate the great occasions, which in the specific Vajrayana context means the tenth day of the waxing and waning moon. It is therefore part of the samaya of mind to offer feasts and tormas on these days. The third, and final part of the samaya of mind is discretion, which is not to expound Vajrayana to those that have incorrect views or antipathy toward it. The reason for this is that if you explain Vajrayana to those who distrust it, then not only will it not help them, but it will harm them and their distrust will grow. That is why Vajrayana is supposed to be practiced with discretion. These are the samayas of mind.

The *samayas of quality and activity* are to dedicate torma daily to the protectors, as is done in the daily practice of Mahakala; to dedicate torma monthly, which would usually involve an extensive form of what is called fulfillment liturgy; and also the yearly elaborate Mahakala torma offering. The monthly one is normally done on the twenty-ninth day of the lunar month and the yearly one is normally done from the twenty-seventh to the twenty-ninth days of the twelfth lunar month. To do the daily, monthly, and yearly Mahakala torma offering is the way to keep the samayas of quality connected with the wealth deities and samayas of activity connected with the protectors or dharmapalas.

Further samayas are as follows. The *samaya of freeing yourself through realization* is to look continually at the nature of your own mind. This does not necessarily mean that you should try to maintain a constant recognition of your mind's nature, but at least in the beginning you should try to flash on the nature of your mind at all times of the day. In other words, do not limit looking at the nature of your mind to formal sessions nor to specific times of day but try to find brief moments throughout your day in which you look at the nature of your own mind. The *samaya of ripening, or benefiting others* through compassion, is to train yourself in the practice of tonglen, taking and sending, in order to enhance compassion and love for others and to actually benefit others in accordance with your ability and their needs, through helping people understand Dharma or, if possible, through providing empowerment, transmission, and instruction.

Always make the aspiration that all of those beings with whom you have any kind of connection, any being who has seen you, heard you, ever thought of you, or has ever touched you in any way, that all of these beings be reborn in Sukhavati, the realm of Amitabha. To make such aspirations is the Mahayana samaya of stirring and emptying samsara from the depths. The reason why, in making this aspiration, you specify that it is for beings with whom you have a connection rather than merely, as we usually do, all beings without exception, is that it is much more difficult to beneficially affect beings with whom you have no connection. This is why when a teacher is asked to provide some service, such as the transference of consciousness for someone, it is important that some connection be made, whether through an offering or in some other way, by the person to be benefited by the teacher. The connection can be positive or negative, but there has to be some connection for the aspiration, in this case the aspiration that beings be reborn in Sukhavati, to affect the person.

The chapter concludes with the remarks, "This brief summary of samaya and the other vows, clear in its distinctions but easy to practice, was written on the ninth day of the month of Trum, in the Horse year, by Raga Asya, who is Karma Chakme. Lama Tsondru Gyamtso, who requested it, took it down as dictation. If there is anything wrong with this, I confess it before the learned. Through the merit of this, may all beings perfect the three vows."

Questions and Answers

STUDENT: You spoke this morning about the monk who cut the briars and how this act went against the Buddha's teachings. I have never heard those teachings about not cutting plants before. Will you elaborate on that?

RINPOCHE: There is no particular objection to cutting grass or trees at the level of genyen, the laypeople, or getsul, the novices. When it comes to the ordained level, there is a strong objection to cutting trees or bushes, and there is a provision regarding this. Although it is objected to for those at the level of the ordained monk, there is a provision to cut trees if it is needed in terms of a major comfort issue. If it is in the interest of the community of monks, the sangha, or if the tree causes some problems to others, such as being poisonous and causing sickness, then there is a provision that it can be cut. Otherwise ordained monks cannot cut trees. This morning we were talking about an ordained monk who, out of anger, cut the trees. That is not permissible. Buddha said that anything that grows should not be cut. It does not necessarily mean that anything that has grown, such as a tree, is a living being; however, it is possible that the tree may contain life. Buddha said there are many beings that depend on the tree or there may be some element or spirit that may be attracted to living there. If you cut a tree, then many lives can be harmed or destroyed.

STUDENT: When you violate any vows, how do you make up for that kind of mistake?

RINPOCHE: There are many different teachings on how to purify violations and restore the violated commitments or samayas. It is very rare to find someone who has never violated any commitment. If one confesses every day and if one really tries to purify every day, I can guarantee you that there will be no implications from this violation. That is why Buddhists are always very busy practicing. It can be like in an individual's life, he or she must work and earn a living to maintain himself or herself. This is like the purification and restoration of violated samayas.

STUDENT: I have heard some people say that bodhichitta, or true loving-kindness and compassion for other living beings, cannot be truly experienced until one has reached enlightenment. Would you speak about loving-kindness and compassion for the unenlightened as well as for the enlightened? How does it differ, if at all?

RINPOCHE: The aim of developing loving-kindness and compassion is enlightenment. That is the ultimate goal; it does not mean that loving-kindness and compassion are experienced at the last minute. On the contrary, if you try to develop loving-kindness and compassion, I feel certain that as you progress, you will have better experiences as time goes on. It does not mean that something will decrease. If you keep working hard, you will have a better experience and a better realization. In other words you will have a better result. It is not something solid that you will achieve the minute you become enlightened.

STUDENT: I can understand what Rinpoche says regarding confession, purification, and compassion. In terms of purification, what kind of practice should one do when one does not have access to a lama or a teacher?

RINPOCHE: The best practice to purify and restore the violated commitment is to confess to your teacher, but if your teacher is not easily available, then you can use a representation, such as a statue or a thangka of Buddha, and confess to the representation. If you do not have such an object, then you can visualize that you are confessing before all the buddhas and bodhisattvas. Even if they are not there physically, from the level of the dharmakaya buddhas, they see you and hear you just as we see and hear each other right here.

STUDENT: I would like to clarify something: are the self-liberating vows you spoke of this morning the same as the lay precepts?

RINPOCHE: The self-liberating vows, or pratimoksha vows (so sor thar pay dom pa), are the vows of individual liberation of the genyen (lay), getsul (novice), and gelong (fully ordained.) They do not include the altruistic attitude. Their aim is for individual liberation based on the fear of suffering and fear of the lower realms. This is their motivation. In the Tibetan tradition, when you take any vow, you are supposed to think that you will take all vows for the benefit of all sentient beings. There is not really a basis on which it can be regarded as an individual escape method. By doing this it becomes part of the bodhisattva vow.

STUDENT: As Western students we are encouraged, but not required, to take the lay precepts. We are given the option of taking one or two or three or all of them. We are not required to take them before we take the bodhisattva vow. Is there a reason for this?

RINPOCHE: We spoke this morning about genyen Dorje Dzinpa, or gelong Dorje Dzinpa. *Genyen Dorje Dzinpa* refers to the lay teacher of the vajra holder, exemplified by Sakya Trizin, Dudjom Rinpoche, or Marpa. All are examples of those who are married and have a family and who first received the lay precepts, then the bodhisattva vow, then the tantric vow. The difference with the gelong Dorje Dzinpa is that the gelong are fully ordained monks, exemplified by His Holiness Dalai Lama and His Holiness Karmapa. I must be honest and tell you that it is very difficult to find a pure gelongma or gelong today. At one time in Tibet, the environment was very conducive to such things. Today, even in Tibet, the environment is much changed. When the time was very good, the monks, especially the ordained gelong monks, did not have to worry about their livelihood. Their food, clothing, medical needs, and everything else needed was provided. Their only concern was their practice and the observance of all the samaya commitments they made. Now, unfortunately, you have to work for your livelihood and since you have to observe all these two hundred fifty-three different moral rules, you cannot be an ordained monk. The environment is not very favorable; therefore to have a pure ordained monk is very difficult.

STUDENT: In the Kagyu tradition you talked about how the three vows could be separate in some ways or exist independently in a person. It leads me to wonder if in our ordinary lives we were also benefiting beings in some way by our aspiration. Related to the idea of aspiration, could we be fulfilling the bodhisattva vow and yet not be being completely true to our lay precepts? Although we are not doing very much for beings in our ordinary lives, are we benefiting them through our practice or aspiration?

RINPOCHE: Yes, aspiration is very important. Even at the lay level, if you have the bodhisattva vow but cannot do much on a practical level, to have the aspiration to benefit beings is very important. In accordance with Buddhist practices, motivation is very important, especially for people such as us who are more or less beginners. To have the right motivation is very important. Whatever you do, if your dedication is for the benefit of all sentient beings, then it will plant a tremendous seed that can really grow bigger and bigger.

No one is perfect at the beginning, at the moment when they take the precepts or vows. We can think of ourselves as infants, who can breathe and move a bit, but besides that can do almost nothing. Of course, in time the infant grows and becomes a fully functioning adult. In the same way, continuing to have a positive aspiration and working bit by bit increases our growth as a practitioner.

STUDENT: I have a general sense that, on higher levels of development and wisdom, the quality that one really needs to develop on one level is the quality that one gives up when going to the next level. It becomes an impediment. Are these vows something that you are saying are dependent on one's level of development? Does that mean that these vows are relative to the level of consciousness that we are at and that, later on, we do not need to be held by them in the same way, such as in the relative and ultimate aspect of this?

RINPOCHE: When you take the vows, you first take the self-liberating vows, then the bodhisattva vows, and then the tantric vows. But this all depends on what kind of motivation you have and how you perceive the vows. When you take the self-liberating vow, if you think only of benefiting yourself, then it is just the self-liberating vow, no more and no less. If you take the self-liberating vow for the benefit of all sentient beings, that means that your scope is bigger, you are more open-minded, and your vow becomes more like the bodhisattva vow. When you take the bodhisattva vow and then you also practice visualizations, recite mantras, and dedicate the merit for all sentient beings, then you have also joined the tantric level. When you take vows at the tantric level, it includes the three vows because, right from the beginning, you have had thoughts for the benefit of others. You have developed by taking the bodhisattva vow, and now you are at the tantric level. The self-liberating vow has become less important at this point. It has become a part that has led to your higher level. If there is something wrong with the vow at the self-liberating level, this has less implication because you have already reached higher levels and have incorporated all the vows. It depends on the motivation you generate.

If you take the self-liberating precept only to benefit yourself, then it is very fragile, and violation can destroy the vow. If you take the bodhisattva vow of loving-kindness and compassion thinking only of yourself, then it becomes more fragile and easier to violate and destroy. If you take the tantric vow just to recite mantras and obtain benefit for yourself, that is technically tantric, but it does not have too much significance. In contrast to this, if, at the self-liberating level, you start thinking to benefit others, you have become like a Mahayana practitioner at the bodhisattva level. At the bodhisattva level, you can move to the tantric level. It all depends on motivation. Rinpoche gave an example this morning. He spoke about the mahasiddha Saraha, who was a great hunter who used to hunt and kill deer. At the relative level, he was hunting and destroying animals and therefore violating the self-liberating vow, which prohibits killing. He violated the bodhisattva vow because he killed animals and did not show loving-kindness and compassion. But he was actually killing the animals out of great, inconceivable loving-kindness, and as a result the animals did not have to be reborn in the lower realms. The moment the animal was killed, the mahasiddha transported its consciousness to a higher realm, so the deer did not have to be reborn again as part of cyclic existence. This can be perceived at whatever level you wish to consider. If you wish to consider the self-liberating level, Saraha did a terrible thing, violating all the vows. On the absolute truth level, he was one of the mahasiddhas and he liberated the deer he killed.

STUDENT: If it is that easy to become enlightened, just to be killed by a mahasiddha, then why don't we all have access to that? I thought it meant that the being only went to a higher rebirth, not necessarily to enlightenment. Are you saying that the deer were actually enlightened?

RINPOCHE: It is not clear if the deer became enlightened at that point, but I can positively say that the deer eventually became enlightened.

STUDENT: You spoke about vajra hell and said that the way one goes there is if one rejects the teachings and violates the commitments of one's teacher regardless of whether that teacher is good or bad. Is that correct? In a case in which there really is a teacher who is harming students and a student turns away from the teacher, does the student necessarily go to vajra hell? Are there exceptions?

RINPOCHE: It all depends on what teachings the vajra master gave. If he gave undistorted, unadulterated, pure, perfect teachings to his students, then definitely the student can go to vajra hell. It is completely dependent on the teachings. If the teachings were distorted, false, or misleading, then it is unclear who will go to vajra hell. Unfortunately, these days it is extremely rare to find a perfect teacher who has accomplished such a level, but it all depends on his teachings. It does not matter if the teachings are at the level of self-liberating, bodhisattva, or tantra, as long as the teachings are pure, without any mistakes, and not misleading, they have to be accepted very seriously. It is something like one's father. A father can be a handsome, brilliant, rich, and wonderful person or a father can be ugly, unintelligent, and poor, but that person is still the father, no matter what else he may be. He has become the vehicle to produce his children. His qualities notwithstanding, he has fathered us, so we have to accept him.

STUDENT: Can you confess anything to the vajra teacher and will it be purified just by confession alone?

RINPOCHE: By confession alone, it is unclear whether you would be purified from the root, but it is definite that you will have reduced its potency and the danger of its growing bigger. Your repeated confessions ultimately lead to being able to purify. By confessing once, you have reduced the danger of its growth, but only repeated confession can lead to uprooting it.

STUDENT: Recently things have been happening to me that prompts a question regarding stealing. I am not actually stealing, but it seems that I am. The situation is that people have been making mistakes. I purchased an article of clothing and when I returned home, I realized that I had not been charged the full price. Right away I was pleased. Then I thought that it really was not good, since someone was going to be negatively affected. I thought I would not return the money to the company because they have enough money. I decided to give the money to a charity. When I thought about it, I realized that my intentions there are not right either because I am putting too much emphasis on worrying about whether the company has enough money or not. I am confused regarding that situation. The other experience was that I got an extra five bags of corn meal. I thought they had made a mistake and they did not charge me. The question arose as to what I would do with that. I thought that I would bring it to a food bank, but then I thought that someone else was going to suffer. I am confused about the situation. I probably should pay for it and then bring it to the food place.

RINPOCHE: Right from the beginning you never thought of stealing, so it cannot be regarded as stealing. Upon realization that there had been a mistake, you felt joy. If you continue thinking that way, it may become part of stealing because you know there was a mistake and yet you feel good about it. Instead of that, if you give to the charitable organization, that would be the best solution.

STUDENT: It would be good to go back to the store and give them the money.

RINPOCHE: I would like to share a personal experience with you. I was in North Carolina and bought a silver plate. I picked up two plates by accident, not realizing that the two were together. I gave it to the cashier and the cashier also thought it was a single plate. I brought it home and gave it to Thrangu Rinpoche. After inspection, Thrangu Rinpoche remarked that there were two plates. I brought one of the plates back to the same cashier who had helped me. The cashier felt insulted and embarrassed, and there were people who accused her of not being able to sell things properly. It probably jeopardized her position. In case there is danger of that, it may be better for you to give the value of the item to a charitable organization.

STUDENT: I have a general question about empowerments. Could you explain about wang, lung, and tri?

RINPOCHE: *Wang* is the empowerment of body, speech, and mind. It is to empower you to practice that special deity. *Lung* is the oral transmission from the lineage that started with Vajradhara and continues on without any break. It has its own significant blessing and you must get the oral transmission. This is the link in the practice from Vajradhara to you. *Tri* is teaching the practice, the visualizations, mudras, mantras, and ritual objects.

STUDENT: You referred to certain levels of beings on up to arhats and buddhas. Where are the wrathful deities within this pantheon? I understand that at one time they were demons that actually preyed upon people, but then Padmasambhava got them to protect the lineage. I have always had a hard time putting my faith in beings that I knew were once demons that we changed against their will. Have these beings since become enlightened and are they now buddhas? I know that they also represent aspects of our own nature. I would appreciate your commenting on that.

RINPOCHE: Not all wrathful deities are exactly the same things. Basically peaceful and wrathful deities, however, are of the same nature. They are the display, in a peaceful or wrathful form, of the same fundamental wisdom. All awakened deities are equally awakened. They are all the display of the same fundamental wisdom, which can manifest as a peaceful deity (in order to benefit those who will be inspired and tamed by a peaceful deity) or as a wrathful deity (in order to benefit those who will be inspired and tamed by a wrathful deity). In the same way, this wisdom can manifest as a male deity or a female deity. The differences between a peaceful deity and a wrathful deity, a male deity and a female deity, are all in the appearance of the deity but not in the actual nature of the deity, which only manifests as it does for the benefit of those particular beings that are connected to it. These are all equally displays of the same awakening.

This wisdom can arise, as well, not as a single figure but as a principal figure surrounded by a retinue, in which case it appears as though the retinue is in some way inferior to or subservient to the principal. For example, the deity can appear as a buddha, peaceful or wrathful, surrounded by a retinue of bodhisattvas, dakas, dakinis, and protectors, but all of these are displays of the same fundamental wisdom. Their wisdom is manifesting as a chief deity and retinue, again, as a display for the benefit of others. Buddhas are perfectly capable of manifesting as bodhisattvas if it is beneficial for beings, but this does not mean that they are not, in fact, buddhas.

Awakened wrathful deities are no different from awakened peaceful deities except in appearance; however, there was something else you mentioned that is true. There were spirits that were bound by Guru Padmasambhava. These were spirits who, at the time, were somewhat malevolent and who were tamed and bound by him, placed under oath, and they have since served to assist practitioners in accordance with their promise and commitment. These are not the same as wrathful deities. These are called mundane protectors. They are called mundane protectors because at the time at which they were bound by oath they were not awakened beings. They were mundane beings. It is uncertain whether they are still mundane beings. Some of them may have, since that time, attained awakening, but they are classified as mundane because they were initially bound by oath. These function to help and assist practitioners. But they are different from wrathful deities, who are embodiments of awakened wisdom.

STUDENT: If we are trying to embody peace and compassion, of what benefit is it to invoke wrathful deities? Is this like Shiva in the Hindu pantheon?

RINPOCHE: We all want to attain a state of mind that is utterly peaceful. What prevents us from enjoying that at present and what prevents us from attaining it is the presence of kleshas and mental afflictions within our minds. These are obviously strong enough and powerful enough to control us and prevent us from attaining the peace of mind we seek. These kleshas not only bring harm to us but they bring harm, indirectly, to others as well. Clearly we need to overcome these in order to attain true piece of mind. In order to overcome them, we need a wisdom that is stronger and more powerful than the kleshas. This is the wisdom embodied by the wrathful deities. The wisdom itself is not wrathful, but it is the power and effectiveness of that wisdom that is displayed in the form of wrathful iconography.

STUDENT: I am wondering what our approach to taking the vows should be. If we were going to take vows, for instance the lay precepts, what should our attitude be as we go into them? Should we feel that we could really keep them, or should we go into them with the feeling that we should do our best to keep the vows but that confession is an option if they are broken?

RINPOCHE: The difference in presentation of vows, including the refuge vow, is based on the merit and motivation of those who take them. Vows can also be viewed differently according to the different vehicles. The vow of a lay disciple, or upasaka, is the vow of refuge— taking refuge in the Buddha, Dharma, and Sangha—and in addition, one or more of five lay precepts. The number of precepts you take corresponds to your degree of confidence and your ability to keep them. There are basically two possible ways that you can view taking the vows. One way is to think, "For the benefit of all beings and in order to remove the suffering of all beings and establish all beings in buddhahood, I will take these vows and will, at all costs, keep them until I attain buddhahood." When you take the vows with that attitude, it makes you what is called an upasaka bodhisattva or an upasaka, or lay disciple of the Mahayana. Another way that you can take the vows is to think, "I wish to achieve liberation from samsara and therefore I will take these vows and will, at all costs, keep them for the duration of this life." That makes you an upasaka of the common vehicle. The ceremony is the same. The difference is what you are actually thinking when you take the vow. Because the Mahayana upasaka vow is of greater benefit, when I give the refuge vow, I use the Mahayana ceremony, but that does not guarantee that everyone that is taking the vow at that time is taking it in the Mahayana way.

STUDENT: That is not quite what I meant. What I thought I heard yesterday was that it is beneficial to take the vows even if you break them further down the line, since you can confess and repair the vow and you still have more benefit for yourself and other beings than if you had never taken it at all. If that is so, do we go into the vow with the attitude "I can do this and never break my vow," or do we go with the attitude that "I will do my best, and since I might break my vow, I can always confess that, thereby giving the most benefit to beings?"

RINPOCHE: It is taught that if you take a vow and you break it, it is better than not having taken it at all, in the sense that samsara will have an end for you. Because you did take the vow, then you have made a connection with it, which will eventually cause you to be liberated from samsara. But *eventually* here means after a great deal of suffering, because the result of breaking any vow you take is to be reborn, definitely, in lower realms and to remain there for a long time and experience a great deal of suffering. In a sense, you can say that it is better than having no connection whatsoever, but it is not a very happy situation. You should never take a vow with the thought that you will just do your best. You should take the vow with the thought that no matter what happens, you will keep the vow, no matter how sick you become and no matter how much you suffer, you will keep the vow. If you have an unconditional commitment to the vow, then no matter what happens, you will still keep it. If your commitment to the vow is conditional, if you think that you will do your best but you do not know how it will work out, then it will not take very much to cause you to lose the vow. The firmer the resolve, the better it is. It is important to remember that these vows you take are a great source of benefit, not only for yourself but also for others, not only in this life but in future lives, and they are a necessary container for your practice as a whole. Having a vow with a conditional commitment is like having a container of grain with the lid not properly on; eventually something will spill out. Having a vow with an unconditional commitment is like having a container of grain with the lid properly on so that it is sealed shut and nothing can get out.

STUDENT: Recently I had a disagreement with my family. Although I handled it better than I usually do, I showed a real display of anger with my brothers. I tried to talk to my mother, attempting to enlighten her before I am enlightened. It brought about some chaos. I cannot be with them for long periods of time because I begin to suffer as they do. Can you give me some advice about this?

RINPOCHE: This is an experience that is characteristic to all beings within samsara. When we are attempting to interact beneficially with others, because we still have kleshas and they still have kleshas, we are loaded and ready to go off whenever they get angry enough with us to ignite our anger. When two people trigger each other's anger in that way, it is like oil encountering a fire. Everything just gets worse. This happens to us, in one way or another, all the time. The best solution is to respond with greater compassion for everyone in the situation when you see what is happening. When you try to talk to someone else for their own good with good intentions that are responsive to their needs, oftentimes they not only do not listen to you but they respond with aggression. If you can see that they are misguided in misjudging your intentions and that that's why they respond to you aggressively, this could give rise to greater compassion for them because you see that their anger is coming from a misunderstanding on their part of what you are attempting to do. If you understand that it is coming from ignorance, that will help you to not get angry. In this specific situation, however, it may be the best thing for you to maintain some distance from these family members and instead pray for them. When you attempt to talk to them, do so in a very simple and careful way. Do not say too much. If you are trying to give them advice, then give it to them in very small pieces, very carefully, and stop as soon as you start to feel resistance. In that way, gradually you may be able to develop better communication with them. From your own side, the experience of doing so will give you an even clearer picture of how samsara works, how much we all suffer, what beings are like, and therefore the benefit and importance of practice and going for refuge to the Three Jewels. It is unfortunate, but we cannot simply put a stop to the self-destructiveness of others simply through our wishing to do so.

STUDENT: When I first came to the Dharma many years ago, I had the opportunity to take many vows. I was encouraged to take them. No one ever told me that you would go to the lower realms for breaking any of them. My question is: if you do not know when you take the vows what all the consequences are, is the karmic result if you do violate them the same as if you knew about it? Can you renew the vows with this knowledge? This is in regard to all three vows.

RINPOCHE: There are four causes of violating any vow. They are ignorance of what the commitment is and how to keep it, an irreverent attitude thinking it is irrelevant whether you keep the vow or not, disrespecting the vow, and kleshas that prevent you from keeping the vow when you want to. Of these, breaking a vow through ignorance, through not knowing what the vow was or how to keep the vow properly, cannot be said to be without negative consequences, but it is not as karmically negative as breaking a vow out of irreverence. Breaking a vow out of ignorance, breaking a vow out of carelessness, or breaking a vow out of being overpowered by your kleshas are all negative, but they are not as bad because they are not as deliberate as breaking a vow out of irreverence. The reason why breaking a vow out of irreverence is the worst, is because you are actually breaking the vow in two ways. You are breaking the vow and you are also developing an incorrect view of the Buddha, Dharma, and Sangha by thinking that the vow does not matter.

STUDENT: Yesterday you talked about the importance of genuine respect. I would like to ask you how we can develop and accomplish this equal respect and also how we can maintain it. The story that caught my attention was about the idea that even if the world ended, you would honor these threads from these sacred robes because the beings led a sacred life. I want to know how to apply that.

RINPOCHE: The basic point of that section of the teaching was the preciousness and value of Dharma. Because Dharma is so precious, so valuable, and so rare, those who practice it are precious and valuable, simply because there is no practitioner who has not gained at least one quality, however slight it may be, through the practice of Dharma. No matter where you would place yourself within the ranks of practitioners, something has happened to you as a result of your contact with Dharma. That is why every member of the sangha, in the widest use of the term *sangha*, is to be respected. That is one reason. That is why great gurus of the past have demonstrated respect for even ordinary members of the sangha in extreme ways. Both Shamar Chokyi Wangchuk, the Sixth Shamar Rinpoche, and the great translator Lochen Rinchen Zangpo, used to demonstrate their respect for the common sangha by placing on the top of their heads the mats on which the sangha sat in order to receive the blessing of the sangha. They also placed on their tongues a little bit of the dust found in the shrine rooms.

As you mentioned, when Buddhadharma disappears from this world — which does not mean the end of the world — the robes worn by the sangha will not be left in the world. They will be taken by gods and will be enshrined in stupas in the god realms. All of this is simply because the effect that Dharma has on anyone who practices it is so precious that it is always to be respected. As well, a genuine practitioner will never think, "I need more respect." As it was taught by the Kadampa teachers, the practice of Dharma is "leaving and joining the dogs." You totally surrender any concern with or need for social position or respect of any kind. If you regard yourself as a dog and not a person, if you regard yourself as low and inferior, automatically you will have faith and respect for others. That automatically produces qualities in you, since you see what is good around you. If you think that you are wonderful and that you are superior, learned, intelligent, and so on, then all of this is pride. You will be unable to see the qualities of others or, if you do, you will react to them with jealousy and competitiveness. It is said, "Leaving the people and joining the dogs makes you a god." By giving up any concern with social position, you become worthy of the highest position because you are without arrogance. Basically it is through having no pride that we start to develop the qualities of a bodhisattva. It is obviously true that there are more intelligent people and more awakened or mature people, but every one of us, regardless of what else may be true, has buddha nature, and therefore every one of us is fundamentally worthy of respect. Not only that but since everyone has buddha nature, showing respect to anyone, no matter who they may be, is a source of merit because, in their nature, they are no different from the Buddha. For that reason, a serious practitioner of the Vajrayana will take the view that, as is said, "all beings are buddhas. There are no sentient beings here at all." Because you are focused on what is true of beings in their essence, that their nature is the same as that of a buddha, because you are focused on that, then that is how you start to experience others. In short, the more we focus on the buddha nature of others, the more respect there will be in the sangha.

Going for Refuge, Which Protects from All Danger and Fear

The next chapter opens with the Sanskrit invocation NAMO RATNA TRAYA YA, "Homage to the Three Jewels." Karma Chakme then tells his disciple Lama Tsondru Gyamtso, "Listen without distraction."

Although all beings seek refuge in one way or another, few people understand all the different ways we can go for refuge and what their varying significances are. We are always taking refuge in something we perceive to be a source of protection, whether it be immediate, temporary, or permanent. When we are small children, we seek the protection of our parents. We go for refuge to our parents from the time we can walk and talk.

Ordinary people in the world seek the refuge or protection of powerful human beings and powerful nonhuman beings as well. People in most cultures believe in some form of powerful spirits, entities that may or may not be associated with their locality, and seek their intercession and protection. These spirits may not exist at all, in which case going for refuge to them does not lead to anything whatsoever. On the other hand they may actually exist, but they still can only afford some kind of temporary benefit. Similarly all religious people take refuge, whether they call it that or not, in whatever is regarded as the primary focus of refuge or protection in their particular religious tradition.

The point is that this attitude of seeking the protection of some kind of higher power does not in itself mean that the source of refuge you are directing yourself to can give you the protection you are seeking. For example, in Tibet before the Buddhadharma was taught, people sought refuge from the various gods and spirits that were worshiped at the time. All of these ways in which we seek protection or go for refuge, when they are concerned with some actual being who is more powerful than ourselves, will bring some temporary benefit. Just as the parents of a child can protect that child from some suffering, all of these sources that we seek to take refuge in can benefit us in some way.

What no source of refuge other than the Three Jewels can do is to protect us from the sufferings of samsara. This is because in order to protect beings from the sufferings of samsara, the source of refuge must itself be free from those sufferings. Whenever you go for refuge to someone or something that is not in itself liberated, it can at most bring temporary benefit.

The reliable or actual sources of refuge in the Buddhist context are what are called the Three Jewels. All three of these are genuine sources of refuge; however, only one of them is considered to be an ultimate source of refuge, and that is the Buddha. Dharma is a genuine source of refuge, but it is not an ultimate source because Dharma is like a path or road on which you must travel to get to a certain destination. Once you have reached that destination, you no longer need that path. You will not turn around and go back the other way along the same path. Therefore Dharma is not considered an ultimate source of refuge. It is, however, necessary.

In the same way, the Sangha, the community that functions as friends, companions, and guides on the path of Dharma, is also not an ultimate source of refuge because the members of the sangha themselves are not fully freed from samsara—that is, they are not yet buddhas. If they were buddhas, they would be called Buddha and not Sangha. Being called Sangha, by definition, they are, at the most, only partially liberated. Therefore they, too, are only a temporary focus of refuge.

Ultimately the only final source of refuge is Buddha, because a buddha has two characteristics that are unique. The first is that a buddha has removed, cleansed, or purified all defects, all ignorance, all mental afflictions, and all karma. The second is that a buddha has brought to full perfection or full bloom all possible qualities. Because of this perfect freedom and perfect blooming, a buddha is unique.

Another way of putting it is that a buddha has conquered the dangers that are posed by the four maras. The four maras are the four things that afflict us in samsara: death, the kleshas, the skandhas, and what is called the deva putra mara, or the attachment to pleasure. Because of that, the Buddha possesses complete and unlimited wisdom, such as the six types of supercognition and so forth.

A buddha is therefore far beyond samsara. Saying that a buddha is beyond samsara is more than saying that a buddha is liberated from it. Of course a buddha is liberated from samsara in that he has exhausted the cause of samsara, which is the mental afflictions, and he has exhausted fundamental ignorance itself. This means that he is not only liberated from samsara but he is also liberated from the one-sided nirvana of the Shravaka or Pratyekabuddha arhats, who have exhausted the mental afflictions but not fundamental ignorance. Because buddhas are beyond both samsara and nirvana, they can, through their great kindness, like that of a mother for her children, continually regard all sentient beings in samsara all of the time. Not only do they see everyone and everything, they also possess the ten powers unique to a buddha. Because buddhas possess the wisdom and the actual ability to benefit beings, they are the supreme and most worthy or suitable source of refuge.

It is necessary to understand that the source of refuge has to possess that which you are trying to gain from it. To take refuge in something that does not possess the qualities you wish to achieve would be like expecting gold to fall from the sky. Since gold is not present in the sky to begin with, holding your hand out and waiting for it to fall is a waste of time. Thus it is appropriate to go for refuge only to the Three Jewels.

The Three Jewels are understood in different ways within the Buddhist tradition. There are, first, the views appropriate to the different vehicles or levels, and then there are the various views of the different schools.

The first and most fundamental way of looking at the Three Jewels is that which is found in the pratimoksha. Here, the word *pratimoksha* refers to the rituals and view of the common or lesser vehicle, the Hinayana. From the point of view of the pratimoksha,

Buddha is the historical nirmanakaya, Shakyamuni, who attained enlightenment 2,500 years ago at Bodhgaya in India. Dharma is his teaching; it is his turning of the dharmachakra, specifically the first dharmachakra, which is his teaching of the four noble truths. Sangha consists of the Shravakas and Pratyekabuddhas, especially those who have achieved any of the four results of the Hinayana path. These results are: (1) entering the stream, which means attaining some degree of stable realization; (2) returning once, which means having only one more lifetime before attaining arhatship; (3) nonreturning, which means being close to the attainment of arhatship in this lifetime; and (4) the actual attainment of arhatship. From the point of view of the Hinayana these are the actual Three Jewels: the historical Buddha, the teaching of the four noble truths, and those who have attained or are close to attaining arhatship.

From the point of view of the common vehicle, the actual Three Jewels are represented by what are called the relative or symbolic Three Jewels. These are as follows: (1) the stupas and images that are symbols of the Buddha and that remind you of and commemorate the Buddha; (2) the letters or written words of the Dharma, which you venerate because that is where you acquire or learn Dharma (for example, in the Hinayana you are taught to venerate the written words, to place the texts above your head, not to put them on the ground or under your clothing, and so on); and (3) all those who wear the robes of the ordained (this means that whatever the robes are in a specific culture, the people who wear those robes, in addition to the very robes they wear, are venerated because they represent the Sangha).

The second special feature of the refuge vow of the common vehicle is its duration. According to the pratimoksha, when you take refuge, you do so for this lifetime only. The vow extends from the moment at which you take it until the time of your death. This means that in future lifetimes you need to retake the vow of refuge.

A third feature is your motivation for taking refuge. According to the pratimoksha, your motivation is that you fear the suffering of samsara. You wish to escape from samsara because it is so much suffering; therefore you alone go for refuge to the Three Jewels.

The Mahayana view of going for refuge is different in regard to the view of the sources of refuge. Buddha in the Mahayana context is not only the nirmanakaya, the historical Buddha Shakyamuni, he is also the trikaya, which is to say, Buddha is both the dharmakaya and the rupakaya, or form body. The rupakaya includes the sambhogakaya, or body of complete enjoyment, and the nirmanakaya, or body of emanation. Thus from the point of view of the Mahayana, Buddha is the two or three bodies or kayas. Dharma is the Mahayana Tripitaka, which means the three collections of Mahayana teachings: the Mahayana Vinaya (training), the Mahayana Sutrayana (discourses), and the Mahayana Abhidharma (teachings on the nature of phenomena). The Sangha in the Mahayana context comprises all the bodhisattvas who have attained at least the first bhumi. Thus all bodhisattvas abiding on any of the ten bhumis are the Mahayana Sangha. That is the Mahayana view of the Three Jewels.

Another distinction that makes the Mahayana view of refuge superior to that of the pratimoksha is the duration of the vow. It is not merely for this lifetime but lasts from the moment you first take the vow until you attain buddhahood. The reason for this is that in the pratimoksha, the taker of the vow — that is to say the container for the vow — is the person's body and mind together. When that person dies and that body dies, it is considered that they can no longer maintain the vow because the receptacle is gone. According to the Mahayana, the taker of the vow — and the container for the vow — is primarily the person's mind, and the mind does not die. Therefore you keep the vow, you retain the vow, from the moment you take it until you fulfill it by achieving buddhahood.

In addition, in the Mahayana your motivation for taking the vow is not merely to protect yourself from the sufferings of samsara but to bring about the protection of all beings from suffering through the achievement of the liberation and awakening of all beings. That is the way the refuge vow is viewed in the Mahayana sutras.

In the Mahayana tantras there is, yet again, a distinct view of the vow of refuge. In the first two of the four levels of tantra, which are called the kriya tantra and the charya tantra, the Three Jewels are viewed in basically the same way as in the Mahayana sutras, or at least the Buddha is. The Buddha is viewed as the trikaya: the dharmakaya, the sambhogakaya, and the nirmanakaya. The Dharma, however, is specifically the kriya tantra and charya tantra teachings. The Sangha is those who have accomplished awareness mantra, which is to say those who have become dakas and dakinis through the practice of the mantras of kriya tantra and charya tantra.

The duration of the vow of refuge and the motivation of the vow of refuge, in kriya and charya tantra, is the same as in the Mahayana sutras.

The Vajrayana is characterized by, among other things, an additional set of tantric teachings known as yoga tantra. In the view of yoga tantra, Buddha is considered not merely the trikaya but also the buddhas of the five families, or what are called the five victors. Dharma is the yoga tantra teachings, and Sangha is the male and female bodhisattvas who abide in the mandalas of the five buddhas.

The fourth and highest level of Vajrayana tantras is called anuttara yoga tantra, or highest yoga tantra. In the view of anuttara yoga tantra, Buddha is identified as the embodiment of the five kayas, or five bodies. These consist of the three kayas (the dharmakaya, the sambhogakaya, and the nirmanakaya) together with a fourth (the essence kaya, or svabhavikakaya, which is the unity of the first three) and a fifth (the kaya of great bliss, or mahasukhakaya, which is the quality of the other four). Dharma is the tantras of anuttara yoga, the tantras of secret mantra. Sangha is the supermundane, or awakened, dakas, dakinis, and dharmapalas.

In the highest reaches of the anuttara yoga tantra, which is the tradition of special instructions, there is a further understanding of the vow of refuge. According to this tantra, the Three Jewels are nothing other than one's own root guru. Why do we say this? We say this because the mind of the guru is the actual Buddha, the wisdom of all buddhas. Therefore the mind of the guru is the embodiment of all buddhas. The guru's speech is obviously the source of all Dharma, so the guru's speech is the Dharma. The guru's body is the embodiment of the Sangha, because the guru is the foremost member of the Sangha. The qualities of the guru are what are represented by the various mandalas of the yidams, and the guru's activity is that of the dakas, dakinis, and dharmapalas.

From the point of view of the tradition of special instructions, all other sources of refuge are seen merely as the display of the guru. Ultimately, at this level, one goes for refuge to the guru alone. For this reason you find in the liturgies statements like, "The guru is the Buddha. The guru is the Dharma. In the same way the guru is the Sangha. The guru is the source of all." In guru yoga practices and guru sadhanas, in particular, you will find everything phrased in this way. For example, in the guru sadhana of Milarepa, you go for refuge to Milarepa. You generate the bodhichitta of wishing to attain the state of Milarepa, and so on.

From the point of view of special instructions, you and all other beings go for refuge to the guru. You think that you and all beings simultaneously take refuge in the guru. Your motivation for doing so is to bring yourself and all beings to the state of the guru, the state of Vajradhara, in this body and in this lifetime. This is the view of the vow of refuge found in the tradition of special instructions within anuttara yoga and particularly embodied in guru yoga tantras.

Another understanding of the vow of refuge found in the highest reaches of Vajrayana is expressed in the very secret teachings of ati yoga, in which the Buddha is the dharmakaya Samantabhadra. The Dharma is the 6,400,000 tantras of ati yoga. The Sangha is the awareness-holders, the dakas and dakinis.

The motivation for the vow of refuge is that one goes for refuge to establish oneself and all sentient beings without exception in the state of buddhahood in one instant of simultaneous hearing and realization. Although this form of going for refuge is most commonly associated with the Dzokchen tradition, it is not unique to it. We find this form in guru yoga practices, such as the Milarepa sadhana, in such formulations as "Grant your blessing that I attain full awakening at this very moment, on this very seat," and so on.

Each vehicle has a different way of understanding and meditating upon refuge. In the pratimoksha tradition, you do not visualize Buddha, Dharma, and Sangha in the sky in front of you. The reason for this is that a buddha is omniscient. A buddha has unobstructed and unlimited wisdom, so a buddha is aware of each and every being all the time. A buddha sees and hears everything. It is impossible that a buddha could fail to be aware of someone going for refuge or supplicating him. Therefore, from the point of view of the common vehicle, there is no need to visualize the Buddha in front of you because buddhas know exactly what beings are thinking and exactly what beings are saying. In whatever realm they may be, they are aware of us.

As it says in the aspiration prayer for rebirth in Dewachen by Karma Chakme, a buddha understands without mistake every single word spoken by every sentient being. From that point of view, because buddhas are omniscient, you do not need to visualize or summon them to get their attention. You already have it. Thus from the point of view of the common vehicle, taking refuge consists mainly of thinking about the meaning of and reciting the words of the refuge vow.

From the point of view of the Mahayana sutras, you could think of it in the same way. Because buddhas are omniscient, you do not need to visualize them or summon them. Ultimately there really is no need to attempt to get the attention of a buddha. However, in order to gather the accumulation of merit, when you are actually taking a Mahayana vow such as the vow of refuge or bodhisattva vow, you should engage in as much preparation as possible. It is traditional when taking the bodhisattva vow, which is when you also take the Mahayana vow of refuge, to carefully prepare the room in which the vow is going to be given, to set up extensive offerings, and, if possible, to spend an entire day before the vow in gathering the accumulations. Then, having consecrated the place and the offerings, you formally invite Buddha Shakyamuni, and by extension all other buddhas and bodhisattvas. In their presence you take the vow of refuge and the bodhisattva vow. At the conclusion of the ceremony you can either request the buddhas and bodhisattvas to depart or you can simply stop visualizing them.

In the three lower tantras—kriya tantra, charya tantra, and yoga tantra—you take refuge in the context of a yidam practice of those levels of tantra. You visualize in the sky in front of you the particular yidam surrounded by all the buddhas and bodhisattvas. Above the head of the yidam in front of you, you visualize your root guru, which in this context is the person from whom you received the empowerments, transmissions, and instructions for that yidam practice. You visualize the root guru in the form of the lord of the family of that particular yidam. In the presence of the guru and the yidam you take the vow of refuge. At the conclusion you either request the deities to depart or you simply stop visualizing them. In these lower tantras you do not dissolve the sources of refuge into yourself.

Taking the vow of refuge in the anuttara yoga tantra is similar to what is done in the lower tantras. You visualize the yidam, in this case the yidam of anuttara yoga, in the sky in front of you. Again, you visualize the root guru in the form of the lord of the family of that yidam above the yidam's head, surrounded by all buddhas and bodhisattvas and all the other deities of that yidam's mandala, gathered like clouds. In the presence of all these you go for refuge.

In the particular tradition connected with the anuttara yoga of Mahamudra, the visualization of the sources of refuge is slightly more extensive. It involves visualizing a lake in front of you, and from the center of this lake emerges the trunk of a wish-fulfilling tree that has five main branches. On the central branch you visualize your root guru, in the form of Vajradhara, as the principal figure surrounded by all of the lineage gurus. To his right you visualize Buddha Shakyamuni surrounded by all the other buddhas. To his left are all the bodhisattvas, the Mahayana Sangha. Behind the guru you visualize the Dharma in the form of texts. In front of the guru you visualize all the yidams of the four classes of tantra. Below them are the dakas, dakinis, and dharmapalas. This style of visualizing the sources of refuge that is used in the Mahamudra preliminary practices is very common and is found in other traditions and practices with slight variations.

For example, the practice of White Tara or the practice of Chenrezik in an extensive form is similar to this. Instead of visualizing the root guru as Vajradhara, you would visualize the root guru as Amitabha. In any of these visualizations of the sources of refuge you do not need to separately invite the wisdom deities, the actual beings. The reason for this is similar to the reason why, in the Hinayana context, there is no need for visualizing the Buddha: because when you bring a buddha to mind, you are actually in the presence of that buddha. Consequently there is no need to separately invite the wisdom deities. Recognizing this, but also visualizing them in front of you, you go for refuge with the confidence that you are in their presence.

Other traditions, such as Dzokchen, have visualizations of the sources of refuge that are basically the same as in Mahamudra. In some of them you do not visualize the wish-fulfilling tree, while in others you do. Aside from slight differences, it basically comes down to the same thing. For example, in some Dzokchen systems, instead of visualizing the root guru as Vajradhara, you would visualize him as Samantabhadra in form, but essentially it comes down to the same thing.

In any of these higher tantric visualizations of the sources of refuge, you dissolve the sources of refuge into yourself at the end of the session. Specifically they dissolve into your heart. Then, having mixed your mind with the minds of the sources of refuge, you look directly, simply, and straightforwardly at your own mind. When you look at your own mind, you will see that it has no substantial existence.

However, the mind is not merely an insubstantial nothing. It is awareness; it has an innate cognitive lucidity, which is why we call it mind. This innate characteristic, the cognitive lucidity of the mind, is the sambhogakaya.

In addition, this cognitive lucidity is not an invariable, single thing; it expresses itself or emerges in an unlimited variety of expressions or cognitions. That is the nirmanakaya.

The inseparability, or unity, of these three, which is the svabhavikakaya, or essence body, is the nature of your mind. The nature of your mind as it really is, is the Buddha, the embodiment of the four kayas. Discovering this within your mind is the ultimate way of going for refuge to the perfect buddha.

When we say "going for refuge to your mind," this does not mean you are going for refuge to your mind in the sense of the mind that thinks without control. You are going for refuge to the nature of your mind. In the same way, when you discover the emptiness that is your mind's nature, you discover the mother of all buddhas, Prajnaparamita, which is beyond description, beyond thought, and beyond imagination. Discovering this within your own mind is truly going for refuge to the Dharma.

Dharma has two aspects: the Dharma of tradition and the Dharma of realization. The Dharma of tradition exists in order to enable people to develop realization. The discovery of this nature within your own mind is truly going for refuge to the Dharma because it means gaining access to the Dharma of realization. In the same way, when you discover the Buddha and the Dharma within your own mind, you become a full-fledged member of the Sangha. In the Mahayana, a true member of the Sangha is a bodhisattva because he or she has realized the nature of things. In a similar way, when you recognize the nature of your mind, you become a member of the Sangha. This is going for refuge to the Sangha in the ultimate or fullest way. That is why in the tantras it says, "Your mind is the supreme source of refuge."

This does not mean that your confused thoughts and your kleshas are sources of refuge. They are sources of samsara, and they have been so from beginningless time. But the nature of your mind, which is the source of all realization, is the true source of refuge. By recognizing this nature you attain buddhahood. This is why it says in the liturgies, "I go for refuge to the ultimate nature and goodness," which refers to the essential emptiness, characteristic lucidity, and unimpeded expression of the mind itself. This is the ultimate or absolute vow of refuge.

The chapter concludes with the colophon "This little song of going for refuge arose in my mind on the evening of the third day of the twelfth month in the Year of the Horse, and was written down by Tsondru Gyamtso."

Questions and Answers

STUDENT: Would you please tell us how we can do our prostrations with quality? I have a hard time with that. When I do them slowly, I seem to be able to concentrate more on the visualization and whole-heartedly try to prostrate. Then there is another side of me thinking about the 111,111 prostrations. I do not want to be too slow by only doing thirty a day, but once I speed up, I tend to lose the quality side of it. Is there a balance to it?

RINPOCHE: With any practice it is important to be as profoundly involved as possible. In a sense this means a certain type of one-pointed concentration. In the case of a practice like prostrations, one-pointedness is not the same as what it is in the practice of tranquillity, or shinay. In the practice of prostrations, one-pointedness essentially consists of maintaining the confidence that the sources of refuge are actually present and maintaining the motivation or intention with which you are prostrating, paying homage with body, speech, and mind in order to bring about the liberation of all beings. What needs to be maintained as much as possible throughout is the confidence of the presence, of the sources of refuge, and the motivation for which you are doing the practice.

The existence of the set numbers, required numbers, of these practices is to inspire diligence. Having a goal in terms of number enables you to practice more. Nevertheless as you indicated in your question, if you become too concerned with the number alone and you allow your mind to wander too much during the practice, forcing yourself to do a great deal of it but letting your mind wander, the problem is that even though you may complete the requisite number, you may regret the way you did the practice and you may think that you did the hundred thousand but you do not really know if you did them properly or not. In order to maintain balance between one-pointedness and diligence of the numbers, try to maintain your motivation for doing the practice throughout the session. By doing so, even if you only do fifty prostrations in a day, because your motivation for all fifty will have been bodhichitta, you will feel satisfied with your practice.

What is especially important is the type of diligence that is called "the diligence in continuous application," which means that day after day, year after year, you keep practicing. You never allow your practice to degenerate or diminish. For example, whatever amount of prostrations you begin with, you may increase it, but you never allow yourself to do less than that. That type of practice is the most effective. Although the length of our lives is uncertain, nevertheless if you keep on practicing in that way, you will come to the end of it. When you do so, you do not need to regret how you performed the practice.

STUDENT: My hours here are my first steps in learning the way of Buddha, Dharma, and Sangha. I do not yet recognize the kind of state of unconditional commitment that I feel is required in order to take refuge. What task might you appoint me in order to prepare to undertake that?

RINPOCHE: As you say, you cannot be expected to have an unconditional commitment to something with which you are unfamiliar; it is best to allow your commitment to grow gradually. It will grow if you expose yourself impartially to experiences and sources of learning that will inspire it. We cannot see all of the six realms of samsara, but we can see part of the human and animal realm. If you observe the life of people and animals, you will see the truth of Dharma because you can see how much everyone is suffering and how what happens to us is beyond our control. We do not choose to be born and we certainly do not choose to die. As you become more and more familiar with the suffering, the anxiety, and the lack of freedom of beings, you will become more confident that the Buddha, Dharma, and Sangha are authentic sources of refuge.

We do many things throughout our lives. We spend the early part of our lives trying to learn to do the things that we spend the rest of our lives doing, and then we die. That is basically the history of human life in brief. You learn how to do things, hoping that they will make you happy. You do them and they do not make you happy. You are never done, and then you die. No matter how much you achieve, you never achieve success because there is always more. Whether you die rich or poor, whether you die young or old, you did not finish. Nobody ever finishes. We can never prevent death. At best, we can delay it for a very short amount of time. Looking around at what is going on will gradually give you confidence. You can also study Dharma books, such as *The Jewel Ornament of Liberation*, and *The Life of Milarepa*. Your trust will grow.

Every one possesses the seed of full awakening. This basic nature, this potential, is the source of all goodness. The problem that we face is that we have never recognized our basic nature for what it is. We have never taken full advantage of it. Having become aware of it, if you start to develop it, then all qualities will increase and you will definitely attain awakening. This increase of qualities is something that you can directly experience within yourself.

Buddha, as our primary source of refuge, refers to a being who became awakened. All buddhas started out as sentient beings. The difference between sentient beings and buddhas is that buddhas recognized their true nature and made use of it in such a way that they were able to eliminate all defects and maximize all qualities. We have the same basic nature as any buddha. If we go through the same process, we will definitely achieve the same results. For example, the flowers on the table in front of me are extremely beautiful, but there was a time when those flowers were not beautiful nor were they even flowers. They were just seeds. Normally we would say that a seed and a flower are two very different things. But the only way that you can ever get a flower is by planting a seed because the seed has within it the innate potential to become that flower with all of its color and beauty. In the same way, every one of us has the innate potential of becoming Buddha, of becoming fully awakened. The difference between a sentient being and a buddha is no greater than the difference between a seed and a flower. Although they seem different, if they are cultivated correctly, the transformation from seed to flower or from sentient being to buddha will definitely occur.

STUDENT: In the ngondro liturgy for refuge and prostrations, just preceding the repetition of the refuge prayer there is a prayer that basically says, "I take refuge in the essence of the embodiment of the body, speech, mind, qualities, and activities of all the buddhas, etc." Until this weekend I never realized that qualities and activities might actually be something different. I was reading it as mind qualities and activities, as in qualities of the mind and activities of the mind. Could you explain the meaning of taking refuge in qualities and activities or help clarify this for me?

RINPOCHE: That section of the refuge is actually a long introduction to the refuge vow and is not repeated. It basically makes the point that the root guru, together with the lineage gurus, is the all-inclusive source of refuge. It says "the essence of the body, speech, mind, qualities, and activity of all the tathagatas of all times and places is the source of all the eighty-four thousand heaps of the genuine Dharma and the embodiment of the arya sangha." All of those things refer to the guru. The point of saying body, speech, mind, qualities, and activity of all buddhas means not only the embodiment of all buddhas, but also the embodiment of every single quality of all buddhas. The idea here with this list of five things is simply to be all-inclusive. The point of this is that the guru is the embodiment of all sources of refuge. To understand this, however, and to understand what we mean by a guru or lama, especially in the Mahamudra context, you must understand that the guru is not simply the person that you have met, the person with whom you could hold a conversation. The guru is much, much more than that. In the Mahamudra tradition the guru is considered to be Vajradhara. That is why when we do ngondro practice, we visualize our root guru as Vajradhara.

Vajradhara is the dharmakaya. Vajradhara is the source of the lineage and the source of all qualities. The guru is the person from whom we receive this lineage, the person from whom we receive what began with Vajradhara. So the qualities of which Vajradhara is the source are received by us from our root guru. This is why we represent the root guru as and consider the root guru to be Vajradhara. If you were to visualize your root guru as an ordinary person, as you physically perceive him or her, you would start to project a feeling of impurity and imperfection onto that image and might think that your guru is not that different from yourself. You would naturally start to have less faith. Whether or not the guru has defects, you will perceive them as long as your feeling of the guru is limited to that flesh-and-blood body that you can see with your eyes.

The dharmakaya, which is the source and nature of all qualities, is without defect. Vajradhara has no defects whatsoever. When we take refuge, we visualize two Vajradharas. The one at the beginning of the lineage is the actual Vajradhara. Then we visualize our root guru also as Vajradhara because just as Vajradhara is the source of the lineage, our root guru is our source of the lineage and therefore has the same function for us and is of the same kindness to us as Vajradhara himself.

The Generation of Bodhichitta, Which Is the Great Path of Awakening

The reason bodhichitta is referred to as the great path of awakening is that once bodhichitta has been generated, it is certain that the individual who has generated it will at some point attain buddhahood. It is also certain that without the generation of bodhichitta, buddhahood cannot be attained. Bodhichitta is actually the substance of the path to awakening, and for this reason it is called the great path.

The chapter begins with the invocation NAMO GURU BUDDHA BODHISATTVA YE, "Homage to the gurus, buddhas, and bodhisattvas." Karma Chakme then tells his disciple who requested this teaching, "Lama Tsondru Gyamtso, listen without distraction." If you really wish to practice the genuine Dharma, then you must engage in this great path. It is the path that has been traveled by all buddhas of the past, it is the path of all buddhas of the present, and it is the great path on which all buddhas of the future will travel. In short, all who have attained the perfect awakening of buddhahood have done so only through the generation of bodhichitta of the Mahayana. The generation of bodhichitta is the moment at which the practice of awakening or buddhahood begins. All buddhas of the past, all buddhas of the present, and all buddhas of the future, who all began as ordinary individuals like ourselves, began the process of awakening through their initial generation of bodhichitta. Therefore if we generate bodhichitta, we begin the same process of the same awakening.

Bodhichitta is generated through the taking of the bodhisattva vow. There exist two traditions of the bodhisattva vow. These are commonly known as the tradition of Nagarjuna and the tradition of Asanga. These two teachers are therefore called the two chariots of bodhichitta. The bodhisattva vow of Asanga was transmitted by Buddha Shakyamuni to the bodhisattva Maitreya, who passed it on to Asanga. This tradition of the bodhisattva vow is called the tradition of extensive deeds. The other one, the tradition of Nagarjuna, was received from the bodhisattva Manjushri, who received it from the Buddha, and is called the tradition of the profound view.

The *tradition of extensive deeds* depends upon a great deal of preparation. The view in this tradition is that the generation of bodhichitta is such a momentous event that it is like inviting a universal emperor or monarch into your home. The home in this case is the person, and the monarch is bodhichitta. If you were to invite a universal monarch into your home, you would probably renovate it first so that it would be as beautiful as you could make it. You would certainly clean it, decorate it as much as possible, and set up a very beautiful throne. You would not invite a universal monarch without making such preparations, and even if you did, he or she would probably not show up. From the point of view of the tradition of extensive deeds, the tradition of Maitreya and Asanga, you can only generate bodhichitta if you have prepared yourself in that way.

According to this tradition, bodhichitta will not arise in anyone's mind without preparation. Therefore in order to take the bodhisattva vow in this tradition, you must have received and be maintaining one of the several varieties of pratimoksha vows, or vows of individual liberation. You also need to have previously studied the Mahayana teachings, the Mahayana Tripitaka, so that you understand fully the implications and significance of what you are doing. Also, when this tradition of the bodhisattva vow is given, extensive preparation, such as very elaborate offerings and other procedures for gathering the accumulation of merit, must be performed. In addition, the ceremony of the bodhisattva vow itself is very elaborate and quite long.

The other tradition of the bodhisattva vow, which is the one that is more commonly observed, is the *tradition of the profound view*. In this tradition, the view of bodhichitta is that it is so wonderful that it is like a seed that will survive in any soil. For that reason it is thought that anyone who sincerely wishes to generate it and can actually participate in the ceremony and repeat the words of the vow after the preceptor will generate bodhichitta. This tradition of the profound view is much more easily and much more widely given.

Ideally, in both cases the vow must be received from a guru who holds and maintains a lineage of the bodhisattva vow, whichever lineage is being passed down. In extreme cases, when it is utterly impossible to encounter a teacher, if someone wishes to generate bodhichitta and they know how to conduct the ceremony, it can be done in the presence of the three supports: stupas as supports of the Buddha's mind, texts that are a symbol of the Dharma, and statues that are images of the Buddha. In cases where teachers and the three supports are unavailable, it can be done in the presence of the visualized sources of refuge. In that case you would visualize the Three Jewels present in the sky in front of you and repeat the vow in their presence.

However it is taken, simply taking the bodhisattva vow once is not enough. This is because you need to protect the bodhichitta from impairment and you also need to cause it to grow in order for it to actually become a continuing cause of awakening. Therefore, so that the vow does not deteriorate and so that the bodhichitta you have generated increases, it is repeated every day. Having once taken the bodhisattva vow, you take it on your own every day thereafter.

One reason for this is that, given the commitments of the bodhisattva vow, it is impossible that ordinary people such as ourselves will not violate it. We are always engaging in slight violations of the bodhisattva vow. All of these minor infractions are repaired through taking the vow every day, and that is one reason why it needs to be done. Bodhichitta is like the crops grown in the northern continent of Uttarakuru. It is said that when you harvest the crops there, they immediately regrow on the spot. Bodhichitta is like that. Although we impair it through minor violations all the time, we can restore it by taking the vow again every day. It is immediately restored.

The reason these two different traditions of the bodhisattva vow exist is that, as is often said, the Buddha was extremely skillful in how he taught. His teaching was always responsive to the actual needs and dispositions of those to whom it was given. There are people who are inspired by very elaborate ceremonies and who regard a simple or relatively informal ceremony of bodhichitta as not enough of a big deal. They would not feel confident in it. There are other people who are much more inspired by a concise form of bodhichitta generation. Because people actually do have these different dispositions, these two traditions exist.

The value of bodhichitta is immeasurable. It is like the legendary elixir that transforms base metals into gold. Such an elixir, by just touching iron or lead, would immediately transform a mass of that metal into pure gold. Bodhichitta is actually like that because in an instant, when it is generated, it transforms an ordinary person into a bodhisattva. As soon as you generate bodhichitta, regardless of who and what you are, you become a member of the family of bodhisattvas. Becoming a member of the family of bodhisattvas means being born into the family of all tathagatas, all buddhas. This means that once you have generated bodhichitta and become a child of the buddhas, it is certain that you will at some point attain buddhahood. Therefore your virtue, regardless of how ordinary or how confused you are, actually eclipses the virtue of Shravakas and Pratyekabuddha arhats because of the power of bodhichitta.

This may seem contradictory, but in fact it is like the situation of a prince or princess born into a royal family. Immediately upon birth that child is a member of the royal family. At the time of their birth they know nothing, they have no power, and they have no authority they can wield. However, they have the potential of all of these things and that is why all the ministers and commoners in the court pay homage to them. Although they are babies, they are still princes or princesses and will eventually be monarchs. In the same way, when you generate bodhichitta, you become genuinely worthy of the veneration of beings of the entire world, including gods or devas. You can withstand and you can digest that veneration. You will not choke on it.

Often when we are treated with respect or veneration, especially in a spiritual situation, we are obscured by this respect and veneration. This is called "the obscuration of spiritual acquisition." For example, when someone asks you to say prayers for them, if you can actually benefit that person, then the offerings you receive will not harm you. If you do not perform the prayers or if you are incapable of bringing the benefit that the person making the offering intends, you become obscured. You accumulate some negativity. It is like misappropriation or a sort of involuntary embezzlement. This does not happen if you have bodhichitta. Even if you are venerated by the gods, the most powerful ordinary beings in the universe, because you have generated the intention to establish every being without exception, including those gods, in a state of full and perfect buddhahood, because your intention is utterly altruistic and noble and unlimited, you are worthy of that veneration and it will not harm you.

Bodhichitta is the aspiration, the wish, and the intention to attain full awakening in order to liberate others—that is how it has been explained by the Victor Maitreya. It has two aspects: the aspiration, which we call aspiration bodhichitta, and the implementation of that aspiration.

Aspiration bodhichitta is the wish to attain buddhahood for the benefit of others. In that sense it is like a hope, a wish, a goal. *Implementation bodhichitta* is the actual accomplishment of that wish generated by going through the process of accomplishing, or bringing about your own buddhahood.

Practically speaking, implementation bodhichitta consists of practicing the six perfections, or paramitas. In order to be called paramitas, they must be motivated by bodhichitta. If we use generosity as an example, when you perform an act of generosity, your intention for doing so must be that you wish to realize full awakening so that you can liberate all beings. Your motivation must be bodhichitta. If your motivation is merely the accumulation of merit for your own benefit, then it is not the perfection of generosity. While you are engaging in the act of generosity, you must not lose sight of this motivation. Afterward the virtue of the action needs to be dedicated to the awakening of all beings. If the beginning, middle, and end of the six virtuous actions (generosity, discipline, patience, joyful effort, meditation, and wisdom) are embraced by bodhichitta, then they become the six perfections (paramitas) and are the practice of implementation bodhichitta.

In the tradition of Nagarjuna, the way that we both initially take the bodhisattva vow and renew the vow on a daily basis is from *The Bodhicharyavatara*. It is found in the collected group chants of the

Karma Kagyu, called *The Clear Daily Practice*, and is also found in the preliminary practices of ngondro. It combines the Mahayana refuge and the generation of both aspiration and implementation bodhichitta into twelve lines. It says, "Until I reach the essence of awakening, I take refuge in the buddhas, and in the same way in the Dharma and in the assembly of bodhisattvas. Just as all buddhas of the past have done, I generate the intention to attain supreme awakening for the benefit of all beings." The first part is the Mahayana refuge and the second part is the generation of aspiration bodhichitta. Then it says, "And just as they have gone through all the stages of the training of a bodhisattva, in the same way I will go through all of those stages." In this way you make the second commitment of the Mahayana refuge, which is the commitment of implementation bodhichitta. The bodhisattva vow according to the tradition of Manjushri and Nagarjuna is included in this short liturgy of twelve lines.

The commitments of the bodhisattva vow have been explained in many different ways. They can be expanded upon almost endlessly and can be summarized in various ways. Here we follow an actual summary that was given by the Buddha himself in the sutra that is called *The Sutra Taught to the King*.

The first commitment of the bodhisattva vow is to rejoice in all of the virtue done by others, including bodhisattvas, arhats, and ordinary beings. One reason for this is that when you rejoice in an action of someone else, you become deeply affected by that action. If it is a negative action, by rejoicing in that action you acquire much the same negative karma as if you had engaged in the action yourself. By the same token, if it is a virtuous action and you sincerely rejoice in it, you accumulate the same merit as the person who actually engaged in that action.

Simply rejoicing in the virtue of others is not enough. You need to engage in virtuous actions yourself. The second commitment of the bodhisattva vow is to dedicate all of your virtue, whatever virtuous actions you engage in, to your own attainment of buddhahood as quickly as possible so that you can establish all beings in a state of buddhahood. According to Buddha Shakyamuni, these two—continually making the aspiration that dedicates all of your virtue to your attainment of buddhahood in order to bring all beings to a state of complete awakening, together with rejoicing in the virtue of others— include all of the commitments of the bodhisattva vow.

There are three types of aspiration bodhichitta. The first type of bodhichitta is called *monarchical bodhichitta*. A monarch first protects himself. By doing this, he secures his power and is able to effectively protect his subjects. The aspiration to attain buddhahood yourself so that you can thereafter bring all beings to that state is the way a monarch thinks.

The second type of aspiration bodhichitta is called *the bodhichitta of a captain of a ship*. The captain of a ship reaches his destination at the same time as his passengers. This type of bodhichitta thinks, "May I and all beings attain buddhahood simultaneously." This is slightly more altruistic and therefore considered slightly superior to monarchical bodhichitta.

The third type of bodhichitta is *shepherdlike bodhichitta*. The shepherd guides the flock to its place to graze, making sure that the animals are protected and have grass to eat. Only then does the shepherd eat. At night he brings the animals back to where they sleep. He is the last one home. The shepherd always takes care of the animals first. Someone who generates shepherdlike bodhichitta, which is considered supreme, thinks, "May I bring all beings to a state of buddhahood and only thereafter attain it myself." To generate any one of these three types of bodhichitta as the dedication of your virtue is the second commitment, which goes along with rejoicing in the virtue of others.

The specific training in implementation bodhichitta is the practice of the six perfections, which you need to practice in accordance with your own ability. There are aspects or forms of the six perfections that we cannot presently engage in. The point is to do our best. Aspiration and implementation bodhichitta together comprise what is called relative bodhichitta.

The second aspect of bodhichitta is absolute, or ultimate, bodhichitta. In the writings of great scholars and mahasiddhas there is some dispute over whether absolute bodhichitta can be generated by ritual. In essence all concur that you generate absolute bodhichitta when you directly realize the correct view of emptiness. The realization of emptiness is equivalent to the generation or realization of absolute, or ultimate, bodhichitta.

The main practice of bodhichitta is the practice of taking and sending, or tonglen. It is through this practice that bodhichitta can be most effectively furthered. In *The Bodhicharyavatara* it says, "As long as you do not completely exchange your own happiness for the sufferings of others, not only is there no way for you ever to attain buddhahood but you will never even experience happiness within samsara." The aspiration to exchange your happiness for the sufferings of others is the essence of taking and sending. It is the only way to attain buddhahood, and it is the only way to attain any kind of happiness, because altruism is the cause of happiness, and selfishness is the cause of suffering.

However, the actual exchange of one's own happiness for the suffering of others, actually taking on the suffering of others, is in most cases impossible. It is also inadvisable for individuals who have not attained at least the first bhumi. When you attain the first bhumi or first bodhisattva level, you can easily remove at least some of the sufferings of others through the creation of emanations and so on. Until then it is inadvisable to attempt to actually, or physically, exchange your happiness for the sufferings of others. The reason is that this can become more of an impediment to your progress than a benefit to the other person.

In one of his previous lifetimes, Shariputra, the disciple of the Buddha, was practicing as a bodhisattva, which is to say that although he had generated bodhichitta, he had not yet attained the first bhumi. In order to obstruct his attainment, Mara came to Shariputra in the form of a Brahmin and said, "I have need of someone's right hand." Because Shariputra had such great compassion and was trying so intensely to practice the Mahayana path, he thought, "Well, I'll give him what he wants." So he said to this Brahmin, "Okay, you can have mine, just cut it off." The Brahmin said, "I am not allowed to actually cut you. I am a Brahmin. So I need you to cut it off yourself"" Shariputra put a razor in his left hand and cut off his right hand and with his left hand gave what was formerly his right hand to this Brahmin. The Brahmin said, "This is disgusting. I cannot accept something handed to me with someone's left hand. I can only accept things from someone's right hand. You cannot hand me your right hand with your left hand. It is no good." He took Shariputra's severed right hand and threw it in Shariputra's face. Of course Mara was just trying to be difficult and to make it impossible for Shariputra to do something virtuous, and he succeeded. He discouraged him so much that in that lifetime Shariputra entirely gave up the Mahayana path. He thought, "Well, if I cannot help even one being without becoming discouraged, what point is there in my aspiring to liberate all beings?"

The point of the story is that as long as we have not attained at least the first bhumi, which comes with the direct realization of the selflessness of all phenomena, our fixation on our own existence and our own welfare is simply too strong. It does not permit us to engage in this type of altruistic conduct without the considerable danger of our becoming resentful or regretting what we have done or even developing intense antipathy toward the path. This is a serious problem. Once you have become realized, you can do whatever you want in order to benefit others. Until that happens, you cannot practically engage in this sort of bodhisattva conduct.

As ordinary individuals, rather than attempting to physically exchange our happiness for the suffering of others, we need to do so through visualization practice. Developing the intention is effective because all things rest on one's intention. By developing the intention to exchange yourself for others, you gain much of the benefit of actually doing it. This is true with both virtuous and unvirtuous states of mind. For example, suppose I generate the thought "I would like to kill every single sentient being. I would just like to murder them all." Of course I cannot do that, but generating that thought is still negative because it is going to move me in that direction and it will cause me to be reborn in lower states. In the same way, even though you cannot actually remove the suffering of each and every sentient being, generating the aspiration to do so is very powerful.

In accordance with this, in order to practice taking and sending, we use the breath. We coordinate the visualization of exchanging ourselves for others with our breathing. When you breathe out, you think that all of your happiness and all of your merit, in short all the causes of happiness and all the happiness that results from the causes of happiness, leaves you and dissolves into each and every sentient being. The cause of happiness is virtue and the result of virtue is happiness. What you are thinking, what you are imagining and aspiring to when you do this, is that you wish every being achieve both the cause of happiness and the result of happiness.

This aspiration that all beings possess the causes of happiness and happiness itself is what is called *maitri*, or love, in the Buddhist tradition. When this aspiration is unlimited, when it is directed equally and impartially to all beings without exception, it is called *boundless or immeasurable love*. If you meditate on that, if you cultivate that kind of love continually, you become impervious to the aggression of others, the harm of fire, water, weapons, and poison. You naturally attract other beings because you are so loving. You attract human beings, gods, and spirits. Of course the final result of this kind of immeasurable love is that you will attain buddhahood, but the immediate result is that you will be reborn as some kind of god, such as Brahma, the king of gods. This does not mean that you will become some kind of cosmic tyrant. It means that you will be reborn with an altruistic mind as a practicing bodhisattva, in a very powerful position where you can help.

This kind of love is the best armor you can wear, because as long as you have it, you are impervious to the attacks of Mara. Simply because you are free of selfishness, you are concerned with others. Therefore the weapons of Mara cannot touch you, in the same way that an empty sky is impervious to any kind of weapon. No matter how many arrows you shoot at the sky, you can never really pierce it, because there is nothing there to be pierced.

We see this in the story of Milarepa. In the first section of *The Songs of Milarepa*, it says that he entered his cave and found it to be full of demons. He tried to banish the demons by visualizing himself as a deity and reciting mantras. But this had no effect; they fed on the power of his mediation and became even worse. When he generated a truly altruistic love and compassion for those demons, he actually swallowed them up. He swallowed up their aggression, and they had to leave. In the same way, this attitude of love is the best way of protecting yourself from all harm.

The other aspect of taking and sending is what you do when you breathe in. When you breathe in, think that all of the wrongdoings and all of the obscurations of all beings, which are the causes of suffering, and all of the suffering that afflicts all beings, which is the result of wrongdoing and obscurations, all this is pulled out of them and dissolves into you. You think that the result is that all beings are forever free from the causes of suffering, which are wrongdoings and obscurations, and that they are also free from the results of wrongdoings and obscurations, which is suffering itself. This aspiration that all beings be free from suffering and its causes is immeasurable or boundless compassion.

This compassion that is impartial, boundless, and unlimited is the beginning of and the real cause of your attainment of buddhahood. It is the seed that will grow into buddhahood. After that, as you pursue the path, this state of mind of compassion is the condition that will lead you to the attainment of buddhahood. Not only is it the seed you are cultivating, it is also the act of farming the seed, because it provides the water, the manure, the sunlight, and all the conditions that cause that seed to grow.

When you attain buddhahood, compassion is the gate through which you benefit beings. It is the cause of all the activities for the benefit of others in which a buddha engages, just like the crops that grow from seeds through the application of nurturing conditions. Therefore buddhahood is born from compassion.

Shravaka and Pratyekabuddha arhats are called "the children of the Buddha's speech," because their attainment is born from the Buddha's teachings. Bodhisattvas are called "the children of the Buddha's mind." All buddhas are called "the children of the bodhisattvas," because buddhas are born from bodhichitta. A buddha becomes a buddha through the full ripening of bodhichitta, the altruistic wish to bring all beings to buddhahood. That is the cause of buddhahood. All bodhichitta, as well as the bodhisattvas that maintain and generate bodhichitta, are born from compassion. Buddhahood comes from bodhichitta, and bodhichitta comes from compassion.

Therefore, as it says in *The Madhyamakavatara*, "Compassion is the root of all Buddhadharma. It is the root of all Dharma and the root of all of the qualities of a buddha."

Compassion is like the golden wheel that is held in the hand of a chakravartin. A chakravartin is a universal monarch, and as the name implies, a chakravartin holds a wheel, or chakra, that distinguishes him. It is his emblem. It has the magical property of summoning all his wealth and splendor. Anyone who holds that golden wheel in his hand is immediately surrounded by all the splendor, wealth, authority, and luxury of a chakravartin. In the same way, any person, regardless of his social status, culture, ethnicity, gender, or age, who has great compassion, will possess all of the qualities, all of the dharmas of a buddha. This has been explained in the sutras.

The difference between a person who has bodhichitta and a person who does not have bodhichitta is great. Although they appear to be the same, the person who has bodhichitta is substantially different. If you throw a small ball of iron into water, it will sink to the bottom. In the same way, someone who does not possess bodhichitta, with even a little bit of wrongdoing will be cast into a lower rebirth. On the other hand, consider a ship, which is also made of iron. It has much more iron than the little iron ball, but it will not sink. It will stay afloat on top of the water. In the same way, someone who possesses bodhichitta as their motivation will not be reborn in lower states. Even if he or she appears to have accumulated a great deal of wrongdoing, this will not cause the person's downfall. This is because if bodhichitta is the motivation, not only neutral actions but also most of the actions that would be considered negative will be transformed into virtuous actions. This refers to the fact that sometimes a person with bodhichitta will act for the benefit of others in a way that seems rough or unkind. If their motivation is genuinely altruistic and if it is done for the benefit of others, they will not be coarsened, afflicted, or obscured by the roughness of their actions.

This is the essential key to the practice of Vajrayana. All of the accoutrements and all of the techniques in Vajrayana practice, the practices of union and liberation, all the manipulation of phenomena, and so on, are very powerfully virtuous and very conducive to awakening, provided they are motivated by bodhichitta. The key to Vajrayana being a tool for awakening is the motivation of bodhichitta. Therefore bodhichitta is the root of all secret mantra, the root of all Vajrayana. Thus, Chakme Rinpoche writes, "Tsondru Gyamtso, keep this in your mind."

This is extremely important because if Vajrayana is practiced without bodhichitta as a motivation, it is not going to lead to awakening. All of the elaborate and powerful Vajrayana practices, such as the sadhanas of Chakrasamvara, Hevajra, and Guhyasamaja in the New Translation tradition, or the sadhanas *The Eight Dispensations, The Collected Thoughts of the Guru*, and Vajrakilaya, in the Old Translation tradition — all of these powerful and famous practices of secret mantra, if practiced without bodhichitta, will only succeed in turning you into some kind of little sorcerer. This is because you empower yourself through these practices; you become a kind of powerful and charismatic person, but your motivation is incorrect.

Therefore at this point the text says, "All tantrikas of the future, if you do not understand this, even though you spend your whole life doing sadhana practice, forget about attaining buddhahood in one lifetime. This will not even lead you in the direction of awakening." Any kind of Vajrayana practice that is not motivated by bodhichitta is like a very sophisticated technological implement in the hands of someone who does not know what to do with it. This is because if you do not have bodhichitta, you do not understand the very basis of tantra. It would be like putting me in the cockpit of the most sophisticated airplane ever developed. I can assure you there will be problems. There is nothing wrong with the airplane. It is wonderful. It works. It can do anything you want. But I do not know how to fly it. If you let me fly that plane and I take off, I am going to hit the ground at a time and place other than that intended. Vajrayana is like that. There is nothing wrong with the techniques of Vajrayana. They are effective, they are profound, but the skill of using them rests upon the presence of bodhichitta.

In the same way, if you engage in all kinds of austerities for the purpose of spiritual attainment, keeping flawless moral discipline and vows and keeping all the samayas you accumulate, if you lack bodhichitta, none of this will further you on the path to awakening.

At the very best, you might attain the state of a Shravaka or Pratye-kabuddha. As long as you do not possess bodhichitta, even if through shamatha practice you acquire ESP, this is not going to help you attain buddhahood. You would just become some kind of saddhu in the marketplace who impresses others with his power. You might acquire the title of rishi, but it is not going to lead you to buddha-hood. Even if you succeed in assembling a large number of disciples, that is not going to help you attain buddhahood. You would just become like the bhikshu Mahadeva, who caused the division of the sangha two thousand years ago. Even if you were to succeed in attaining the eight great mundane siddhis, this is not going to lead you to awakening. You are just like a common mundane magician who can manipulate phenomena. Therefore Lingje Repa said, "The attainment of the eight great mundane siddhis is amazing, but it is not very useful in the attainment of awakening."

We have seen that if you possess bodhichitta as your motivation, any path you undertake, whether it is the path of the sutras or the path of the tantras, will be effective. If you do not possess bodhichit-ta, because the very essence of the path is not present, any path you undertake will be ineffective. This is the reason there seem to be so few people attaining enlightenment or becoming siddhas nowadays.

When we think of the history of the Buddhadharma, and of Vajrayana in particular, we can think of innumerable siddhas in India and also in Tibet. Nowadays there seem to be comparatively few, which may lead us to the mistaken conclusion that Dharma has somehow become stale or ineffective and that it does not work any-more. This is not the case. All of the teachings that were in India and were transmitted to Tibet are upheld and available today. His Holiness the Dalai Lama is the upholder of all the traditions of Buddhadharma that were carried to Tibet. His Holiness the Gyalwa Karmapa is the holder of the Kagyu lineage and tradition. His Holiness Minling Trichen Rinpoche is the head and upholder of the Nyingma tradition, and their Holinesses Sakya Trizin and Sakya Dakchen are the holders of the Sakya tradition. Each of them main-tains all of the traditions for which they are responsible, ensuring that the transmission remains unbroken.

Questions and Answers

STUDENT: There are times where I meet people or am in situations where I feel like I want to help people, but because of my capabilities, I think I am very limited. Sometimes I think I do not have enough compassion or bodhichitta because I did not extend myself enough. There are times when I feel as though I have helped up to a point, but beyond that you cannot do much. It is almost like your giving up on the person. You feel like you are supposed to keep helping them but you are also, at the same time, feeling that you cannot do it any more. Part of you feels like maybe you do not have enough compassion or bodhichitta for his person. What do you do in cases like this?

RINPOCHE: Sometimes you have to be very sure that you know what kind of effect an effort to help someone is going to have before you decide whether or not to do it. If you are unsure exactly how much help the person needs, you may be better off not helping them. Sometimes people do not want to be helped and they just get angry, so you may do more harm than good. Once, when we were in New York City, we saw a woman attempting to bring her shopping home. She had so many bags that she was dragging them, not even carrying them. Bardor Rinpoche went up to her and attempted to pick up some of her bags and help her. She became furious and said, "I can take care of it. I can carry it. I do not need any help." And yet she was dragging them along the ground because she could not pick them up. In the same way, sometimes it happens that people do not need help or they do not think they need help and they do not want it.

STUDENT: There are also cases where people do ask for help and you are helping them and it gets to a point where the help you give them results in their not trying to help themselves. They might even go to different teachers and ask them the same questions repeatedly. The person might be given the same answer from all the teachers, but the person still does not really follow what they are advised. Sometimes I feel like they are still trying to hold on and ask for help.

RINPOCHE: You have to let people like that be. You can pray for them. You have to have the aspiration that they be able to get it together and that they be able to benefit themselves and others and practice Dharma properly, but there is not much you can actually do to help them.

STUDENT: I had a situation during the summer where I was working for my father and we had someone there, a tradesman, who was giving me a very hard time because he felt that I was just given things by my father and that it was very easy for me. He was extremely rude and insulting and it made me very angry. I specifically tried not to insult him, but I eventually had to say to him, "Look, either stop it or leave." He got very upset. As it happens, my father showed up at that time, so the incident did not go any farther. I almost felt that it was at the point where it was going to become a physical confrontation, and that it almost had to become that because I couldn't just let him insult me, walk all over me, and so on, for various reasons, both on a personal level and in terms of the other people there. I felt extremely frustrated. It still bothers me a lot when I think about it. It is still very disturbing. I do not really know what to do. I could not just leave and it was a very difficult situation.

RINPOCHE: The job you get is largely a function of your merit as an individual accumulated in previous lives. Whether the circumstance of your acquiring a position is your right by birth or your training and qualifications is ultimately irrelevant. When someone says the sorts of things that that person was apparently saying to you, usually they are motivated by jealousy. Someone who is that jealous and that aggressive is probably coming out of a long series of rebirths in lower realms, and is possibly headed for another long series. Certainly, at this point, they are profoundly unhappy, otherwise they would not be occupying their mind in that way. When you reflect upon the fact that the person is certainly more unhappy than you are, it will make you feel less angry, you will feel more compassion for him, and you will be inspired to pray for his welfare. When people abuse you verbally, you have to allow what they say to go in one ear and out the other and not assume that just because someone says something, that it is necessarily true.

Also, this happened in the past. No doubt, when this person said these things to you, you felt hurt and depressed. The words that they said to you, however, are gone. They no longer exist. Words leave no physical trace. All they leave is an imprint in our memory, and what maintains that imprint is your fixation on the feelings you had when those words were said. If you let go of that fixation, there will be nothing left of it.

The Cooling Shade: Placing Others Under the Protection of the Three Jewels

The next chapter of this text is called simply "The Cooling Shade." It describes how to place others under the protection or the refuge of the Three Jewels. It begins with the invocation NAMO RATNA TRAYA YA, which means "Homage to the Three Jewels."

The topic is introduced using the image of a parasol that shades one from the burning rays of the sun, with the parasol representing the compassion of the Three Jewels. The top part that sticks up like in an umbrella is here an ornamental, golden peak, representing the precious and abundant qualities of the Buddha, Dharma, and Sangha. Below that peak is the actual silken fabric of the parasol itself, which is like divine silk, because it has the power to protect all beings. This power comes from compassion combined with the aspiration made by the Buddha, Dharma, and Sangha.

This parasol of the protection of the Three Jewels is something that you hold over others' heads to protect them from the burning rays of the sun. You hold up this parasol by the golden handle of devotion, allowing it to shade others and protect them from the heat of samsara. The methods that are described in this chapter can be used to protect or to pray for either the living or the deceased. These methods work because, as we have seen, buddhas are constantly regarding all sentient beings all of the time. Buddhas never stop regarding and benefiting beings. The manner in which buddhas regard all beings is utterly impartial. They have the same consummate loving-kindness for each and every being that they would if that being were their only child.

Generally speaking, we have friends and we have enemies. There are those we favor and those we hold in disfavor. Buddhas do not make such distinctions. Buddhas have the same loving-kindness for all beings and they have completely conquered the hordes of mara, which would otherwise obstruct or prevent them from benefiting beings. Therefore if you request the protection of the buddhas for someone, it is certain that that person will be protected. This is definitely the best way to protect someone. There are elaborate ways you can do this, using special ceremonies and so on, but it can also be done equally effectively using the practices with which you are already familiar. The practice that is used as an example of how to do this is the Mahamudra preliminaries, or ngondro, which most people are familiar with. Each part of ngondro has a method that can be used to benefit others.

Using the first part of ngondro, the practice of going for refuge and generating bodhichitta, you do the visualization and recite the liturgy as usual, but in addition you think that not only you but especially those beings you wish to protect are all going for refuge, joining their palms in an attitude of devotion, reciting the refuge vow, and remaining in an attitude of devotion. You recite the liturgy as usual, and at the end of the session, after you have completed the repetition of the usual refuge vow and the taking of the bodhisattva vow, you recite the single line "We go for refuge to the guru and the Three Jewels" 108 times.

Then, at the end of the session, you think that the sources of refuge melt into light and dissolve, in this case not only into yourself but also into those to be protected. Think that by this occurring, all those to be protected are filled with the blessings of the Three Jewels. After that, rest in the practice of emptiness, which in this case is the recognition that you, those you are trying to protect, and the sources of refuge all have the same fundamental nature and are, in that sense, inseparable.

By doing this, you are practicing both the relative and the absolute ways of going for refuge. The visualization of the sources of refuge, the repetition of the refuge vow, and the dissolution of the sources of refuge into you and into those to be protected comprise the relative refuge. Resting in an awareness of the fundamental equality or sameness of yourself, those to be protected, and the sources of refuge is equivalent to the ultimate or absolute refuge. Practicing like this will definitely cause those whom you designate to be placed under the protection of the Three Jewels.

The second way to use ngondro practice to benefit others is by practicing in a special way the second part of ngondro, which is the meditation and mantra repetition of Vajrasattva. The reason this practice can also be used is that when you are attempting to protect others, you are attempting to protect them from suffering. The cause of suffering is wrongdoing and obscurations. All of the suffering, hardships, and problems we experience in this lifetime and in past and future lifetimes, as well as the suffering that others experience, are caused by our accumulation of wrongdoing and obscurations. When we accumulate these obscurations, and as a result suffer and then become resentful of our suffering, we engage in more wrongdoing, accumulate more obscurations, and suffer more as a result, and so on. This is why we call this samsara, or cyclic existence. The cause leads to the result, and the result inspires us to accumulate further causes, and so on.

If the causes—wrongdoing and obscurations—do not exist, then the result—suffering—will not occur. It will not be experienced. An effective way of protecting others from suffering is to remove the cause of their suffering. The most effective way of purifying obscurations is the Vajrasattva practice.

You do this practice exactly as it is found in the ngondro, which is to say that you visualize Vajrasattva seated above your head. In addition to this, you think that emanating from the Vajrasattva above your head are many other Vajrasattvas, who come to rest or are seated above the heads of those you wish to protect. The beings for whom you do this can be either living or deceased. You visualize them and you think that there is a Vajrasattva seated above the head of every one of them as individuals.

You do the practice as usual, reciting the hundred-syllable mantra, the six-syllable mantra, the words of confession, and so on. There is nothing different to recite. At the end of the usual practice, you do the following special visualization: Think that wisdom ambrosia descends from the bodies of all the Vajrasattvas and purifies not only the obscurations of yourself but especially the wrongdoing and obscurations of each of the other beings individually. Each being whom you wish to protect or purify has a Vajrasattva above his or her head, and each of the Vajrasattvas is purifying the being underneath him. Visualizing this, you recite the six-syllable mantra OM BENZA SATTO HUNG an additional 108 times for the benefit of those to be protected.

At the end of the recitation, as usual Vajrasattva melts into light and dissolves into you. This means that the Vajrasattva above your head melts and dissolves into you, and the additional Vajrasattvas dissolve into the people above whom they are seated. Each person's Vajrasattva dissolves into him or her individually. Having done that, you briefly meditate on emptiness without any thought of what you are attempting to confess or purify, of the person doing the confession, or of the act of confession as having inherent existence.

This includes both the relative and the absolute acts of confession. The relative act of confession is the meditation on Vajrasattva up to and including the dissolution of Vajrasattva into yourself and the others. The absolute or ultimate confession is the resting in the fundamental sameness or equality of that which is to be purified, the person purifying it, and the act of purification. This can actually reduce the negative karma, even the karma of previous lifetimes that others have accumulated.

The third way of using ngondro practice to benefit others is by employing the third part of ngondro, which is the mandala offering. The reason for this is that all of the happiness that we experience in this life and in other lives is a result of our accumulation of merit. You cannot possibly experience even a moment's happiness without the previous accumulation of merit as its cause.

The way to accumulate merit that involves the least difficulty is the offering of the mandala, which is therefore considered the most profound way of gathering the accumulations of merit. If you wish to make others happy, you have to accumulate merit for them on their behalf, and the easiest way to do this is by making the mandala offering.

You do the mandala practice as usual up to a certain point. You visualize the sources of refuge—the Three Jewels—which are the recipients of the mandala offering, in the sky in front of you. When you offer the mandala, you think that the bodies of yourself and all those to be protected, all of the possessions of yourself and those people, and all of the virtues accumulated by yourself and by them in the past, present, and future—all are brought together and offered in the form of billions and billions of worlds. "World" here is visualized as consisting of the central mountain—Mount Meru—and the four continents. You emanate billions of these worlds and you mentally fill each of them with heaps and masses of all the most wonderful, desirable things that are found in the realms of humans and devas.

You offer the mandala as usual following the liturgy. At the end you add the offering mantra GURU DEVA DAKINI RATNA MANDALA TRATITSA SOHA. You recite this mantra 108 times as a specific accumulation of merit for those you are wishing to protect. At the conclusion of the session you think that all of the deities, the sources of refuge, dissolve into you and into those to be protected. This does not mean that you divide them so that some dissolve into you and some dissolve into those you wish to protect. You think that each assembly entirely dissolves into each person. You get a full set of sources of refuge and each of them gets a full set.

Then you meditate briefly on emptiness as before. The first part of this, the mandala offering, is for the accumulation of merit on behalf of others. The second part, the meditation on emptiness, is for the accumulation of wisdom on behalf of others. Through increasing the two accumulations, you will increase their prosperity.

The most effective way of blessing or consecrating the body, speech, and mind of yourself and others is the practice of guru yoga. This of course is the practice or cultivation of devotion. You can use the fourth part of ngondro, guru yoga, to benefit others in the following way.

You visualize the root and lineage gurus above your own head just as you usually do in guru yoga practice. You do the practice, reciting as many of the two supplications as you wish. At the end of the regular practice, before you dissolve the gurus into you, you repeat the first line of the second supplication, LAMA RINPOCHE LA SOL WA DEP, "I supplicate the precious guru." You repeat that one line 108 times for the benefit of those for whom you are praying. You visualize the root and lineage gurus above your head only; do not visualize them above the heads of those to be protected. While reciting this mantra, you think that rays of light emerge from the bodies of the root and lineage gurus above your head. The rays of light enter into the tops of the heads of all of those to be protected and drive out all of their wrongdoing and obscurations in the form of black tar or goo right out the bottoms of their feet. These rays of light fill their bodies and dissolve into them. Consequently their bodies become crystalline, stainless, and luminous.

You visualize this while reciting that one-line supplication, thinking that the blessings of the gurus are actually entering into these people for whom you are praying. At the end of the session, the root and lineage gurus dissolve into you as usual. Chakme Rinpoche says, "I have not seen anywhere an instruction that you dissolve the root and lineage gurus into the others." They just dissolve into you. The reason for this is that you are the person whose devotion is powering or fueling this practice. It is not necessarily the case that those you are praying for have devotion. They might not be Buddhists at all. They might not have any connection with the gurus to whom you are praying, but you can still pray for them because you have that connection. However, because they do not necessarily have the connection, at the end of this practice, you dissolve the lineage and root gurus into yourself, not into them.

This method of using the four ngondro preliminary practices to protect others or to bring others under the protection of the Three Jewels is found in commentaries of both the New and the Old, or Sarma and Nyingma, traditions. Karma Chakme Rinpoche writes, "I have actually heard these instructions from my kind root guru, so do not think that I just made this up and wrote it down."

The reason this is important is that people go around saying, "When will I experience the compassion of the Three Jewels?" They say this all the time without realizing that you have to know how to bring that about. You have to know how to ask, how to call for the compassion of the Three Jewels. If you do not have a drumstick, the drum is not going to make any sound.

Karma Chakme concludes the chapter, "Therefore, at the exhortation of Tsondru Gyamtso, this was composed by the retreatant called Raga Asya, Karma Chakme Rinpoche, on the evening of the twenty-seventh day of the tenth month, in the Year of the Wood Snake."

Questions and Answers

STUDENT: I want to clarify my understanding of the refuge practice. You said that we need to add a certain liturgy about going for refuge to the guru and the Three Jewels. Does that come right after the taking of the bodhisattva vow?

RINPOCHE: Yes, it is that one line—"We go for refuge to the guru and the Three Jewels"—and it is inserted after the bodhisattva vow has been taken.

STUDENT: When we are practicing the refuge section of ngondro for the benefit of others, should we be visualizing the sources of refuge in any special way?

RINPOCHE: The fundamental attitude in going for refuge should be one of desperation. Samsara will never come to an end—which is to say that for all beings, including yourself, there will never be a time of freedom and happiness—unless a method of liberation is found. The first part of the attitude we take in going for refuge is a feeling of sadness and renunciation. The second part is the recognition that all the methods we might employ to bring about our liberation depend upon, or start with, going for refuge to the Buddha, Dharma, and Sangha.

How do we view the Buddha, Dharma, and Sangha in the context of the Mahamudra preliminaries? Essentially the Buddha is viewed as the trikaya, the three bodies. Dharma includes both tradition and the realization that that tradition brings; it also includes both the Dharma of sutra and the Dharma of tantra. Sangha includes the Hinayana sangha of the Shravaka and Pratyekabuddha arhats, but is primarily made up of all of the male and female bodhisattvas that abide on the ten bhumis. It is the exalted Sangha of the Mahayana. Of course, the attitude with which you go for refuge is that you are doing so not temporarily, such as for this life alone, but until you have attained perfect awakening or buddhahood. You are not going for refuge just to free yourself from samsara but rather because you can then liberate all beings.

STUDENT: Some of us recently received the empowerment for Vajrasattva. According to the ngondro practice, we are supposed to complete the going for refuge before practicing Vajrasattva; therefore what portion of the Vajrasattva can be done daily to keep the commitment of the empowerment? And do we get to count whatever we do and add it to the number of repetitions we do in the future?

RINPOCHE: You should work as hard as you can on the prostrations until you finish them. Of course, prostration practice is very difficult, but you do eventually get to the end of it. The prostration practice can prevent rebirth in lower states, and the physical discomfort of doing prostrations, as considerable as it may seem to be, is far less than the physical discomfort of rebirth in the lower realms.

For someone who is still doing prostrations and wishes to recite the Vajrasattva mantra in postmeditation while walking around or working, either as an observance of the commitments of the empowerment or in order to generally purify themselves, that is fine. However, you should not consider it part of the accumulation of the Vajrasattva mantras for the ngondro. Until you finish the first part of ngondro, you should not begin the liturgy for the second part, and any mantras you recite in postmeditation are not counted for the accumulation.

There is a saying that it is better to have a cup of grain than a large vessel of grain that is mixed with sand and grit. If you have just one cup of grain, it is very easy to cook and you have something you can eat. If you have what seems to be a much larger vessel of grain but do not know how much of it is actually grain and how much of it is sand, grit, and small stones, it is very unwieldy. You do not know how much you have or if you can actually ever use it to cook and eat.

In the same way, if you approach Vajrasattva practice by just sort of trying to say the mantra a lot in postmeditation and trying to count that as Vajrasattva practice, you are ending up with something that is unwieldy. The practice is mixed with the distracted mind of postmeditation, so it is not really meditation practice and also you have no idea how many you have said. You may have said a lot, you may not have said many at all. You will not have much confidence in your own practice if that is the way you approach it. It is much better to take things one step at a time and to concentrate on one thing at a time so that you know what you have done and know where you are.

STUDENT: How appropriate is it to do the Vajrasattva practice without having first taken the bodhisattva vow?

RINPOCHE: Having received the empowerment, it is okay to do Vajrasattva practice without having separately taken the bodhisattva vow. Anytime you take any Vajrayana empowerment, it includes the generation of bodhichitta, which is a kind of bodhisattva vow. Nevertheless if you separately take the bodhisattva vow, it will make your practice much more powerful and definite. The custom in the Tibetan Buddhist tradition is that every ritual and every personal practice begins with the renewal of the vows of refuge and bodhichitta. When you are taking an empowerment, at the beginning of the empowerment you are instructed to have bodhichitta as your motivation. There is always generation of bodhichitta in the early stages of the empowerment ceremony. In addition, at the conclusion of the ceremony you are instructed to dedicate the virtue of the empowerment to the awakening of all beings. In a sense, the bodhisattva vow is included. Nevertheless it is necessary at some point, for your practice to be full-fledged, to take the vow as a separate commitment.

STUDENT: I am a little confused about the instructions on using the Vajrasattva practice to benefit others. Could you please review that?

RINPOCHE: When you begin the Vajrasattva practice and you visualize Vajrasattva above your head, you immediately think that Vajrasattvas are emanating and appearing above the heads of those to be protected. Essentially, they appear simultaneously with the Vajrasattva above your own head. Then you go through the practice as usual, concentrating on the purification. You recite the hundred-syllable mantra however many times, and the six-syllable mantra however many times, and then the liturgy of confession. After the liturgy of confession, you again recite 108 of the six-syllable mantra, this time concentrating on the purification of those to be protected. After that the Vajrasattva above your head melts into light and dissolves into you, and at the same time the Vajrasattvas above the heads of those to be protected dissolve into them individually.

STUDENT: I have heard conflicting instructions. In the usual ngondro practice you only do 216 recitations of the hundred-syllable mantra. Therefore do you only do 108 six-syllable mantras?

RINPOCHE: What you are asking is about ngondro in general, so do not confuse this with the practice that is being described. When you are doing the ngondro practice of Vajrasattva, what you are accumulating is hundred-syllable mantras. The repetition of the six-syllable essence mantra at the end of that is for the purpose of repairing any incorrect repetition or pronunciation of the hundred-syllable mantra. Therefore the six-syllable mantra is customarily chanted 108 times regardless of how many or how few hundred-syllable mantras you have chanted.

STUDENT: I am dedicated to Dharma practice and I understand the importance of it. The problem I have is that while sitting daily on the meditation cushion, my meditation becomes a little bit solidified. It becomes like automatic prayer. How can that become more alive and more inspired? In addition, after about half an hour my knees and back start hurting me and I find myself wanting to do the practice faster just because I am experiencing a little bit of physical pain.

RINPOCHE: It is good that you are devoted to and committed to Dharma, but devotion is easily lost if there is no real understanding of Dharma or of how to practice it. By this I mean that the problems you are describing in your first question mean that you have no certainty, no real conviction. If there is that kind of conviction, the practice will never become stale or solidified in the way you are describing. Nevertheless this is true for all of us in the beginning. We always start out lacking conviction because it only comes through experience. Once that conviction is gained, you become absolutely certain that the path you are pursuing will lead to awakening, at which point there is no problem with staying fresh and in focus. To some extent this is a question of habit. As you practice more, the habit of practice and the habit of the insight of practice will increase. The problem we face is that if we allow ourselves to become distracted while we are practicing, we amass bad habits as well. It can become easier and easier to get distracted, and eventually it can become sort of automatic. Therefore it is important to employ the faculty of alertness, which defends or protects our mindfulness.

The function of alertness is to recognize distraction, and once you have recognized it, you simply return to the meditation, to the technique. This return to the technique should be done gently. It is not a question of attempting to force your mind back. Working with your mind is a little bit like working with a timid bird. If you extend your hand and invite the bird, eventually it will jump onto your hand. But if you thrust your arm out in a hurry and try to grab the bird, it will fly away. Therefore in returning to the technique, do so without attempting to force your mind.

With regard to your second question, there are two things that might be happening. The first thing, which is probably the more likely, is that your body is not yet used to the physical position of practice, in which case there is no alternative but to gradually allow yourself to get used to it. Only maintain the meditation posture as long as you can do so without discomfort, and gradually that period of time will increase as your body gets more used to it. The other possibility is that you have some kind of physical injury or condition that is causing the pain, in which case attempting to prolong the sitting period could exacerbate whatever problem it is. If it is because of an injury or health condition, then you should rely upon the guidance of a physician in determining what posture to use in practice.

Nowadays we have all kinds of problems with our minds and with our bodies when we practice. The great practitioners of the old days, who seem to have all but disappeared now, did not worry about these things because they had this certainty that I spoke about earlier. They had an attitude that was completely hard-headed and uncompromising. They thought, "I do not care if I get sick or even if I die. I will just keep practicing until I attain awakening." Because they had that kind of attitude, they did not have the problems that we face. Since we do have these problems, however, we have to deal with them individually and appropriately for each particular situation.

Dispelling All Obstacles: Visualizations to Benefit Others

This next chapter essentially explains three different ways of using deity meditation to remove the obstacles of others. The chapter begins with the invocation NAMO MAHA KARUNA KA YE, "Homage to the Great Compassionate One," which refers to Chenrezik. In the prior chapter the metaphor that was used was of a parasol; here it is the metaphor of a breeze.

A wish-fulfilling tree called Gorshisha is found on the Mountain of the Potala. The Mountain of the Potala is the island pure realm of the bodhisattva Chenrezik, or Avalokiteshvara. The wish-fulfilling tree is moved by the breeze of profound instructions, causing its beautiful or delicious scent of benefit and happiness to pervade all the hundred directions. In other words, these instructions are like a breeze that causes the scent of that tree, which is like the compassion of Chenrezik, to pervade everything.

The actual instructions begin as follows: We have reached the age of bad times in which there is fivefold degeneration. People are afflicted by sickness, demons, bad luck, and all kinds of unpleasantness. Sudden adversity and obstacles of all kinds afflict people. In response, the custom arose of people bringing offerings, whatever they can gather, to teachers and requesting that they pray for them, perform visualizations, and so on for their benefit. This custom has developed as a response to the fact that people have problems that can be benefited by prayers and meditations being done for them by teachers.

Having received those offerings, if you (as the teacher to whom the people have turned) do not perform some special visualization for their benefit, then you are deceiving them. Another difficulty is that among the visualizations you might do, a lot of them are going to cause more problems than benefit. For example, in order to help someone who is ill, you might perform the practice of chö, or "cutting through." The problem is that if you do this practice, it is very hard to withstand the upheaval it is going to bring. When you practice chö intensely, it produces a lot of fear and possibly hallucinations or actual dangerous occurrences. You have to have the courage and the confidence of the view that will enable you to withstand the occurrences that arise. If you do not, and most people do not, then having done chö will actually harm both you and those for whom you are praying.

Furthermore, most patrons of Dharma feel that they are afflicted by spirits who do not like the Buddhadharma. If you try to do some sort of exorcism ritual and meditation to remedy this, the dharmapalas do not like it because it is as if you are trying to turn them into your own personal bodyguards. In addition, if the person has a strong occurrence of negativity running through his or her life and you try to magically manipulate this, you actually put your own life in danger.

Therefore, for all these reasons, in answer to people's prayers, you need a form of practice or visualization that is not going to harm you and is certain to benefit them. That which is extolled for this in all the tantras is authentic of origin, brings immediate and obvious benefit, and is adorned with profound instructions. Chakme Rinpoche guarantees it from his own experience. This means that the instructions Chakme Rinpoche is about to present are not just found in texts that are past history; it is something he can guarantee because he has practiced them himself.

His instructions for the first of these practices are to visualize yourself as some form of Chenrezik, whichever form you are most familiar with. It could be Gyalwa Gyamtso, the red Chenrezik; it could be Four-Armed Chenrezik; it could be Thousand-Armed Chenrezik or Two-Armed Chenrezik—whichever one you are used to. In addition, above the head of the sick or afflicted person, seated on a moon-disk seat, you visualize the bodhisattva Chenrezik in the following specific form: He is white, with one face and two arms. His right hand is extended in the gesture of bestowal of protection. His left hand holds a white lotus by its stem. He is seated with his legs crossed and is adorned with all the usual silk clothing and jewelry. In his heart you visualize above a moon disk the syllable HRI surrounded by the mantra, which is facing outward.

Then you visualize rays of light emerging from the syllables in Chenrezik's heart, and you invite all the wisdom deities, especially Chenrezik himself, from the realm of the Potala. They dissolve into the Chenrezik above the afflicted person's head. Then you recite a supplication that says, "Great bodhisattva, who bestows protection and fearlessness upon the fearful, Arya Avalokiteshvara, I pay homage to you. I pray that you free this person (say the person's name) from the dangers of sickness and affliction."

After the supplication you visualize ambrosia descending from the body of Chenrezik, purifying all the sickness and other afflictions from which that person is suffering and filling his body with well-being. Visualizing this, the mantra that you recite is OM MANI PEME HUNG. Then say the person's name and the name of the sickness or affliction. You continue with SHANTIM which means "purify," and KURU YE, which means "to do", and SOHA, which means "may it be." You recite this mantra as many times as you can. At the end, you think that the deity Chenrezik above the person's head melts into light and dissolves into that person.

The sources for this are *The Lotus Sutra, The Vajra Funjura Tantra*, and also the terma of the Nam Chö, the tradition of terma from which our Amitabha and Medicine Buddha practices come.

The second of the three visualizations given in this chapter is drawn from the commentaries on *The Kalachakra Tantra*, especially from the commentary that is called *Stainless Light*. In this visualization you would normally visualize yourself as Vishvamata, who is the consort of Kalachakra. In this case, you would visualize yourself as Vishvamata alone, without Kalachakra accompanying her. As Thrinley Rinpoche writes, "Because it is also a nondual tantra, you can visualize yourself as that particular form of Avalokiteshvara known as Gyalwa Gyamtso." In any case, you visualize that rays of light from your heart emanate outward, and at the end of each ray of light is another Vishvamata. She is white in color with one face and two arms. In her right hand she is holding a vase, in her left hand she is holding a white lotus, and she is riding on a white elephant.

You then visualize that she rides out on the tips of the rays of light and comes to rest above the person you are trying to protect. This is primarily concerned with the alleviation of the suffering of ill or afflicted people. You visualize that she pours ambrosia from the vase in her hand, with which she washes away all of the sickness affecting that person, causing all of their sickness and demonic obstacles to be purified and causing their body to become completely cleansed like a vessel of crystal. While this is going on, you visualize that many other emanated goddesses who accompany Vishvamata are singing songs of praise and auspiciousness and sending down a rain of flower petals. Visualizing this, there is no liturgical recitation, but there is a mantra, the Vishvamata mantra with something added to it. It is OM TREM VISHVAMATA SOHA. Then you say the name of the person for whom you are praying and you say the name of their sickness or demons, then SHANTIM KURU YE SOHA, which means, "May they all be pacified."

The number of mantras you recite is up to you. It depends upon the seriousness of the person's illness and the amount of time at your disposal. At the end you can dissolve the deity Vishvamata either into the ill person or back into yourself. Chakme Rinpoche gives his sources, and he does so because he does not want you to think that he just made this all up. There is a specific empowerment for this visualization found in a collection of empowerments called the *Druptop Gyamtso*, or *Ocean of Sadhanas*. The visualization is explained in general in the commentary on *The Kalachakra Tantra*. It is explained in detail in the commentary *Vimilaprabha*, or *Stainless Light*, which was written by the rigden Peme Karpo of Shambhala. In this particular text, the practice is explained as a way of dispelling all of the sixteen dangers, not just sickness.

Next Karma Chakme Rinpoche talks about his own experience with this visualization so that you will understand that it actually works. A patron of his suffered from an obscuration of his vision because of an imbalance of the three humors; he suffered from too much phlegm. Chakme Rinpoche performed this visualization one period a day for one month. During that time the patron had a dream that a woman dressed in white clothing washed him, and the next morning his vision was somewhat clearer. Day after day his vision improved more and more until his obscuration was completely cleared up. Chakme Rinpoche writes, "Therefore I have acquired certainty as to the effectiveness of this visualization."

The third visualization given in this chapter makes use of the deity White Tara. In this practice you would normally visualize yourself as White Tara. However, if you wish, if you are more comfortable doing so, you may visualize yourself as Chenrezik in the usual form. It does not matter. In either case, rays of light emanate from your heart, and these rays of light invite White Tara from the Potala. She comes to rest above the head of, or in front of, the ill person. You supplicate her, which can be in your own words, for the pacification of whatever danger or affliction is affecting that person. You visualize that from her body a stream of milk-like amrita descends, dissolving into the afflicted person and purifying all of the sickness, demons, and so on. If you wish, while visualizing this, you can recite praises to Tara, such as KORWA LE DROL TARE MA, and so on. However, this is not necessary. In either case, you recite the mantra TARE TUTTARE TURE but before you say SOHA, you insert the name of the person and the name of their sickness or demons, and KURU YE SOHA. This means, "May all of their sickness and demons be pacified." At the end of performing the visualization, you think that Tara dissolves into the person, specifically into the part of their body that is afflicted by the sickness. For example, if the person has a toothache, then you think that Tara dissolves into the person's tooth, and so on.

This White Tara visualization comes from the Kadampa tradition. In that tradition it has been taught that in the experience of many Kadampa geshes, simply doing that visualization once, for one period, will alleviate the sickness of the afflicted person. However, this might not be the case nowadays. This is because we have less confidence in the teachings, or sometimes it is because of impurities in our samaya, which causes the power to be less effective. Also, if the visualization is done by someone without compassion, it will not have the same effect.

This visualization can be used for any of the sixteen dangers, which include things like water, abysses or cliffs, fire, predators, political persecution, and so on. You can apply it to any of those dangers. Consequently when you are traveling to a dangerous place or on a dangerous road, or if someone else you know is doing so, you can visualize White Tara above yourself or above that person, or directly in front of you or that person. In this case, Tara would be making the mudra, or gesture, of bestowing protection, and you would alter the mantra to include whatever particular danger you are seeking protection from. In other words, you would take out the words *sickness* or *demons*, and insert *dangers on the road*, or whatever the problem is.

This is taught in the large text that is called *The Hundred Thousand Praises to White Tara*, and it is also taught in the *Cha Tupita Tantra* and has been carried down through our lineage as an oral instruction. This means it has continued to be practiced as an actual method and is not merely found in old texts. Again, Chakme Rinpoche writes, "This White Tara visualization is a summary of all the teachings from commentaries and instructions of the lineage, as well as based upon my own experience."

He then sums up his teaching, and regarding the visualizations he says, "The virtue of these three methods or instructions is that they do not harm the person who performs them. That is to say, sometimes some procedures or ceremonies you might perform for others might be risky to yourself, but these are not. Furthermore, they are beneficial to the person for whom they are performed, not only immediately but also in the long term. Because the deities being used in these visualizations are wisdom deities, a connection is established with the person being prayed for so that they can be reborn in a pure realm, or at the very least establish a strong connection with that deity."

Then he concludes the chapter by saying, "This was written down by the diligent one, who is able to write down these instructions through his great exertion, even in the freezing cold." As most of you will remember, this refers to the circumstances under which this book was dictated. It was dictated to the person who requested it, Lama Tsondru Gyamtso, who received each chapter as dictation while sitting outside Chakme Rinpoche's retreat hut in the depth of winter.

Thus it was written down by Lama Tsondru Gyamtso on the evening of the eighth day of the tenth month in the Year of the Wood Snake.

Questions and Answers

STUDENT: In regard to the concise practice to benefit others through the short Chenrezik, is this practice available as a text?

RINPOCHE: The application that was taught is not a separate Chenrezik practice that replaces the ordinary Chenrezik practice. It is not a short or concise or convenient form of Chenrezik practice. There is a difference between a practice and the application of a practice. This is an application. As such, there is no separate liturgy to be used other than the supplication and the mantra that were given in the teaching. The supplication is long enough that you may find it unwieldy to use, in which case just recite the mantra. The mantra to be recited is OM MANI PEME HUNG (the person's name) (the sickness) SARMA SHANTIM KURU YE SOHA. That is sufficient. If you cannot remember that, it is sufficient to simply recite the mantra visualizing Two-Armed Chenrezik above the person's head, specifically focusing on that person's welfare, that person's benefit. It is not really a liturgical practice like the Chenrezik puja we do here as a community.

STUDENT: Is it better to do the Chenrezik practice or the Vajrasattva practice for the specific purpose of purifying illness?

RINPOCHE: The Vajrasattva practice would be better.

STUDENT: Karma Chakme says that he helped people by doing this practice. I thought it was impossible to purify someone else's karma. I need to understand this.

RINPOCHE: You actually can benefit someone else in this way, but there has to be some kind of established connection, which can either be a mundane or a Dharmic one. This is why the custom in Tibet was that if you became ill or if someone in your family became ill and you were requesting prayers from a lama, you would go to the lama with offerings. The purpose of the offerings was to establish some kind of karmic connection between the teacher and the sick person so that benefit could be given effectively. This is also why you can successfully pray for the longevity of your teacher. If someone is your teacher and you are his disciple, you have established a connection with him. This means that your prayers for his longevity will be more effective than those of someone who has no connection. It also means that when a teacher prays for his disciples, he can benefit them greatly. It is similar to the wires that transmit electricity: As long as there is some kind of wiring present, the electricity can travel. That is how it works.

The River of Ambrosia That Purifies Obscurations: Vajrasattva Practice

This chapter begins with the Sanskrit invocation NAMO VAJRASATTVA YE, "Homage to Vajrasattva." As is the case with the other chapters, there is an injunction to the disciple who is writing it down to listen, only here it says, "Listen, Lama Tsondru Gyamtso, we have great hatred for our enemies."

People have great hatred for their enemies. We wish to bring about their downfall, and even if we succeed in doing so, we are dissatisfied. We want to kill them. We want to eradicate them utterly and make them nonexistent. The general point here is that we are constantly thinking about trying to do in or to outdo our enemies.

If you think about it carefully, enemies, such as thieves and so on, are our best friends. As Shantideva said, "There is no evil like anger, and no virtue like patience." One of the implications of that statement is that without enemies, we have no real opportunity to practice patience, no real opportunity to practice impartial loving-kindness and compassion. Rather than resenting our enemies, we should actually feel gratitude toward them. Furthermore it says in the text that all those who are our enemies in this lifetime have, throughout many previous lifetimes, been our kind parents; and also within this lifetime it is not uncommon for enemies to turn into friends. The most an enemy can do to us is kill us, which they can only do once. Once they have killed us, we are dead. They cannot kill us again and again. There is one enemy, however, that can kill us more than once and that harms us throughout all of our lifetimes. That enemy is our own wrongdoing. This enemy can not only kill us, it can actually cast us, and has cast us, into hell innumerable times. There we are killed not only once, we are killed and revived again and again. If you are concerned with enemies, understand that your own wrongdoing and obscurations are your true enemies. If you are concerned with doing in your enemies, try to do this one in.

Wrongdoing, if not confessed and purified, even if very slight at the time it was done, accumulates interest. It actually grows as each day and each year passes, which is why it is said that even the small wrongdoings of the foolish are heavy. If we confess wrongdoing, even if it is not completely purified by the confession, it will not increase and will actually decrease over time. That is why it is said that even the great obscurations and wrongdoings of the wise are light. Anything we do that is wrong, no matter how slight it is, if it is not confessed, will increase over time; it will never just disappear by itself. The imprint of any single act of wrongdoing, regardless how minor the action itself, in the absence of confession, will abide for a billion kalpas without disappearing. The results of our actions ripen only for us. They do not ripen for the earth. They do not ripen for a stone. They ripen in the aggregates, sense fields, and elements of the individual who performed the action.

On the other hand, there is no unvirtuous action so horrific that it cannot be purified by confession. For example, the king, Ajanta Shatru, which means "Unborn Enemy," or "Already an Enemy Before He Was Born," killed his own father, who was an arhat; created a major schism in the sangha of the Buddha; and with malevolent intent drew blood from the body of the Buddha. Yet through one act of confession he was able to purify all of this. Another example is Angulimala, "Necklace of Fingers," who killed 999 people and collected a finger from each of his victims, which is how he got his name. Nevertheless he was able to purify this wrongdoing by one single act of confession.

You might ask how it is possible that such heinous crimes can be purified by such brief moments of sincere confession. It happens in much the same way that a single spark is able to burn a large mass of hay. It was taught by Buddha Shakyamuni that a confession can purify any wrongdoing. In order to do this effectively, however, you need a method, and the method of confession is what is called the four powers.

To be authentic and fully effective, any act of confession must contain all four of the following components. The first is called *the power of reliance or support*. This means taking as the witness for your confession "supports," or representations of the Buddha's body, speech, and mind that have blessings, such as a statue of the Buddha, a volume of Dharma, and a stupa, which have blessings when they have been properly prepared and consecrated. Alternatively, you could rely on some other support, such as a Vajrayana mandala or your guru. If you lack any of these and wish to perform a confession, you may visualize all the buddhas and bodhisattvas, which means you simply invite them to witness your confession. This is valid because, with their omniscient wisdom, buddhas and bodhisattvas can actually hear anything that is intentionally addressed to them by a sentient being.

The second power is *the power of regret*. This means sincerely regretting unvirtuous actions as intensely as you would regret having drunk poison. If you were to drink poison, the type of poison for which there is no remedy and which will definitely cause your death, having discovered that you had drunk it, you would certainly wish you had not done so. Your wish must have that degree of intensity. In truth you have more reason to regret unvirtuous actions than you do to regret drinking poison, because drinking poison will kill you, but it will do so only once. Unvirtuous actions not only cause your death once, they eventually cause it innumerable times.

The third power is the actual mechanism or procedure of purification, *the power of remedy for harmful actions or conduct*. This can be any virtuous action whatsoever that is specifically dedicated to purification. It can be physical acts of virtue, such as prostration or circumambulation. It can be verbal acts of virtue, such as the recitation of scripture, liturgies, and mantras. Among these, the meditation and mantra recitation of Vajrasattva is considered supreme for purification.

The fourth power is the one we have the most trouble with. It is usually translated as *the power of resolution*, but you can call it a commitment or a promise. It means that you have a strong commitment never to commit the wrongdoing again. This is the hardest thing for us because the nature of unvirtuous actions is that they are habit-forming. When you do something wrong, one of its results is that it reinforces the habit to do the same thing again. The position we often find ourselves in is analogous to that of children who are constantly being given clean clothes and as soon as they put them on, they immediately run out and five minutes later they are filthy again. Every time we confess our wrongdoing, we immediately go out and do it all over again.

Unfortunately, even though we have the other three powers, if this fourth power is not present, we will not successfully purify our wrongdoing. For example, certain attitudes can obstruct this power, such as the arrogant thought "I can take care of this action of wrongdoing, I can handle it, it is not that important, it is not that big a deal," or "I am clever enough, or strong enough, to withstand its effect."

Another attitude that can obstruct the power of resolution is actually being proud of whatever it was one did. I do not know how prevalent it is in this country, but in Kham, in eastern Tibet, it was quite common to be proud of unvirtuous things one had done, especially if they were "macho." For example, it was not uncommon to overhear someone casually saying, "Yeah, when he said that, I stabbed him immediately." Such a person would be just as likely to say OM BENZA SATTO HUNG right after stabbing their victim, which certainly calls into question how much they really meant to purify their wrongdoing, since thereafter they would brag about it. In any case, if there is a lack of commitment, a lack of resolution, then even though one takes measures to purify or counteract the wrongdoing, they will not be successful.

Another attitude that can be problematic is the thought "I have to do such-and-such thing as part of living in the world, but I will purify it later." The thought "I can confess it and purify it later" presents a threefold problem. First of all it is habit-forming. If we do it once because we think we have to, we may thereafter do it again because we liked doing it. Second, the length of our lives is uncertain, and there is no guarantee that we will be alive long enough to confess or purify the wrongdoing. The third problem is that if we go through our lives that way and let the accumulation of our wrongdoings creep up on us bit by bit, we can end up being smothered or crushed under a mountain of wrongdoing from which it may seem almost impossible to escape. In any case, it is taught that if we do not have the resolution that will keep us from repeating the unvirtuous action, whatever it is, we will not be able to purify it even though we have admitted or confessed it.

The primary method that we use for the act of confession is the hundred-syllable mantra of Vajrasattva. If you are in retreat and are doing something else as your main practice, you would recite the hundred-syllable mantra every day between sessions at least twenty-one times. That way your previous wrongdoing, including violations of commitments, will not increase. Chakme Rinpoche adds that this is not simply an arbitrary number he alone has made up, but is taught in all of the Indian and Tibetan texts on this subject and was taught by all the scholars and siddhas from India and Tibet. It is also said in several places, for example in *The Tantra of Hayagriva* that reciting the hundred-syllable mantra even once will purify all your wrongdoing. It makes sense to interpret this statement as meaning that the mantra would have this degree of effectiveness by reciting it with the utmost conviction, but realistically speaking, we probably cannot expect that to happen for us. It is, however, by no means impossible.

There is a story from the eastern part of Tibet. In Golok there was a householder who had a family, and like many people of that region, in order to sustain his livelihood, he occasionally killed people. He had killed eighteen people and eighteen horses. Nowadays we do not think of that as being very much, because often those who are responsible for the deaths of many people are responsible for deaths in much larger numbers. In the old days and in eastern Tibet, killing eighteen people was generally considered quite an accomplishment. At the end of this man's life, as he was ill and dying, his family members went to him and said, "Father, you know you have done some bad things in your life. Maybe you should do something about it before you die." And he said, "Good idea! Somebody pass me a mala." One of the family members handed him a mala, and very slowly he said OM MANI PEME HUNG one hundred times—one mala's worth—and then he handed them back the mala and relaxed. He said to his family at that time, "You know, I only killed eighteen people and eighteen horses. Chenrezik is a lot tougher than that. I think he can take care of it." Because he had so much faith and was sincere in his confession, he was reborn in the Potala, the realm of Chenrezik.

It all depends upon our degree of faith. The usual number that is given for the effective recitation of the hundred-syllable mantra is 100,000. It is also taught that nowadays all of the numbers that are found in the tantras need to be multiplied by four. The reason for this is that we live in a time of degeneration, which means that our kleshas are much stronger. We engage in much more wrongdoing in general than people did in the past. At the same time, our faith has actually decreased, so while we have more to purify, it is harder for us to purify anything because of our attitude. Therefore it is taught that it is best if you can recite the mantra 400,000 times; this will be extremely effective. Even if someone has committed a root violation of samaya, which is a fundamental violation of the commitments of Vajrayana, if they recite the hundred-syllable mantra 400,000 times, unmixed with other speech (which means that they are doing it in formal meditation sessions, not just reciting it while they are walking around and talking), their violation will be purified. This is taught in both the old, or Nyingma, and the new, or Sarma, traditions.

At this point Chakme Rinpoche offers a compassionate concession to the needs of individuals. He says that if you find the hundred-syllable mantra too difficult to recite, you may recite the six-syllable mantra, OM BENZA SATTO HUNG, 600,000 times, and it will have an equivalent effect of purification.

Karma Chakme Rinpoche now describes why one might want to do such purification. It is taught that someone who has committed a root violation of samaya in this lifetime will be reborn in a specific hell realm. In the sutras this hell realm is called Shambhala hell, and in the tantras it is called vajra hell. It is said to be to the northeast of Avichi, which is the lowest of the eight regular hot hells. It is seven times worse than the worst of the eighteen regular hell realms. It is a state of inconceivably great suffering that is completely uninterrupted. We do not even know how truly bad it is or how long it lasts because the Buddha refused to speak of it in detail. The reason he refrained from describing this hell was that he found that when he started to talk about it, bodhisattvas, out of their compassion for beings, started to vomit blood and die on the spot. Nevertheless all of the violations of samaya and other wrongdoing that we have engaged in that might cause us to be reborn in this hell will be purified and you will not be reborn in that hell realm if the Vajrasattva practice is conducted with a clear visualization and with the full number of the six-syllable or hundred-syllable mantra. This was taught in *The Vajrapani Tantra*.

For people like ourselves who are afflicted by a large amount of ferocious or intense wrongdoing, this instruction of Vajrasattva is more valuable than a hundred or even a thousand wish-fulfilling jewels. Legend tells us that there exists a wish-fulfilling jewel that will fulfill any wishes upon request, but this practice is even more precious than that because it can purify or remove the fundamental reason behind all of our suffering.

At this point Chakme Rinpoche says, "Therefore, Lama Tsondru Gyamtso, perform great benefit for beings and always teach this practice at the beginning of any course of instruction." Regardless of whatever practice you do, you will see that close to the beginning of all of them the instruction in the practice of the hundred-syllable or six-syllable mantra of Vajrasattva is always presented. The reason is that the most fundamental condition for the rest of the practices to be effective is an initial effort on our part at purification. Chakme Rinpoche gives an analogy for this. He says that if you are dying wool, for example a wool blanket, before you dye it, you have to thoroughly clean it and get all the dirt out, otherwise the color will not take. The dye will not take hold because it will be inhibited by the dirt. If it is properly cleaned and prepared, then the color will be beautiful, exactly as you intend. What this analogy is implying is that if you prepare yourself through the purification practice of Vajrasattva, then whatever further practice you engage in will have the full effect it is supposed to have, and all of the indications of your practice's effectiveness that are described in the traditional commentary will be present in your own experience.

Once you purify wrongdoing and obscurations, it is actually easy to generate meditation experience and realization. For example, if you are meditating upon the path of method, which is to say the six dharmas of Naropa, it was said by the mahasiddha Talung Thangpa, who founded the Talung Kagyu, that the best way to ensure the successful generation of bliss and warmth is to accomplish the practice of Vajrasattva. If you wish to practice meditation on a wrathful deity, such as Gonpo Bernakchen or Palden Lhamo, and if you have engaged in the purification practice of Vajrasattva, then there will be no obstacle arising when you pursue the main practice and it will only be a source of benefit for yourself and others. It will go smoothly and there will be no upheaval. In short, the cause of everything that goes wrong for us — our sickness, demons, and afflictions of all kinds — is our previous wrongdoing and obscurations.

Often we become somewhat superstitious and say, "I am experiencing an obstacle. Where did this obstacle come from? Oh no, an obstacle!" But all obstacles stem from our own previous wrongdoing, therefore it says in the text, "If you have no wrongdoing and obscuration, then how could sickness or obstacles ever arise for you? Where would they come from?" That is why Vajrasattva practice is the single most effective and most profound method of averting obstacles and misfortune. When we practice yet do not experience the results described in the practice manuals, it is because we are obscured, because we have not gone through the necessary practice of purification. This is because the signs or indications of the practice are in fact themselves obscured by our obscurations.

Therefore the most profound single method for increasing our realization and our experience of purity or sacredness is the Vajrasattva meditation. The only reason that we do not see Mahamudra, that we do not see the nature of our mind as it is right now, is because of our obscurations, which in this case stem from what is called connate, or coemergent, ignorance. If we remove those obscurations, which can be done most effectively through the practice of Vajrasattva, there is nothing preventing us from seeing the nature of our mind as it is, and we will. Therefore there is no more profound method of generating realization of Mahamudra than the Vajrasattva practice. Chakme Rinpoche concludes this part of the chapter by saying, "There is no point in my continuing to say the same thing in many other ways. In short, it is taught that you can attain full buddhahood through this method alone. Therefore, Tsondru Gyamtso, practice it."

THE ACTUAL INSTRUCTION IN THE USE OF THE HUNDRED-SYLLABLE MANTRA

Now we come to the second part of the chapter, which gives the actual instruction in the use of the hundred-syllable mantra. This part of the chapter also begins with a Sanskrit invocation, NAMO GURU VAJRASATTVA YE, "Homage to the guru, inseparable from Vajrasattva," and, as usual, the injunction "Listen, Lama Tsondru Gyamtso." Chakme Rinpoche gives an explanation of the four parts of the meditation on Vajrasattva and the recitation of his mantra. The stages of the visualization are also very important. Thus this practice of Vajrasattva has many levels, or many styles of practice. These are described as outer, inner, secret, and very secret because they correspond to levels of development, degrees of merit, degrees of diligence, and so on. Nevertheless we must begin with the outer level of Vajrasattva practice, and only when we have become accustomed to and familiar with that is it possible to go on to the others.

The first of these four, then, is *the outer practice of Vajrasattva*, which is the Vajrasattva practice with which we are familiar. It is the style that we employ in the preliminary practices. For this purpose, you begin by visualizing yourself in your ordinary form, and above your head you imagine a white lotus flower on top of which is a moon disk. Standing upright on top of the moon disk you visualize a brilliantly white and luminous HUNG syllable from which radiate innumerable rays of light, which make offerings to all buddhas and bodhisattvas, thus purifying the obscurations of all sentient beings. These rays of light are then withdrawn back into the HUNG, which is now suddenly transformed into Vajrasattva, who is also brilliantly white in color, or, as it says in the text, "the color of crystal." This means not that he is without color but rather that he is insubstantial, translucent, and almost transparent, so that you can see through him;

you can see his inside from the outside and his outside from the inside. He is adorned with silken garments and much jewelry. His right hand holds a golden vajra to his heart, while his left hand holds a silver bell, the top part of which is a vajra, to his left hip. He is seated with his legs half-crossed, which is to say that his right leg is extended slightly forward. Next, having visualized him, you think that from his body, and especially from his heart, rays of light radiate outward, and these again make offerings to all buddhas and bodhisattvas, this time inviting all of them in the form of light to dissolve back into Vajrasattva, who at that point becomes inseparable from all buddhas and bodhisattvas.

Next, as a result of your devotion and supplication to Vajrasattva, ambrosia issues forth from his heart in the following manner: You visualize in the heart of Vajrasattva a moon disk on top of which is a white HUNG syllable, and surrounding that is his hundred-syllable mantra. Through the force of your supplication, you think that from the syllable in his heart a stream of wisdom ambrosia flows forth. This fills his entire body. The excess that cannot be contained by his body flows out through the big toe of his right foot. The ambrosia flowing out of his toe enters you through the aperture at the center of the top of your head, and as it fills your whole body, it drives out all of your wrongdoing, all of your obscurations, in the form of filth and impurities that are expelled primarily out of your lower door and out of the soles of your feet. You can visualize the obscurations, impurities, and traces of wrongdoing in the form of a smoky liquid, such as creosote. As this is expelled or driven out of you, you think that it dissolves under the ground. Continuously visualizing that, you recite the hundred-syllable mantra, or if that is too difficult, you may simply recite the six-syllable mantra of Vajrasattva.

At the conclusion of each cycle of purification, you think that your body is completely emptied of all obscurations, which also means all substantiality such that your body has become, for example, a crystal vessel filled with milk-like ambrosia. This does not mean that you think that your body is made of crystal. It means that it is insubstantial and translucent so that, for example, it is a little bit like a crystal vase filled with milk. At the conclusion of each session of the practice, you think that Vajrasattva addresses you as follows. He says to you, "Child of good family," and then addresses you by name, "your wrongdoing and obscurations have been purified." Having said that, he melts into light and dissolves into you. The reason you visualize Vajrasattva dissolving into you at this point is that once all of your obscurations have been removed, in essence you have become identical to Vajrasattva. It is therefore appropriate, once you have removed the obscurations, to think that he dissolves into you since you are no longer separate from him anyway. Then you rest in the confidence of your inseparability from him and look at the nature of your mind. That is the outer practice of Vajrasattva, and it is not unique to our Kagyu tradition. It is found in the preliminary practices of most traditions. The source of it is the tantras, both the new tantras and the old tantras.

The second aspect of Vajrasattva practice is *the inner Vajrasattva practice*, which is essentially similar except that instead of having one Vajrasattva who embodies all five buddha families, you have five Vajrasattvas, specific to the five families. Therefore in the same way as before, you visualize yourself in your ordinary form and you think that above your head is a lotus; however this time the lotus has only four petals. On top of not only the center of the lotus but of each of the four petals is a moon disk, so that there are five moon disks altogether, and on top of each of these is a syllable. On top of the moon disk in the center of the lotus is a white OM. On top of the moon disk on the petal to the front is a blue HUNG. On top of the moon disk to the right is a yellow SO, or SWA. On top of the moon disk to the rear is a red AH, and on top of the moon disk to the left is a green HA. As before, these syllables are transformed into Vajrasattva, which means that you do the same visualization as you did the first time with the radiation and collection of rays of light, the offerings, and so on. In this case, however, there are five syllables and five transformations. The syllables become the Vajrasattvas of the five families. The OM in the middle is transformed into the white Vajrasattva of the Buddha family, who is often referred to as Buddhasattva, and is essentially the Buddha Vairochana. The HUNG is transformed into the blue Vajrasattva of the Vajra family, who is also known as Akshobhya.

The SO is transformed into the yellow Ratnasattva of the Ratna family, who is Ratnasambhava; the AH into the red Padmasattva of the Padma family, who is Amitabha; and the HA into the green Karmasattva of the Karma family, who is Amoghasiddhi.

They look the same as the Vajrasattva in the outer practice, with two differences. The first difference is that they are each a different color, as was explained. The second is that although they are holding their scepters in the same position as Vajrasattva, the scepters they hold vary. In the case of Buddhasattva, who is in the middle, in his right hand he is holding a golden wheel to his heart, and in his left hand he is holding a bell to his hip, but the upper part of the bell is not a vajra or half-vajra but a golden wheel. In the case of Vajrasattva, he is holding a vajra and bell as usual. In the case of Ratnasattva, he is holding a jewel to his heart, and in his left hand a bell, of which the upper part of the handle is a jewel. In the case of Padmasattva, he is holding a lotus to his heart with his right hand and with his left hand he is holding a bell of which the handle is a lotus. In the case of Karmasattva, he is holding a double vajra or a crossed vajra to his heart in his right hand, and in his left hand he is holding a bell, of which the upper part, the handle, is a crossed or double vajra. The adornments and ornamentation are the same as they were in the outer practice. All five Vajrasattvas have the same silken garments and jewelry. They are all seated in the posture of royal ease, which means that it is essentially the same as in the outer practice, with the right foot extended forward, except that there is more grace to the posture of the upper body, so that they are slightly leaning in a very, very graceful way. In the heart of each, on a moon disk, is their individual syllable, which is to say the syllable from which they emerged or from which they were transformed, and each of these syllables is surrounded by their particular hundred-syllable mantra.

Each of these five Vajrasattvas has a slightly different mantra, which we will get to in a minute. As in the outer practice, from the syllables in their hearts, rays of light radiate outward, and these make offerings to all the buddhas and bodhisattvas, who are included in the five families, throughout all the realms in all directions. When it says "all buddhas and bodhisattvas included in the five families," this means all buddhas and bodhisattvas in all realms without exception. This is because there is no buddha or bodhisattva that is not included in the five families, just as there is no pure realm anywhere that is not included in the pure realms of the five families. Thus all of these are venerated, and as before, they dissolve into light and are summoned back and become inseparable with the five Vajrasattvas above your head.

Then, just like in the outer practice, as a result of your devoted supplication you think that ambrosia descends from the syllables in the hearts of the Vajrasattvas. In this case, because there are five Vajrasattvas, the ambrosia is of five different colors. The ambrosia descending from the Buddhasattva, in the center, is white; from the Vajrasattva, in front, is blue; and so forth. All of these five colors of ambrosia enter into your body through the aperture at the center of the top of your head as before and fill your entire body. These purify individually all the wrongdoing and obscurations that you have accumulated through the five poisons. The white ambrosia, which comes from Buddhasattva, purifies ignorance. The blue ambrosia, which comes from Vajrasattva, purifies anger. The yellow ambrosia, which comes from Ratnasattva, purifies pride and greed. The red ambrosia, coming from Padmasattva, purifies desire. Finally, the green ambrosia, coming from Karmasattva, purifies jealousy and all of the actions, wrongdoing, and other obscurations that you have accumulated through these five poisons.

The only reason for rebirth in the six realms is the presence of the five poisons. If the five poisons are completely eradicated, then you will not be reborn in the six realms. Sometimes the six realms are referred to as the five destinies, or the five paths, because they come from these five poisons. Therefore you think that as a result of these five poisons and the karma accumulated through them, which is being fully eradicated, the causes of rebirth in the six realms have been cut off, as though a door has been closed. When the ambrosia fills your body, you think that this ambrosia of five colors is the embodiment of the five wisdoms. Furthermore, while you are reciting the mantra, you think that, at the same time, these Vajrasattvas of the five families are reciting their individual mantras, and that the sound of them fills the universe, purifying the obscurations of all beings. So in the case of this inner practice, not only your obscurations but also those of other sentient beings are being purified simultaneously.

The five mantras are as follows: The basic form of the mantra is the hundred-syllable mantra and the six-syllable mantra with which you are familiar. In the case of Buddhasattva, instead of OM VAJRASATTVA SAMAYA . . . and so on, it is OM BUDDHASATTVA. In other words, where you would say Vajrasattva, you substitute Buddhasattva. That is the hundred-syllable mantra of the Tathagata, or Buddha family. The six-syllable mantra that corresponds to that is OM BUDDHASATTVA HUM. Next is the Vajrasattva mantra of the Vajra family. This is the same as the usual mantra, except that instead of being OM VAJRASATTVA SAMAYA . . . it is HUM VAJRASATTVA SAMAYA . . . and so on. The six-syllable mantra of the Vajra family is the usual one: OM VAJRASATTVA HUM. The Ratnasattva mantra of the Ratna family is SO (or SWA) RATNASATTVA SAMAYA . . . . Thereafter anywhere that you would say VAJRASATTVA, you would substitute RATNASATTVA. The six-syllable mantra of the Ratna family is OM RATNASATTVA HUM. The Padmasattva mantra of the Padma family is AH PADMASATTVA SAMAYA . . . and so on. You substitute PADMA wherever there would otherwise be VAJRA. The six-syllable mantra of that family is OM PADMASATTVA HUM. Finally, the Karmasattva mantra of the Karma family is HA KARMASATTVA SAMAYA . . . and so on, and the six-syllable mantra is OM KARMASATTVA HUM. You recite those mantras as much as you can.

At the conclusion of the session you perform some liturgy of confession. Three are suggested here. The longest of the three you could perform, if you have time and access to the liturgy, is called *The Agonized Confession of Rudra*, which is a fairly long confession liturgy. If not, you can recite the latter chapter of *The Confession Tantra*, which is slightly more common. Again, it is not that short and goes "OM, supreme wisdom body . . ." and so on. If you wish to recite something more concise than either of those, you can recite the stanzas of confession from the Seven Branches found in *The Aspiration to the Conduct of Excellence*. This is the second, longer seven-branch liturgy that occurs in the Green Tara practice.

At the conclusion of that, you think that the Vajrasattvas of the five families melt into light and dissolve into you and you rest without conceptual focus. This is to say, you rest in a direct experience of your mind's nature of Mahamudra. The scriptural source for this inner practice of Vajrasattva is *The Tantra of Emptying the Depths of the Hells*, and it contains the essence of that tantra. That is the inner practice of Vajrasattva.

The third style of Vajrasattva practice is *the secret practice of Vajrasattva*. Again you visualize yourself in your ordinary form and, as before, above your head you visualize a lotus. This time, however, on top of the center of the lotus you do not visualize a moon but rather a sun disk. The reason for this is that in this form of the practice Vajrasattva is semiwrathful, which is to say that he is not entirely peaceful in appearance the way he was in the two previous practices but instead a mixture of peaceful and wrathful. Above that sun disk you visualize a HUNG. It is white, as it was in the first Vajrasattva practice, and after it emerges, it is transformed into Vajrasattva in the same way as in the two previous practices, which is to say that rays of light radiate outward from it, making offerings to all buddhas and bodhisattvas and purifying the obscurations of all beings; then these rays of light are drawn back into the HUNG, which is transformed into your guru in the form of Vajrasattva Heruka.

Heruka means that Vajrasattva is semiwrathful in appearance. He is white in color and luminous. He has one face and two arms. However, instead of having two eyes as he did in the first two practices, because he is wrathful he has three eyes, the additional one being in his forehead. He is smiling but also frowning wrathfully at the same time. In the previous practices part of his hair was bound in a topknot while the rest flowed freely downward. Here, because he is wrathful, his hair is upswept as though by the wind. In the previous practices his tiara or crown had five jewels set in gold, which represented the five buddha families. Here, in place of the jewels he has five skulls, which also represent the five buddhas, and they are each topped by a diadem. Also, in the previous practices Vajrasattva was holding a vajra to his heart with his right hand. Here in his right hand he is holding a vajra, but he is holding it aloft into space. In his left hand, instead of a bell he has a skullcup, which he is holding not at his hip but in front of his heart. He is adorned with jewelry that is very similar in design to the jewelry worn by the peaceful Vajrasattva, except that in the case of the peaceful Vajrasattva it is made out of gold whereas here it is made out of bone. Instead of having silken garments, he has a skirt made of tiger skin and a shawl made of elephant skin. He has a consort, Vajratopa, who is bright red in color. She is adorned with bone ornaments similar to his and has no other garment or ornamentation. She is in union with the "father" and in her right hand she is holding a hooked knife while in her left hand, a skullcup. You may visualize Vajrasattva seated, in which case he is seated in the posture of royal ease, or else you can visualize him standing, in which case he is standing with his right leg bent and his left leg outstretched.

In any case, Vajrasattva and his consort abide in the midst of a mass of oscillating flames and light that emerge from their bodies. In the heart of the father you visualize a moon disk on top of which, as before, is a white HUNG syllable surrounded by his mantra. Here again, the Vajrasattva mantra is slightly different. As before, from the syllables in his heart, rays of light emanate that invite all gurus, yidams, and dakinis. Having been invited, they dissolve into both the father and the mother, both Vajrasattva and Vajratopa. This causes them to become even more majestic, splendid, luminous, and radiant than they were before, and also causes their bliss to expand such that from the juncture of their union there flows forth a stream of ambrosia. In this case the ambrosia is identified with bodhichitta.

As in the previous practices, this ambrosia or bodhichitta enters your body via the aperture at the center of the top of your head. As before, it fills your body, expelling and purifying all wrongdoing and obscurations and expanding your own realization as well as your experience of well-being and warmth. The mantra that is recited for this practice is called the Heruka Hundred Syllables. It begins OM SHRI HERUKASATTVA SAMAYA . . . and so on. It is slightly different, and if you do not wish to recite the hundred-syllable mantra, you can recite the short mantra. In this case the short mantra is OM AH GURU VAJRASATTVA HUM. At the conclusion of the session of reciting the mantra of purification and doing the visualization, you recite the standard liturgy of confession. This is also found at the conclusion of the ngondro practice of Vajrasattva. You say, "Protector, through ignorance and bewilderment I have contravened and violated samaya."

You should address Vajrasattva as "protector" for two reasons. The first is that his function is to protect you from suffering by removing the traces of your wrongdoing. The second is that one of the qualities embodied by his semiwrathful appearance is his effectiveness in protecting beings. You admit all wrongdoing. Here you are specifically referring to your contravention and violation of your samaya. Again you say, "Guru Protector, please protect me." Then you say, "O Vajra Holder, the principal embodiment of great compassion, I go for refuge to the principal protector of beings," which is to say the principal figure who removes the suffering of beings. *Vajra Holder* here is a synonym for Vajrasattva, and you refer to him as the principal or the chief because he is the principal deity or means for the purification of the wrongdoing of sentient beings. After saying that, you think that your guru in the form of Vajrasattva Heruka melts into light and dissolves into you, after which, as in the first two practices, you rest free of conceptual focus. That is the secret practice of Vajrasattva, which is found in both the new and the old tantras and in both the oral and the treasure traditions.

The fourth practice of Vajrasattva is *the very secret Vajrasattva practice*. This is different from the first three in that while there were great differences among them, they were nevertheless all forms of preliminary Vajrasattva practices. They all had in common the fact that you visualized yourself initially in your ordinary form and visualized Vajrasattva, in one form or another, above your head, purifying you from outside and from above you. This next Vajrasattva practice is the type you would do, after completing the preliminaries, if Vajrasattva were your main practice.

Here you initially dissolve all appearances, including the appearance of your own physical body, into nonconceptuality or into emptiness. From within that state or expanse of emptiness you think that you re-arise in the form of Vajrasattva. Here you do not visualize yourself in your ordinary form with Vajrasattva above your head, but instead, from the very beginning of the practice, you visualize yourself as Vajrasattva. In this case Vajrasattva is in his peaceful form, smiling, with one face and two hands. The form of the deity here is identical to the form in the outer practice of Vajrasattva. The difference is that instead of visualizing the deity above you, you identify yourself, your own body and mind, with the deity. In addition, above the head of yourself as Vajrasattva you visualize the buddhas of the five families. You are Vajrasattva, and the buddhas of the five families are seated above you. Vajrasattva is adorned with golden jewelry and silken garments as usual. He is holding a vajra to his heart with his right hand and a bell to his hip with his left. Here it is specified that the upper garment of Vajrasattva is of white silk. He also has a lower skirt of silk, of which the color is not specified, and he is seated in the posture of royal ease; however, his seat or throne is slightly different here. In the case of the ngondro Vajrasattva, he is seated on a lotus and moon disk. Here you also visualize yourself as Vajrasattva seated on a lotus and moon disk, but the lotus is supported by a golden throne, which is upheld by eight elephants. Traditionally the elephants upholding the throne are deities of the Vajra family. You may not have visualized this during the preliminary practices, because the idea of having eight elephants above your head might seem somewhat oppressive.

As in the ngondro practice, in the heart of Vajrasattva, which in this case is your own heart, you visualize a moon disk. Standing upright on top of the moon disk is the syllable HUNG surrounded by the hundred-syllable mantra. The way in which the hundred-syllable mantra is placed on the moon disk here, according to the tradition of instruction, is slightly different from the way it is in the preliminaries. There the mantra does not turn, and because of the length of it, in order to make it easy for visualization, it is visualized spiraling inward, not as one circle but as a coil or spiral. Here the mantra is to be visualized as one circle consisting of the hundred syllables. It is written so that it will turn to the right. The easiest way to say it is that it is facing outward and will turn to the right.

As in the other practices, having visualized the syllables in your heart, rays of light radiate up from them inviting all buddhas and bodhisattvas, who dissolve into you as Vajrasattva, and especially into the mantra in your heart. Think that the mantra starts to turn. As it turns, ambrosia streams from it as before and fills your body as Vajrasattva, driving out all your wrongdoing, obscurations, sickness, demons, and everything out of the pores of your skin. As in the other practices, these obscurations are visualized as all sorts of crud and filth. All of this is expelled out, leaving your body utterly stainless and luminous in the form of Vajrasattva, like a vessel of crystal. Visualizing this, you recite either the hundred-syllable or the six-syllable mantra.

With regard to the emphasis on the use of these two mantras, traditionally people primarily use the hundred-syllable mantra of Vajrasattva for the bulk of the session and, at the end of the session, recite the six-syllable mantra of Varjasattva as many times as appropriate, for example one hundred times.

At the conclusion of the session, you make offerings and perform praises to yourself as Vajrasattva in the following way: Thinking that you emanate offering goddesses or dakinis from your heart and that they make the seven usual offerings to you, you recite the offering mantras, OM VAJRA ARGHAM . . ." and so forth. Then you think that these same offering goddesses sing praises to you as Vajrasattva. Thinking that, you yourself recite the praise, which is one stanza.

The meaning of it is as follows. VAJRASATTVA MAHASATTVA, is the first line and it says that Vajrasattva is a great being, or "sattva," because he is utterly pure and embodies the purity that is the nature of all things.

The second line says, "First Vajra, Samantabhadra." The meaning of this is that Vajrasattva's status or nature or realization is not the result of his having emerged from confusion through pursuing the path. From the very beginning of time Vajrasattva, who is also known as Samantabhadra, the primordial buddha, has been completely pure, completely awakened. Therefore he is called the First Vajra.

The third line says, "Vajra, all tathagatas." In being the primordial buddha, in being that essential nature of purity itself, he is, in a single form, the embodiment of the vajra nature of all buddhas without exception.

Finally you say, "Homage to Vajrasattva." This is called "the praise," and at this point you think that the deity as yourself simply dissolves, and you rest without any kind of conceptual focus. You do not request the deity to depart. The reason for this is that, in the understanding of this practice, your nature and the nature of Vajrasattva have from the very beginning been identical. Once you have identified yourself with Vajrasattva through or in the practice, asking him to depart would be meaningless, since from the very beginning he has been your own nature. For example, if you pour water into water, you can no longer separate them, and any attempt to divide the second water from the first water will be fruitless.

In the most extensive form of Vajrayana practice, which is the practice of the combined mandala of the eight dispensations, there are 725 deities. The essence of the 725 deities is the 100 peaceful and wrathful deities. The essence of the 100 peaceful and wrathful deities is what is called the 25 deities, or 25 families, and the essence of this is the five buddhas, each of which has a fourfold retinue. The essence of the five buddhas is Vajrasattva, who is called the all-embracing single family. Therefore it is understood that by meditating on Vajrasattva you are simultaneously meditating on all deities, all buddhas, and all mandalas. By accomplishing, or realizing, Vajrasattva you accomplish or realize all deities, all mandalas, and all buddhas. Therefore this very secret practice of Vajrasattva is considered to be the essence of all of the tantras and teachings of the eight dispensations and the peaceful and wrathful deities.

The chapter indicated four Vajrasattva practices: outer, inner, secret, and very secret. It now gives a fifth, which is called *the Vajrasattva practice of suchness*, or of the nature. The reason this was not enumerated as a phase of Vajrasattva practice at the beginning is that, strictly speaking, it is not a Vajrasattva practice at all, and you will see why. All things, meaning all things that we call relative truth or "the deceptive truths," are infallible in their interdependence. This means that because they have no inherent existence, because they are produced by causes and conditions, any change in the causes and conditions that affect or control them or bring them about will change those things that are affected by them. It is for that reason that these practices—the outer, inner, secret, and very secret—are effective in the purification of obscurations. In short, because obscurations and the traces of wrongdoing that are brought about through causes and conditions have no inherent existence, they can be purified through changing the conditions.

One of the implications is that ultimately speaking, from the point of view of the definitive meaning, from the point of view of the nature of things (which could be called Mahamudra), because wrongdoing and obscurations are only relative truths, only deceptive truths, only true for deluded cognition, they have no real existence. From the point of view of the ultimate nature, there is no such thing as wrongdoing and there is no such thing as confession because from the very beginning wrongdoings and contraventions of samaya, downfalls, and so on have never had any inherent existence.

Practically speaking, this means that your fundamental nature, which is the nature of your mind and the nature of all things, is free of any kind of substantial entity or substantial existence. In that sense one could say that it is like space. Something that is insubstantial cannot be affected by anything else. For example, whether there are bright, cheerful clouds in the sky or dark, threatening clouds has no effect whatsoever on the space of the sky itself. Nevertheless from our point of view these things seem to affect us. The reason for this is that as long as we operate under the illusion or false imputation of substantial existence or substantial entity, we experience things in a deluded way. In that deluded way, which we call relative truth, there is consistency and there is definitely a result of actions. Ultimately, however, things have always been utterly pure. Not pure in the sense of something that was dirty and got cleaned up, but pure in being the dharmadhatu, or expanse that is the nature of all things, which is free from, or beyond, any substantiality or insubstantiality.

From that point of view, virtue, which is like bright clouds appearing in the sky, really brings no benefit and wrongdoing does no harm. This is not true in our experience, however. Virtue brings tremendous benefit and wrongdoing brings tremendous harm. Nevertheless neither affect our fundamental nature, which remains the same regardless of what we do and therefore regardless of what we experience as a result. If you engage in wrongdoing, you end up going to the lower realms, but even if you are burned in hell for aeon after aeon, your nature has not been affected in the slightest nor has it degenerated to any degree. If you cultivate the path, you eventually attain supreme awakening, samyaksambodhi, but even if you attain that, your nature has not improved in the slightest degree in any way.

In short, the nature of your mind is like space in the sense that, not being substantial, it is not truly affected by anything that occurs within it. Ultimately wrongdoing, or "that which is to be confessed," the person performing the confession, and the act of confessing are all beyond elaboration. They have no true existence. If you realize that, this is the ultimate confession. This is taught in the first chapter of *The Tantra of Stainless Confession*. If you actually want to put this into practice, it is done simply by looking at your mind without prejudice or assumption, and relaxing in that act of looking.

In order to show that he did not come up with this himself, Karma Chakme Rinpoche quotes Tilopa's *Mahamudra Upadesha*, or *Instructions on Mahamudra*. About this Tilopa said, "The darkness accumulated throughout a thousand aeons is dispelled in one instant by the illumination of one lamp or torch. In the same way, at the very instant at which you realize your own self-aware mind to be the clear light, all of the ignorance, wrongdoing, and obscurations accumulated throughout innumerable aeons are burned up." Therefore this is referred to as the torch of the teachings, or the torch of the doctrine.

No matter how long a place has been without light, as soon as a light is turned on, it becomes light at that instant. The amount of time that has passed is no longer relevant. The darkness does not need to be separately removed; it is removed simply through the act of illumination. In the same way, all wrongdoing and obscurations fundamentally obscure the nature of your mind. Once the nature of your mind is recognized, that in itself removes all obscurations. Therefore the entire process we go through of purification of the obscurations, gathering the accumulations of merit and wisdom, and the effort to receive the blessing of the root and lineage gurus—the purpose and function of all of this without exception is to bring us to a realization of the nature of our mind. It is that realization itself that truly and finally removes all of our obscurations. Therefore that realization is called the torch of the teachings.

That quotation refers to this aspect of purification, which is called the ultimate purification, or purification in suchness. It is possible because your mind in itself — that is to say, the nature of your mind — is indestructible. It is indestructible and unchangeable because it is without any substantial entity or substantial existence whatsoever. Finally realizing the nature of your mind, therefore, is realizing what is called the true vajra. All of the uses of the word *vajra*, including the one in the name Vajrasattva, are metaphorical and refer to this nature. To understand that is to realize what is really meant by the concept of "vajra." The cultivation of that realization, the cultivation of that familiarization with and meditation on that nature of your mind, is the true "Vajrasattva." This is what is really meant by the vajra-being, or Vajrasattva.

Therefore, at that level of purification in suchness, one does not look for purification from outside oneself. One simply observes one's mind. One simply fosters the experience and recognition of the nature of one's own mind. That is the ultimate meditation and mantra recitation of Vajrasattva.

In summation, we have discussed the five styles of Vajrasattva practice described in this chapter: the outer, inner, secret, very secret, and ultimate or natural Vajrasattva. If you practice them properly by reciting the requisite number of mantras and doing your best to have a clear visualization, there is no doubt that all of your wrongdoings and contraventions of commitments will be purified. By practicing in this way, you make your human life meaningful. Although we have wasted innumerable lifetimes up to this point, and therefore have not attained awakening, if we make good use of our present human life, then we ensure at least our eventual awakening. Certainly, having engaged in such practices in this lifetime, you will proceed from happiness to happiness, which means that you will not be reborn in lower states and will gradually progress along the path until you attain buddhahood.

When you do a practice such as Vajrasattva—that is, a practice of purification—there are likely to be indications in your experience of something happening, some kind of change occurring in you. These indications can take different forms. What is explained in the text are indications that we would normally find pleasant and that we would assume mean that the practice is going well, and they do. You should not, however, think that everyone is definitely going to have the same experience of the practice.

The typical signs described in the text are that you will feel physically well; you will feel vigorous, tranquil, and at ease. At the same time, your mind will become clearer than it was before. You will experience an attitude of renunciation because you will experience a recognition of the futility of samsara and the value of liberation. At the same time, you will have greater faith or confidence through an appreciation of the qualities of the Three Jewels and a wish to attain those qualities yourself. Also, some kind of meditation experience or possibly realization will arise apparently spontaneously within you through doing the practice. For some individuals there will be experiences like this, which occur in the waking state, or direct experiences of the mind. For others there will be dreams that indicate that you are going through a process of purification, for example dreaming that you are washing, or putting on bright or white, new, clean clothes. You could dream that you are drinking some kind of ambrosia or milk, or dream that you are flying. All of these are considered to be indications, in this context, of purification. You could have all kinds of positive experiences like that, an increase in your experience of sacredness, and so on.

Not everyone is going to experience purification as a pleasant thing. Because purification is the removal of the imprints of previous wrongdoing, you could experience it as somewhat unpleasant. You could find that your mind is becoming more and more agitated as you continue the practice. You could actually even experience some kind of external upheaval in the circumstances of your life. It is natural for us, when this happens, to assume that we are doing something wrong, that we are doing the practice wrong or that we are not doing it enough or something like that, otherwise these bad things would not happen. That is not necessarily the case. Do not forget that when you are doing a practice like Vajrasattva, because you are purifying your previously accumulated negative karma, that karma may show up in your life. This is like washing dirty clothes. When you immerse dirty clothes in the washing solution, initially they seem to get even dirtier because the dirt starts to emerge from them, and they may even smell. But they are not getting dirtier; this is the beginning of the dirt coming out of the clothes. If these experiences arise for you while you are doing a purification practice, be patient. Recognize that it is the eradication of negative karma, not the accumulation of it, and continue to do the practice.

That completes the chapter on the Vajrasattva practices of purification.

Questions and Answers

STUDENT: You mentioned that a violation of a root samaya is particularly serious. What is a violation of root samaya?

RINPOCHE: The generic meaning of a samaya violation is that when you are practicing Vajrayana, if you violate the commitments, which form the parameters for the practice, then the practice will not work. No qualities will arise as a result of the practice. A root samaya violation is defined as one that eradicates all benefit from the practice. A branch samaya violation is one that diminishes, impinges upon, or impairs the benefit of the practice. Thus if you violate branch samaya but not root samaya, there will be benefit to the practice but there will also be problems because of the violation. If you violate root samaya, there will be no benefit whatsoever to the practice of Vajrayana. The most important of the root samayas—the first of the fourteen root samayas that are commonly enumerated—governs your relationship with your root guru. Therefore the most fundamental definition of a violation of root samaya is to sincerely, that is to say from the depths of your heart, turn against the guru—his body, speech, or mind.

STUDENT: Is it necessary to have the Vajrasattva empowerment for all of the different stages of the Vajrasattva practices?

RINPOCHE: Generally speaking, Vajrasattva empowerments are required in order to do the inner forms of Vajrasattva practice, such as the inner and secret practices, and so on, but are not, strictly speaking, required in order to do the outer practice. The main form of Vajrasattva practice we do, and that with which we must begin, is the outer practice, which is found in the ngondro preliminaries.

STUDENT: Is there a separate liturgy for each of those practices, or could someone do them using the ngondro liturgy?

RINPOCHE: There are liturgies for all of these different aspects of Vajrasattva practice, although they are not exactly what was described in the chapter of the manual we were discussing today. For example, there is the practice of sang thik Vajrasattva, or "the secret essence of Vajrasattva," which is kind of a combination of the secret and the very secret form of it, and so on.

STUDENT: If one knows the ngondro practice and is familiar with the visualizations and one does not have that much time, is it okay to skip the liturgy and just do the Vajrasattva visualization and the mantra?

LAMA YESHE: Do you mean when you are accumulating Vajrasattva recitations as done in ngondro?

STUDENT: No, I mean afterward, when one has completed that.

RINPOCHE: That is fine.

STUDENT: Compared to understanding the purification of sickness and wrongdoing or the breaking of samaya, I find it hard to understand what the demons are that I am trying to purify, so I find it hard to relate to them. Can you offer some explanation of what demons are and how we can relate to them?

RINPOCHE: The term that has been translated "demon" here is *dön*, which has a slightly more specific reference. There are both outer and inner döns, or demons. Outer döns are when, as a result of your previous accumulation of negative karma, you are actually harmed by others. These may be beings with bodies, such as other people, or they may be apparently disembodied beings that somehow affect you. Then there are inner döns, and these are your five kleshas.

STUDENT: If we are then asked to purify, or imagine the purification of, our kleshas, is that one and the same as purifying our demons?

RINPOCHE: Essentially yes, because if you purify the kleshas, there will be no basis for the appearance of harm from others in the external world.

STUDENT: I know that a lot of things are serious wrongdoings, but other than those I am always in question, thinking, "Is this wrong, or is it right?" I have a lot of problems with that on a daily basis. It is similar to the story you told about knifing somebody and then simply saying, OM VAJRASATTVA HUM. Is there a book on wrongdoings?

RINPOCHE: There is a sutra taught by the Buddha that is called *The Sutra of a Hundred Actions, (or Karmas)*, and one of the purposes of that sutra is to delineate what constitutes virtuous and unvirtuous actions. But I have to tell you that it is very hard to understand that sutra, so it might not be that useful. Fundamentally what needs to be understood about actions is that any action that is motivated by a mental affliction, such as anger or aversion, including irritation, or any action that is motivated by ignorance, is unvirtuous. It is because of that, as you indicated in your question, that we have so much trouble recognizing our constant minor unvirtuous actions, because the very nature of an unvirtuous state of mind is that it is obscured and obscuring. It covers up its own unvirtuousness through its being an ignorant state of mind, which is one that is not fully aware of itself. Although this manifests in our experience and our behavior in all kinds of ways, it often manifests as a feeling of irritation or frustration, which many of us know best as getting angry at yourself or getting angry at an inanimate object. Normally we would not think of that as unvirtuous because we are not directly harming anyone else, but it is an unvirtuous state of mind because it is ignorant and also because it is founded upon aggression or aversion. In any case the fundamental root of all of these unvirtuous states of mind and unvirtuous actions is ignorance, and ignorance by its nature is the hardest to recognize.

STUDENT: This is in reference to confession and the form it should take, for example the way to work with confession that is most complete and helps develop the resolve not to repeat habitual patterns. If I were to go into all the things I have done wrong, not to mention all the right things that I did not do, it would take too much time. Instead can I go on to some of the things I was doing right. Is this okay?

RINPOCHE: What you say is precisely true. None of us can actually remember all of the wrongdoings we have engaged in, even in this lifetime. Even if we could remember them, enumerating these actions one by one would take almost forever. In addition to that, we have been accumulating this kind of negativity throughout beginningless time and we have no memory of all of the things that we have done prior to this current lifetime. Nevertheless we do bear the imprints of those actions and are at risk of experiencing their results unless we confess them. Therefore any act of confession has to be stated in such a way, in such language, that it is inclusive of all of the actions, all of the wrongdoing that you have ever committed in any way. So the specific liturgy can vary, but it will always include the words and the ideas that "I confess all of the unvirtuous actions or wrongdoing I have performed throughout beginningless time, or throughout beginningless samsara, with body, speech, and mind." You also have to be aware, when you are making or performing the confession, that you cannot remember all of the wrongdoings you have committed. You are directing the confession to all buddhas and bodhisattvas with the understanding that since they are omniscient, they can and do remember all of your unvirtuous actions even though you do not. You are essentially saying, "All of those actions that I have ever done wrong, which you know about in detail but I do not remember, I am confessing and admitting. May I never perform any of them again." With such an attitude that is all-encompassing, you can actually purify all of your previous actions.

STUDENT: Is the Chenrezik visualization, when you have him over your head and he sends the purifying rays to remove your obscurations, similar to or the same as the Vajrasattva? Specifically, if you feel that you need more purification, can you extend the part where you get the flow of amrita, or do you need to do a totally separate sadhana, such as Vajrasattva?

RINPOCHE: You can definitely do the practice of Chenrezik in order to purify wrongdoing and obscurations, and you should not think that it is necessary to shift to a different practice in order to do it. Ultimately all of these deities, all of these practices, have the ability to purify anything because they are all fundamentally embodiments of the same nature, the same wisdom. For example, because it says that Vajrasattva is the embodiment of all deities, it also follows logically that Vajrasattva is present in all other deities, so that when you meditate upon Chenrezik, he is no different in essence from Vajrasattva. If any one of them includes all of them, then it must follow that they are all included in any one. With regard to the technique of the Chenrezik practice, immediately before you recite the mantra, you recite the section of the liturgy to which you were referring, in which you say, "Rays of light come from the body of the Noble One and purify . . . ," and so on, and you describe the purification not only of your wrongdoing and obscurations but of your perception, so that the entire realm becomes Sukhavati and all beings become Chenrezik. You can continue with this visualization while you recite the mantra, continue to visualize Chenrezik above your head, continue to have the rays of light purify you and all beings, and transform your perception as well. This does not have to be done just briefly and then discarded.

STUDENT: I would like to return to the subject of the four powers. You taught that if you do not have 100 percent regret, then you are not going to get the result, so that you really have to have those first three powers before you even get to the fourth power. I know, sometimes, that something is not right and that I should regret it, but I do not really want to regret it. Is there any way that I can generate more of a sense of regret in my practice?

RINPOCHE: You are perfectly correct in saying that the reason we have so much trouble generating the power of resolution not to commit an action again is that we lack sufficient remorse. You are absolutely correct in saying that. Therefore you are also correct in saying that we need to exert ourselves in some way in cultivating regret or remorse for our wrongdoing. The first step is to recognize what we are doing, which means thinking about it until we are certain what it means to say that any act of wrongdoing only leads to suffering. There is never any real profit or benefit in it; it always leads to suffering. The second step is actually to contemplate the details of what suffering really means, especially in its more intense form. To this end you can turn to books such as *The Jewel Ornament of Liberation* or similar texts in which the sufferings of the hell realm, the preta realm, the animal realm, and so on are described in detail. When you study this material, you need to actually imagine it. You need to contemplate it in the sense of imagining yourself in your present body experiencing the sufferings described in the text. When you are doing this kind of practice, you imagine yourself as you are now in this body being in whichever hell realm it is, and at the same time you bring to mind how little tolerance you have for pain. We find the idea of being stuck by a pin or a needle, such as when we get an injection, really nerve-racking. We do not want anything like that to happen to us. Imagine being immersed in a fire that destroys you again and again and again, for aeon after aeon after aeon. In the same way, you can use your imagination to put yourself through any of the sufferings of any of the realms, especially the lower realms.

What is important to bring to mind when you are doing this contemplation is that that which experiences the suffering is the same mind that experiences the human realm today. The way you experience sensations is pretty much the same. Of course, the environment is different and the body is different because the environment is different. But the way that the body experiences sensation, its degree of sensitivity to pain, is if anything, greater and more sensitive than what we experience in the human realm. Fundamentally what this comes down to is a belief. If you actually believe in the results of actions, you will have no trouble generating regret for unvirtuous actions or wrongdoings because you will know what they lead to. If you have that regret, you will have no problem resolving not to repeat the action. It is like discovering that you had drunk a deadly poison—you would experience intolerably strong regret for having done so, as well as the wish to do anything possible to remove the poison. It depends on how much you believe it. If you think, "Well, there is a slight possibility that what I drank had poison in it, but I do not really know," then of course your regret will be less strong, and as a result your resolution will be less strong and intense. It comes down to whether or not you really believe in karma.

STUDENT: My question is on the subject of virtuous as opposed to non-virtuous action. A large part of my life is in the business world, and I am looking to increase that action in the workplace. There are certain principles that I observe now, such as not misrepresenting myself or the company I work for and trying to make all transactions increase the other person's confidence or peace of mind. I am cognizant that I work for a company that has a certain agenda, which is making more money, and that is fine with me, but I am looking for some way to align the teachings with my work on a daily basis, like a kind of meditation in action.

RINPOCHE: Living in this world you must support yourself. None of us have any choice about that. In your case, that involves business, and as you have indicated in your question, one has a certain amount of freedom of choice to pursue business in an ethical way. Specifically, your commitment to not deceiving others and trying not to hurt or harm others is admirable, and I rejoice in it. One thing you might try, as much as you can afford it, is to give to poor people and others who are needy. That can help. It not only helps them, but it also helps you maintain a freedom from negativity in connection with the business. The act of working, pretty much regardless of the occupation, can be virtuous, unvirtuous, or neutral. It depends not only on the effect it has on others but also on the motivations with which you work. Often in business, because it is by nature competitive, competitiveness arises, and that can bring about a situation of negativity to some extent. You need to reflect continually on this, and determine to work with your motivation.

STUDENT: My question concerns the relationship between bodhichitta and the four different kinds of visualizations. Unless I misunderstood, in the first, outer Vajrasattva practice, we are seeking to purify ourselves. At the other extreme, at the other end, the visualization also involves the purification of others. I recognize that for someone like me it would be a hard enough task simply to purify myself. However, in the context of the aspiration of the bodhisattva vow and bodhichitta, doesn't the visualization also involve directly seeking to purify others as well?

RINPOCHE: As you indicated in the way you asked the question, the explicit presence of the purification of the obscurations of others in some of the Vajrasattva practices and the absence of it in others is designed to correspond to the level of ability and the level of maturity of different practitioners. Although we have all taken the bodhisattva vow, our actual altruism and resolve to benefit others even at the expense of our own welfare, is quite weak until we have purified the majority of our obscurations. Therefore it may not be appropriate for every practitioner to focus too much on that initially; it may be asking too much of them. Although we take the bodhisattva vow early on, we have to start small, so to speak, start gradually in our implementation of that vow. For example, in the past, when people were cultivating their paramita of generosity, when someone was frightened by even the smallest act of giving something of theirs away to someone else, they were taught to begin by passing a coin back and forth between their own two hands. This may sound childish, but in fact there are people for whom even that is such a big deal that their hands shake when they do it because they are so unaccustomed to giving anything away.

The preliminary practices are intended to be appropriate for beginners, people who are at the beginning levels. In the outer Vajrasattva, which is part of the preliminary practices, the purification of others is not specifically built in. This does not rule out your visualizing that all beings are simultaneously purified along with you. Were it specified in the practice, then you would have to visualize that, which might be too much. There are some people who are innately compassionate and altruistic. Such people can, from the very beginning, from their first encounter with Vajrasattva practice, think that they are purifying others along with themselves. When someone has that kind of innate altruism, it comes from having a habit of compassion and an aspiration to it from previous lifetimes. Most of us are simply not born altruistic. Most of us are pretty selfish, and in fact we tend to delight in harming others, for the most part.

STUDENT: My mother is ninety-one and because of her acute arthritic pain she has very little enthusiasm about continuing life, although she does not have any great desire to end her life or to die. I tried to engage her in conversations when I was visiting her recently, about how she feels about her life and whether there were still some unfinished goals she would like to attend to, but she is pretty unresponsive to any kind of conversation I attempt to engage her in. Now that we have had these teachings about confessions and purification of wrongdoing, I am wondering if there is any way, with her not being Buddhist, that I might be able to enhance her transition, which perhaps is rather imminent?

RINPOCHE: Because you are connected to your mother by descent, what you do can affect your mother very much, especially if you intend it to. Practically the best thing you can do for your mother is to pray for her yourself. Pray for her easy transition. The best ways you can do this are by using the two mantras: the OM MANI PEME HUNG mantra of Chenrezik and the Amitabha mantra OM AMI DEWA HRI. In addition you can blow gently on your mother's head while saying these mantras; this causes her to be blessed by the mantra. Also, if it will not irritate her, try saying the mantras in her hearing, even just once or twice.

STUDENT: In the practice of confession and purification, is there any importance or emphasis placed on restitution where that would be possible?

RINPOCHE: Restitution will definitely help in the purification of wrongdoing. Actual restitution, manifest restitution, of course, will help, but so will the motivation of restitution, which is the thought that the merit of purification is dedicated to all beings, but primarily to those that you have harmed.

STUDENT: I understand that the Vajrasattva practice is the best way to do confession. Is there a practice that a beginning student, or perhaps someone who is not even a practitioner yet, can begin immediately in order to do confession, knowing that it is possible that one's life could end tomorrow?

RINPOCHE: The two situations you describe are quite different. If someone is a practitioner but is not yet doing Vajrasattva practice, that is one situation. If someone is not a Dharma practitioner at all, has not taken the vow of refuge, and so on, then that is a very different situation. It is hard to prescribe any mode of confession for a non-Buddhist from a Buddhist point of view. However, for practitioners who are not yet doing Vajrasattva practice, you can simply visualize the Buddha, Dharma, and Sangha in front of you. Think that they are present and that they witness your confession, and then perform the confession. As part of the remedial-conduct aspect of the confession, you can recite whatever mantra you wish, such as OM MANI PEME HUNG or OM AMI DEWA HRI, and so on. Again, the hardest thing about confession is the regret. Without the regret there will not be the commitment, and therefore the purification will not take place. The key to regret is that before you begin the accumulation aspect of the preliminaries, or ngondro, you should seriously and intensely contemplate the four thoughts that turn the mind, because only through doing so will you be inspired enough to have stable renunciation for samsara. The four thoughts need to be contemplated to the point that what you previously regarded with attachment you now regard with revulsion and disgust. Only at that point will you have sufficient revulsion to truly regret your actions.

STUDENT: Is the aspiration to purify oneself the key to developing regret, and is this to be cultivated before the practice of ngondro begins?

RINPOCHE: It is important and beneficial to have the aspiration to purify your wrongdoing and obscurations, but you do not need to stop there just because you have not yet begun the preliminaries. Again, what is most important is to recognize how serious a problem wrongdoing is. Once that recognition is established, then any virtuous action is an act of purification. As it said in the text, "Any virtuous action or practice will suffice." Therefore it can be circumambulation, prostration, anything you like.

STUDENT: In practicing for the benefit of others who may be ill or in some other type of dire situation, you indicated that one should visualize the person, mention their name, and then identify the problem. At this point, can we be effective using these practices to benefit others?

RINPOCHE: You do not do these practices unless you have done a lot of the specific yidam practice with which they are connected, so in the case of White Tara you must have already recited at least one million mantras. They will not really work otherwise because you have not been empowered to do them. What is more normally done by people like ourselves is that when we want to pray for someone, we pray for them. We say whatever mantra and whatever prayer and think, "May so-and-so's sickness be pacified" and in addition to that "May the sufferings of all sentient beings be pacified." That is the way that brings certain benefit, regardless of our degree of training, simply through the power of our genuine or altruistic bodhichitta. It not only benefits that person, it benefits us, and indirectly it benefits all sentient beings. The three application visualizations, which were taught in the eighth chapter of this text, are basically for use by those with some experience and realization, and they are very effective when performed by someone like Chakme Rinpoche himself, who was a mahasiddha. Because of his attainment, when he visualized something, it really took effect for that other person. Although these methods are in themselves very powerful, we cannot assume that our doing them would have the same benefit as his doing them.

On the other hand, it is not the case that there are no benefits in our doing a visualization like that, provided it is done with one-pointed focus and the genuine intention to benefit the other person. There is a story that one year, when Jetsun Milarepa was in retreat in the mountains, his retreat location was cut off by snow for six months, from the valley in which his lay disciples were living. During that period, because he was cut off from all food and so on, they assumed that he had passed away. To commemorate him, they performed a service, including a feast offering, and later, when the snow melted and they encountered him again, he asked them, "What did you all do on such-and-such a day? Because starting on that day for about one month, I was so full, I had no wish to eat anything at all." From that it is evident that when, with one-pointed faith and compassion, we perform some type of ceremony or visualization, it can actually affect the person who is the focus, such as bardo beings and so on. That is why we dedicate food and burned offerings and so on to bardo beings.

STUDENT: How can Vajrasattva be the essence of all the deities?

RINPOCHE: Since all the deities are different manifestations or appearances of the same single wisdom, the wisdom of the dharmadhatu, the differences in their appearance, such as their different colors, costumes, scepters, and so forth, are concessions to the different needs or dispositions of different beings.

STUDENT: Why, then, is Vajrasattva the essence?

RINPOCHE: When it is said that the essence of all deities is Vajrasattva, it is not referring to Vajrasattva in the sense of a specific iconographic depiction showing a certain color, a certain position, and holding certain scepters; it is referring to that which Vajrasattva represents and embodies. The vajra part of Vajrasattva's name indicates the unchanging nature of all things, while the sattva part indicates the unwavering compassion that is the effect of the realization of that nature. Thus essentially when we say Vajrasattva, what we are really referring to is the unity of compassion and emptiness, which could be called buddha nature, or could be called the dharmadhatu, or could be called the dharmakaya, whatever you wish to call it. But in essence it is that which manifests as any and all deities, and the particular manifestation of form bodies depends upon the needs of those beings for whom those deities are manifested.

STUDENT: Then why does Vajrasattva represent, or is specifically associated with, purification?

RINPOCHE: Because it is through buddha nature, or the recognition of that expanse that is the nature of all things, that we purify obscurations. That nature has never, from the very beginning, been obscured, and therefore when it manifests in a form body as Vajrasattva, it manifests as the embodiment of that saving from obscuration. The problem is that because we are dualistic, we think that these different forms, or these different deities, are different in essence and nature. We think when we hear the name Vajrasattva that it refers to a specific form, which is a white deity who is sitting in a certain posture, holding certain things, and so on. But once you grasp that all yidams are manifestations of the same wisdom, the same nature, which appears in distinct forms merely to correspond to the aspirations of different beings, then you have grasped the root of purification through Vajrasattva.

I will give you an analogy, one that is imperfect, so it cannot be taken too far, but imagine that there are one hundred containers of water lying outside in the sunlight and each of them has been dyed a slightly different color. Some are different shades of red, others different shades of blue, and so on. Each of them will, from a certain angle, have a reflection of the sun in it, and each of those suns will appear slightly different because of the color of the dye in the water. The essence of the sun that is reflected in all of them is not really different; in each case it is the same sun. What are appearing in the vessels of water are simply different, or distinct, reflections of the same fundamental thing. In the same way all of these different deities are manifestations or reflections of the same fundamental nature. That is indicated in practice when, for example at the end of a practice, the deities dissolve one into another and finally into oneself. It is appropriate to visualize Vajrasattva dissolving into oneself because one's own nature, the nature of one's own mind, is that nature that Vajrasattva embodies or represents. Thus because Vajrasattva has never been separate from you, it is appropriate to visualize that he dissolves into you. We tend to think that we and the deities are different or that the deity is something outside or separate from ourselves. We also think that there are differences among deities, that some are somehow more powerful or better than others, but this is all because of a dualistic fixation that is based upon being deceived by relative truth. From the ultimate point of view of Mahamudra, all deities simply represent this same fundamental nature or buddha nature, which can be called many things. It can be called awareness, it can be called Samantabhadra, and so on.

STUDENT: Do the purification and realization happen simultaneously?

RINPOCHE: Yes, but neither occurs all at once. To the extent that obscurations are purified, there will be realization of the nature. However, until all the obscurations have been purified, the realization of the nature, while authentic, will not be complete. That is why there are different stages and paths.

The Mandala Offering, Which Accumulates a Mountain of Merit

Karma Chakme Rinpoche opens this chapter on the mandala offering with the Sanskrit invocation NAMO RATNA GURU YE, "Homage to the precious guru." This chapter is addressed to a different student of Karma Chakme, Pema Tupkey, who is referred to in many of his writings. It is evident from the beginning of this chapter that he was present along with Lama Tsondru Gyamtso in listening to the teaching. Thus it begins, "Listen, Pema Tupkey. There is only one cause for the arising of well-being and happiness in this and any lifetime, and that is the accumulation of merit."

Anything pleasant that arises in your experience, such as pleasant external circumstances, good health, and prosperity, without exception arise from a cause, and the only possible cause of such things is your having previously accumulated merit. If you do not accumulate any merit, such experiences and circumstances cannot possibly arise for you because there is no cause that will bring about their arising. Everything good that happens to us, that affects us, is the result of our accumulation of merit. The teaching continues, "Therefore it is of the utmost necessity to gather the accumulation of merit. Even the splendor of the body of a buddha, the major and minor marks and signs of physical perfection that grace the body of a buddha at the time of awakening, results from the accumulation of merit."

Not only in our ordinary situation do all pleasant experiences come from our accumulation of merit, but also the observable characteristics that adorn the form and features of a buddha, their majesty and splendor, result from our accumulation of merit on the path. Even though you may have completed the Vajrasattva practice, which is designed to purify obscurations, you still need to go further and accumulate merit. The removal of obscurations itself is not sufficient, in the same way that preparing the field is not enough to grow the crops—you have to actually plant the seeds. Removing obscurations is like preparing a field; the accumulation of merit is like the planting of the seeds.

There are innumerable methods of gathering the accumulation of merit, but it is taught that there is no way more effective or more profound than the offering of a mandala. All other conventional ways of accumulating merit involve using composite things or giving away or offering composite things, and therefore entail some kind of limitation or have some kind of taint about them. Making offering to the Three Jewels, being generous toward those who are in need, dispersing offerings to the sangha, and serving the sangha, such as providing tea during a group practice, and so on—all of these things, of course, accumulate merit, as does creating images, such as having thangkas painted or statues made. The problem with these is that because they involve your actually giving up something, they are all basically tainted. There are individuals who can give things away without any kind of reservation or klesha, but they are very rare.

This "taint" that is spoken of comes about in three ways. In the first place there is the taint that results from the fact of your having an attachment to the process and to the object of giving. Second, for many of us, in order to acquire the funds we use to finance that which we give away, there has been some kind of prior wrongdoing involved in their accumulation. Third, when we are actually giving, there is always some difficulty involved, and this can produce some kind of resentment in us afterward, or in any case there is always the danger that we will regret our giving in some way. We are always doing good things and afterward thinking, "Well, I should not have done so much, I should not have given so much." The offering of a mandala does not involve these problems, because all you are doing is moving piles of rice around. You are not actually giving up anything at all externally. Therefore there is no more profound or effective way to gather the accumulation of merit than the mandala offering, a simple, physically oriented practice.

Chakme Rinpoche points out that this is not only his opinion. He quotes Lingje Repa who was the founder of the Drukpa Kagyu. "Futhermore, all of the sutras and tantras — and within the tantras, both the old and the new tantras — are in agreement that the offering of a mandala is the most convenient and most effective way of gathering the accumulation of merit. Therefore it is most appropriate to practice it."

Like the practice of Vajrasattva, there are different levels or styles of mandala offering practice: the outer mandala, the inner mandala, and the secret mandala. As in the case of the Vajrasattva practice, they correspond to different levels of previous training, different dispositions, and so on.

The first of these is the *outer* mandala. To offer the outer mandala, you visualize all buddhas and bodhisattvas as present in the sky in front of you. If you actually have the materials for a mandala offering, the mandala plate and the grain and so forth to be offered on it, then you physically offer it. This would involve the thirty-seven-pile offering, or whichever form of the mandala offering you are doing. If you do not have these materials, the outer mandala can be offered simply through the mandala gesture or mudra that we commonly use before teachings.

In either case, when you are offering a mandala, you imagine that it is the entire world consisting of the four continents and Mount Meru and including all of the wondrous possessions of humans and gods. You offer not just one of these worlds; you offer billions and billions of them. Think that you offer everything fit to be offered throughout the billion worlds in the entire realm that is the activity of the Buddha. You offer it by thinking that you give up all of these things and present them as offerings to the buddhas and bodhisattvas. By doing so, you accumulate merit that is the same as what you would accumulate by physically offering all of these billions of worlds and everything they contain to buddhas and bodhisattvas. The reason this is the case is that you are not actually accumulating the merit through physically presenting these things to buddhas and bodhisattvas, for they have no desire for material things of any kind. You accumulate the merit through your willingness to offer everything, through your intention. The intention is just as well articulated or manifested through your symbolic offering as it would be through a physical or actual offering, therefore you accumulate the same merit.

In the practice of the outer mandala, you do not normally dissolve the field of accumulation into yourself at the end. You either request that the deities depart and return to their own places or you simply stop visualizing them and let them dissolve into freedom from conceptual focus. In any case, because it is entirely symbolic, this practice of the outer mandala is free from any kind of stain or taint of resentment.

With the *inner* mandala practice, as with the practice of the outer mandala, you visualize the Three Jewels in the sky in front of you. In this case, it is specified that it be all gurus, all yidams, and so forth. The inner mandala is different from the outer mandala in that you are not offering the outer world; you are offering the inner world of your body. In that sense it is similar to the practice of chö, or severance; however, there are many differences as well. For example, in this practice, unlike in chö, you do not need to separate your awareness from your material body. In the practice of chö you begin by doing the transference of consciousness; here you do not need to do that. You simply visualize your body, just as it is, as the mandala of the world and offer it as such. In detail, you conceive of your four limbs as the four continents; of your spine as Mount Meru; of your skin as the golden ground that is the foundation of the world; of your central channel, or avadhuti, as the wish-fulfilling tree; of your heart as the wish-fulfilling jewel; and so on. In the practice of chö there is a very, very detailed list of correspondences between your various organs, sense organs, and so on, and the different things that are found in the mandala offering. Here the list is basically the same. In general, the entire contents of your body, your flesh, blood, bones, and all of your organs, are seen as an unlimited variety of desirable things that normally belong to the gods and humans. These would include the sixteen offering goddesses and innumerable offering substances that produce undefiled well-being; you offer all of those things. At the end of offering the inner mandala, you think that the deities who are the recipients of the offerings dissolve back into you.

The third type of mandala offering is the *secret* mandala offering. As in the outer and inner mandala, you visualize the field of accumulation in the sky in front of you. Again it is specified that this includes all gurus and yidams gathered like masses of clouds. To make the offering, you first visualize your mind as a wish-fulfilling jewel. The reason for this is that just as the wish-fulfilling jewel is said to be the source of all that is needed or wished for, your mind is the source of all things. Therefore for the purpose of making the secret mandala offering, the offering of mind, you visualize your mind as a wish-fulfilling jewel, and you think that constantly emanating from that wish-fulfilling jewel, which is actually your mind, are innumerable offering substances similar to the offerings produced by the aspiration of the bodhisattva Samantabhadra. In the aspiration of the bodhisattva Samantabhadra the offerings that are produced are first of all innumerable in number and variety. Beyond that, each and every one of them multiplies itself exponentially so that each one produces ten more of its kind, and each of those ten produces ten more, and each of those ten produces ten more, so that each offering produces tens, and hundreds, and thousands, and tens of thousands, and millions, and billions. Thus you think that in that way, emanating from your mind in the form of a wish-fulfilling jewel, is an unlimited variety and number of offerings such that they fill all the realms throughout the universe to the limits of space. You think that these are constantly offered to all buddhas and bodhisattvas of all places and all times. That is the secret mandala offering.

In this way you can continually practice the outer, inner, and secret mandala offerings. When you reach that point in your practice, in order to accumulate merit, you should practice this intensively for a week or two weeks or a month, if possible, in strict retreat, and in any case with the utmost concentration.

As in the case of the Vajrasattva practice, there will be some indication of your having accumulated merit. In this case the signs are first of all what you will experience in the waking state, and secondly what you will experience in your dreams. In the waking state you will find that you feel happy and cheerful, and your mind will be lucid and clear. You will not feel particularly hungry, even though you do not seem to need to eat as much as before. You may dream of the sun or the moon rising. You may dream of holding aloft flags or banners of silk, or you may dream that you are blowing a conch shell, or that you are sitting on a throne. You may dream that you are wandering through a field of flowers, and here it says "flowers that are not red." The reason for this is that dreaming of walking through a field of red flowers is sometimes considered a sign of imminent death, so any other color is okay. Or you might dream that you are in a place where there is a great harvest, or that you acquire some jewels or something very, very precious.

All of these are signs of your having gathered the accumulation of merit, but as with Vajrasattva, you should not mistake these for an indication that you are done. They merely show that you are moving in the right direction. Until you attain full awakening or full buddhahood, you need to continue to gather the accumulation of merit.

Therefore even after you finish making the mandala offering as the major focus in your practice, you should continue to make it every day, which could mean, if you can, doing the extensive mandala offering (the thirty-seven-pile mandala offering) or if not, just the one stanza of the brief mandala offering, or if you cannot do that, even just the mandala-offering mantra. Whichever one of these you do, if you do it one hundred times every day and visualize the mandala offering those hundred times as well, then you will continue to gather the accumulation of merit.

Now we come to the presentation of our specific practice of the mandala offering according to the Mahamudra tradition. According to this tradition, when you are doing the mandala offering as it is found in the Mahamudra preliminaries of the ngondro, you need two mandala plates. One is called the accomplishment mandala, and the other is called the offering mandala. *The accomplishment mandala* is placed on the shrine as a support or focus for your visualization of the deities who make up the field of accumulation, and since there are basically five groups of these deities, you therefore place five piles of grain on the accomplishment mandala. Because this has to last for the duration of your practice, traditionally we use five small tormas instead of the five piles of rice.

Next you visualize the accomplishment mandala as a palace made entirely of precious materials. Inside it, seated on five thrones, you visualize the principals of the five aspects of the field of accumulation surrounded by their retinues. On the central throne you visualize your guru in the form of Vajradhara, surrounded by all the other root and lineage gurus. To his right you visualize Buddha Shakyamuni, surrounded by all the other buddhas. To the left of Vajradhara you visualize the principal heart disciples of Buddha Shakyamuni, surrounded by all the other members of the Sangha. To the rear, you visualize the Dharma in the form of books. And at the front, you visualize the yidam, surrounded by all the other yidams taught in the tantras. Also in the palace, in between these five groups, you visualize all the dharmapalas. You may either think that simply through visualizing them they are automatically present because of their omniscience (as is presented in the ngondro liturgy itself), or, if you wish, you can insert an actual liturgy of invitation, request to be seated, and so on. Either is appropriate. Then, in the presence of that assembly and to that assembly, you perform the offering of the mandala. At the end of the session you dissolve the assembly into yourself rather than requesting them to depart, as in the conventional outer mandala. That is *the mandala offering of relative truth*, and that is true also of the outer, inner, and secret mandalas, presented earlier. All of them are the mandala offering of relative truth, which gathers the accumulation of merit.

The mandala offering of absolute truth is how you gather the accumulation of wisdom. This is done by looking at your mind with your mind. As in the equivalent part of the Vajrasattva instruction, you simply allow your mind to look at itself, at its own nature. You rest in that, relaxed, without distraction. That is how you gather the accumulation of wisdom. Essentially what this means is that you rest free of concept or conceptual elaboration in your mind's natural state, which is called Mahamudra.

It is best if these two practices, the accumulation of merit and the accumulation of wisdom, be combined, mixed, or done simultaneously. This is to say that while visualizing the field of accumulation and gathering the accumulation of merit, you also rest in a direct experience of your own nature. Since that is difficult, it is also acceptable to alternate them. This means that for the body of the session you gather the accumulation of merit according to relative truth. At the end of the session, after dissolving the field of accumulation into yourself, you look at the nature of your mind and gather the accumulation of wisdom according to absolute truth. In any case, it is of the utmost importance that from now until the actual attainment of awakening, both of these elements, the accumulation of merit and the accumulation of wisdom, be represented in your practice.

At this point Chakme Rinpoche inserts a quotation from Tilopa to show that this is not merely his own opinion but is a traditional teaching of our lineage. It says, "Naropa, do not be separate from the two wheels of the chariot, the gathering of the two accumulations, until you attain full awakening." The meaning of this is that just as a chariot needs to have two wheels in order to function as a vehicle, your practice has to include these two elements, the accumulation of merit and the accumulation of wisdom, in order to function as a vehicle or path to awakening. When you actually fill up with these two accumulations, once you have a good stock of them, everything else will happen automatically. You will automatically have realization of the nature of all things. Automatically your insight into the nature of things and the particulars of things will increase. Automatically your wishes will be accomplished in accordance with the Dharma. Automatically you will understand the meaning of the teachings of the Buddha. Automatically you will be passing through all of the various paths and stages that are delineated in those teachings. And finally, you will come to attain supreme awakening. That completes the presentation of the mandala offering, "which is a mountain of merit."

Questions and Answers

STUDENT: In the Chenrezik practice as it relates to mandala, is there a short mandala practice and a seven-branch prayer where you are making offerings and you say "I and everything else," or does the word *mandala* only relate to the specific kind of layout of the offerings?

RINPOCHE: The daily practice of Chenrezik includes offerings in the seven branches. It does not specifically include a mandala offering, although if you are able to remember it while reciting the offering branch, you can include in your visualization the offering mandala as part of it, but it is not specifically mentioned in the liturgy. The nyungne practice of Chenrezik, which is more extensive, does include the mandala offering in addition to the seven branches.

STUDENT: In the teaching on mandala practice there was a section that was related to offering the body. As I recall, there were correlations to the regular mandala practice that one learns, that the heart is the wish-fulfilling jewel, and then it was continued as in chö, and so forth. Could you fill that in? I have not received the chö teaching, so I do not know what correlates to what.

RINPOCHE: What was presented is sufficient for the inner mandala itself. Aside from the heart being the wish-fulfilling jewel, the spinal cord being Mount Meru, and the four limbs being the four continents, no details were given. You simply think that all of your innards take the form of all the splendid possessions of gods and humans, and that is enough.

STUDENT: What color is the wish-fulfilling jewel? Is it blue?

RINPOCHE: The custom seems to be to depict it as blue, when it is depicted, but its wish-fulfilling quality has nothing to do with its color. The defining characteristic of a wish-fulfilling jewel is that it can fulfill one's wishes in an instant, which might also include its changing color — if you wanted it to be red, for example.

The Guru Yoga That Is a River of Blessings

The next chapter begins with the Sanskrit invocation NAMO MAHAMU- DRA YE, "Homage to Mahamudra." Then Chakme Rinpoche address- es his disciple: "Lama Tsondru Gyamtso, listen. Because devotion is the source of meditation, meditation on guru yoga is known to be extremely important."

THE GURU AS THE OBJECT OF SUPPLICATION

To begin with, one has to recognize or determine who the guru, the object of supplication, actually is. It is therefore necessary to under- stand the varieties among gurus. There are essentially five different types of gurus, and these are explained in this part of the text. The first is *the person from whom you take the vow of refuge*, from whom you take the most fundamental upasaka, or lay ordination, the person who, as it is said, "cuts your hair." That guru should be a bhikshu, if there are fully ordained monks or bhikshus present in the area. If there are none, then it can be a shramanera (a novice) or an upasaka (a lay disciple). In the absence of a bhikshu, these others are allowed to give the vow of refuge. Thus the first type of guru is the person from whom you take this vow. Such a person is very kind to you because he or she has given you the vow of refuge.

The second type is *the khenpo or preceptor from whom you receive an active ordination*. This is either the preceptor from whom you received the novitiate ordination, which is called "leaving home," or the pre- ceptor from whom you received full ordination, which is called "completing the approach, or process." The ordination must be given in the presence of a certain number of fully ordained monks, depending upon where it is given. If it is in a central country, that is to say a place where there is a great monastic sangha, there must be twenty-one monks present at the ordination. If it is in a borderland, which from the Dharmic point of view means a place where there are very few monastics, it can be as few as five. Strictly speaking, the ceremony can be conducted by as few as two, the preceptor and the instructing master. In actuality if it is any less than five, you will receive the vow but the two who ordain you will incur a minor violation, which is like a misdemeanor. In addition, to receive monastic ordination, you must be without the specific impediments that disqualify a person for ordination, and again, the situation is the same: You receive the vow, but the preceptors commit a misdemeanor. For the authentic pratimoksha vow, or vow of individual liberation ordination, to be transmitted to someone, they must have an actual stable renunciation of cyclic existence and the wish to be free of it. If they do not have that, then the vow they receive is, in a sense, not the full, authentic vow of pratimoksha.

With regard to the guru who transmits the pratimoksha vows—the refuge, upasaka, and monastic vows—regardless of how great that person's qualities may be, he or she is not regarded as Buddha. From among the Three Jewels, such a person is regarded as Sangha because the person is fulfilling the function of the Sangha. This means that you should regard the preceptor from whom you receive any form of pratimoksha vow as the foremost member of the Sangha.

Now we come to *the guru who administers the bodhisattva vow.* According to the Mahayana, that person must possess the bodhisattva vow and must hold its lineage, which means two things: They must have received it, and they must not have committed a root violation or impairment of it. If they possess those two qualifications, it does not matter whether they are a monastic or a householder, they are qualified to give the bodhisattva vow. However, as in the case of the pratimoksha preceptor, those gurus who transmit the vows according to sutra, regardless of how great their personal qualities may be, are regarded merely as "spiritual friends," or as bodhisattva members of the Sangha.

Generally, it is taught that the attitude you should have toward your preceptor, the one who gives you the pratimoksha vow, is the same as toward a parent, for example a father. The attitude you should have toward the one who teaches you the sutras, for example the one who gives you the bodhisattva vow, is to consider them as a physician and to consider yourself to be like a person who is ill and requires the attention of a physician. There is no greater view of the guru than that.

Next, we come to *the guru who transmits Vajrayana, or secret mantra,* to you. This fourth type of guru is specifically the one from whom you receive empowerment. Whatever that guru may be, regardless of his or her possession of personal qualities, the one from whom you receive any empowerment should always be regarded as the deity or yidam of that empowerment. This is clearly presented in many empowerment texts, which were composed in India, many of which contained the words, "Do not view the guru and the yidam as different from one another. If you view them as the same, you will definitely be able to receive sacred siddhi or attainment." The meaning of this is that all attainment comes from viewing the guru as the yidam. Therefore regardless of the guru's personal qualities, if you receive empowerment from that person, that is how you should view them.

There is a traditional story in our lineage that once, while in the presence of his guru Naropa, Marpa had a vision of his yidam, which was the deity Hevajra. Naropa was of course aware that Marpa was having this vision and he said to Marpa, "To whom will you prostrate first? To me, the guru, or to your yidam?" Marpa thought, "Well, I can usually see the guru when I am in his presence, but I only rarely see the yidam. Therefore I will prostrate to the yidam." However, that reasoning was mistaken, and as a consequence, Naropa prophesied the following: "Your Dharma lineage will flourish like the current of a great river, but your family lineage will vanish like a flower that appears in the midst of the sky." Indeed we know that Marpa's family lineage did die out, even though he had had seven sons by that point, while his Dharma lineage did not.

Thus it is taught that if you view the guru and yidam as the same, you will attain siddhi in accordance with the practice of that yidam, but if you view the yidam as superior and other than the guru, it is very difficult for the practice to be successful. This needs to be pointed out, because it is not uncommon for us to think that the guru is just a person whereas the yidam is something spectacular, something wonderful, something supermundane. If you hold the guru and the yidam to be very different in that way, your practice will not lead to the attainment of siddhi. It makes no difference whether the guru who bestows empowerment is a buddha or a sentient being. What makes a difference is your attitude, your degree of faith. If you actually view the guru as the yidam, then you will receive all of the blessings and all of the attainments and siddhis that come from that yidam. Therefore it is said that in the Vajrayana it is our faith that produces the attainment, not the actual qualifications of the guru. This is because when you view a guru as a deity, it benefits you, it affects you, whereas it does not actually bring any benefit to, nor does it particularly affect, the guru himself. It is simply a method that leads to your accomplishment or your realization of that deity. As an illustration of this, Chakme Rinpoche recounts an event in the life of Milarepa when his students came to him and said, "Of whom are you an emanation? Of which buddha or bodhisattva are you an emanation?" And he said, "I have no idea myself of whom I am an emanation. It is quite possible that I am an emanation of a sentient being from one of the three lower realms, but if you view me as Vajradhara and supplicate me in that way, you will receive the blessing of Vajradhara." That is the understanding we have of the guru of secret mantra in general, which is to say, the guru who bestows empowerment.

The fifth and final type of guru is *the guru of Mahamudra*, which is to say the teacher from whom you receive the transmission of Mahamudra. Unlike the guru of Vajrayana in general, the guru who teaches Mahamudra cannot be just anyone because the qualities of Mahamudra can only be transmitted, or pointed out, by someone who has realized them. Just as you can only make tsa tsa in a mold that has the characteristics that you want to come out in the tsa tsa, so it is taught that for Mahamudra, in contrast to Vajrayana in general, the teacher or guru must have realization.

Unfortunately, in the present age of degeneration, we face the problem not only that such realized teachers are not necessarily easily available but, even more, that we have no way ourselves of determining whether someone has realization, especially since even though they may have realization, we ourselves lack trust, or confidence. Even though a teacher may be perfectly realized, we might not believe it or have confidence in them. Therefore if you are unable to find or connect with a teacher who you are absolutely certain possesses perfect realization, you should not think that this disqualifies you as a recipient of Mahamudra teachings. What you are instructed to do in that case is, having received the Mahamudra transmission, which could even be instruction based entirely on a text, to then view the teacher as whichever guru of the Mahamudra lineage you have the most faith in. It could be Gampopa or any of the Karmapas, such as Dusum Khyenpa, or if you are a practitioner of another Kagyu lineage, it might be Lord Gotsangpa, for example. Traditionally, in the Karma Kagyu it would most likely be someone such as Gampopa or one of the Karmapas. In that case, having received the transmission from a holder of the lineage, you would consider that figure of the lineage in which you have the greatest confidence to be your root guru, and you would supplicate him as such. According to the statements of the great teachers of the Kagyu lineage, this attitude or approach will produce Mahamudra realization. This was taught out of compassion and a realistic sense of the needs of future generations of Kagyu practitioners.

You can supplicate any member of the Kagyu lineage as your root guru and hold them as such, but in that case, you should visualize your present teacher in the form of the historical guru or in the form of Vajradhara. The reason for this is that if you view your present root guru in his actual form, because we tend to project a sense of limitation and aversion onto an ordinary human form, you will receive in your experience not only the qualities for which you are praying but the reflection of your own negative projections. Thus in order to receive the qualities and blessings of realization, without any reflection whatsoever of negative projections, it is best to view your root guru in the form of a deity, such as Vajradhara, and not in the ordinary form in which you perceive him. In any case, the method that produces realization for someone who has no realization, which is to say that causes realization to grow, increase, and be perfected; the method that dispels all impediments and protects you from all sidetracks and mistakes; the method that blesses and consecrates your body, speech, and mind; that enables you to accomplish your wishes without any impediments; that causes you to be attended and assisted by all of the protectors of your lineage — the supreme method for all these things is guru yoga.

Guru yoga is presented in four topics, which are outer guru yoga, inner guru yoga, secret guru yoga, and very secret guru yoga. The first of these is the outer guru yoga, which has three varieties: the visualization of the lineage gurus as stacked one above the other, the visualization of the lineage gurus as a crowd surrounding the root guru, and finally the visualization of the root guru alone as embodying the entire lineage.

OUTER GURU YOGA

Stacked Visualization: How to Visualize the Lineage One Above the Other

The first to be presented is how to perform guru yoga visualizing the lineage one above the other. If you have received empowerment for a yidam practice, then you would visualize yourself as that yidam when you are doing guru yoga. For example, in the Kagyu tradition if you have received the empowerment to do so, you visualize yourself as Vajrayogini when you are doing guru yoga. If you have not received this empowerment and are just beginning with the preliminary practices, then you visualize yourself in your ordinary form. In either case, you visualize your root guru above your head in the following way.

On a precious throne upheld by eight snow lions, on top of which is a lotus and moon disk, is seated your root guru in the form of Vajradhara. This is to say, you visualize Vajradhara and think that he is your root guru, your personal guru, appearing in that form. Then, as the name of this technique indicates, you visualize the entire lineage, one above the other, above him. His teacher is above him, and his teacher's teacher is above him, and so on until you reach the original Vajradhara from whom the lineage descends on the top. They are visualized one above the other just like pearls on a string.

When visualizing the root and lineage gurus in this way for guru yoga, you do not need to invite them. Normally when you are doing yidam practice, you visualize the yidam and subsequently you invite the actual yidam and dissolve it into your visualization. The visualization is called the samayasattva or samaya deity; and the invited, actual deity is called the jnanasattva, or wisdom deity. Here it is understood in the attitude toward guru yoga that it is unnecessary to invite the gurus because they are always present whenever they are thought of, like the reflection of the moon in a body of water. All the bodies of water automatically will have the reflection of the moon in them provided that they are positioned so that the moon can be reflected in them. It is not necessary for the moon to be separately invited into each pool of water. In the same way, whenever you think of the guru, the guru is present. It is sufficient in guru yoga practice to recognize that from the very beginning, the visualized or samaya guru and the wisdom guru are inseparable.

The main part of the practice of guru yoga is supplication or prayer to the guru, which can take several different forms depending upon the specific practice or liturgy of guru yoga that you are using. In the most elaborate form, this consists of a long supplication to the entire lineage, each member of which will be mentioned by name, as in our Mahamudra preliminaries. Here we focus on one specific type of supplication, which is used in our Mahamudra preliminaries and is also found in many preliminary practices of both the Sarma and the Nyingma schools. It is called the Ma Nam Zhi Kor, or the four manams. *Ma* and *nam* are simply the first two words of each of the four lines of the supplication. *Ma* means "mother" and *nam* is the first part of the word for "space."

The next part of the text is a commentary on this prayer. I will give you a translation of the prayer so that you will understand the commentary:

All sentient beings, my mothers who fill space,
supplicate the guru, the precious Buddha.

All sentient beings, my mothers who fill space,
supplicate the guru, the pervasive dharmakaya.

All sentient beings, my mothers who fill space,
supplicate the guru, great bliss, the sambhogakaya.

All sentient beings, my mothers who fill space,
supplicate the guru, compassion, the nirmanakaya.

The text explains the meaning of this supplication, which although commonly used is seldom explained. The first point, which should be obvious by looking at the structure of the supplication, is that you are not praying for your own benefit. You are not praying because you want to be happy or you want to be free of samsara. You are praying on behalf of all beings.

Wherever there is space, there are sentient beings; and wherever there are sentient beings, they are afflicted by ignorance, mental afflictions, and karma. Essentially what this supplication consists of is praying that every sentient being throughout the universe realize Mahamudra.

Let us consider the second line first. "All sentient beings, my mothers who fill space, supplicate the guru, the pervasive dharmakaya." What does it mean to refer to the guru as the pervasive dharmakaya? The dharmakaya is called pervasive because all buddhas are the same in the dharmakaya. In this sense there is only one dharmakaya for all buddhas. It is called Samantabhadra, "the all good," and is shown as Samantabhadra; it is called Vajradhara and shown in that form; it is called the Great Mother, Prajnaparamita. It is called the youthful vase body; it is called the primordial buddha. And so on. All of these names are styles of depiction that indicate this same dharmakaya, which has from the very beginning been awake, and that is the dharmakaya of every buddha. The mind of your guru is nothing other than that. Therefore the mind of your guru is that pervasive dharmakaya that is the mind of all buddhas. That is what is meant by the dharmakaya guru.

The next line says, "All sentient beings, my mothers who fill space, supplicate the guru, great bliss, the sambhogakaya." The sambhogakayas, or bodies of complete enjoyment of all buddhas without exception, no matter how many buddhas there are, are what we call the five sambhogakaya buddhas, or the sambhogakaya buddhas of the five families. There are no sambhogakayas that are not included in that. Regardless of which buddha it is, his sambhogakaya is the five sambhogakaya buddhas. Therefore, that is also the sambhogakaya of your guru. That is what is called the sambhogakaya guru.

"All sentient beings, my mothers who fill space, supplicate the guru, compassion, the nirmanakaya." Nirmanakaya is unlimited and innumerable. We can say one dharmakaya and we can say five sambhogakayas, but because nirmanakaya is a direct response to the needs of individual beings, there are in a sense as many nirmanakayas as there are beings to perceive them. The sambhogakaya is experienced only by buddhas and bodhisattvas, who have pure perception, but the nirmanakaya, because it is a spontaneous response to the impure or ordinary perception of ordinary beings, is in a sense completely unlimited in how it might appear. We can attempt to sum it up by saying that according to the sutras there are three types of nirmanakaya. These are called supreme nirmanakaya, born nirmanakaya, and made nirmanakaya.

The *Abhidharma* talks about a billion worlds like our own; it also states that "billion" is the number that corresponds to the activity of a single nirmanakaya buddha. According to the basic presentation, as each of the thousand buddhas of this fortunate kalpa appears in this world, he will also appear simultaneously in a billion other worlds— not only buddhas but also the great bodhisattvas like Avalokiteshvara, Arya Tara, Guru Padmasambhava, Vajrapani, and Manjushri. There are a billion of each of these as well. In fact there are even more worlds, since this figure of a billion drawn from The *Abhidharma* is merely symbolic. Elsewhere it is said that the field of activity of a single supreme nirmanakaya is sixty-two times the number of grains of sand in the river Ganges. In all of those worlds, all of those buddhas, all of those bodhisattvas, and all of those Guru Padmasambhavas are emanations of Avalokiteshvara. The meaning of this is that Avalokiteshvara (Chenrezik) is the embodiment of the compassion of all buddhas, and compassion is the source of all compassionate activity. That is why you refer to the guru as compassion, the nirmanakaya guru.

At the same time, Avalokiteshvara, Padmasambhava, and our root guru, Karmapa, are three different names for the same thing. They are of the same nature, clearly predicted by Buddha Shakyamuni himself, all of which is included in what we call the nirmanakaya guru.

This is the same in essence as the fathers and sons of the Kagyu lineage. It is for this reason and with this intention that in the *Guru Yoga of the Four Sessions*, Gyalwa Mikyo Dorje wrote, "I supplicate you who are the principal figure in the boundless realms. I supplicate you who pervade all realms with your emanations. I supplicate you who surpass our thoughts, our expectations, and even our hopes." This and similar parts of the *Guru Yoga of the Four Sessions* refer to the fact that the guru, the Karmapa, is all-pervasive.

All of this is included in what is called the *supreme nirmanakaya*. In the histories of the previous births of Buddha Shakyamuni there are many stories of the Buddha having been born in ways that were directly responsive to the particular needs not only of particular beings but of particular species, for example, taking birth as a fish, taking birth as a rabbit, taking birth as a person in a difficult social position, and so on. All of those are what is called *born nirmanakaya* or *nirmanakaya of birth*.

In the billion worlds that the text speaks about, each of the countries that we know in this world, especially the ones connected with Dharma, have an equivalent. Therefore they say that in those billion worlds, there are a billion Tibets, and in each of those Tibets, just as in the Tibet of this world, there are the two principal supports, which are the two Jowo. There are two images of the Buddha that were offered by the two queens of Songtsen Gampo. The one offered by the Chinese queen was Jowo Shakyamuni, which is an image of Buddha Shakyamuni, and the other one, which was offered by the Nepalese queen, is an image of the Buddha Akshobhya, and is therefore called Jowo Akshobhya. There are such famous supports in each of the billion worlds, and not only those two, but also all of the properly created and consecrated images of the Buddha, including thangkas, stupas, and so forth. All such things are considered nirmanakaya because they are emanations or agents of the buddhas' activity. They are what are called *made nirmanakaya* or the *nirmanakaya that is constructed*.

That which is in essence a buddha or a bodhisattva can manifest in any emanation that is appropriate to benefit beings. The reason for this is that buddhas have to manifest in such a way that we can communicate with and relate to them. For example, if a person were to walk into the midst of a group of animals, the animals would be frightened and run away. Consequently in order to benefit those animals, a buddha needs to take birth as that type of animal. Buddhas and bodhisattvas can display any form of imaginable emanation. Within human society, they can take any place and fulfill any role — as monarchs, as ministers, as religious teachers, and so on. An emanation is not a one-step process. There will be an emanation of a buddha, and that emanation can produce other emanations, which are called secondary emanations. Those can produce still others, which are called tertiary emanations, and each level of emanation can produce further and further, so you get four, five, six, and seven.

There are examples of this where great teachers such as Jamgon Kongtrul Lodro Thaye the Great, and Jamgon Khenytse Wangpo produced five simultaneous emanations. The point of all of this is that such buddhas and bodhisattvas are not hesitant or afraid to take birth, and therefore go through death, in order to benefit even one single being. They have no hesitation whatsoever about this. When the Eighth Gyalwa Karmapa, Mikyo Dorje, was asked how many emanations he had, he answered, "Well, just in Tibet about 500,000." Of course, there was only one Mikyo Dorje, there was one Karmapa who was the throne holder, but he had emanations and secondary emanations and so on spreading out to that number. All of this is included in what we call the nirmanakaya guru, so when you are supplicating in that line, that is what you are referring to.

To return to the first line—"All sentient beings, my mothers who fill space, supplicate the guru, the precious buddha"—you are specifically thinking of your own root guru because, according to the anuttara yoga tradition of the Vajrayana, your root guru is the embodiment of all buddhas. The reason that the mind of the guru is the embodiment of all buddhas is because if the mind of the guru is the dharmakaya, which is the wisdom of all buddhas, it follows that the mind of the guru embodies all buddhas. Since the guru is the source of Dharma, the speech of the guru is the embodiment of all Dharma. However the guru may manifest, whether as a monastic or as a chakravartin, the body of the guru as the foremost member of the Sangha is the embodiment of the whole Sangha. The qualities of the guru are what manifest as the yidams and other deities, and the activity of the guru is what manifests as dakinis and dharma protectors.

All of this is included in the guru alone, which is why we say, "The guru is the Buddha, the guru is the Dharma," and so on. If you supplicate the guru alone, you are automatically supplicating all the rest because they are included in the guru. If that is the way you understand this supplication, the Ma Nam Zhi Kor, then it is to be used as the principal supplication. Therefore in the Mahamudra preliminaries, you accumulate 100,000 of that supplication. Alternatively, you can use a supplication addressed to any of the fathers and sons of the lineage. For example, in the Mahamudra preliminaries there is a second supplication composed by the first Gyalwa Karmapa, Dusum Khyenpa, LAMA RINPOCHE LA SOL WA DEP, which is also included. You can also recite the name mantra of the guru, which in the case of the Mahamudra preliminaries consists of the short supplication to the Karmapa, KARMAPA KHYENNO. In the Mahamudra preliminaries you do all three of these. After every Ma Nam Zhi Kor supplication, you say KARMAPA KHYENNO, so you accumulate 100,000 of each.

At the conclusion of the session, you think that ambrosia streams from the bodies of the lineage gurus and the root guru and enters through the aperture at the top of your head, filling the channels of the wheel of great bliss (the mahasukha chakra) inside your head.

This first empowerment purifies all physical obscurations and grants you the vase empowerment, which makes you capable of accomplishing *vajra body*. The ambrosia next fills all of the channels in the throat, purifying the obscurations of speech and granting you the secret empowerment, which makes you capable of accomplishing *vajra speech*. Next the ambrosia fills all the channels in the heart, purifying the obscurations of mind, granting you the empowerment of knowledge, and making you capable of accomplishing *vajra mind*. Then it fills all the rest of the channels in your body, from the navel down to the bottoms of your feet. This purifies all of the wrongdoing and obscurations of body, speech, and mind acting in conjunction. Through this you receive the fourth empowerment, the precious word empowerment, which enables you to accomplish the *essence body*, which is the *vajra nature*.

You think that all of the lineage gurus melt into light and dissolve into your root guru. The root guru melts into light and dissolves into you. At this point you rest in the confidence that the body, speech, and mind of all of those root and lineage gurus and your body, speech, and mind are completely inseparable as though water had been poured into water. Corresponding to the degree of your confidence—which means the degree of faith with which you supplicated the gurus during the main body of the session and therefore the degree of confidence you have in their having dissolved into you—corresponding to this, there will definitely arise some kind of meditation experience, maybe realization. Having enough confidence is sufficient; you simply do not need to attempt to alter or control what arises as a result of that devotion.

This is how to perform guru yoga by visualizing the lineage one above the other, and how to receive empowerment at the end in the form of one single stream of ambrosia, which is one of the ways that the empowerment at the end of guru yoga is sometimes visualized. This technique, the stacked visualization of the lineage is basically the same in the Sarma and Nyingma guru yogas with some slight differences in the individuals represented.

Meditating on the Guru Surrounded by the Lineage Gurus, Gathered Like a Crowd

First you need to understand the different aspects of lineage, what constitutes a lineage. There is a difference in the way lineage is reckoned in the Nyingma teachings as opposed to the Sarma teachings.

In the Nyingma teachings, the lineage must be sixfold. The first of the six is "the lineage of the thought or wisdom of the victors, the buddhas." This is the lineage that has passed from the dharmakaya Samantabhadra to the sambhogakaya buddhas of the five families. It passed from all of the buddhas who have appeared in the past up until now, which is to say the sixty-five buddhas that are described as having appeared in the past, especially the twelve buddhas who have appeared in this realm. This is all in the context of the Dzokchen tantras, where this is explained. The point is that this lineage is passed from one buddha to another simply through the intention of it being passed. No form of communication, no form of gesture or symbol, is necessary. It passes from one buddha to the next buddha to the next buddha simply by the presence of the intention through which each buddha completely recognizes and receives the meaning of Dharma. Therefore it is called *the lineage of the intention or thought of the victors.*

The second lineage, which starts with Garab Dorje is passed down to Shri Singha; the eight great vidyadharas of India; Guru Padmasambhava; and his disciples, such as Mandarava. In the case of such individuals, the transmission of the lineage occurs through the display of a very simple symbol or sign, such as a gesture of the hand, which causes the recipient of the lineage to receive the complete transmission and to understand the complete meaning of Dharma. It is therefore called *the symbol lineage of the vidyadharas, or holders of awareness.*

The next lineage, *the lineage of entrustment of the dakinis,* arises when wisdom or karma dakinis physically entrust teachings to appropriate individuals. This can be done in two ways. One way they transmit the teachings is to entrust the "dakinis' parchment," which consists of small scrolls in which there are scripts that have no recognizable letters and do not mean anything in any human language. Their function is to cause the teachings to arise in the mind of the recipient. The other way in which they transmit teachings is through handing a book, such as an entire volume of teachings, to the recipient master who is receiving it. In either case, as soon as the scroll or volume is placed in the hand of the receiving master, they immediately understand all of it. They receive the complete transmission, and in fact they become the inheritor or owner of those Dharma teachings.

The next lineage concerns the subsequent discovery of such teachings. Individuals who received empowerment, transmission, and instruction from Guru Padmasambhava, either in India or in Tibet, were in many cases empowered by him through ceremonies of empowerment and through the making of powerful aspirations on his part and on the part of the disciple. They were empowered by him, upon their subsequent rebirth, to rediscover teachings they had previously received from him. The way this works is that the aspiration and empowerment are done so that the discovery will happen when the particular teachings will most benefit the people of that time. It will be discovered by the rebirth of the particular disciple who was originally given those specific teachings. Usually this involves an emanation of Guru Padmasambhava appearing in the vicinity of the person who discovers it. The emanation, who is not the discoverer himself, will do something to reawaken the person's habits, making the person capable of finding it. This is called *the treasure lineage of aspiration.*

Many things have to come together for the discovery to occur and to be most fruitful; it requires a lot of interdependence and auspiciousness. Essentially, the factors that determine whether or not these things will come together are the merit and receptivity of the people at that time, because the discovery is designed to benefit those people. If they are receptive to the teachings in general and will be receptive to that teaching in particular, the discovery will occur without impediment, and the teachings can be spread, but it has to be done without any kind of violation of the circumstances. In other words, if the signs that indicate it is appropriate to look for and retrieve the treasure are not present, it may not be retrieved at all, but when the signs are present and it is retrieved, it is practiced by the discoverer and transmitted to his disciples and brings great benefit.

The final lineages are what are transmitted from that point onward. The discoverer passes on the lineage, and then it is called *the ultimate lineage of dispensation*, or *the passing on of the true meaning*. Or else it might also be called *the lineage of compassion and blessing*.

Great individuals, such as the great teachers of today, receive the complete empowerment, transmission, and instruction of those teachings and then transmit them in their complete and elaborate forms to the next generation. Because that involves primarily oral transmission, it is called *the oral lineage of individuals*.

In this tradition it is considered important that the actual texts be used when giving empowerments, transmissions, and instructions, and it is important that the texts be actually read and not just recited from memory. The reason is that this brings or maintains the blessing of the original dakini scroll, which was the source for all this. In the Nyingma tradition it is considered to convey more blessing if it is done that way. It is said in that tradition that the best lineage will have all six of these lineages included in it.

In the Sarma, or New Translation, school there are two types of lineages: the Sutrayana and the Mantrayana (Vajrayana). Within the Sutrayana, there are several lineages of the bodhisattva vow. There is *the lineage of profound view*, which originated with the bodhisattva Manjushri and was taught by him to Nagarjuna, and by Nagarjuna to Arya Deva, and so on. Another lineage of the bodhisattva vow, *the lineage of extensive deeds*, is the lineage of Maitreya passed to Asanga, Vasubandhu, and so on. There is also the *short lineage of the bodhisattva vow*, which was passed by Manjushri to Shantideva and by him to the Sumatri Dharmakirti, to Atisha, to Geshe Dromtonpa, and so on. Those are all lineages of sutra.

The Sarma School classifies the lineages of Vajrayana into three — the long lineages, the short lineage, and the lineages of pure appearance or vision. In the context of our own Kagyu lineage, the *long lineage* of tantra refers to the four lineages that Tilopa received in India from human teachers, the Vajrayana lineages of Nagarjuna. The *short lineage* consists of the one that Tilopa received directly from Vajradhara himself, and passed on to Naropa and so on.

It is called the *lineage of pure vision* (or *pure appearance*) when Kagyu gurus have received teachings directly from their yidam or from previous mahasiddhas, who are no longer present, such as Guru Padmasambhava.

In most cases, the teachings were received as a vision while these masters were awake; not in the form of dreams. There is no discussion whatsoever about the validity of a sacred or pure-appearance lineage received when the master is awake. There has been discussion in the past, Chakme Rinpoche writes, about the status of lineages received by a master in a dream. Some logicians have said that if someone receives a lineage in a dream, such as an empowerment or a transmission or both, it is all right for them to practice it, but it is not all right for them to transmit it unless they have attained the first bodhisattva level. However, according to the Third Gyalwa Karmapa, Rangjung Dorje, and the Fifth Gyalwa Karmapa, Dezhin Shekpa, regardless of whether the person has or has not attained the first bodhisattva level, if they have certainty about the validity of what they have obtained, then in fact it is better than their having attained it in an ordinary way in the waking state. For example, when someone receives a complete transmission and empowerment from their yidam during a dream, this is in a sense more extraordinary than their having received it in a conventional way. Karma Chakme Rinpoche here passes on something he was told by Ngawang Tashi Paldrup, that if you think about it, neither waking-state appearances nor dream appearances are real anyway. They are both like dreams. Therefore it is acceptable to transmit a lineage that has been received in a dream. In any case, that is the meaning of *the lineage of pure appearance*, which is the third type of lineage according to the Sarma, or New Translation, school.

The Actual Visualization of the Lineage as a Crowd

Now that we have figured out what the lineage is, the way that you actually perform the visualization of the lineage as a crowd is as follows: As before, you visualize your root guru above your head on a lotus-and-moon-disk seat. Again, you visualize your root guru in the form of the deity, which in the case of the Mahamudra ngondro would be in the form of Vajradhara. Surrounding the root guru, you visualize all of the lineage gurus and all other gurus with whom you are connected in their ordinary forms, for example, you visualize Tilopa and Naropa as Indian mahasiddhas.

As in the previous guru yoga practice, no separate invitation is necessary. They are actually present the instant you recollect or visualize them. You then supplicate using either the lineage supplication or a short supplication. In the previous section, the Ma Nam Zhi Kor supplication was explained. Here the supplication KARMAPA KHYENNO is explained.

The word *karma*, part of the name of the Gyalwa Karmapa, is Sanskrit. Literally translated it means "action," but if we translate it according to the context here, it means that the Karmapa is the embodiment of the activity of all buddhas. Our lineage consists primarily of the Gyalwa Karmapa, so the recitation of KARMAPA KHYENNO is a supplication to all of the Karmapas. The other members of the lineage are only assisting in the performance of the activity of the buddhas, therefore in this one supplication, KARMAPA KHYENNO, you are actually and simultaneously supplicating the entire lineage. It is therefore sufficient in itself as a supplication.

At the conclusion of the session of guru yoga, the deities in the retinue, the lineage gurus and so on, dissolve into the root guru. Then, from the forehead of the root guru, visualized as Vajradhara, rays of white light are emitted, which dissolve into your forehead, purifying your physical obscurations and granting you the empowerment and blessing of body. Then from the throat of the guru, rays of red light are emanated, which dissolve into your throat, purifying obscurations of speech and granting you the empowerment and blessing of speech. From the heart of the guru rays of blue light are emanated. These dissolve into your heart, purifying your mental obscurations and granting you the empowerment and blessings of mind. From the navel of the guru, rays of yellow light are emanated, which dissolve into your navel and purify obscurations that equally affect body, speech, and mind, granting you the blessings and empowerments of qualities. Finally, from the lower abdomen of the guru, rays of green light are emanated, which dissolve into your lower abdomen, purifying the cognitive obscurations and granting you the empowerment and blessing of activity. Then you think that in a state of great joy, the guru melts into light and dissolves into you. As before, you simply rest in the nature of your mind.

This is how to meditate upon the lineage as a crowd, gathered in a mass around the guru. It is in accordance with all the various traditions of guru yoga. When you are doing guru yoga in this way, surrounding the lineage you can visualize the eighty-four mahasiddhas of India, the twenty-five disciples of Guru Padmasambhava, all sorts of mahasiddhas, vidyadharas, and so on. You can think that they are all there.

In the stacked visualization, the empowerment took the form of ambrosia descending through your body. Here it takes the form of rays of light. Empowerment by rays of light is in accordance with kriya tantra.

In the guru yoga visualizing the lineage as a crowd or assembly, we went into a detailed presentation of what constitutes the lineage according to the Nyingma tradition and also according to the tradition common to the Sarma and Nyingma. Within the context of the third type of outer guru yoga—visualizing the root guru alone as the embodiment of all sources of refuge—the understanding of what constitutes a root guru will be presented, based primarily upon the Kagyu tradition.

The Visualization of the Root Guru Alone as the Embodiment of All the Sources of Refuge

In order to do this type of guru yoga where you visualize the root guru alone as the all-sufficient embodiment of the Three Jewels, you need to correctly determine exactly who your root guru is. In order to do this, you need to understand what constitutes a root guru. Nowadays—and although Chakme Rinpoche is referring here to the time in which he was living and writing, the seventeenth century, it refers all the more, by extension, to our present time—monastics in particular and practitioners in general view as their root guru the person from whom they received the vow of refuge or the preceptor from whom they received the vows of refuge, upasaka, shramanera, or bhikshu. Although many people think of it in this way, this is not taught in any sutra or tantra. A preceptor is a preceptor, a root guru is a root guru, and they are different.

All the different traditions hold the general view that what constitutes a root guru is a teacher who is a "threefold vajra holder." What this means is the teacher from whom you received the vows of the three vehicles. Therefore if you received the pratimoksha vow—the genyen, getsul, or gelong vows—either all three or any one of them, plus you received the bodhisattva vow, plus you received the complete four empowerments of any given tantra from a single teacher, that person is the threefold vajra holder because you have received the vows of the three vehicles from them. According to most traditions, that is the person that you should consider to be your root guru.

In the specific context of Vajrayana, the threefold vajra holder is someone from whom you receive the complete four empowerments for your yidam, the reading transmission of the root tantra, the commentaries, and the practical instructions for doing the sadhana of that yidam. That is the view according to most traditions, however if that were true, we would have many root gurus, because after all, we receive empowerments, transmissions, and instructions over the course of our lives not from one teacher but from many. Does that mean that we have more than one root guru? According to the Kagyu tradition, the answer is no.

In the particular tradition of *the ultimate lineage*, or *the lineage of the true meaning* of the Kagyu, even if you receive ordination or vows from a teacher and you receive oceans of empowerments and transmissions from them, or they teach you a great deal about learning in the sciences and other areas of knowledge and are very kind to you;

even if you receive all of this from one teacher, your kind guru, they are not necessarily your root guru. Therefore it is said in the Kagyu lineage songs, "I have had one hundred kind gurus but only one true root guru." In the same way, even a teacher who gives you instructions for your practice, who points out the nature of stillness and occurrence, and the nature of the experiences of bliss, lucidity, and nonconceptuality, such a teacher is kind, but they are not your root guru. Someone only becomes your root guru when, based on their instruction, you achieve direct realization of the nature of your mind. According to the Kagyu tradition, that is the single criterion for someone's being your root guru.

Because that is the criterion, it is irrelevant how much time you have spent with them or how many empowerments you have or have not received from them. You might recognize the nature of your mind simply through seeing their face, simply through meeting them, or simply through hearing a little bit of their speech, possibly not even formal teachings. You might recognize the nature of your mind through receiving a blessing, as is commonly given in a public blessing where the palm of the hand is placed on the top of your head. Maybe you hear some teaching from them or receive a very brief empowerment from them. It might even be someone you never actually meet; you might actually receive a letter from them or something like that. However it happens, when you directly and nakedly recognize the nature of your own mind, the person who causes that to happen is your root guru. According to the Kagyu tradition, such a person alone is considered your root guru.

There is a great deal of historical evidence for this position in our lineage. Lord Gampopa studied for many years with eminent teachers of the Kadampa tradition, and based on their instruction he achieved a level of tranquillity such that he could remain seated in meditation for seven days without moving. Nevertheless because he did not achieve realization of the nature of his mind under their guidance, he did not consider the Kadampa teachers his root guru. His root guru was Jetsun Milarepa.

In the same way, Gampopa's student Lord Phakmo Drupa studied with the great hierarch of the Sakya tradition, Drakpa Gyaltsen, and based upon his instruction, he perfected the meditation experiences of bliss, lucidity, and nonconceptuality. He did not however, fully recognize the nature of his mind under Drakpa Gyaltsen's guidance, but did so later under the instruction of Gampopa; therefore he considered Gampopa alone to be his root guru.

A few generations later in our lineage, the great mahasiddha Urgyenpa had already attained so much common siddhi that he was renowned as a mahasiddha who had mastered many traditions and teachings. He could display miracles at will. Urgyenpa met Lord Karma Pakshi, the Second Karmapa, when he was already in his fifties and only spent two days with him. He considered Karma Pakshi to be his root guru because during those two days he received the full transmission of the ultimate lineage of the Karma Kagyu. He did not receive any elaborate empowerments from Karma Pakshi. In fact all that Karma Pakshi did was to fill a plate with barley, stir it with a riding crop that had been consecrated using the Gyalwa Gyamtso practice, and then place these on top of Urgyenpa's head. Normally you would not consider a plate filled with barley or a riding crop as implements of empowerment. He placed them on Urgyenpa's head and spoke some words of impartation — the impartation of command, the impartation of the lineage — and immediately at that moment Urgyenpa gave rise to supreme genuine realization. At that point Karma Pakshi handed him a copy of the texts that he had composed pointing out the trikaya, called *Karmapa's Pointing Out the Trikaya*. Handing him that, Karma Pakshi said, "Uphold my lineage." That was the transmission of the ultimate lineage. They were only together for two days, and yet Urgyenpa is the person who follows Karma Pakshi in the ultimate lineage of unity, the ultimate lineage of the Karma Kagyu. He was considered by the Third Gyalwa Karmapa, Rangjung Dorje, to be his root guru.

Rangjung Dorje did not receive all of the empowerments, reading transmissions, and textual instructions from Urgyenpa because Urgyenpa had never received them. He received those things from another disciple of Karma Pakshi, called Nyenre Gendun Bum. Nevertheless Rangjung Dorje's root guru was Urgyenpa because Urgyenpa held the true or ultimate lineage beyond words. In the same way, the Sixth Gyalwa Karmapa, Tongwa Donden, had two main disciples, one of whom was Jampal Zangpo, who composed our lineage supplication, and the other one was the first Gyaltshap Rinpoche, Paljor Dundrup. They were co-disciples. They studied together with Tongwa Donden and they received all of the same empowerments and all of the same transmissions at the same time. Nevertheless, because Paljor Dundrup did not give rise to perfect realization under the direct instruction of Tongwa Donden, whereas Jampal Zangpo did, Jampal Zangpo comes next in the lineage. Paljor Dundrup gave rise to realization under the instruction of Jampal Zangpo when he went over the teachings they had both received simultaneously from Tongwa Donden. Therefore it was necessary that Jampal Zangpo, who otherwise would not have been in the direct lineage, take his place in the lineage of the Sixth Karmapa before Paljor Dundrup.

In the Kagyu lineage we do not reckon the lineages we have received separately, thinking that this different lineage of empowerment comes from these different masters and this lineage of transmission comes from these different masters. Although such things are important for the individual empowerments and transmissions, we do not think of those as our lineage. We think of our lineage as the ultimate lineage, which includes the essence of all of it. The reason for this is that when you generate realization of your mind's nature, at that moment you receive the real empowerment, because at that moment you give rise to the wisdom that is the meaning of all empowerments. That wisdom is the supreme essence and the root of the meaning of all of the Tripitaka and all of the four tantras. All of these teachings exist in order to transmit this one recognition, this one wisdom. To recognize the nature of your mind through someone's instruction or blessing is called *the transfer of the blessings of the ultimate lineage*, or the empowerment that transfers the blessings of the ultimate lineage.

This is emphasized particularly in the Kagyu tradition, but it is not unknown in other traditions. In the context of the Nyingma school, the same empowerment that is the transfer of blessings is called *the empowerment of the display of awareness* and again refers to the recognition of the mind's nature. When you receive that, you have received the essence of all empowerments and all transmissions, therefore you consider the person from whom you receive that to be your root guru. Examples of this can be found even today. His Holiness the Sixteenth Gyalwa Karmapa gave the same empowerments and teachings to all of his heart sons and close disciples; nevertheless in his letter predicting his rebirth he said he would be accepted by Lord Amoghasiddhi, referring to Situ Rinpoche by his personal name. The implication is for this ultimate lineage to be unbroken, it has to be continued by the one person who received it, which was Situ Rinpoche. That is why His Holiness the Seventeenth Gyalwa Karmapa has gone to the great difficulty of traveling all the way back to India from Tibet. The reason for this is that he must receive the ultimate lineage from the person who received it from his previous emanation, and that is Situ Rinpoche.

The Actual Visualization of the Root Guru Alone

When you are actually doing this form of guru yoga, where you visualize the root guru alone, you visualize your guru, as before, seated above your head on a lotus-and-moon-disk seat. If your root guru is one of the "fathers and sons" — that is to say, someone who is definitely and obviously a buddha — then it is appropriate to visualize the guru as you see him, in the form that you visually perceive him. This is appropriate because it will only increase your faith and your pure perception of your guru. If it is a root guru about whom you or other people have reservations (in other words, one that you might perceive as imperfect), if you have any reservations about visualizing this person in his ordinary form, then you had better visualize him as in the Kagyu ngondro, as Vajradhara.

Visualizing the root guru alone, either in his ordinary form or as Vajradhara, you think that inside his head at the level of the forehead is a white OM, in his throat is a red AH, in his heart is a blue HUNG, and in the center of his body at the level of the navel there is a yellow HO. From these four syllables, rays of light radiate and invite all buddhas, bodhisattvas, lineage gurus, yidams, and dakinis—all of whom dissolve into the root guru. Reflecting on the fact that the root guru is the embodiment of the Three Jewels, generate devotion, then supplicate the root guru. The supplication that is suggested here is the third supplication found in the Mahamudra preliminaries: LAMA RINPOCHE LA SOL WA DEP, "I supplicate the precious guru," and so on. You can also use the Ma Nam Zhi Kor, or the name mantra, KARMAPA KHYENNO.

At the conclusion of the session, from the OM inside the guru's head a white OM radiates outward and this dissolves into your head, granting you the empowerment of the guru's body. From the AH in his throat a red AH is emanated, which dissolves into your throat, granting you the empowerment of his speech. From the HUNG in his heart a blue HUNG is radiated, which dissolves into your heart, granting you the empowerment of his mind. Finally, from the HO behind the navel, a yellow HO is emanated, which dissolves into your navel, granting you the complete fourth empowerment. As in the other practices, think that the guru melts into light and dissolves into you, and then rest in the experience of your mind's nature without any alteration or contrivance. This means that with the confidence that the guru has dissolved into you, you do not attempt to impose any concept on the meditation experience, such as good or not good or what you expect to discover and so on.

This approach of visualizing the root guru alone as the embodiment of all buddhas is the essence of all instruction on guru yoga. These three techniques are all techniques of what is called outer guru yoga.

INNER GURU YOGA

The second section of guru yoga is the inner guru yoga, and like the outer guru yoga, this has three parts. Inner guru yoga is not superior to outer guru yoga, and it is not that outer guru yoga is incomplete or less efficient. The inner guru yoga is designed for someone who has received the empowerments, transmission, and instruction of a yidam practice, has fully completed the required number of mantras of that yidam practice, and is able therefore to visualize themselves as a yidam with relative ease. This way of doing guru yoga is for such a person.

The basis of the practice of inner guru yoga is to visualize yourself as the yidam deity, whichever is your yidam deity, and especially to visualize that the body of the deity is completely hollow. This is to say, the external form or features of the deity are like a hollow enclosure, such as a tent or a balloon. The inside of the yidam's body is completely hollow. The reason you are visualizing this is to recollect the fact that the yidam's appearance is without any substantial existence.

The yidam is the display or representation of the qualities of dharmakaya, which is the absolute truth. The appearance of substantiality is relative truth, and it is bewilderment. If you visualize the yidam as something substantial, a flesh-and-blood form, then you are degrading something that is a representation or display of absolute truth into an impure display of relative truth. Many of the problems people have when they attempt to do deity practice are connected with this. An example of this is the thought that, "Well, if I move my hand, then I have to visualize the yidam as moving his or her hand." This is a sign of having missed the basic point of yidam practice, which is that it is the insubstantial appearance of the qualities of dharmakaya in that particular form.

Nirmanakaya Guru Yoga

You visualize yourself as the yidam, and in the center of your body at the level of the heart, you visualize a precious throne upheld by eight snow lions. On top of that you visualize a lotus flower, and on top of the center of that a moon disk. Seated on that, you visualize your root guru in the form of the nirmanakaya Buddha Shakyamuni, with the complete appearance of Buddha Shakyamuni. His right hand is extended over his right knee in the earth-pressing gesture, and his left hand is in the gesture of meditation. He is adorned with the three robes of a monastic. In the three places of the body of the root guru as Buddha Shakyamuni, you visualize three syllables, a white OM, a red AH, and a blue HUNG. Think that from those three syllables rays of light are emanated outward, and they summon all nirmanakaya buddhas throughout the universe, such as the thousand buddhas of this fortunate aeon. All of them dissolve back into the root guru in the form of Buddha Shakyamuni, who is visualized in your heart. The supplication is the nirmanakaya supplication from the Ma Nam Zhi Kor, "All sentient beings, my mothers who fill space, supplicate the guru, compassion, the nirmanakaya." You recite that for the bulk of the session. At the end you think that the Buddha, in essence your root guru, melts into light and dissolves into you.

The benefits of the nirmanakaya guru yoga are that your morality will become pure, which means that any previous violations of morality will be repaired, and future violations will not occur. You will be able to benefit the Buddha's teaching. You will have the ability to do so, and all of the necessary circumstances to enable that to occur will be arranged. This is the first part of inner guru yoga, called nirmanakaya guru yoga.

Sambhogakaya Guru Yoga

You visualize yourself as the yidam, and again in your heart you visualize the lion throne, lotus, and moon disk. Seated on top of that, in your heart, you visualize your root guru, this time in the form of the principal sambhogakaya buddha, Vairochana, who is brilliant white in color and adorned with the silken garments and jewelry of the sambhogakaya, like Chenrezik or White Tara. His hands are in the teaching mudra. Again, rays of light from the HUNG in his heart, and so on, radiate outward, inviting all of the sambhogakaya buddhas, such as the buddhas of the five families, all of whom dissolve back into Vairochana in your heart.

This time the supplication is the sambhogakaya line from the Ma Nam Zhi Kor. At the end, as before, you think that Vairochana melts into light and dissolves into you, and you simply rest relaxed without any conceptual focus. The benefits of the sambhogakaya guru yoga are that you will be able to stay put. Being able to stay put means that when you are trying to do some kind of Dharma activity or practice, such as trying to remain in retreat or trying to do some study, it often happens that your mind gets restless and that you want to go somewhere else. This restlessness will be prevented by this practice. In addition, you will be able to hold your ground, which means that you will be able to fulfill your activity in that specific institution or practice place, and finally this will give rise to the experience or wisdom of bliss emptiness. That is the sambhogakaya guru yoga.

Dharmakaya Guru Yoga

As before, you visualize yourself as your yidam. In the heart, you visualize a lion throne, lotus, and moon disk, and on top of that you visualize your root guru seated in the form of the dharmakaya Vajradhara, with all of the usual ornaments. He is the color of the sky, holds the vajra and bell crossed in front of his heart, and so on. Again, rays of light shoot out from his heart, inviting all the dharmakayas of all buddhas, all of whom dissolve into Vajradhara in your heart. For this guru yoga it is especially important to think, "My root guru is just dharmakaya. He really does not even have form. The perception of him as form is just my mistake. He is really the dharmakaya." Giving rise to the certainty that your root guru is the actual dharmakaya, then you recite the dharmakaya line from the Ma Nam Zhi Kor.

At the end of the session, think that the root guru melts into light, which means that you have maintained a bare apprehension of characteristics. In other words, you are thinking of the dharmakaya as the dharmakaya, but you are giving it form—scepters, costumes, ornamentation, and so on. You simply let go of that, which here is called causing it to melt into light, and you mix the guru's mind and your mind. Then rest relaxed, without any kind of alteration or contrivance, in whatever experience arises in your mind through mixing it with that of the guru.

The benefits of dharmakaya guru yoga are that the pure aspect of your mind will be distinguished and separated from the dregs of your mind. The pure aspect of your mind is awareness, the dharmakaya, while the impurities are thought, bewilderment, and confusion. Through doing this practice, the sediment will be separated from the pure aspect, and the naked experience of cognitive lucidity and emptiness will arise. That is to say, a direct experience of your mind's nature, unfiltered by any kind of preconception, will arise, the unity of cognitive lucidity and emptiness. That is the dharmakaya guru yoga.

These three inner guru yogas, together called *the trikaya guru yogas*, come from the text *The Fivefold Mahamudra*, which is one tradition of Mahamudra that we practice. This part of the text concludes with the instruction, "Tsondru Gyamtso, if you want to give rise to experience and realization, practice these." This means that not only Lama Tsondru Gyamtso but also anyone who wants to generate meditation experience and realization would be well advised to practice these.

The text continues, "The supreme guru yoga and the guru yoga of the yidam are the root practices of the secret tradition, which is the most secret oral aspect of the Kagyu tradition. In fact, you do not even chant them aloud; there is not even a liturgy that is recited. Therefore, if it is unfitting even to chant them aloud, how could you expect me to write about them here?" Other than that, there are several other guru yogas that could be called secret and very secret, but because people have different degrees of experience of practice and understanding of Dharma, there is no need to go into them.

Ultimate Guru Yoga

The text now discusses the results of guru yoga, also called the ultimate guru yoga. The point is that any form of guru yoga practice, such as the outer guru yoga, the inner guru yoga, and so on, will lead to realization. Whatever style of guru yoga you are doing, whatever the specific practice involved, at the end the guru dissolves into you and you mix your mind with the mind of the guru through thinking that the guru's mind has dissolved into yours and that they are inseparable and indivisible. Through the power of the blessing of your devotion to the guru, and the thought that the guru's mind has dissolved into yours, the experiences and realizations that arise through that technique or in that context are considered free of impediment and free of defect. Sometimes we might give rise to meditation experiences that are somehow faulty or defective, but the experiences that are born of this type of devotion and mixing your mind with the mind of the guru are considered trustworthy.

Aside from mixing your mind with the mind of the guru, you do not have any kind of attitude or preconception about what that mind, the mixed mind of the guru and you, consists of. When you are simply resting without alteration, you discover that it has no substantial characteristic. It has no form; it has no color; it has no substantial existence whatsoever. Therefore you can call it empty, or emptiness. That emptiness of your mind is the dharmakaya, the dharmakaya guru.

Although this mind is empty in the sense that it has no substantial existence, you do not discover this through thinking "empty." You do not come into it with that preconception. You discover it precisely because you are free of preconception and free of concept. Although it is empty of substantial existence, that does not mean it is nothingness, because at the same time your mind is self-aware. It is aware of itself, and its cognitive lucidity appears or manifests to itself. That is the sambhogakaya guru.

This cognitive lucidity is not limited or unitary in its manifestation. The cognitive lucidity itself manifests in the totality of your experience, which is unimpeded by any kind of limitation. In this sense, the quality of the display of your mind is like the display on the surface of a mirror, which is unlimited by all of the things that are reflected in it. Nevertheless, all of those images reflected on the surface of the mirror have no substantial existence. They do not exist in, behind, or in front of the mirror. In the same way, although your mind is completely insubstantial, because of its cognitive lucidity, it nevertheless manifests as a continuous and unlimited display. That unlimited display is the nirmanakaya guru.

When we talk about these three things, they are conceptually distinguished or isolated from one another. This might lead to the conclusion that they are three different things, but in fact they are not. The openness of the mind is at the same time its capacity to cognize and to display, therefore these three are fundamentally the same thing. This is the fourth body, the svabhavikakaya or essence body.

With regard to the relationship between the mind of the guru and your mind, it is acceptable and appropriate to think that the guru's mind dissolves into yours because the nature of the guru's mind is exactly the same as the nature of your mind. You can distinguish between the guru's mind and your mind simply based on the fact that the guru's body and your body are different. For example, there is water in India and there is water in Tibet. We can distinguish between them. We can call them Indian water and Tibetan water, but the water itself, the chemical composition of water in and of itself, is the same.

The distinction you make between two bodies of water based on geography is like the distinction you make between the mind of the guru and your own mind. They are in different bodies, but they are the same in that the nature of the guru's mind and the nature of your mind is emptiness beyond elaboration. Therefore when you mix your mind with the mind of your guru at the conclusion of the session of guru yoga, you no longer experience a separation between yourself and the guru. In the songs of the Kagyu this is called "not finding an object of supplication." The guru has dissolved into you and is no longer outside you to be supplicated.

This is also expressed in the teachings of Guru Padmasambhava when he said, "Self-awareness is Amitabha; its unimpeded clarity is Avalokiteshvara; and the self-liberation of thought is Padmasambhava." When he says, "Self-awareness is Amitabha," it means the nature of your mind, the emptiness, and its insubstantiality is the dharmakaya, which here is being given the name Amitabha. There is at the same time an unceasing cognitive lucidity that is not a lucidity to something outside itself, but it is lucid to itself. That is the sambhogakaya, which here is called Avalokiteshvara. The self-liberation of thought, the appearance of thoughts within the recognition of the mind's nature, is the nirmanakaya, which here is called Padmasambhava.

Such statements refer to the mixing of the mind with the mind of the guru, with the result of the recognition of the nature of that mind. If you realize this through doing guru yoga practice, then your devotion to the guru becomes what is called "the devotion of dharmakaya," because finally it becomes devotion to the mind of the guru, which is the dharmakaya and which is also never separate from you. Because the nature of that mind is the same as the nature of your mind, from that point onward you are never separate from the guru. This is therefore called the "guru yoga of the nature," or the "ultimate guru yoga."

Whenever you wish to see your guru, simply look at the nature of your mind, because the nature of your mind is the actual nature of the guru. If you see the nature of your mind, you have seen all buddhas, because that nature of your mind is the dharmakaya, the dharmakaya of all buddhas. That is why in the Kagyu tradition it is considered of far more importance to see the nature of your mind than it is to have a vision of a yidam. If you have a vision of a yidam without having seen the nature of your mind, then you might think you are seeing one yidam, or that you also have to see all the others separately. If you see the nature of your mind, you see the dharmakaya, which is the actuality of all yidams, of all buddhas, of all gurus, and so on.

This section concludes, "Therefore, Tsondru Gyamtso, take as your continual practice the dharmakaya guru yoga."

GURU YOGA IN DEITY PRACTICE

The last section of the chapter on guru yoga also begins with the invitation "Lama Tsondru Gyamtso, who emphasizes faith and devotion, listen." The reason why the emphasis on faith and devotion is mentioned at this point is not only to say that Tsondru Gyamtso strongly possesses these qualities but to point out that they must be emphasized. The practice of guru yoga, through which faith and devotion are generated, is the most important form of practice. At the same time, without faith and devotion, you cannot effectively practice guru yoga. If someone with no faith and devotion attempts to practice it, nothing much will happen.

The "jewel of many colors" is a legendary jewel that will adopt the color of the surface on which it is placed. Here it is used as an analogy for the way devotion to the guru can be used in conjunction with deity practice. The jewel is the guru and one's devotion to the guru. Placing the jewel on a surface that transforms its color is like visualizing the guru as a deity.

In the same way, by visualizing the glorious guru in the form of whichever deity you wish, you will receive the blessing of that form on which you are meditating. The point here is that the effectiveness of any deity meditation depends upon considering that visualized deity to be your root guru taking that particular form. For any deity practice to be effective, it has to be a form of guru yoga.

"That precious wish-fulfilling jewel, although it has no thought, if it is placed on top of a victory banner, will rain down jewels, food, and clothing. In the same way, that precious guru, when placed at the top of the victory banner of your devotion and supplicated with intense devotion and yearning, will rain down both common and supreme attainments." The guru is like the legendary wish-fulfilling jewel that, if properly supplicated, will produce whatever is needed or wanted without thought of preference or partiality. Just as the wish-fulfilling jewel has to be placed on a victory banner for the blessing to be received, in the same way, supplication with devotion causes the blessings of the guru, and therefore all common and supreme attainments, to arise spontaneously, just as supplication of the wish-fulfilling jewel causes the rain of food, clothing, and wealth.

Karma Chakme Rinpoche now goes through the ways that you can apply this guru yoga to specific purposes. For example, if you wish to purify wrongdoing, visualize the guru as Vajrasattva, which is what we do in the second part of the preliminary practices, where the Vajrasattva that you are visualizing above your head is identified with your root guru. The purpose of this is to purify wrongdoing. If you wish to purify obscuration, visualize the guru as Akshobhya. If you wish to pacify sickness, visualize the guru as the Medicine Buddha. This will be most effective if your wish to pacify sickness is not merely to pacify your own sickness but to pacify the sicknesses of all sentient beings and the causes of those sicknesses. If you wish to pacify demonic disturbances, visualize the guru as Vajrapani; if you wish to exhibit miracles, visualize the guru as Guru Padmasambhava; and if you wish for wealth, visualize the guru as Jambhala.

In all these cases, the motivation has to be altruistic. If you are wishing for wealth or for the ability to perform miracles for your own benefit and gratification, it is simply not going to work. However if you wish for the necessary resources or for the ability to perform miracles to benefit beings and the teachings, then visualizing your root guru in the indicated form and supplicating them will be effective.

From one point of view Jambhala is a mundane deity, and from another point of view he is supermundane. Here, in visualizing the guru as Jambhala you are thinking of him as supermundane. In the same way, if you wish to increase your longevity, visualize the guru as Amitayus. If you wish to perform great benefit for beings, visualize the guru as Avalokiteshvara. If you wish for a great insight, visualize the guru as Manjushri. If you wish to establish the doctrine and firmly plant the Buddha's teachings, visualize the guru as the Lord of the Doctrine, which refers to Buddha Shakyamuni. If you wish to pacify a danger, visualize the guru as Tara.

The point of all of this is that you should not think that you can only visualize the guru in one form. You should not think, "Well, the guru is Vajradhara, so it is not acceptable to visualize him as Chenrezik or Buddha Shakyamuni," or "The guru is Buddha Shakyamuni, so I should not visualize him as Chenrezik." You can visualize your guru as any of these wisdom deities and you will receive the blessing of whatever deity you visualize him as. For example, by visualizing the guru as Vajradhara, we receive the blessing of Vajradhara.

In any of these cases, in essence it is always your root guru visualized in the form of whatever deity you wish. By meditating on the guru and supplicating the guru in the particular form that is suited to your particular purpose, you will accomplish that activity efficaciously. Karma Chakme Rinpoche mentions that this is not something he is making up, but that it is found in the teachings of our lineage, in a text that is called *The Treasury of Devotion*. He says that he has received the transmission of that text and he is merely setting forth what it says there.

In the practice of guru yoga, there are slightly different ways you can visualize the guru, which Chakme Rinpoche has just described.

Now there is a presentation of the various places they can be visualized. The general custom is that when you are supplicating the guru, you visualize him above your head, and when you are making offerings to the guru, either physically set-out offerings or mentally imagined offerings, you visualize him in the sky in front of you. Throughout the day you can visualize the guru in the center of your heart. If you are ill, you may visualize the guru wherever you are ill. For example, if you have a headache, visualize your guru in the midst of your head; if you have a toothache, in the midst of the afflicted tooth. If you are terrified of something, visualize the guru in the place that you associate with your terror, the place that is the source of your terror. By doing any of these things, all of the problems, illness, fears, and so on will be pacified. It mentions specifically in the text that even if you have a toothache, visualize your guru in the midst of that tooth as the Medicine Buddha. Chakme Rinpoche finishes this part of this section saying, "Tsondru Gyamtso, keep these applications of guru yoga in mind."

He concludes the whole presentation of guru yoga with, "If guru yoga is practiced sincerely, not merely with your mouth, in other words, whatever form of guru yoga you practice, whether outer, inner, or secret, whatever particular tradition it is, it must be practiced more than as something you are just saying without really meaning it. It has to be sincere. Sincerity means that it is practiced with a degree of yearning and devotion that is almost intolerable."

If you start with great yearning and devotion in the practice of guru yoga, your yearning and devotion will increase more and more. Eventually, through the practice of guru yoga, you will get to the point where you cannot think about anything except the guru. At that point, you will come to a very different and far superior understanding of the relationship between your root guru and all other buddhas and teachers. You will recognize that all buddhas and bodhisattvas throughout the universe are merely the emanation of the guru, because you will see that the guru is the embodiment of them all. At that point, all sense of preference and partiality will be swept away, and when you hear about learned or noble individuals, rather than thinking of them as some object of jealousy or competitiveness, you will see them as emanations of your guru. When you hear about the power or blessing of deities, such as the effectiveness in protection of Dharma protectors and dakinis, you will no longer think that they are something outside or other than your guru. Instead you will recognize that they are the emanation of your guru, emanated for the purpose of activity.

The meaning of this is that as long as we have not properly practiced guru yoga, we will have a sense that the guru is just a person and that the deities are somehow superior. When you properly practice guru yoga, you recognize that all of the deities, Dharma protectors, and so forth, are merely emanations or displays of the qualities and activity of your guru. They are not superior to the guru; in fact, they are not other than or outside the guru.

Ultimately you will recognize this is true, because the guru is the embodiment of all buddhas. Once you have completely resolved within the depths of your heart that the guru is the embodiment of all of the Three Jewels, then there will be no limit to your devotion, and you will never be satisfied with your veneration of the guru. You will never think, "I have offered the guru enough. I have praised the guru enough." Even were you to offer your own flesh and blood as an offering to the guru, that would still not be enough for you.

Whenever you think of the guru and supplicate the guru, you will cry uncontrollably. There is actually a saying about this, "If your eyes are dry, you are not a Kagyupa." You will think that you are going to explode with devotion, as though your flesh and bones were going to blow up. It is more than you can stand. When devotion reaches that degree of intensity, even if you try to prevent meditation experience and realization from occurring, you will not be able to. Regardless of how little interest you have in their arising, because of your devotion they will arise automatically.

In most of your meditation experience and throughout your dreams, you will continually meet your guru, receive empowerments and transmissions from him, receive predictions from him, receive instructions on how you should avoid certain problems or impediments, how you can enhance your practice, and so on. When you dream of the guru, the particular expression and gestures of the guru will indicate what you should do and what is going to happen.

In many tantras, such as *The Display of Ati*, it says that the precious and kind guru should be visualized above the head or in the midst of one's heart. By doing so, you will attain all of the qualities of a thousand buddhas. The first point here is that the visualization of the guru is the essence of the visualization of any deity. By visualizing the guru, you will attain the blessing and the qualities of a thousand buddhas.

"Better than millions of recitations of any mantra, is one supplication to the guru." This does not mean that the recitation of mantra is meaningless or has no benefit. The distinction being made here is between the recitations of deity mantras based on the misunderstanding that they are somehow other than your guru, and the simple act of supplicating the guru with the recognition that the guru is the embodiment of all buddhas and all deities.

If you think that the deities you meditate on are other than your guru and are better than your guru, then you will get less out of millions of deity mantras than you will get out of one moment's supplication to your guru. If you have confidence when you are supplicating the guru that your guru is the embodiment of all deities, and if you recognize that the deity is nothing other than your guru displayed in that form, then automatically the recitation of the mantra is supplication to the guru, and this distinction does not apply.

In that way, the benefits of supplication to the guru are unlimited and immeasurable. For that reason, in Kagyu tradition the principal practice is supplication of the guru.

The chapter ends with the following prayer: "Through this presentation of the practice of guru yoga, in the future may there be many practitioners who, through possessing devotion, receive a rain of blessings and give forth the good crops of experience and realization." Karma Chakme concludes, "May this be taught to many and may it bring unceasing benefit for beings." That completes the chapter on guru yoga.

Questions and Answers

STUDENT: In reference to the story about Marpa, I am wondering what Marpa should have done. Should he have bowed to the guru first? Or, because there is no separation between the guru and the yidam, should he have bowed to both simultaneously?

RINPOCHE: What he should have done was to bow simultaneously to both in the recognition of their inseparability.

STUDENT: How does one visualize the guru as the deity without actually having the vision, as Marpa did?

RINPOCHE: In general this is possible without having a vision of the yidam because you take the attitude that the form or appearance of the guru you normally experience is the nirmanakaya; that the speech of the guru is the sambhogakaya, which is the yidam; and that the mind of the guru is the dharmakaya. In that way the guru is the embodiment of the Three Jewels, the three kayas, and of course, all yidams. More specifically, the instruction is to view the guru as the yidam you received from that guru at the time of empowerment. At that time you were instructed to visualize the guru as the yidam and you were provided with sufficient details about the yidam's appearance, otherwise the empowerment process becomes impractical, because you are viewing the empowerment implements, such as the painted icons and so on, as the actual deity, and the guru as some kind of servant of that deity, which is inappropriate.

In the practice of guru yoga, toward the end of the practice all of the other members of the assembly, such as the Three Jewels— the Buddha, the Dharma, and the Sangha, —eventually dissolve into the guru. This visualization is done to remind you of the fact that although the Three Jewels and so forth appear distinct, they are all emanations or embodiments of the guru's wisdom.

STUDENT: At that time, should we also see all the surroundings as the mind of the guru?

RINPOCHE: When you are engaged in the actual profound path of Vajrayana, then you are instructed to view all that appears and exists as the display of the body, speech, and mind of the guru, but this instruction is not necessarily emphasized at the time of the preliminary practices.

STUDENT: In the Chenrezik practice, you are visualizing Amitabha above your head. Since Amitabha is kind of the head of the Padma family, and Chenrezik came from him, is that sort of like a form of guru yoga? I mean, when you become Chenrezik, and you still have Amitabha over your head.

RINPOCHE: It would be hard to say that the practice of guru yoga is completely present in visualizing Amitabha above your head, but it is present in the recitation of the lineage supplication at the beginning of the practice.

STUDENT: In the Chenrezik practice, in the part where you are visualizing yourself as the deity, you really cannot be the deity because if you were the deity, you would be enlightened. I do not understand.

RINPOCHE: As long as we are not free of dualistic fixation, we fixate upon the appearances of things and their apparent characteristics, which cause us understandably to have the attitude that "the deity is pure and I am impure, therefore I cannot be the deity. The deity and I are inherently separate." However, all of the qualities of which the deity Chenrezik is the embodiment are inherent or innate within your own nature. In other words, your fundamental nature or your fundamental being is already the essence or the nature of Chenrezik. This nature pervades all things, including all appearances, all sounds, and all thoughts, consequently in our nature all appearances are already the body of Chenrezik, all sounds are already the mantra of Chenrezik, and all thoughts are already the wisdom of Chenrezik. In order to bring about the direct experience of that, we do the practice.

STUDENT: Does that mean that no matter how terrible one is at the visualizing part, if one just keeps doing it, eventually it will happen?

RINPOCHE: Yes.

STUDENT: When you spoke of the nirmanakaya multiplicity of emanations, does that include all realms simultaneously when a buddha emanates.

RINPOCHE: Yes, there are such emanations throughout the six realms, and they will take the particular form most appropriate to benefit beings in each particular realm.

STUDENT: Does that include both animate and inanimate, such as rivers and trees?

RINPOCHE: Definitely, it also includes inanimate objects. As you see in the aspiration chapter of *The Bodhicharyavatara*, bodhisattvas aspire to take the form of whatever will benefit beings or alleviate their particular sufferings, therefore buddhas and bodhisattvas can emanate as medicine or medicinal substances or as fruit-bearing trees in order to alleviate hunger, and so forth.

STUDENT: Rinpoche, my question has to do with the description of teachings that arise in a dream and teachings that arise when awake. My question is, when they arise during what is called awake, is that a *mind ter*, or is it an actual creation-and-completion practice. Is it ordinary? You did say that it can happen in an ordinary way. What I am asking is, when you draw a difference between dreaming and awake, is it a vision that happens spontaneously when awake or is it a realization that comes from an ordinary practice of a bodhisattva?

RINPOCHE: The reason these visions happen for these great masters and bodhisattvas, whether they occur in the waking state or during a dream, is that they have purified most all of their afflictions and cognitive and karmic obscurations. The one result of that purification is that they see much more and they do it much more clearly. As a result, under various circumstances, these visions can occur for them. It is not necessarily directly related to their practice at that time. They are not intentionally trying to bring about the vision. They are not thinking, "I want to see such and such a deity," or anything like that. Usually it seems that they are resting their minds in a state of simplicity, and from within that state the vision arises.

STUDENT: The text differentiates between the dream and the ordinary awake state. The way you are saying it now, it sounds like it is all the same if you have a vision.

RINPOCHE: It would be pretty much the same whether you are dreaming or awake, which is the reason why the whole question of dream revelation is raised in this chapter, to take exception to the view that it is that much different. When we dream, we are doubly confused, we are doubly bewildered. We are intoxicated by the state of sleep and the state of dreaming. Nevertheless, because of the removal of their obscurations, these great masters are not; their minds are as lucid during the state of sleep as when they are awake. What arises for us is dreams that reflect habits; what arises for them are visionary experiences. There is not that much difference between a vision while their body is asleep and a vision while their body is awake because their mind is pretty much the same thing. Of course, an observer would see a difference. In the one case, the lama would be asleep and in the other case he would be awake. From their point of view, however, there is no difference.

STUDENT: Earlier today you taught us that there is one criterion only by which one defines one's root guru, and that is the teacher with whom one experiences the nature of mind. My question is, does this mean in a permanent sense, or does it mean the first glimpse? Does it mean the first time any teacher is able to impart that experience to you? Maybe it lasts five minutes; maybe it lasts eight hours.

RINPOCHE: In this case, it refers to an unchanging and full realization of the mind's nature.

STUDENT: Do we say, then, that if we have not had that experience that we have not yet met our root guru?

RINPOCHE: It is true. Until you have an unchanging realization of the nature of your mind, you do not yet have a root guru, according to the Kagyu tradition. Until that realization occurs, you can take as your root guru the person from whom you have received, from the Vajrayana point of view, the empowerments, transmissions, and instructions for your principal yidam practice, or otherwise the person from whom you have received the three vows — the pratimoksha, the bodhisattva, and the samaya vows.

STUDENT: I guess this question refers to the other method — not the Kagyu method — of determining one's guru. A friend of mine said that she had heard that a teacher and a student should examine one another for three years. I had not heard this before, and I wondered about that.

RINPOCHE: This custom is recorded as having occurred at the court in China, when one of the emperors wished to take teachings from Sakya Pandita, but he insisted on examining the qualities of the lama for three years before he would take him as his teacher. After three years he was satisfied that Sakya Pandita was an eminent guru, and then Sakya Pandita in his turn said, "Well, I now have to examine you for three years." Unfortunately during those three years Sakya Pandita passed away.

That is the story, but I do not know if there ever really was a specific custom of doing it that way in general. For one thing, in order to make such an examination of the teacher, you would require great intelligence, great prajna to be able to do it. Otherwise, no matter how many years you spend doing it, you might not be able to understand. Then there is the danger, as we saw in the story, of impermanence taking effect within the six years.

STUDENT: For those of us in this lineage who have not taken all of the vows you talked about regarding the guru, should we not look to or feel that His Holiness, the Karmapa, is our root guru?

RINPOCHE: That is fine, especially if you have the attitude that His Holiness is the embodiment of the activity and wisdom of all buddhas.

STUDENT: Is it proper, then, to request from the teacher you are working with at some point to be shown the nature of your mind? Or will that happen spontaneously?

RINPOCHE: There is a custom of requesting your principal teacher to give you what is called a pointing-out instruction. They can do it, but the problem is not the pointing out of it, it is the recognition of it. They may point it out, but the question remains as to whether or not you will actually recognize what is pointed out. The major factors that enable recognition, authentic recognition, to take place are the things that are accomplished during the preliminary practices of ngondro. It is for this reason that so much emphasis is placed on these practices. The purification of obscurations, the gathering of the accumulations of merit and wisdom, and the entrance into you of the blessing of your guru and his lineage, all of these things are necessary for there to be any real possibility of recognition taking place. Normally this happens once the preliminaries have been completed.

Many people do receive pointing-out instructions from various teachers, and in some cases they actually recognize the nature of their minds. In many cases, what happens is they have a kind of experience that is impressive to them, and what is happening is they are receiving a kind of a blessing, but they are not really recognizing the nature of their mind. Often what happens is they simply leave the ceremony or the occasion with a sense of confidence, "Now I have received the transmission," or "I have received the instructions from my guru. Now I really have something." This can be more a sense of just possessing some special secret than anything else. There was a Sikkimese man who could not read Tibetan, and he had received one stanza of instructions from a Tibetan teacher, and he carried this around with him in his breast pocket, saying, "I have the instructions of my guru with me all the time." However, he could not read them.

STUDENT: During the discussion of inner guru yoga, at the end of the session of the three varieties it was said that the guru then melts into you. I am not sure what that means. You have the guru visualized inside you at your heart level. Where exactly is the guru melting into?

RINPOCHE: It means the distinction between the guru and you no longer exists.

STUDENT: The question of "root guru" was something I wanted to discuss because I have a real problem with this. I always feel like I am never going to find a root guru. During ngondro I had flashes of all the many wonderful teachers I have seen. I will flash on His Holiness the Sixteenth Karmapa. I will flash on Chogyam Trungpa Rinpoche. I will flash on Lama Norlha, and it's like, who is Vajradhara up there? I just cannot keep a visualization of a root guru during the preliminaries, and yet we have just been told that the preliminaries are necessary in order to have just that obstacle removed. Would you comment on this, please?

RINPOCHE: Vajradhara is the embodiment of all of the Three Jewels because he is the dharmakaya of all buddhas. Therefore automatically Vajradhara includes all of the teachers with whom you have any connection. It is not that you are not including the human teachers who have been your actual sources of Dharma transmission. It is that Vajradhara is the embodiment of all of them, and by viewing

Vajradhara as your root guru, which automatically means that you are thinking of all of your individual teachers as part of Vajradhara, then you are cultivating a pure outlook toward your teachers that would otherwise be somewhat difficult.

As ordinary individuals, we naturally tend to experience things as somewhat impure, we tend to project impurity rather than purity onto our experiences and onto the people we encounter. As long as you think of your root guru as an individual, a person, you will tend to think of him as ordinary, and you will tend to project all kinds of attitudes and expectations and reservations and things on your guru. There will be a lot of watching out for what the guru is doing to see if he is what you want or not. You think, "Oh, he is mad at me," or "He likes me," or you think, "Boy, he is really wrong. How could he say that or do that?" or you think, "Oh, he is really right. That is exactly what I wanted him to do."

As long as you have all those thoughts, you are allowing the limitation of your projections to be placed on the growth of your devotion. On the other hand, if you view your guru as Vajradhara and think that the form of Vajradhara represents the kindness of all of your gurus, the function and kindness of all of your gurus embodied into one form made entirely of light, and not a corporeality, which therefore cannot be a basis for your projection of liking the guru's form or not liking it; and also that it is simply the embodiment of the wisdom of emptiness, then that will be the most effective thing for the increase of devotion.

STUDENT: When you say "nature of mind," is that equivalent to buddha nature?

RINPOCHE: Yes. They are synonymous terms.

STUDENT: Vajradhara is the dharmakaya representation, and then you have nirmanakaya and sambhogakaya, which you related to Chenrezik and Amitabha. However, all of these always contain all of everything else, so what is the point in separating things into nirmanakaya, sambhogakaya, and dharmakaya?

RINPOCHE: The reason for the isolation of different forms that correspond to the kayas, or bodies, is to depict degrees of purity in the outlook of the perceiver of the aspects of Buddha. One thing was that you were confusing two lists that were given this morning. One list was Vajradhara as dharmakaya, Vairochana as sambhogakaya, and Buddha Shakyamuni as nirmanakaya. The other one was Amitabha as dharmakaya, Avalokiteshvara as sambhogakaya, and Padmasambhava as nirmanakaya. It does not really matter. The point you make is still true.

The reason they are distinguished in this way is to make a distinction between the purity of perception of different observers. In a sense that which is perfectly pure is the dharmakaya, and this is experienced by a buddha himself. Then there is the pure experience of a buddha by another being, a bodhisattva, which is the sambhogakaya, and then there is the experience of a buddha by a being of impure perception but with good karma, which is the nirmanakaya. Then there is the further experience of a buddha, which is indirect, where the being does not have enough good karma to encounter the nirmanakaya and so encounters an emanation or is somehow benefited indirectly by the activity of the buddha. To depict these different levels of perception of a buddha, these different forms are presented.

STUDENT: The triad with Amitabha, Chenrezik, and Padmasambhava — is that a Kagyu point of view? Amitabha and Chenrezik are both in the lotus family, and I wondered if there was any buddha family relationship?

RINPOCHE: The designation of Amitabha as the dharmakaya, Chenrezik as sambhogakaya, and Guru Padmasambhava as the nirmanakaya is a common one that is shared by the Kagyu and Nyingma schools, and although these three deities are, when classified as to family, of the Padma family, this classification is not limited to a description of the Padma family.

STUDENT: I need further clarification on how we view the root guru, because this question comes up a lot at our center. Can you differentiate between "spiritual friend" and how that might be different from the root guru? I am also trying to get a definitive understanding regarding who the root guru is. You seem to be saying that in the absence of a teacher who has pointed out the nature of one's mind in an unchanging way, you may then view as your guru the preceptor of the four empowerments of your yidam; and in the absence of that, the one who offered you the three vows; and in the absence of that, His Holiness as the embodiment of all buddhas. There seem to be many, "if not this, then this." Is there anything definitive, or is it simply that we need to see whomever we see as the embodiment of all buddhas. Is that sufficient?

RINPOCHE: First, the difference between what is called a spiritual friend and a root guru is great. The term that is translated into English as *spiritual friend* literally means "a virtuous friend." It is used to refer to any spiritual teacher who is a positive influence on you, which can mean almost any level of intensity of positive influence. Essentially, the function of a spiritual friend is to show you the path. The function of a root guru is to bring you to the end of the path, and that is the difference between them. One shows you the beginning and the other one brings you to the end.

With regard to how you actually identify your root guru, the way it was explained in the text is that an individual's root guru, according to the common tradition, the tradition common to all lineages, is to consider as your root guru that person from whom you receive all three levels of ordination: pratimoksha vows, the bodhisattva vow, and the samaya vows that are received at the time of full empowerment. If you receive all three of those from one person, according to the traditions in general, that person may be considered your root guru.

Within the specific context of Vajrayana teaching, if you receive empowerment, transmission, and instruction from one person, then this person is called the guru of threefold kindness, and you may certainly consider such a person your root guru. The uncommon Kagyu tradition is to consider the person through whose speech or actions you are caused to recognize decisively and in an unchanging way the nature of your mind to be your root guru. It does not matter if he brings you to that point through giving you a lot of empowerments, transmissions, and instructions or not. If he causes you to recognize the nature of your mind, he is your ultimate root guru in the uncommon sense.

You have a common way of reckoning your root guru, and an uncommon way. With regard to His Holiness, for anyone who has great and unchanging faith in His Holiness, it is perfectly acceptable to regard him as your root guru, because to say the least, he will never let you down. It is never a bad choice of a guru. So definitely, it is more than appropriate to consider His Holiness your root guru.

In addition to that, there may be other individuals who are kind to you with whom you have a connection based on aspirations from the past and so on, and those are also your teachers.

STUDENT: Should you view them all as essentially being the embodiment of the buddha nature of all buddhas? For instance, I try to see you as being inseparable from His Holiness Karmapa, who in turn is inseparable from Vajradhara.

RINPOCHE: It is said to be acceptable to view someone in that way if you have unchanging faith and devotion, because regardless of the characteristics of the teacher, if you have that great devotion for them, you receive great blessing. From the point of view of the teacher, it may be unfitting, but from the point of view of the disciple, I would have to say it is acceptable.

STUDENT: Do the buddhas believe in chi?

RINPOCHE: In the context of Vajrayana, it is spoken of, definitely.

RINPOCHE, TO HIS STUDENTS: I want to say something about this whole business of signs and dreams. Normally I never say anything about this except in a particular context when teaching people, and in retreat I usually do not talk about it either. The only reason I have mentioned it now is that it exists in the present text, therefore I am required to go through it. However, there is a danger in talking about signs and so on, because as soon as you mention to people that there are signs that can happen when you do practices, they tend to develop anxiety and hope about the arising or absence of such signs. As soon as you pollute your practice with that kind of hope and that kind of agitation about what kind of signs or experiences you are going to have, you put a block in the way of the practice. It is actually better in general not to talk about signs. That way people have no expectations.

Dedication

I pray that the Lama's life be excellent,
That his supreme life be long,
And that his activity increase and spread,
Bless us that we remain inseparable from the Lama.

By this merit may all become omniscient,
From this attainment, after defeating evil faults,
Through the endless storm of birth, old age, sickness, and death,
May we liberate all beings from the suffering in the three worlds.

Glossary

ABHIDHARMA (Skt.) [Tib. chos mngon pa]   Higher Dharma. The part of the Tripitaka that contains the scholarly analysis of phenomena. See also TRIPITAKA.

ABSOLUTE TRUTH   See TWO TRUTHS.

AFFLICTIVE EMOTIONS   See KLESHA.

AGGREGATES   See SKANDHA.

AMITABHA (Skt.) [Tib. 'od dpag med]   Buddha of Boundless Light. One of the five dhyana buddhas, who correspond to the five buddha families. He presides over the pure realm of Sukhavati and is lord of the Lotus family. Rebirth in his pure land guarantees complete enlightenment in one lifetime. See also DEWACHEN.

ANIMAL REALM   See SIX REALMS.

ANUTTARA YOGA TANTRA (Skt.) [Tib. bla na med pa'i rnal 'byor]   The highest of the four categories of tantra in the Sarma, or New Translation, school of Tibetan Buddhism. Examples of anuttara yoga are the Karma Pakshi, Hevajra, Chakrasamvara, and Kalachakra tantras.

ARHAT (Skt.) [Tib. dgra bcom pa]   Worthy one. An arhat is one who, having exhausted all defilements and mental afflictions, passes into nirvana.

ASANGA (Tib. thogs med)   Asanga lived in India during the fourth century CE and established the Yogachara school with his brother, Vasubandhu. After twelve years of retreat, he received a vision of Maitreya and subsequently wrote the five Maitreya texts, which have had a profound impact on Mahayana Buddhism.

ASURA REALM   See SIX REALMS.

ATISHA (982–1055 CE)   Atisha Dipamkara Shrijnana was a renowned Buddhist scholar and teacher at the monastic university, Vikramashila, in India. He was invited to Tibet in 1043, where he founded the Kadampa school and wrote his most influential work, *The Lamp for the Path to Enlightenment*, which teaches the gradual path to enlightenment.

AVADHUTI (Skt.) [Tib. dbu ma]   Central channel; a subtle channel of the body.

AVALOKITESHVARA (Skt.)   See CHENREZIK.

BARDO (Tib. bar do)   Intermediate state; most often referring to the period between death and rebirth. There are six bardos: the bardo of birth, dreams, meditation, the moment before death, the bardo of dharmata or suchness, and the bardo of becoming.

BENZA (Tib. ba dzra)   Tibetan transliteration of the Sanskrit word *vajra*.

BHIKSHU (Skt.)   See GELONG.

BHIKSHUNI (Skt.)   See GELONGMA.

BHUMI (Skt.) [Tib. sa]   A level in the series of stages of spiritual development of a bodhisattva on the path to buddhahood. The Mahayana tradition recognizes ten such levels, often called the bodhisattva levels; the Vajrayana recognizes thirteen.

BODHGAYA (Skt.) [Tib. rdo rje gdan]   A town in Bihar, India, where Buddha Shakyamuni attained enlightenment under the bodhi tree. The Mahabodhi Temple was built there during Ashoka's period. Bodhgaya has been a major pilgrimage site for centuries.

BODHICHARYAVATARA (Skt.) [Tib. byang chub sems dpa'i spyod pa la 'jug pa]   *The Way of the Bodhisattva*, composed by Shantideva, an Indian pandita, who lived between 650 and 750 CE. A major text and a great classic of Mahayana Buddhism, the text is a guide to cultivating enlightened mind for the benefit of all beings.

BODHICHITTA (Skt.) [Tib. byang chub kyi sems]   Mind of awakening. Relative bodhichitta is the desire to practice the six paramitas to attain buddhahood for the benefit of all sentient beings; absolute bodhichitta is immediate insight into the emptiness of phenomena.

BODHISATTVA (Skt.) [Tib. byang chub sems dpa'] In the Mahayana tradition, a bodhisattva dedicates his or her existence throughout all rebirths to the attainment of enlightenment in order to liberate other beings who are suffering in samsara. The bodhisattva ideal is in contrast to the way of arhats and Pratyekabuddhas, who attain nirvana solely for their own benefit.

BODHISATTVA VOW (Skt.) [Tib. byang chub sems dpa'i sdom pa] The essence of the bodhisattva vow is to preserve the mind of bodhichitta that sincerely wishes to benefit all beings, not merely for the temporary alleviation of sufferings but to bring all beings without exception to a state of full and complete awakening. The bodhisattva vow is received from a master who has maintained the vow unbroken.

BÖN (Tib. bon) The religion of pre-Buddhist Tibet, believed by its adherents to have been introduced by Shenrap from an area located in what is now Persia. Bön now reflects many aspects of Tibetan Buddhism but still retains a distinct identity.

BUDDHA SHAKYAMUNI (Skt.) [Tib. sha kya thub pa] Sage of the Shakyas. The historical buddha was born a prince into the Shakya clan in the fifth century BCE. Upon attaining enlightenment at Bodhgaya, Buddha Shakyamuni taught the Dharma. He is the fourth of the thousand buddhas of the present era.

CHAKRASAMVARA (Skt.) [Tib. 'khor lo bde mchog] A main yidam that belongs to the anuttara tantra set of the New Translation school, who is associated with practices for mental purification and the transformation of obstacles. His consort is Vajravarahi (Dorje Phakmo).

CHAKRAVARTIN (Skt.) [Tib. 'khor los sgyur ba'i rgyal po] A universal ruler; a king who propagates the Dharma.

CHARYA TANTRA (Skt.) [Tib. spyod rgyud] The second of the four tantras of the New Translation school of Tibetan Buddhism. It emphasizes external ritual with internal visualization. See also ANUTTARA YOGA TANTRA, KRIYA TANTRA, and YOGA TANTRA.

CHENREZIK (Tib. spyan ras gzigs) [Skt. Avalokiteshvara] The bodhisattva who embodies the compassion of all buddhas. Chenrezik is the patron deity of Tibet. Both His Holiness Karmapa and His Holiness Dalai Lama are manifestations of Chenrezik.

CHÖ (Tib. gcod)   Meditation practice in which the meditator offers his or her body in order to overcome the false belief in and attachment to the ego, including the fear associated with the ego's dissolution. The practice was widely taught by Machik Lapdrön, who received it from the Indian teacher Phadampa Sangye.

CHOKYI WANGCHUK (Tib. chos kyi dbang phyug)   The Sixth Shamar Rinpoche, Karma Chakme Rinpoche's guru.

DAKA (Skt.) [Tib. dpa' bo]   Male counterpart of the dakini.

DAKINI (Skt.) [Tib. mkha' 'gro ma]   Sky-walker. Female tantric deity who fulfills enlightened activities and who protects and serves the Buddhist teachings and practitioners. Dakinis transmit secret teachings to select practitioners when the time is ripe.

DEVA PUTRA MARA   See MARA.

DEWACHEN (Tib. bde ba can) [Skt. Sukhavati]   The pure realm of Amitabha Buddha, located in the west. See also AMITABHA.

DHARMA (Skt.) [Tib. chos]   The teachings of Shakyamuni Buddha; one of the Three Jewels in which one takes refuge. It is also a term for "phenomena," "truth," "law," etc.

DHARMADHATU (Skt.) [Tib. chos dbyings]   The all-encompassing space, without origin or beginning, in which emptiness and interdependent origination are inseparable.

DHARMAKAYA   See KAYA.

DHARMAPALA (Skt.) [Tib. chos skyong]   Protector of the doctrine. Fierce and powerful, the Dharma protectors vow to guard the Dharma and its practitioners. Dharmapalas are *wisdom protectors*, who are emanations of buddhas or bodhisattvas, and *mundane protectors*, who are virtuous samsaric beings.

DORJE PHAKMO (Tib. rdo rje phag mo) [Skt. Vajravarahi]   The embodiment of wisdom, she is one of the main yidams of the Kagyu lineage and the consort of Chakrasamvara.

DUSUM KHYENPA (Tib. dus gsum mkhyen pa) [1110–1193]   The first Karmapa. Dusum Khyenpa was a student of Gampopa, who empowered him to practice Hevajra and Mahamudra. He

received the Kalachakra and the lam dre teachings from Virupa.
See also KAGYUPA, KARMA KAGYU, and KARMAPA.

DZOKCHEN (Tib. rdzogs chen) [Skt. maha ati]   The Great Perfection is
the highest yana of the Nyingma school. Taught by Garab Dorje,
it is the ultimate way to achieve direct realization of the clear and
luminous quality of mind itself.

EIGHT CONSCIOUSNESSES (Tib. rnam shes tshogs brgyad)   The five
sense consciousnesses are sight, hearing, smell, taste, touch, and
body sensation. The sixth is mental consciousness; the seventh is
afflicted consciousness, the klesha mind; and the eighth, the
alaya, is the ground consciousness.

EMPOWERMENT (Tib. dbang bskur) [Skt. abhishekha]   Empowers, or
authorizes, the student to engage in a specific Vajrayana practice.
It must be conferred by a Vajrayana master who embodies the
teaching of the lineage.

EMPTINESS (Tib. stong pa nyid) [Skt. shunyata]   In the second turning of the wheel of Dharma, the Buddha taught that neither external phenomena nor internal phenomena have any real or
inherent existence and are therefore "empty."

FIVE DEEDS WITH IMMEDIATE RESULT   See FIVE NEGATIVE STRAIGHT-
THROUGH ACTIONS.

FIVE NEGATIVE STRAIGHT-THROUGH ACTIONS (Tib. mtshams med lnga)
Actions that cause the doer to assume immediate rebirth in the
lowest quarters of hell without passing through the bardo. These
are killing one's mother, killing one's father, killing an arhat,
intentionally causing a buddha to bleed and doing so with the
desire to harm, and causing a schism in the sangha.

FIVE POISONS   See KLESHA.

FORM KAYA   See KAYA.

FOUR IMMEASURABLES (Tib. tshad med bzhi)   Also called the four
inconceivables or the four boundless qualities. They are unlimited love, boundless compassion, unsurpassable joy, and
fundamental impartiality.

FOUR NOBLE TRUTHS (Tib. 'phags pa'i bden pa bzhi)   First sermon taught by the Buddha, at Sarnath, India. The four noble truths are the truth of suffering, the truth of the causes of suffering, the truth of the cessation of suffering, and the truth of the path leading to the cessation of suffering.

FOUR ORDINARY FOUNDATIONS   See FOUR THOUGHTS.

FOUR POWERS (Tib. stobs bzhi)   To be authentic and fully effective, any act of confession must contain all four of the following components—the power of reliance or support; the power of regret; the power of remedy for harmful actions, which is any virtuous action specifically dedicated to purification; and the power of resolution, or the intention never to repeat the wrongdoing.

FOUR SPECIAL FOUNDATIONS   See NGONDRO.

FOUR THOUGHTS THAT TURN THE MIND (Tib. blo ldog rnam bzhi)   They are reflection on precious human birth, impermanence and the inevitability of death, karma and its effects, and the pervasiveness of suffering in samsara.

GANACHAKRA (Skt.) [Tib. tshogs kyi 'khor lo]   Literally, "wheel of gathering." A ritual feast offering, part of many sadhanas.

GANDI (Skt.)   A wooden gong, which when beaten with a wooden stick, calls the community to come together for work, ceremonies, and other matters.

GELONG (Tib. dge slong) [Skt. bhikshu]   A fully ordained Buddhist monk.

GELONG DORJE DZINPA (Tib. dge slong rdo rje 'dzin pa)   *Gelong* refers to the vows kept by the fully ordained, and *Dorje Dzinpa* refers to the tantric samayas. Clear examples of ordained monks who are Vajrayana practitioners and turn the wheel of the tantric teachings are His Holiness the Dalai Lama and His Holiness the Gyalwa Karmapa.

GELONGMA (Tib. dge slong ma) [Skt. bhikshuni]   A fully ordained Buddhist nun.

GELOPMA (Tib.) [Skt. shikshamana]   A postulant nun. Women are required to take the vows for a postulant nun, which are taken after the vows for a novice nun and before the vows of full ordination. See also GETSULMA and GELONGMA.

GELUK (Tib. dge lugs) One of the four main lineages of Tibetan Buddhism and the most recent of the New Translation schools, founded by Tsongkhapa (1357–1419 CE).

GENERATION AND COMPLETION (Tib. bskyed rim and rdzogs rim) Two stages that are the means and knowledge of Vajrayana practice. The creation phase, the visualization, is based on pure perception (perceiving sight, sound, and thought as deity, mantra, and wisdom). The completion stage is resting in the natural state of mind.

GENYEN (Tib. dge bsnyen) [Skt. upasaka] A Buddhist layman who is given this status by taking refuge in the THREE JEWELS. He maintains precepts and gives alms to ordained sangha.

GENYEN DORJE DZINPA (Tib. dge bsnyen rdo rje 'dzin pa) *Genyen* refers to the vows of the lay practitioner, and *Dorje Dzinpa* refers to the tantric samayas. Genyen Dorje Dzinpa are tantric teachers who are not ordained. This includes highly respected lamas such as His Holiness Sakya Trizin of the Sakya tradition and His Holiness Dudjom Rinpoche of the Nyingma lineage.

GENYENMA (Tib. dge bsnyen ma) [Skt. upasika] A Buddhist laywoman, who is given this status by taking refuge in the Three Jewels. She maintains precepts and gives alms to ordained sangha.

GETSUL (Tib. dge tshul) [Skt. shramanera] A novice monk.

GETSULMA (Tib. dge tshul ma) [Skt. shramaneri] A novice nun.

GOD REALM See SIX REALMS.

GURU YOGA (Tib. bla ma'i rnal 'byor) A practice of devotion to the guru culminating in receiving his blessing and becoming inseparable with his mind. It is also the fourth preliminary practice of the Vajrayana ngondro.

HELL REALM See SIX REALMS.

HINAYANA (Skt.) [Tib. theg pa dman] The vehicle or path in which practitioners contemplate the four noble truths and the twelve links of interdependence with the aim of achieving liberation from the sufferings of samsara. The only Hinayana school that survives today is the Theravadin.

HUMAN REALM See SIX REALMS.

HUNGRY GHOST REALM   See SIX REALMS.

INTERDEPENDENT ORIGINATION (Tib. rten 'brel) [Skt. pratityasamutpada]   The doctrine that nothing exists independently, but only comes into existence dependent on previous causes and conditions. See also TWELVE LINKS.

JAMBUDVIPA (Skt.) [Tib. 'dzam bu gling]   The southern of the four principal continents in Buddhist cosmology.

JETSUN (Tib. rje btsun)   A title indicating a master, teacher, or lord; for example, Jetsun Milarepa.

KADAMPA (Skt.) [Tib. bka' gdams pa]   A tradition brought to Tibet by Atisha at the end of the first millenium. The Kadampa school, which emphasized the gradual path, has not survived as an independent school, but rather has been absorbed into the other schools.

KAGYU (Tib. bka' brgyud)   The teaching lineage, whose teachings and practices are passed down through a succession of realized teachers. The Kagyu traces its lineage back to the mahasiddha Tilopa, who received the teachings directly from Vajradhara. The Kagyu are particularly known for their many great yogis as well as the monastic tradition that began with Gampopa (1079–1153). One of the four main lineages of Buddhism in Tibet and one of the three main schools of the New Translation school, the Kagyupa school is subdivided into four greater and eight lesser lineages, not all of which have survived to the present day.

KALACHAKRA (Skt.) [Tib. dus kyi khor lo'i rgyud]   The literal meaning is "wheel of time." A deity manifested by Shakaymuni Buddha at the request of the king of Shambhala. Kalachakra is an anuttara yoga tantra. Receiving the empowerment is thought to guarantee rebirth in Shambhala.

KARMA (Skt.) [Tib. las]   Action. The universal law of cause and effect according to which one inevitably experiences the results of one's own positive and negative actions.

KARMA KAGYU (Tib. ka rma bka' brgyud)   The supreme Kagyu sect under the leadership of the Gyalwa Karmapas. It was established, in the twelfth century, by the first Karmapa, Dusum Khyenpa (1110–1193), one of Gampopa's students. See also KAGYU and KARMAPA.

KARMAPA (Tib. ka rma pa)   The Gyalwa Karmapa, is the head of the Karma Kagyu lineage of Tibetan Buddhism. The present Karmapa, Ogyen Trinley Dorje, is the seventeenth in an unbroken lineage that began with Dusum Khyenpa. The Gyalwa Karmapas, who embody the activity of buddhahood, were prophesied by both Buddha Shakyamuni and Padmasambhava. A manifestation of Chenrezik, they are pure examples of wisdom and compassion, and have revealed their realization as scholars, yogins, artists, and poets. See also KAGYU, KARMA KAGYU, and DUSUM KHYENPA.

KAYA (Skt.) [Tib. sku]   The three natures, or "bodies," of buddhas. The three kayas are the nirmanakaya, or emanation body, by which buddhas appear in physical form in the realm of sentient beings; the sambhogakaya, or enjoyment body, through which buddhas appear to bodhisattvas; and the dharmakaya, which is the unoriginated wisdom beyond form, which manifests in the sambhogakaya and the nirmanakaya. There is a fourth kaya, the svabhavikakaya, or the body of essential nature, and it expresses the ultimate unity of the three aforementioned kayas. The term *rupakaya*, "form body," refers to both the sambhogakaya and the nirmanakaya. There is a fifth kaya as well, the mahasukhakaya, or body of great bliss, which is the quality of the other four kayas combined.

KHENPO (Tib. mkhen po)   Title of someone who has completed the advanced studies of Buddhism.

KLESHA (Skt.) [Tib. snyon mongs]   Emotional obscurations. The three primary kleshas, the *three poisons*, are attachment or desire, aversion or anger, and ignorance or delusion. Along with pride and envy, they are referred to as the five kleshas.

KRIYA TANTRA (Skt.) [Tib. bya ba'i rgyud]   Action tantra. The first of the outer tantras; focusing on cleanliness, purity, and correct behavior.

Lotus sutra, Sutra of the Lotus of the True Doctrine (Tib. dam pa'i chos padma dkar po'i mdo) [Skt. Saddharma-pundarika-sutra] A foundational text of Mahayana Buddhism in which the Buddha explains the principles underlying the unity of the three yanas and the concept of skillful means in adapting the teaching to the capacities of different beings.

LUNG (Tib.) Reading transmission given to a student by a lineage holder, which is a necessary preliminary to doing the practice.

MAHAMUDRA (Skt.) [Tib. phyag rgya chen po] Literally, "great seal." A meditation practice particularly emphasized in the Kagyu tradition, Mahamudra is the direct experience of the empty, luminous, and pure nature of mind.

MAHASIDDHA (Skt.) [Tib. grub thob chen po] Great adept; the highly realized masters in the Vajrayana tradition. Also refers to the eighty-four great and eccentric mahasiddhas who lived in India between the eighth and twelfth centuries CE and who reached great spiritual attainment through the diligent practice of tantra. Tilopa and Naropa are two of the eighty-four mahasiddhas.

MAHASUKHAKAYA See KAYA.

MAHAYANA (Skt.) [Tib. theg pa chen po] The "greater vehicle." The teachings of the second turning of the wheel of Dharma in which shunyata (emptiness) and compassion for all beings are emphasized. See also BODHICHITTA, BODHISATTVA.

MAITREYA (Skt.) [Tib. byams pa] The buddha of the future, who at the present time resides in Tushita, a heavenly realm, from which he emanates manifestations into other realms. He will take birth as the fifth buddha of the present era.

MANDALA (Skt.) [Tib. dkhyil 'khor] Symbolic representation depicting the palace of a particular deity. These circular diagrams are sometimes elaborately executed with grains of colored sand and are used for empowerments and elaborate meditation practices. The mandala offering, the third of the four special foundations, perfects the accumulation of merit by repeatedly offering the entire universe to the sources of refuge.

MANJUSHRI (Skt.) [Tib. 'jam dpal dbyangs] The bodhisattva

manifesting the perfection of wisdom and thus a frequent figure in the prajnaparamita sutras of the Mahayana tradition. He is shown wearing sambhogakaya ornaments and holding a flaming sword in his right hand and a text in his left hand.

MANTRA (Skt.) [Tib. sngags]   Sacred sounds representing various energies that symbolize and communicate the nature of a deity. Mantras, which are manifestations of the speech aspect of enlightenment, range from single syllables to lengthy combinations. OM MANI PEME HUNG, the mantra of Chenrezik, is among the most widely practiced.

MARA (Skt.) [Tib. bdud]   Mara is anything that obstructs the practice of Dharma and seduces you into abandoning your practice in favor of worldly activities. The first of the four maras is the deva putra mara, which is attachment to and craving for pleasure. The second, the klesha mara, causes one to take rebirth in the six realms of samsara. The third is called skandha mara because the skandhas or aggregates are the cause for the presence of suffering. The fourth one is the mara of death.

MENTAL AFFLICTIONS   See KLESHAS.

MILAREPA (Tib. mi la ras pa)   This famous yogi (1040–1143) is one of the greatest and most celebrated teachers in Tibetan Buddhism. Despite having accumulated heavy negative karma in his early adulthood, he became the student of Marpa and attained full awakening in one lifetime. He then composed the *100,000 Songs*, spontaneously created to elucidate his experience of realization. His students include Gampopa and Rechungpa.

MOUNTAIN DHARMA (Tib. ri chö)   Refers to serious retreat practice, especially solitary retreat in the mountains. The essential point of mountain Dharma is to abandon all concerns of this life and to undertake solitary retreat with the intent of experiencing the nature of your mind.

MOUNT MERU (Tib. ri rab lhun po)   The giant mountain at the center of the Buddhist world system that is surrounded by smaller mountains, lakes, oceans, and the four continents. Meru, or Sumeru, is visualized as a vast peak, and serves as the focus of mandala offerings.

NAGA (Skt.) [Tib. klu]   Powerful serpent beings who inhabit waters and are often the custodians of treasures, either texts or actual material treasures.

NAGARJUNA (Skt.) [Tib. klu sgrub]   A leading Buddhist philosopher in the interpretation of shunyata, the founder of the Madhyamaka school, and the author of *The Fundamental Treatise of the Middle Way*. Lived in India in the late second century CE.

NAM CHÖ (Tib. gnam chos)   Literally, "Sky Dharma." A tradition of terma.

NAMTHAR (Tib. rnam thar)   Literally, "records of liberation." Biographies of the enlightened masters of Tibet containing the spiritual path by which the master attained enlightenment, most often written by their disciples.

NGONDRO (Tib. sngon 'gro)   The preliminary practices of Tibetan Buddhism in which the practitioner begins the Vajrayana path, performing 111,111 repetitions of refuge prayers and prostrations; 111,111 Vajrasattva mantras; 111,111 mandala offerings; and 111,111 guru yoga practices. The preliminary practices prepare the student for the successive stages on the Vajrayana path.

NIRMANAKAYA   See KAYA.

NIRVANA (Skt.) [Tib. mya ngan las 'das pa]   The extinction of the causes of samsaric existence—false ideas and afflictive emotions—accomplished by spiritual practice and resulting in liberation from cyclic existence. See also SAMSARA.

NYALWA DORJE DEN (Tib. mnyal bar do rje gdan)   Vajra hell, where the suffering is limitless and unbearable.

NYINGMA (Tib. rnying ma)   The "old" school, or ancient translation school, which represents the Buddhist teachings as they were first translated into Tibetan from Sanskrit and other languages. This school began in the eighth century CE with Padmasambhava, who buried terma, or hidden treasures, to be discovered at the appropriate time in the future by tertons, or treasure discoverers. Dzokchen is the highest meditation practice in the Nyingma tradition.

NYUNGNE (Tib. smyung gnas)   The fasting practice of Thousand-armed Chenrezik, the bodhisattva of infinite compassion.

PADMASAMBHAVA (Skt.) [Tib. pad ma 'byung gnas, gu ru rin po che] Literally, the "lotus-born" buddha of Uddiyana, who brought the Vajrayana teachings to Tibet in the ninth century CE. He subdued the negative forces of Tibet, founded the Nyingma school, and concealed Dharmic treasures (terma) for the benefit of future generations.

PALDEN LHAMO (Tib. dpal ldan lha mo) [Skt. Shri Devi] Female Dharma protector, the only female of the eight Dharma protectors.

PARAMITA (Skt.) [Tib. pha rol tu phyin pa] Reaching the other shore, transcending concepts of subject, object, and action. The six paramitas, or the six perfections, are the transcendent actions of generosity, discipline, patience, exertion, meditation, and knowledge. The ten paramitas include these six plus means, strength, power, and wisdom.

PARINIRVANA (Skt.) [Tib. yongs su mya ngan las'das pa] Final nirvana, the highest nirvana, which is entered at death once having achieved complete enlightenment.

PRAJNAPARAMITA (Skt.) [Tib. shes rab kyi pha rol tu phyin pa] Transcendent knowledge. The Mahayana teachings on the cultivation of insight resulting in the direct realization of emptiness.

PRATIMOKSHA VOW (Skt.) [Tib. so sor thar pa] Literally, "individual liberation." The self-liberating vow that constitutes the basic ethical commitments of a lay disciple, a novice, or a monastic.

PRATYEKABUDDHA (Skt.) [Tib. rang sangs rgyas] A solitary realized one. A Hinayana arhat who concentrates on his or her own liberation and contemplates the twelve links of interdependence.

PUJA (Skt.) [Tib. mchod pa] Buddhist ceremonies that range from the very simple to the most elaborate. See also SADHANA.

RAGA ASYA (Skt.) Sanskrit for Karma Chakme.

RANGJUNG DORJE (Tib. rang 'byung rdo rje) The Third Karmapa (1284–1339), renowned for his texts used extensively in the Kagyu lineage, among which are *The Aspiration Prayer of Mahamudra of Definitive Meaning*, *The Profound Inner Meaning*, and *Treatise on Buddha Essence*.

RENUNCIATION (Tib. nges 'byung)   The stable renunciation of samsara, which means that what you previously regarded with
attachment you now regard with revulsion and disgust because
you recognize the futility of samsara and the value of liberation.
See also FOUR THOUGHTS and FOUR POWERS.

ROOT GURU (Tib. rtsa ba'i bla ma)   According to the anuttara yoga tradition of the Vajrayana, your root guru is the embodiment of all
buddhas because the mind of the guru is the dharmakaya, the
wisdom of all buddhas. Since the guru is the source of Dharma,
the speech of the guru is the embodiment of all Dharma. Whether
the guru manifests as a monastic or as a chakravartin, the body
of the guru as the foremost member of the sangha is the embodiment of the whole sangha. The qualities of the guru are what
manifest as the yidams and other deities, and the activity of the
guru is what manifests as dakinis and Dharma protectors. In
Karma Chakme's Mountain Dharma your root guru is defined as the
teacher who points out the nature of your mind.

RUDRA (Tib. ru dra)   The demon of ego clinging. In Tibetan Buddhism, the personification of the destructiveness of ego.

RUPAKAYA   See KAYA.

SADHANA (Skt.) [Tib. grub thabs]   Literally, "means of accomplishment." A Vajrayana liturgy and method for one of many deities
that includes chanting, visualization, and mantra recitation. See
also PUJA.

SAKYA (Tib. sa kya)   One of the four main schools of Tibetan Buddhism. The lineage, headed by His Holiness Sakya Trizin, is
passed from father to son. It emphasizes lam dre teachings and
Buddhist logic.

SAMANTABHADRA (Skt.) [Tib. kun tu bzang po]   Literally, "all good."
One of the eight great bodhisattvas, he is an emanation of
Vajrasattva, and the primordial dharmakaya buddha for the
Nyingma lineage.

SAMAYA (Skt.) [Tib. dam tshig]   Sacred word or vow. The sacred
commitment of Vajrayana is primarily to one's root guru and to
the practice one has committed to, but also to the sangha.

SAMBHOGAKAYA   See KAYA.

SAMSARA (Skt.) [Tib. 'khor ba]   Cyclic existence, in which ordinary beings are trapped in an endless cycle of rebirth in the six realms, which contain endless suffering. The state of ordinary beings bound to suffering by attachment, aggression, and ignorance. See also NIRVANA.

SAMYAKSAMBUDDHA (Skt.) [Tib. yang dag par rdzogs pa'i sangs rgyas] Completely and perfectly awakened.

SANGHA (Skt.) [Tib. dge 'dun]   The community of practitioners who have taken refuge in the Three Jewels. Also, the noble sangha of realized ones.

SARMA (Tib. Sar ma)   The New Translation school, which includes the Kagyu, Geluk, and Sakya schools. These schools rely on the texts of the second propagation, brought by Rinchen Zangpo.

SECRET MANTRA (Tib. gsang sngags)   Refers to the Vajrayana.

SEVEN BRANCHES   Stanzas of confession from the "Seven Branches," found in *The Aspiration to the Conduct of Excellence*, a part of many sadhanas.

SHAMATHA (Skt.) [Tib. zhi gnas]   Literally, "calm abiding." Tranquillity meditation in which the meditator uses techniques, such as following the breath, to attain a calm and focused mind. See also VIPASHANA.

SHARIPUTRA   Highly regarded arhat and foremost disciple of Buddha Shakyamuni, he was known for his attainment of wisdom and his exemplary qualities of compassion, patience, and humility. The Buddha declared that Shariputra was a perfect disciple.

SHINAY (Tib.)   See SHAMATHA

SHRAMANERA (Skt.)   See GETSUL.

SHRAMANERI (Skt.)   See GETSULMA.

SHRAVAKA (Skt.) [Tib. nyan thos]   Early disciples of Buddha Shakyamuni, the Shravakas practiced meditation and contemplated the Buddha's words, which they actually heard because they were present at that time. The Shravakayana was the first yana.

SHUNYATA (Skt.) [Tib. stong pa nyid]   Emptiness. Conceptual frameworks are empty of any true essence or self, are dependent on causes and conditions, and thus lack inherent existence.

SIDDHI (Skt.) [Tib. dngos grub]   Accomplishment. The eight ordinary siddhis show mastery of the mundane everyday world; the supreme siddhi is enlightenment.

SISTER PALMO   A Western woman, a devotee of His Holiness the Sixteenth Karmapa, was ordained by His Holiness as Gelongma Kachok Palmo, but was known as Sister Palmo. With His Holiness, she helped to found and operate a school for young lamas. Initially, some forty young tulkus from the four traditions of Tibetan Buddhism attended the school, acquired English, and were able to greatly benefit many Westerners. She traveled with His Holiness to the West in 1974. Sister Palmo was responsible for making available many early translations of sadhanas and prayers. She also significantly helped the Tibetans in their early years in India.

SIX DHARMAS OF NAROPA (Tib. na ro chos drug)   Naropa taught Marpa these tantric practices, which are an important part of the Kagyu teachings and a standard practice in the traditional three-year, three-month, three-day retreat. They consist of tummo, illusory body, dream yoga, clear light, bardo, and phowa.

SIX REALMS (Tib. khams drug)   The six realms of samsaric existence as shown on the Wheel of Life. The god realm is the highest of the six realms, where beings are dominated by pride and suffer because they will fall to the lower realms. In the asura realm, the beings are dominated by jealousy and envy and suffer as a result of their constant quarreling and fighting. The human realm is characterized by desire and attachment, and although the beings suffer from ceaseless struggle, it is the best rebirth because one has the opportunity to practice Dharma. The animal realm is dominated by ignorance and stupidity; beings there suffer from constant fear. The hungry ghost realm is dominated by greed, and the preta beings suffer terribly from hunger and thirst. The lowest of the realms, the hell realm, is dominated by hatred and aggression, and the beings endure intense suffering.

SIX-SYLLABLE MANTRA   Usually refers to OM MANI PEME HUNG, the mantra of Chenrezik. In *Karma Chakme's Mountain Dharma*, it often refers to the six-syllable essence mantra of Vajrasattva, OM BENZA SATTO HUNG.

SKANDHA (Skt.) [Tib. phung po lnga]   Literally, "heap." The five skandhas, or aggregates, are form, feeling, conception, formation, and consciousness. In the confused state, we cling to one or another aspect of these five as a concrete self. When the skandhas are actually seen for what they are, no self is found in them, either singly or taken together. In Vajrayana they are correlated to the five buddhas of the mandala.

SOHA   Tibetan transliteration of the Sanskrit word *svaha*.

STUPA (Skt.) [Tib. mchod rten]   A monument that contains the relics of the Buddha or high teacher. The stupa symbolizes the dharmakaya, the mind of the Buddha, and can range from small and simple to monumental structures.

SUTRA TAUGHT TO THE KING (Tib. rgyal po la gdams pa'i mdo) [Skt. rajavavadaka]   The Buddha's summary of the commitments of the bodhisattva vow.

SVABHAVIKAKAYA   See KAYA.

TANTRIKA (Skt.) [Tib. ngags pa]   Tantric practitioner.

TATHAGATA (Skt.) [Tib. de bzhin gshegs pa]   Literally, "thus-gone." A fully enlightened buddha.

TATHAGATAGARBHA (Skt.) [Tib. de bzhin gshegs pa'i snying po]   The essence of the tathagatas, it is the seed or essence of enlightenment that all beings have and is what gives them the potential to be a buddha.

TEN UNVIRTUOUS ACTIONS   There are three unvirtuous actions of body: to intentionally kill, to steal or take that which is not offered, and to engage in sexual misconduct. The four unvirtuous actions involving speech are lying, slander, verbal abuse, and mindless talk. The three types of mental unvirtuous actions are covetousness, spite or maliciousness, and wrong view.

TEN VIRTUOUS ACTIONS   These involve abandoning the ten unvirtuous actions and by implication engaging in actions that are the direct opposite, such as saving lives, generosity, speaking the truth, and so on.

TERMA (Tib. gter ma)   Literally, "hidden treasure." These concealed treasures have included texts, ritual objects, and relics, which were hidden mainly by Guru Rinpoche to be discovered at the proper time by a TERTON for the benefit of students.

TERTON (Tib. gter ston)   A revealer of hidden treasures that were concealed primarily by Padmasambhava and Yeshe Tsogyal.

THANGKA (Tib. thang ka)   A Tibetan scroll painting depicting buddhas, bodhisattvas, and other deities, used as religious objects.

THREE JEWELS (Tib. dkon mchog gsum) [Skt. triratna]   The precious Buddha, the precious Dharma, and the precious Sangha.

THREE SUPPORTS (Tib. rten gsum)   Stupas are the supports of the Buddha's mind; texts are a symbol of the Buddha's speech, the Dharma; and statues are the form, or body, of the Buddha.

TILOPA   The great Indian mahasiddha who received teachings directly from the dharmakaya Vajradhara, thus beginning the Kagyu lineage. He subsequently received four lineages from four Indian gurus. The lineage that comes to us is a combination of all four. His principal disciple was the mahasiddha Naropa, to whom he passed his lineage.

TRIPITAKA (Skt.) [Tib. sde snod gsum]   The Buddhist canon. The *three baskets* are the sutra-pitaka, discourses of the Buddha; the vinaya-pitaka, ethics and discipline; and the abhidharma-pitaka, principles of higher doctrine.

TSONDRU GYAMTSO (Tib. brtson 'grus rgya mtso) [Skt. Virya Sagara] The disciple who requested Karma Chakme to teach about mountain Dharma.

TWELVE LINKS OF INTERDEPENDENCE (Tib. rten 'brel yan lag bcu gnyis) The twelve successive phases that begin with ignorance and end with old age and death, based on the principle that nothing exists independently, but comes into existence only in dependence on various previous causes and conditions. See also INTERDEPENDENT ORIGINATION

TWO TRUTHS (Tib. bden pa gnyis)   Relative truth is how ordinary beings perceive phenomena; it is considered true on a conventional level. Ultimate truth is the absolute nature of relative truth, that all phenomena are beyond arising, dwelling and ceasing.

This ultimate truth is emptiness, which is only perceived by realized beings.

UDDIYANA (Skt.) [Tib. u rgyan]   The country to the northwest of ancient India where Guru Rinpoche was born on a lotus flower.

UPASAKA (Skt.)   See GENYEN

UPASIKA (Skt.)   See GENYENMA

VAIROCHANA (Skt.) [Tib. rnam par snang mdzad]   The principal sambhogakaya buddha. Also the name of a great scholar and translator who lived during the time of King Trisong Deutsen. He is one of the main masters to bring the Dzokchen teachings to Tibet.

VAJRADHARA (Skt.) [Tib. rdo rje 'chang]   Dorje Chang, literally "vajra holder." He is the dharmakaya Buddha of the Sarma school.

VAJRASATTVA (Skt.) [Tib. rdo rje sems dpa']   The buddha of purification. The second of the four preliminary practices, which is intended to purify obscurations and wrongdoing.

VAJRAYANA (Skt.) [Tib. rdo rje theg pa]   The indestructible path. The Vajrayana follows the bodhisattva path of the Mahayana and is characterized by an additional set of teachings based on the tantras, which emphasize deity practice using visualization, mantra, and mudra. Also sometimes called Tantrayana, or secret mantra.

VINAYA (Skt.) [Tib. 'dul ba]   Discipline. Part of the Tripitaka, it contains the Buddha's teachings on ethics, discipline, and conduct.

VIPASHYANA (Skt.) [Tib. lhag mthong]   Insight meditation, which develops insight into the nature of reality. See also SHAMATHA.

WHITE TARA (Tib. sgrol dkar)   Female deity whose special function is to promote good health and long life, both for the practitioner and for others. She is white with two arms and seven eyes of perfect wisdom that give birth to enlightenment.

YAMA (Skt.) [Tib. gshin rje]   Lord of Death, the personification of impermanence.

YANA (Skt.) [Tib. theg pa]   Vehicle or path. The three main yanas are the Hinayana, the Mahayana, and the Vajrayana.

YIDAM (Tib. yi dam)   A tantric deity. The yidam is a personal protector of one's practice and a guide to enlightenment.

YOGA TANTRA (Skt.) [Tib. rnal 'byor rgyud)   The third of the outer tantras of the Sarma, or New Translation school.

YOGI, YOGINI (Skt.) [Tib. rnal 'byor pa, rnal 'byor ma]   Tantric practitioners.

Index

Index of Stories Told by Khenpo Rinpoche

Karma Triyana Dharmachakra

Karma Triyana Dharmachakra (KTD) is the North America seat of His Holiness the Gyalwa Karmapa, and under the spiritual guidance and protection of His Holiness Ogyen Trinley Dorje, the Seventeenth Gyalwa Karmapa, is devoted to the authentic representation of the Kagyu lineage of Tibetan Buddhism.

For information regarding KTD, including our current schedule, or for information regarding our affiliate centers, Karma Thegsum Choling (KTC), located both in the United States and internationally, contact us using the information below.

Karma Triyana Dharmachakra's web site, www.kagyu.org, is an incredible resource containing extensive information regarding the activities of KTD, His Holiness Karmapa, and the Kagyu lineage.

Or contact KTD directly at:

Karma Triyana Dharmachakra
335 Meads Mountain Road
Woodstock, NY, 12498 USA
Front Office: 845 679 5906 ext. 10
E-mail: office@kagyu.org
KTC Coordinator: 845 679 5701
E-mail: ktc@kagyu.org

KTD Publications

GATHERING THE GARLANDS OF THE GURUS' PRECIOUS TEACHINGS

KTD Publications, a part of Karma Triyana Dharmachakra, is a not-for-profit publisher established with the purpose of facilitating the projects and activities manifesting from His Holiness's inspiration and blessings. We are dedicated to gathering the garlands of precious teachings and producing fine-quality books.

We invite you to join KTD Publications in facilitating the activities of His Holiness Karmapa and fulfilling the wishes of Khenpo Karthar Rinpoche and Bardor Tulku Rinpoche. If you would like to sponsor a book or make a donation to KTD Publications, please contact us using the information below. All contributions are tax-deductible.

KTD Publications
335 Meads Mountain Road
Woodstock, NY, 12498 USA
Telephone: 845 679 5906 ext. 37
www.KTDPublications.org